THE SINGLE GLOBAL CURRENCY

COMMON CENTS FOR THE WORLD

2014 Edition

Morrison Bonpasse

Single Global Currency Association
Newcastle, Maine, USA

Single Global Currency Assn. (a Maine non-profit corporation)
P.O. Box 390
Newcastle, ME 04553 USA
001-207-586-6078
Morrison Bonpasse, President
morrison@singleglobalcurrency.org
www.singleglobalcurrency.org

The Single Global Currency – Common Cents for the World (2014 Edition)

ISBN-10 0977842673
ISBN-13 9780977842674

REVIEWS AND COMMENTS OF PREVIOUS EDITIONS OF
THE SINGLE GLOBAL CURRENCY–COMMON CENTS FOR THE WORLD

"Bonpasse describes and, where possible, quantifies its benefits, that here can only be summed up:...The progress toward a single world unit is favoured by some current trends... These factors fuel Bonpasse's expectation that the goal of a single currency is in the agenda, so much so that he proposes an operational plan for mobilizing the stakeholders... All of us will see it accomplished, Bonpasse confidently reassures us..."
Antonio Mosconi, Review in *The Federalist Debate,* "Towards a Euro-like Currency for the World," March, 2008.

"Morrison Bonpasse, president of the Single Global Currency Association, based in Newcastle, Maine, and one of the leading proponents of a universal currency, says...that globalization and monetary nationalism are a dangerous combination. 'The benefits of a single global currency far outweigh the costs, so we should start planning now and avoid further risk and crises,' he says.... 'The world's existing multi-currency system must be replaced, and the IMF should explore this idea,' Bonpasse says. 'The only reason the IMF exists is to help the world cope with floating exchange rates.'"
Gordon Platt, in December 2007, *Global Finance* magazine article, "Universal Currency Could Hold Key to Stability and Growth—Single Global Currency."

"With the implementation of a common currency across the globe, all companies in all countries will use the same currency, and therefore the same measure in recording transactions, based on the same accounting standards. That said, the recent book by Morrison Bonpasse entitled, *The Single Global Currency - Common Cents for the World*, is a good start leading to this goal. It is the seed for great things....
I recommend the book to all accountants, and challenge accountants to help implement what is the next generation of accounting."
Ratnam Alagiah, University of South Australia, in the *Journal of Applied Management Accounting (JAMAR)* in Australia, Volume #5, Number 1, Winter 2007, page 69.

"A single global currency would eliminate many problems, such as transaction costs, trade imbalances, currency crises, and speculation. Interested listeners will be fascinated by the historical and cultural background that supports the author's arguments. The language is clear enough for such an esoteric subject, and Christopher Price gives an adequate reading. He enunciates slowly and clearly, and does not get excited about any part of the content. The author is president of a group promoting a single global currency, so there is a lot of energy in the writing, if not in the reading. The topic has an intellectual consistency and a moral foundation that comes across as admirable." T.W. © AudioFile Magazine 2007, Portland, Maine, reviewing the Audio-CD Edition.

"Your book deals with a very interesting topic with a long history that has attracted numerous distinguished minds, including those of Gasparo Scaruffi, John Stuart Mill, John Maynard Keynes, James Meade, Milton Friedman, and Robert Mundell, among others. While some have been in favor of a single currency, others against, all agree that there are costs as well as benefits associated with a single global currency, although they disagree as to their relative magnitudes."
François Bourguignon
Senior Vice President & Chief Economist
World Bank, 8 June 2006, letter to the author

"At Brown, Volcker discusses U.N. probe—As part of graduation weekend activities, the former Fed chairman talks about the investigation he headed into the oil-for-food program in pre-war Iraq.
"...The lecture, titled 'Is the U.N. Up to Its Job?' was among the commencement weekend activities. Brown also is awarding Volcker a doctorate of humane letters....
"At the end of his lecture, Volcker received a standing ovation and a request by a graduating senior for his autograph.
"Then he picked up his paperback copy of Morrison Bonpasse's *The Single Global Currency, Common Cents for the World*, put on his straw hat and prepared to walk."
From the *Providence Journal*
Lynn Arditi, *Providence Journal* Staff Writer ,
Providence, Rhode Island, US, Sunday, 28 May 2006, at http://www.projo.com/cgi-bin/bi/gold_print.cgi

"...a remarkable new book advocating a single global currency."
James W. Dean, Professor Emeritus, Simon Fraser University, 13 October 2006 in a speech in Kyev, Ukraine, at http://www.carleton.ca/economics/cep/cep06-07.pdf

"...In *The Single Global Currency: Common Cents for the World,* Morrison Bonpasse, the founder and president of the Single Global Currency Association, presents a convincing case that it is a moral imperative for the world's 191 nations to join together in a global monetary union and collectively save those economies trillions of dollars by adopting one common currency. Offering readers a comprehensive, but accessible journey through this multi-layered issue, Bonpasse calls for the world to set a goal of making the transition to a single currency by 2024...
"Bonpasse has a conversational style that brings the economic principles and numbers he uses to life. His stated narrative goal for the book is to 'bring simplicity to a complex issue,'

and he is able to do this admirably throughout the course of
300-plus pages....
 "Bonpasse is an ardent and unabashed champion of his
cause, saying, 'you may be reading the most important book
you have ever read, because the topic will save the world—
trillions.' ...this book makes an important contribution to understanding
still more about the enormous benefits that would come from greater
global cooperation."
Tatiana Brailovskaya
Lincoln County Weekly, Maine, US, 26 April 2006

"...A single global currency would, according to Bonpasse, benefit
the world's economies by trillions of dollars since it would
end transaction costs for currency trading and eliminate the
need for and cost of maintaining foreign currency reserves
while creating a dramatic one-time increase in global asset values
by removing risks of currency fluctuation.
"Modeled on the Euro (the currency of the EMU, the European
Monetary Union) which it would replace along with all
other currencies including the U.S. dollar, the new global currency
Bonpasse advocates ideally would eventually,... become the single unifying
unit of exchange, store of value, and unit of account for the entire world....
"Bonpasse's book does a very good job explaining the costs
and inconveniences of the current system of (mostly) national
currencies and fluctuations in exchange rates among them.
 It does not, however, dig very deep into the foundations of fiat money or
how the modern monetary system actually works and so does not engage
very much the considerable obstacles on the way to the single
global currency that Bonpasse promotes.
Will Zachmann, *Duxbury Clipper,* Massachusetts,
US, 17 May 2006

Table of Contents

From the wisdom of John Stuart Mill...

"Let us suppose that all countries had the same currency, as in the progress of political improvement they one day will have....

So much of barbarism still remains in the transactions of the most civilized nations that almost all independent countries choose to assert their nationality by having, to their own inconvenience and that of their neighbours, a peculiar currency of their own."

John Stuart Mill, *Principles of Political Economy with Some of Their Applications to Social Philosophy.* London: 7th Edition, with introduction by W.J. Ashley, 1909, first edition published 1848, full text at http://www.econlib.org/library/Mill/mlP36.html.

Preface

How to Read this Book: The book should be complete and useful without reference to the chapter endnotes, which provide further information with sources and weblinks. However, for those who utilize the endnotes, web links are included to enable purchasers of Kindle or other electronic versions of the book to obtain easy access to referenced materials.

Intended audience: This is a book for every reader of English, including economists. Where its economic analyses and assumptions fall short, it is hoped that economists will move beyond criticism and then present their own estimates and calculations. For example, in Chapter 1 is an estimate of 4.6 percent for the asset value-depressing-effect of currency risk. More thorough calculations of global currency risk are welcomed.

This book is intended for worldwide readership by people who understand that the fluctuating valuations of its multiple currencies, 140 in early 2014, cause recurring problems. It's for those who have observed recurring currency crises and see the risk of more to come, and worse. It's for those who see continuing problems with global imbalances of payments and no reasonable solution in sight. It's for those who would say and ask, like Robert F. Kennedy, "I dream things that never were and say, Why not?"[1]

The 2014 Edition: The 408 page first edition of this book was published in 2006. The subsequent 2007, 2008 and 2009 editions contained the full first edition, together with addenda containing the year's updates of Single Global Currency (SGC)-related material. The 2014 edition updates the 2006 first edition within the original text and adds material where useful. Further editions will be published every five years, i.e. 2019, 2024 etc.

Earlier Editions: The 06 Edition was posted in 2007 on the website of the Single Global Currency Association at "SGC Book" on the left of each page of the Association's website, http://www.singleglobalcurrency.org/book_ecopy.html. The 2007, 2008 and 2009 Editions are now posted there as well.

The first edition is also available at the Munich Personal RePEc (Research Papers in Economics) Archive at http://mpra.ub.uni-muenchen.de/1175/. Similarly, the 2007, 2008 and 2009 Editions are posted electronically in the same archive.

All editions are also available on www.amazon.com, with the 2009 edition available in Kindle format.

Price
The price of this book is set initially in euros, as the euro is the currency which is presently the most promising path toward the Single Global Currency. The euro services the world's second largest economic unit, after the United States, and eventually it will be the official legal tender currency of all European Union countries. The price of the first edition was set at

€16.00 and that has remained the price for each successive edition. (See spreadsheet at end of book for the equivalent price, as of 2 January 2014, of this edition.) This is as close as we can get to the "Law of One Price", meaning that identical goods should cost the same everywhere, if trade were free and without transportation and transaction costs.

<u>Other books exclusively about the Single Global Currency</u>: Until 2009, this book, in its several editions, was the only book in print, and on CDs, in the world entirely devoted to the Single Global Currency. However, in 2009, the Icfai University Press, of Hyderabad, India, published *A Single Global Currency—Perspectives and Challenges* which contains a collection of essays, including "Single Global Currency Origin, Costs and Benefits" by this author.

In 2007 Tina Wenzel published a 23 page booklet entitled *Global Monetary Union – On the political and economic common sense of common cents*. The booklet has several parallels to this book including the use of "common cents" in the title and the introductory quotation from John Stuart Mill.

<u>Capitalization</u>: The terms "Global Central Bank (GCB)" and "Global Monetary Union (GMU)" are capitalized, as are European Central Bank (ECB) and European Monetary Union (EMU). However, while the names of currencies such as the euro, dollar, yen, and yuan are not capitalized, the term "Single Global Currency (SGC)" is capitalized here. It does not yet have a name, such as mundo or eartha, which would not be capitalized, but it IS the subject of the book, and capitalization tends to communicate a sense of importance.

<u>Work of the Author</u>: This book is published by the Single Global Currency Association which fully supports the key message of this book: that the world needs to plan now for the implementation of a Single Global Currency, managed by a Global Central Bank, within a Global Monetary Union. However, the author, and not the association, is responsible for the accuracy and writing of this book.

<u>How important is this book?</u> You may be reading the most important book you have ever read, because the SGC will save the world--trillions.

---

1. The original quote was in George Bernard Shaw's play, *Back to Methuselah*, Act I, *Selected Plays with Prefaces*, vol. 2, p. 7 (1949). The serpent said to Eve, "You see things; and you say 'Why?' But I dream things that never were; and I say 'Why not?' "

President John F. Kennedy quoted these words in his address to the Irish Parliament, Dublin, 28 June 1963. *Public Papers of the Presidents of the United States: John F. Kennedy*, 1963, p. 537.

Senator Robert F. Kennedy used a similar quotation as a theme of his

1968 campaign for the presidential nomination: "Some men see things as they are and say, why; I dream things that never were and say, why not." Senator Edward M. Kennedy quoted these words of Robert Kennedy in his eulogy for his brother in 1968. (*The New York Times*, 9 June 1968, p. 56; Source: http://www.bartleby.com/73/465.html *Respectfully Quoted: A Dictionary of Quotations*, 1989.)

Introduction

> "Perhaps the sentiments contained in the following pages are not yet sufficiently fashionable to procure them general favor; a long habit of not thinking a thing *wrong* gives it a superficial appearance of being *right* and raises at first a formidable outcry in defence of custom. But the tumult soon subsides. Time makes more converts than reason."
> Thomas Paine in *Common Sense.*[1]

The size and endurance of the world's multicurrency foreign exchange system gives it the superficial appearance of being "*right,*" but it's more obsolete than "*wrong*" and will increasingly be subjected to the "reasons" for replacing it with a Single Global Currency. The major questions are the timing and stability of the implementation.

The wordplay in "Common Cents" in the second part of the title, "Common Cents for the World," arose from an email exchange with Michael Federle, Group Publisher of *Fortune* magazine and the author. In his response to an email, Mike wrote on 27 April 2005 that a Single Global Currency "makes all the sense in the world." Seeing the opportunity for a pun, I responded, "Indeed it does. Makes all the cents in the world too." After that, I used the punned form of "cents" a few times and then coined the slogan, "Common Cents for the World." Of course, as with most ideas, this was not the first such use of the punned phrase. In late 2005, Google reported 115,000 "results" for "Common Cents" of which two came from the Single Global Currency Association website. Google now reports 589,000 "results" for "Common Cents." Thomas Paine, author in 1776 of the original *Common Sense,* perhaps would be pleased with the pun and with the common sense goal of a Single Global Currency--with common cents. It made no sense to him for the American colonies to be governed, without representation, by England, and it makes no cents/sense for the world not to implement a Single Global Currency--soon.

"Cents" are actually closer to a Single Global Currency as a word, as that is the term which denominates the coins of fifteen currencies, including those of the European Monetary Union, Singapore/Brunei and the United States.[2] Thus, "cents" are already denominated in countries whose GDPs comprise about 50 percent of the world's total.

The 2,500 year solution: Approximately in the sixth century B.C. people began foreign exchange trading of the increasingly standardized coins of the Western, Indian and Chinese civilizations. Foreign exchange became the fifth wheel of human transactions, accompanying the first four of labor, raw materials, money and energy. For most of those 2,500 years, the multicurrency foreign exchange system seemed to be more of a solution than a problem.

From the beginning two central problems arose in foreign exchange trading:

-What is the value of one coin/currency compared to another, and
-What makes the value of one currency rise or fall compared to
  the others?

Over the next two-and-a-half millennia, the value of traditional foreign exchange trading has grown to $5.3 trillion per day, and traders and economists continue to struggle with those two basic questions. The answers remain elusive. There are thousands of academic articles, and hundreds of books, written by economists about these questions, but none solves either question. None has pulled the Arthurian sword from the economics Rosetta Stone.[3] Through all the analyses, we know a lot more about many aspects and implications of the multicurrency foreign exchange system, but no one consistently knows the values of currencies and no one can predict their ups and downs.

Like the banned pesticide, DDT, the multicurrency foreign exchange trading system was developed to solve a problem--people wanting to trade goods and services which were valued using two different currencies. Like the makers of DDT who responded to the need to kill inconvenient insects, the traders of foreign exchange improved the service so as to efficiently enable the vast increase in convenient trading; but the two basic questions were never solved. Instead, like DDT, the larger and more efficient foreign exchange trading system has become more hazardous and can bring harm to people and economies as values of currencies fluctuate with large, unpredictable variations. One example of such movements is the seesaw relationship of the US dollar and the euro, the currencies of the two largest, most stable economies in the world. After being introduced on 1 January 1999 at the value of $1.17 ($1.16692),[4] the euro descended to its $.83 low against the dollar in October 2000. Then, it increased almost 100% to its high of $1.60 in April, 2008. Since then, it dropped and was in the $1.35 range in early 2014.

The multicurrency foreign exchange trading system will never solve the two problems of valuation and value fluctuations and, like DDT, it must be replaced with something better. The Single Global Currency is the common cents/sense solution. It does not merely answer the two foreign exchange questions; it eliminates them.

If the phrase "moral consequences" had not already been used by Benjamin Friedman's, *The Moral Consequences of Economic Growth*, this book might have been titled, *The Moral Consequences of the Multicurrency Foreign Exchange System*, because further delay in implementing the Single Global Currency, in the face of the evidence of its benefits for the world, becomes a moral issue. If a cure for cancer were readily available, it would be immoral to delay the implementation of such a cure, while continuing further research on cures which are known to be ineffective. Similarly, in a world where vast health, housing and nutrition needs are unmet due to lack of money, it is immoral to delay the SGC implementation, while continuing to focus marginally useful research on the puzzles of the risky and costly multicurrency foreign exchange system. As Ramon Tamames of Spain has said, such research is really about "silly things."[5]

There IS a moral solution to the problems of the multicurrency foreign exchange system, and it's the Single Global Currency, within a Global Monetary Union, managed by a Global Central Bank (termed henceforth from time to time as the "3-Gs").[6] This book will enable readers to understand that solution, and to learn why it is not yet on the international radar screen with an implementation date; and what it will take to get it there. For some, it hopefully will move their understanding from "Why?" to "Why Not?"

Others will ask, "What does this mean to me?" The short answer is that the life of almost every human being will be improved by the implementation of the Single Global Currency, just as those lives are currently diminished by the unpredictable, risky multicurrency foreign exchange system. The most direct effect of the Single Global Currency will be the elimination of currency transaction charges for international purchases and sales, for an annual global saving of about $300 billion. The removal of such charges, if passed on to consumers, will lead to a reduction in the price of internationally traded goods and services.

Dwarfing that benefit will be the opportunity to achieve a one-time increase in the value of financial and other assets worldwide of about $10 trillion through the lowering in interest rates and the elimination of worldwide currency risk. That increase of asset values will contribute an additional $3 trillion in world GDP, which will, in turn, become the foundation for future annual GDP increases. Assuming annual overall GDP increases of 3 percent, that would mean approximately a $90 billion annual increase. When added to the $300 billion in transaction cost savings, that brings the annual benefit to $390 billion, an average of about $50 for every human being, every year. To the extent that the implementation of the Single Global Currency causes minimal harm, such as unemployment for currency traders, those savings can be used to mitigate such harm.

Even with the expectation that those benefits will be spread unequally, they still will benefit everyone on the earth at some level. Even if measurable cash does not flow into everyone's hands, everyone will benefit from the elimination of currency crises.

On the other hand, a failure to implement a Single Global Currency may lead to inevitable currency crises, and even a worldwide currency crisis affecting the US dollar, and the loss of $trillions. The 2007-2009 global financial crisis barely avoided a serious currency crisis.

The book begins with an explanation of the current multicurrency foreign exchange world and its dangers. Chapter 4 introduces monetary unions, and Chapter 5 begins the explanation of the Single Global Currency. There are no economics formulas or graphs in this book. Even the two chapters specifically dedicated to the views of economists, Chapter 3 on the existing multicurrency world and Chapter 6 on the Single Global Currency, are written for lay readers.

The race to land a human on the moon began with US President John F. Kennedy's September 1962 proclamation at Rice University in Texas that it was to be the goal of the United States to land a human being on the moon before the end of that decade.[7] At the time of the setting of that goal, only a maximum of seven years and three months in the future, the United States had launched only two people into orbit, beginning with John Glenn in January and Scott Carpenter in May, and neither flight lasted longer than five hours.

We are now much further along the journey to the Single Global Currency than humans were to the moon in 1962. We now know how to implement the 3-Gs: a Single Global Currency (SGC) in a Global Monetary Union (GMU), with a Global Central Bank (GCB). We have considerable experience with monetary unions, crowned most recently with the euro, which took ten years to implement from the February 1992 signing of the Maastricht Treaty to the 1 January 2002 distribution of the new currency among the people of the European Eurozone.[8] Further, it could be argued that the process took only five years and two months from the 1 November 1993 adoption of the Treaty to the 1 January 1999 implementation of the euro on financial ledgers, but with the new cash not yet in circulation.

The size of the Single Global Currency project should not be daunting, as the Gross Domestic Product or GDP, of the Eurozone economy in 2012 was greater than the GDP of the entire world in the mid-20th century, even when adjusted for inflation. The administrative costs of implementation will be far less than those incurred by the United States when sending an astronaut to the moon, estimated to be equivalent to $159 billion in 2012 US dollars.[9]

By the time the world reaches the "3-G" goals, the multicurrency foreign exchange trading system will have had a run of 2,500 years and it will have long outlived its usefulness. The book will now explore the history, operations, and problems of the multicurrency foreign exchange system, and then why and how it must be replaced. What the people of the world want is stable money, and the Single Global Currency will provide such stability – among other benefits.

ENDNOTES

1. Thomas Paine, *Common Sense, Rights of Man, and other essential writings of Thomas Paine*, New York, NY: New American Library, 2003, p. 3, Introduction.
2. The fifteen currencies belong to: Argentina, Australia, Canada, Eastern Caribbean Monetary Union, Eritrea, European Monetary Union, Gambia, Guyana, Malta, New Zealand, Singapore, South Africa, Sri Lanka, United States, and Zimbabwe. Sources: http://en.wikipedia.org/wiki/Cents and www.google.com for (cents coins currency). The legitimacy of Wikipedia as a source is confirmed by Thomas L. Friedman in *The World is Flat*, New York, NY: Farrar Straus and Giroux, 2005, who said at page 94 that he used this source regularly.
3. The Rosetta Stone was discovered in 1799 in El Rashid (Rosetta), Egypt by soldiers in Napoleon's army while digging to construct an addition to a fort. Written approximately in 19 B.C., the stone contains a decree to

priests in three languages: Egyptian hieroglyphs, a local script called demotic, and Greek. This discovery enabled the first translations of the heretofore undecipherable hieroglyphs. The Stone was donated to the British Museum by King George III, whose common sense in this regard would likely have impressed even Thomas Paine. See http://www.britishmuseum.org/explore/highlights/highlight_objects/aes/t/the_rosetta_stone.aspx
The Arthurian reference is to the legend that Arthur became King of England after pulling a sword from a stone. See http://www.kingarthursknights.com/faq/swordstone.asp
4. The value of the euro was established in the spring of 1999 as equivalent to a precise quantity of each of the currencies of the twelve participating countries, e.g., equal to 40.3399 Belgian francs. See the list of currencies and their values at http://www.ecb.europa.eu/euro/intro/html/index.en.html. On the first trading day of the euro, Friday, 1 January 1999, those 40.3399 Belgian francs, and 1.95582 German deutschmarks, etc., were all equal to 1.16692 US dollars and equivalents in other currencies. From that point forward, all foreign exchange trading with the twelve legacy currencies stopped and trading began with the euro. On Sunday afternoon (GMT), 3 January 1999, with trading beginning in New Zealand on Monday morning local time, 4 January, the euro rose in value to 1.1803 US dollars. See FX Converter at http://www.oanda.com/convert/classic
5. In a conversation with the author in Malaga, Spain, mid-February 2013.
6. The abbreviation "3-Gs" here will save space and perhaps conjure an image of humankind accelerating into a new economic world, freed of the dynamics previously thought to be as permanent as gravity. Incidentally, three Gs (as in: three times the force of gravity) are within the boundaries of space flight where astronauts endure gravitational pressures of approximately 3 Gs, or three times the force of gravity, at launch, but face approx. 6 Gs upon re-entry.
7. For more information about President Kennedy's speech and moon landing goal, see http://er.jsc.nasa.gov/seh/ricetalk.htm
8. The term "Eurozone" is used in this book as shorthand for the countries of the European Monetary Union, which now includes 18 of the European Union's 28 member countries. See http://europa.eu/about-eu/countries/index_en.html.
9. The estimated cost of the Apollo moon voyages in the 1960s was reportedly $25.4 billion in 1960s US dollars. See BBC's "Apollo Missions: The Conclusion," at http://www.bbc.co.uk/dna/h2g2/A830774. The Economic History Association's website www.eh.net has an excellent utility to determine the value of US dollars between any two years between 1704 and 2014. Calculations can be made using the Consumer Price Index (CPI) or GDP per capita or other indices. Using the "Purchasing Power Calculator" which uses the CPI, the $25.4 billion (using the year of the first Apollo landing, 1969), was equivalent to $159.0 billion in 2012. See http://www.measuringworth.com/uscompare/relativevalue.php.

Chapter 1. The Expensive, Complex, and Hazardous Multicurrency Foreign Exchange World[1]

The world has seven+ billion people. Most of them live in the 193 member nations of the United Nations and exchange their goods and services and pay their taxes using the 140 currencies listed at the end of this book.[2] Most of that commerce is within countries or monetary unions which use the same currency (also called a "currency area"),[3] but an increasing amount of that commerce is international and that requires the translation and exchange of value from one currency into another.

In April, 2013 those transactions added up to the daily exchange of the equivalent of approximately $5.3 trillion in what is called "traditional" foreign exchange trading,[4] which is equivalent to $757 for every human being on every working day. These numbers do not include the increasingly popular trading in "non-traditional" "instrument derivative" instruments which total another $2.3 trillion daily. They also do not include the notational value of over-the-counter derivatives, which totaled $693 trillion in June, 2013.[5]

Imagine every human on the earth trading currency worth $757 every working day, after considering that people with an annual income of $250,000 make $685 per day. For perspective, a 2008 World Bank study found that one-quarter of the world's population in 2005 lived on $1.25 a day or less.[6] It would take those people almost two years to earn $757.

For further perspective, let's explore the size of a trillion by looking at units of time. There are 31.5 million seconds in a year, so a lucky person with a Japanese life expectancy of 79 years might live for 2.5 billion seconds.[7] There have been only 70.5 billion seconds since 221 B.C. when China was unified by Qin Shi Huangdi, and the country converted to one currency. One would have to look back to the year 29,676 B.C., toward the end of the Paleolithic Age, when humans were developing languages, to go back 1 trillion seconds. Thus, a trillion is a very large number.

The annual gross domestic product of all the 7+ billion human beings in 2012 was approximately $71.8 trillion.[8] Thus, the dollar equivalent of the world's entire annual gross domestic product is traded as currency, or contracts for currency, every 13 (71.8/5.3) days.

What IS Money, Anyway?

The basic answer from economists is that money is a medium of exchange, a store of value, and a unit of account.

Medium of exchange - Money moves value from one person to another, unless the other person uses a different currency, in which case the money is essentially bartered in the foreign exchange markets.[9] As the value of money across borders fluctuates, its effectiveness as a medium of exchange is impaired.

Store of value - People should be able to leave foreign money on a bureau and it should retain that value over time. However, such value can be diminished or enhanced by fluctuating exchange rates, or if the money is involved in a currency crisis.

Unit of account - Money enables the value of an object or service to be measured and then perhaps compared with something else. This function, too, is subject to fluctuations by foreign exchange rates when that "something else" comes from another country or currency area.

Thus, in our multicurrency foreign exchange world, money fails in all three of its primary functions due to fluctuations in exchange rates. A Single Global Currency would avoid these problems and restore money soundly to its true use and definition. [10]

Trade in Goods and Services

According to the World Trade Organization, total world trade of goods or merchandise in 2011 was $17.8 trillion,[11] or approximately 26 percent of the total value of the world's $69.6 trillion GDP for that year.[12] That trade consists of buying and selling by individuals, corporations, and governments. In short, by almost everyone.

At the individual level, when a Thai citizen purchases a Honda car, s/he or the car dealer needs to purchase yen with bhat. When a South African purchases Brazilian coffee, s/he or the intermediary merchant needs to purchase reals with rands. When a Canadian purchases wine from France, s/he or the distributor must purchase euros with Canadian dollars. All of these transactions require foreign exchange trading at some point in the transaction, i.e. at the consumer, wholesale or larger scale.

Changing Values of Currencies

The values of currencies to each other vary, and despite all the efforts of thousands of economists and speculators, they vary with unpredictable timing and to an unpredictable degree. The title of Dominick Salvatore's article, "The Euro-Dollar Exchange Rate Defies Prediction," presents the problem.[13] Economists often use the term "puzzle" for such intractable problems.[14]

Why do currencies rise and fall in value relative to each other? The short answer is the classic law of economics: Supply and Demand. If the demand for a currency rises, for such reasons as the need to purchase a good or service priced in that currency, its value will rise. The worldwide foreign exchange market is a very special market because of the uniformity of the goods for sale. A euro is a euro is a euro around the world.

For an increasing number of buyers and sellers of currency, the concern is whether a currency will rise or fall in value, so sales and purchases can become part of a self-fulfilling prophecy. If enough people sell currency because they think the value is declining, the value will decline.

Another major factor in currency purchases is interest rates, the foundations for which are set by central banks for each currency. When interest rates rise for a currency, foreigners are more likely to purchase that currency and earn those higher interest rates; and the currency's value will rise.

Note the contrast with other systems of measurement. For example, if a country's factories receive orders, i.e., demand, for 100,000 meters of wire, and the actual production, i.e., supply, was 125,000, the appropriate response would not be to shorten the length of a kilometer to .8 of its former value, in order to bring supply into equilibrium with demand. Such a change would transform the orders for 100,000 meters (pre-adjustment) into orders for 125,000 meters, simply by changing the value of the measurement. Of course, such adjustments of the metric system would make the system useless. [15]

Similarly, changing the value of a currency as a response to changes in supply and demand or economic conditions is not an appropriate response. To satisfy the definition that money is a measurable unit of account, the value of that money must be stable.

Jose Cordeiro cited the early 20th Century economist, Irving Fisher, about the need for stable money, " 'We have standardized every other unit in commerce except the most important and universal unit of all, the unit of purchasing power. What business man would consent for a moment to make a contract in terms of yards of cloth or tons of coal, and leave the size of the yard or the ton to chance.' "[16] While Fisher was writing about the fluctuating purchasing power of a national currency, and not about the fluctuations of foreign exchange values, the quest for stable money shines through.

Illustrating how currency fluctuations can affect prices, this book has been published in five editions, (2006, 2007, 2008, 2009 and 2014) all priced at €16.00. However, the USD price, rounded to the nearest half-dollar, has fluctuated as follows: $19.00, $21.00, $23.50, $22.00 and $22.00. The most notable change for USA purchasers is the change in the price of the book from the original $19.00 to $22.00. That's because, although always priced at 16 euros, the euro was worth $1.37 on 2 January 2014, compared to $1.19 in 2006. The price for US buyers of this 2014 Edition is thus 15.8 percent higher than the 2006 edition, but a drop from the $23.50 price in 2008 when the euro was worth $1.47. The 15.8 percent increase over the eight years since 2006 is not a significant increase, as it means only an annual compounded percent increase of about 1.9 percent. However, the contrast, and the effect of currency fluctuations is shown when seeing that the price has remained exactly the same for Eurozone Europeans for all five editions. In some currencies, such as the Swiss franc, the price of this book declined during the period 2006-2014, from 24.80 CHF to 19.68 CHF, because the value of those currencies increased relative to the euro. However, for most other currencies, the price has increased because of the euro's increased value.

In March 2014, the *Wall Street Journal* reported, "Australian Exporters Benefit From Currency Swing," i.e. a 15 percent reduction in the value of the Australian dollar since its 2013 peak value to the USD of $1.06. Because of that 2013 high valuation, one company, the producer of Yellow Tail wines, suffered its first annual loss in more than 20 years. [17]

At another micro level, a friend secured an education loan in Newfoundland in the early 00's, and then moved to Maine where he was earning wages in US dollars. For several years, the repayments were easier because of the USD/CAN exchange rate. Then came the 2007 rise of the "Loonie," named after the image of the loon on the $1 CAN coin. When the US and Canadian currencies reached parity, and the trend threatened to continue, the payments became more painful until his parents were moved to pay off the entire loan in Canadian dollars. The point here is that currency fluctuations DO make a difference to the lives of ordinary people, and they are often more than a nuisance.

At the macro level, the Swiss Central Bank reported a loss of 3.97 billion Swiss francs [€2.45 billion] for the first quarter of 2008.[18] The loss came because the Swiss franc increased in value, but the other assets held by the bank, including gold, decreased in value. For this small country of 7.7 million, that meant a loss of €318 for every inhabitant of Switzerland, in order to maintain reserves to support a multicurrency system. This might be the basis of a specific public opinion poll question in Switzerland, "Would you be willing to write a check to the Swiss Central Bank to compensate for its nearly 4 billion Swiss franc loss in the value of the reserve assets we use to maintain the global multicurrency foreign exchange system, OR would you prefer a Single Global Currency, where no such losses would occur?"

Home-based "carrying trade."

The real-life effects of foreign exchange fluctuations, inflation and interest rates, in an e-economy can be seen with European mortgages and other loans. In Bulgaria, Romania and Hungary over 50% of all corporate and home loans are made in foreign currencies, usually in euros or Swiss francs. Borrowers make their payments by converting their local currencies into the borrowed currency. The reason for the cross-currency loans is the lower interest rates of the denominated currency, but a problem arises when the value of the euro and Swiss franc rise on the foreign exchange markets, compared to the local currency. The effect is like what happens with adjustable rate mortgages, the payments for which rise when the prime rates rise. In the case of one Budapest homeowner, his monthly payments rose by 10% in two months due to the rise in the value of the euro relative to the Hungarian forint.[19]

Plastic Money and the Appearance of a Global Currency

Despite the continued existence of 140 currencies among the 193 UN members, it is now possible to travel the world and easily engage in small-scale trade with plastic money, such as a Visa card, Maestro card, MasterCard, smartcard, or other cards. Travelers can either pay for goods and services with their cards, which automatically make the foreign exchange translation, or they can go to an automated teller machine (ATM) and withdraw cash in the local currency. It's so easy that it's rarely noticed that there is always a small percentage charge for the foreign exchange transaction--and those charges add up. The irony is that by making such foreign exchange transactions much easier, the public pressure on the central bankers and governments of the world to move to a Single Global Currency may be decreased. Indeed, as one Visa executive stated in 2001, "When Visa was founded twenty-five years ago, the founders saw the world as needing a Single Global Currency for exchange. Everything we've done from a global perspective has been about trying to put one piece in place after another to fulfill that global vision."[20]

4

The World of Currency Trading and the Tools of the Trade

The $5.3 trillion daily trading is conducted primarily at the major exchanges of the world, from East to West: Sydney, Tokyo, Hong Kong, Singapore, Frankfurt, Zurich, Paris, London, and New York.

The Foreign Exchange Committee in New York reports that North American average daily traditional foreign exchange trading in October 2013 totaled $785 billion, which is approximately 15 percent of the world's total. In October 2013, North America had 526,025 daily trades with an average for each currency trade of about $1.5 million.[21] With similar sized trades around the world, that would mean approximately 3.5 million trades per day, worldwide.

The size of the average trade varies by type. The average size of spot transactions in New York, was $1.2 million, while the average foreign exchange swap was for $37.6 million.[22]

The British Foreign Exchange Joint Standing Committee, associated with the Bank of England, reports $1.9 trillion in daily trading of traditional products in London, or 36 percent of the worldwide total.[23]

The foreign exchange worldwide extended market opens on Monday mornings in Sydney, Australia, which is actually Sunday evening, 8:00 p.m. Greenwich Mean Time (GMT), until afternoon on Friday, New York time, which is 10 p.m., GMT. During that period, the market can be said to be open twenty-four hours a day, as trading centers move with the sun from East to West. The sun sets only on short weekends, 10 p.m. Friday (GMT) to 8 p.m. Sunday (GMT), on the foreign exchange trading empire.

It is not known how many foreign exchange traders or brokers in the world. In the US, there are 153,053 retail FX brokers registered with the Commodities Futures Trading Commission.[24] As the ratio of brokers to economic output is likely to be more consistent around the world than the ratio of brokers to total population, and as the US constitutes about 1/4 of the global economy, the number of retail brokers worldwide is estimated to be four times the US number, or roughly 600,000.

What's Actually Traded

The table below shows the breakdown of the daily $440 billion in "traditional foreign exchange" in North America, during April, 2013.

Type	Volume of Trades	Number	Transaction Value Avg.
Spot Transactions	$518.9 billion	510,245	$ 1.0 million
Outright Forwards	$179.3 billion	74,297	$ 2.4 million
Foreign Exchange Swaps	$257.1 billion	6,709	$38.2 million
Totals	$955.3 billion	591,251	$ 1.6 million

These products are defined by the New York Foreign Exchange Committee:[25]

<u>Spot Transactions</u> are single outright transactions that involve the exchange of two currencies at a rate agreed to on the date of the contract for value or delivery within two business days, including US dollar-Canadian dollar (USD-CAD) transactions delivered within one day.

<u>Foreign Exchange Swaps</u> involve the exchange of two currencies on a specific date at a rate agreed to at the time of the conclusion of the contract, and a reverse exchange of the same two currencies at a date further in the future at a rate agreed to at the time of the contract. For measurement purposes, only the long leg of the swap is reported so that each transaction is recorded only once.

<u>Outright Forwards</u> involving the exchange of two currencies at a rate agreed to on the date of the contract for value or delivery at some time in the future (more than one business day for USD-CAD transactions or more than two business days for all other transactions). This category also includes forward foreign exchange agreement transactions (FXA), non-deliverable forwards, and other forward contracts for differences.

<u>Currency Options</u> are over-the-counter contracts that give the right or the obligation—depending upon if the reporter is the purchaser or the writer—to buy or sell a currency with another currency at a specified exchange rate during a specified time period. This category also includes exotic foreign exchange options such as average rate options and barrier options. Not included in totals of "traditional" foreign exchange trading, these instruments are also called "derivatives,"[26] and they were traded at the daily rate in North America of $52.0 billion per trading day.[27]

Most of the currency trading is with a few "pairs" of international currencies: Euro/US Dollar (EUR/USD), British Pound/US Dollar (GBP/USD), Canadian Dollar/US Dollar (CAD/USD) and Yen/US Dollar (JPY/USD).

The Language of Currency Exchange
Every discipline has its special words and special meanings. For a glossary of the terms and phrases in the international economics and foreign exchange world, see Alan Deardorff's online "Glossary of International Economics."[28]

A 2013 headline about foreign currency trading reported, "Dollar Rises Past 103 Yen, a 4-1/2 year high, on U.S. data."[29] However, as this makes US exports more expensive, this "rising" is not good news for the United States and its struggle to conquer its balance of payments problem, but "rises past" sounds positive. A 2005 article, entitled "Yen at 32-month Low as Japan's Small Investors Look Abroad," reported: "In Tokyo, the yen traded as low as 121.39 yen to the dollar, its weakest point since March 2003. It has fallen 16 percent this year, from a high of 101.68 yen to the dollar on Jan. 17."[30] Thus, the yen drops in value as the number of yen required to purchase a dollar increases.

When quoting currency prices, one has to be careful to state what is quoted as buying what. When the price of the euro goes from $1.26 to $1.25, it is said to "drop" or "lose," but if the same change in values of the two currencies to each other is quoted as a change for the price of a dollar from €.7937 to €.8000 then the price of a dollar is rising.

Such a change in value would have many effects which are easiest to see with respect to importers and exporters. When a newspaper headline says, "Euro May Gain on Speculation that ECB is Closer to Raising Rates," it means that the price of the euro relative to other currencies is likely to increase. Where a euro yesterday might cost $1.200, it might be predicted to cost $1.212 tomorrow, an increase of 1 percent. If the entire currency price change is passed on to buyers and sellers at every level, then Eurozone exporters would be hurt because their goods would become more one percent expensive to holders of dollars and importers would benefit because they could buy dollar-denominated goods more cheaply.

The linguistic trick for trading a buy/sell currency pair is that when you are buying one currency you are selling the other. For example, in a euro/US Dollar pair (EUR/USD), the euro is the "base" currency and the dollar the "counter" or "quote" currency. This pairing sequence reflects the US dollar's primary role in the international financial system. If the price of a EUR/USD pair is 1.3715, that means that it costs $1.3715 to purchase a euro.[31] To avoid confusion, the trading of euros and dollars is not quoted in reverse, i.e., a USD/EUR pair. In typical retail pricing, when we say that a cup of coffee costs €1.25 and it is clear what is buying what. We never hear that 8/10 of a cup of coffee will purchase a euro.

Forex Firms and the Get Rich Quick/Gambling Side of Foreign Exchange Trading

Most of the world's currency trading is done by banks and large financial institutions with each other. This is called "interbank" trading. In addition, an increasing amount of foreign exchange trading, called "FX" or "Forex," is done by retail firms and their customers. This activity, called "currency gambling" by *Casino Times*,[32] continues to attract people eager to make quick profits. These firms use software platforms, such as is offered by Reuters, which enable their customers to see nearly as much about the worldwide foreign exchange markets as do the traders among the major financial institutions.

Currency traders are a special breed.[33] One wrote of his oversized role in the international monetary system:

> "What created this market? How did the nations of the world conclude that international currency exchange should be determined by profit-oriented traders sitting in front of computer screens with telephones glued to their ears?"[34]

The retail firms have websites which offer free "practice"[35] or "virtual trading"[36] accounts. One firm has 55,000 individual accounts with an average account balance between $5,000-$10,000.[37] Invites one, "Ready to try currency trading? Open an account with as little as $250. Experience the benefits of FOREX.com."[38] On another website, "Our tight spreads and substantial liquidity are a result of combining quotation streams from 13 of the world's largest foreign exchange dealers which constitute more than two-thirds of the market share in the global interbank market. ... Our forex spreads and substantial liquidity have helped our customers become among the most profitable."[39]

Advertisements on the internet seek to attract people who are interested in making quick money. For example, one approach is to offer a "free" enticement, such as this advertisement translated from the original Italian, "Earn €25 in 1 minute! New traders can also receive FREE: Personal training 1:1 -12 sessions online video training -An eBook exclusive on trading - Fill in your details to get €25 FREE."[40]

A search for "forex trading" on www.amazon.com for books brings up 1,797 books, sorted by "relevance," beginning with
1. *50 Pips A Day Forex Strategy* by Laurentiu Damir
2. *Forex Made Simple: A Step-By-Step Day Trading Strategy for Making $100 to*
    $200 per Day by Alpha Balde
3. *The Forex "Set & Forget" Profit System: It is VERY DIFFICULT TO LOSE with this extremely reliable trading system...* by Mark Boardman
4. *Forex For Beginners* by Anna Coulling, and
5. *An Introduction to Forex Trading* - A Guide for Beginners by Matthew Driver.

Most of these books have the flavor of a Gold Rush, rather than the taste of a system of dealing with real money that real people have struggled to earn and save, and of a market on which the financial stability of the world depends. Perhaps showing the disconnect between the real world and the currency world, a number of surveys of currency traders in 2011-2012 showed that roughly one-third lost money,[41] despite a healthy overall growth in the world GDP of approximately 3.9 percent.[42]

The BarclayHedge Currency Trader Index, which tracks 105 currency trading programs, reported an average gain in 2013 of .95 percent. This was a decline from the 1.71 percent in 2012 and 2.25 percent in 2011.[43]

To reduce risk, some currency traders and mainstream mutual funds have established "currency funds" for investing in currencies or securities denominated in another currency. Fidelity Investments has several such funds, including the "Australian Dollar Currency Fund," "Euro Currency Fund" and "US Dollar Currency Fund. Fidelity states, "Institutional investors, banks, and hedge funds traditionally dominated the currency markets. With the advent of ETFs, individual investors now have the ability to gain exposure to this large and tremendously important asset class."[44] A US bank offers certificates of deposit and savings accounts which can be invested in several currencies.[45] In short, there are many ways to invest in order to profit, or hedge against loss, from the multicurrency foreign exchange system. It has taken much time, effort and money to establish and operate these mechanisms to cope with the foreign exchange system.

While the prospects for gain in the foreign exchange market are appealing, it must be remembered that almost every person's profit in the foreign exchange markets is balanced by another person's loss, and may be considered to be a "zero sum" game.[46] For example, for every person who bought Swiss francs and sold US dollars, there was another who sold Swiss francs and purchased US dollars. For every person who profited when the USD rose against the CHF, another person lost, and vice versa.

Regulation of Currency Trading

In the United States, the Commodities Futures Trading Commission was authorized to regulate trading of currency futures contacts upon its creation in 1974, and pursuant to the "Treasury Amendment" of the same year.[47] Such regulation seeks to protect the general public, and it excludes those transactions conducted among banks and other informed institutions.[48]

The Federal Trade Commission is tasked to ensure that advertising for currency trading conforms to legal standards of truthfulness.

Much of the protection of the system comes from internal rules of the particular regional market or professional associations and committees. In New York, the Foreign Exchange Committee of the Federal Reserve Bank of New York has approximately twenty-five members from the major banks, and other financial services companies in the United States. The Committee's *Guidelines for Foreign Exchange Trading Activities*[49] functions as a handbook for ethical currency trading. Within the banks and other firms, currency trading is guided by internal audit rules and the prospects for regular outside audits.

The New York Foreign Exchange Committee Chair, Mark Snyder, spoke in 2005 of his concern that "retail aggregators" are pulling people into the foreign exchange market who maybe shouldn't be there. He expressed concern for the "reputational risk" to the foreign exchange markets due to negative public opinion about "products or activities." He said, "...there have been media reports and lawsuits alleging that unscrupulous retail foreign exchange aggregators have defrauded their clients."[50]

Indeed, there have been. For example, in 2013, Daniel Lucas pleaded guilty to Federal wire fraud charges after promising three investors that he would double their money in a year with foreign currency trades. He lost money on his $28,000 in trades and spent the rest of the $78,000 on himself.[51]

Rogue Traders

From time to time, large cracks develop in the system, as was the case of John Rusnak of Allfirst Bank in Maryland, US, who had lost $691 million of his employer's money over five years. Rusnak was hired in 1993 as a currency trader and pursued a profit-seeking currency trading strategy based on the belief that the Japanese yen was going to increase in value against the dollar.[52] Previously, the bank conservatively traded currencies primarily for customers who wished to protect themselves against currency fluctuations during the period of a business deal.

For example, if a customer agreed in January to purchase Japanese machinery for 1,000,000 yen on March 1, and the exchange rate was 125 yen to the dollar, the customer would want to ensure that s/he would have to pay the same $8,000 equivalent in March as was negotiated in January. Such protection is called hedging. If the exchange rate changed to 100 yen to the dollar during that period, making the yen 20 percent more expensive, the machinery would cost $10,000, if no currency insurance or hedging were purchased. The hedging could be in the form of an option to purchase 1,000,000 yen on March 1 for $8,000 plus fees plus a risk premium for the risk the seller will take that the currency will, indeed, increase in value by March 1. Such currency insurance might cost an Allfirst customer approximately $500, thus bringing the cost of the machinery to $8,500, but avoiding the risk that it might cost $10,000.

Pursuing the more aggressive strategy from 1993 until 1997, Rusnak's foreign exchange trades seemed to generate income for the bank and for its customers. However, in 1997 he lost $29.1 million and thereafter desperately tried to reverse the tide while concealing his efforts. He continued to lose money until the deception was uncovered in early 2002. Caught and convicted, he served most of his seven and one-half year sentence. He was released in 2009 and has been making repayment installments at the rate of $1,000 per month for the five years of his probation. [53]

In January 2005, the National Australia Bank discovered a 360 million Australian dollar loss due to unauthorized currency trading by four traders. The losses led to a management shakeup and criminal charges. [54]

In January 2006, a long-term J.P. Morgan Chase employee, Terrence Gumbs, was fired and later arrested for making an unauthorized order to sell €385 million on a certain date. He placed the order in an effort to achieve sufficient profits to make up for earlier losses of $300,000. Instead, his foreign exchange contracts cost the bank approximately $6 million. [55]

In August 2007, Joel N. Ward pleaded guilty in California to fraud and money laundering in a scheme which may have defrauded about 100 clients of more than $11 million. His crimes started normally enough as he established his "Joel Nathan Forex Fund" in 2003. He suffered losses and began to pay his original investors with more recent investments, and thus transformed his fund into a Ponzi scheme. By 2006 he confessed to his investors that he had lost it all. The feisty spirit of currency traders was evident when he and 52 of his 93 defrauded customers requested at his 2007 sentencing hearing that the judge allow him to continue currency trading so he could repay his investors. The judge declined the suggestion, and sentenced Ward to nine years in Federal prison. [56]

For the period 2001-2008, the Commodities Futures Trading Commission (CFTC) in the US has estimated that about 26,000 individuals lost approximately $460 million in currency-trading frauds. [57]

The largest currency trading market is in London, and thus the largest temptation to fix prices. In 2013 and 2014 regulators in the US and the UK began investigating allegations that currency traders at the largest international banks had worked together to manipulate currency prices. Even before the investigation was completed, several currency traders had been fired after internal bank investigations. [58] The size of the fraud, which may have begun in 2006, [59] may be as large as the LIBOR-interest rate-fixing scandal which had resulted in record-setting fines of about $3.6 billion. [60]

Speculation Plays Large and Dangerous role

Who are the speculators? They are everyone who buys or sells currency for reasons unrelated to the actual need for currency for financial or trading transactions.

George Soros is probably the world's most famous currency speculator. He was born in Hungary and now lives in New York, where he runs several financial funds and is an active philanthropist. His most famous currency gamble was his bet that the British pound was overvalued in September 1992, and he profited by as much as £500 million. At the time, the Bank of England tried to hold the value of the pound within the range agreed upon as part of the European Rate Mechanism (ERM), roughly at 2.95 deutschmarks. The economic fundamentals in the United Kingdom were weak, and Soros sold pounds short and purchased deutschemarks, meaning that he contracted to sell pounds at a later date, when they would be worth less than at the time of the currency contract. The Bank of England attempted to intervene in the markets by purchasing billions of pounds, but it failed and on 17 September 1992, the British Chancellor of the Exchequer declared defeat and took the pound out of the ERM and let it float on the markets as it has done since then.[61]

One of the world's most successful investors is Warren Buffett, with an entirely self-made personal worth of approximately $53.5 billion.[62] He announced in 2002 that he was pessimistic about the value of the dollar, in view of the large trade and federal government deficits, and that his company, Berkshire Hathaway, was going to speculate in the currency markets against the dollar.[63]

David Leonhardt, of *The New York Times,* reported in 2006 that Buffett lost approximately $1 billion betting against the dollar by investing in other currencies.[64] In recent years, there has been little reporting of Buffett's currency trades, which have presumably declined. One exception came in Berkshire Hathaway's March 2008 report which reported a profit of $100 million from the buying and selling of the Brazilian currency, the real.[65] The company's 2010 annual report showed a profit of $100 million in currency trading involving the Australian dollar.[66] These profits had a zero relationship with the provision of goods and services for customers of the companies owned by Berkshire Hathaway.

Trying to hedge against potential losses in dollar denominated assets, former US Treasury Secretary Robert Rubin invested in assets denominated in foreign currencies,. In 2006, he lost approximately $1 million because the dollar did not decline as predicted. As he said afterwards, "But I don't know. I really don't. I don't think anyone does. It's possible that none of this [large decline of the US dollar] could happen."[67]

On 29 January 2005, Bloomberg.com reported that Bill Gates, the world's richest person, "is betting against the dollar."[68] He was quoted as saying "I'm short the dollar." Without knowing the details of his transactions, he could have gone "short" using different types of transactions. Let's suppose that on Monday, 10 January, he purchased $100 million in euros from a currency dealer in Chicago and promised to pay that person back $100 million in dollars on 10 November 2005. That is, he could have purchased a contract, committing him to deliver $100 million on 10 November. On 10 January 2005, with the exchange rate of

$1.3108/euro he could have purchased €76,289,289. By 10 November, with the exchange rate of $1.1740/euro he could have sold the €76,289,289, but would have been able to purchase only $89,563,626 and thus would have been short $10,436,374, i.e., a loss of that amount. Thus, to perform his contract to deliver $100 million, he would have needed to dip into other assets for the $10,436,374 and cover his loss. Since this dip into the FX markets, Mr. Gates has appeared to steer clear of foreign exchange trading.

Another speculator is the lesser-known Henryk de Kwiatkowski. For his own personal account, he traded a large volume of currency futures over five months, beginning in late in 1994. In the first few trading weeks, he netted over $200 million but then suffered successive daily losses of $112 million, $98 million, and $70 million. In 2000, he sued his brokerage firm, Bear Stearns, in New York District Court for his losses. He was awarded $164.5 million on the theory that his broker should have kept him informed about factors affecting market prices. In September 2001, the Appeals Court for the Second Circuit reversed the verdict and found that Mr. de Kwiatkowski was responsible for his losses and was not an unsuspecting victim. The court noted his "trading experience, his business sophistication, and his gluttonous appetite for risk."[69]

A core message of this book is that the people of the world, and their corporations want stable money. However, speculators are among those who thrive amidst currency volatility as it "creates opportunities to trade."[70] Volatility is such an important measure for speculators and other currency traders that there are several indices to track it, e.g. the Deutsche Bank "Currency Volatility Index."[71]

Related to the world of speculators is the unofficial "black market" for currencies which exists when government seeks to over-control the foreign exchange trading sought by citizens. Typically, the black market in currencies thrives when countries fix the value of their currencies at an unrealistic value. In March 2014, Venezuela was such a country, as the bolivar traded on th black market at a rate approximately "13 times the official rate of 6.3 against the greenback."[72] Indeed, the black market currency values are said to be more accurate reflections of currency values than the nominal values.[73]

One friend recalls that he was in Egypt on a monthly US dollar allowance which he calculated was not sufficient to sustain him if he used those dollars to purchase Egyptian pounds at the official rate. So he took his dollars to the black market and traded them for Egyptian pounds at the higher unofficial exchange rate. He recalls never being so scared in his life, as he watched a dealer take his money and then disappear behind a curtain; and not return for several minutes. The rules in the black market are different from those at Egyptian banks.

Another friend, who is now an economics professor, recalls making money as a young boy in Central America when his grandmother would send him deutschmarks as birthday presents and he would trade them for local currency on the black market rather than at the lower exchange rate at an official bank.

Transaction Costs

Willem Buiter, a supporter of the euro, wrote that "The transaction cost saving advantages of a common currency are familiar…. The usefulness to me of a medium of exchange is increasing in the number of other economic agents likely to accept it in exchange for goods, services and securities. By eliminating the need for the exchange of one currency for another, monetary union saves real resources."[74] Although the concept of the savings from elimination of transaction costs is commonly understood, there are few studies of such savings, and none, worldwide.

What are transaction costs? They are the salaries of the traders and all the corporate infrastructures which support them, and the purchases and maintenance of the computers and all the associated costs of buying and selling complex securities. They are often invisible and have to be calculated.

When I purchased the book, *Le Chateau de Sable,* on the internet, the quoted price in Canadian dollars was $28.00 CAD[75] plus $5.00 CAD for shipping. When the bank statement arrived with the charge of $28.93 USD, it utilized the exchange rate of $.851212, which was almost identical to the Bank of Canada quoted rate for that day. In addition, there was included a $1 CAD "exchange rate adjustment," which works out to be a 3.57 percent transaction charge.

When I purchased Paul De Grauwe's *Economics of Monetary Union* from Amazon.com.uk, the quoted price was £29.99 plus a delivery charge of £6.98 for a total of £36.97. Amazon.com.uk then used the exchange rate of $1.7736 to the Pound, which was very close for the Bank of Canada rate for the day, and my Visa card was billed $65.61. Thus, Amazon.com bundled its foreign exchange transaction charges into its "delivery charge" and it was invisible to me.

Transaction costs are often unbundled or invisible. In her refreshing look at global trade, *The Travels of a T-Shirt,*[76] Pietra Rivoli traces the life of an American T-shirt beginning in the cotton fields of Texas and ending in a second-hand clothing store in Tanzania. The first currency transaction comes when the Texas cotton is sold to China and the second is when the T-shirts are sold back to the United States as finished clothing. The final transaction is when the used T-shirt is sold in bulk to used clothing dealers in Tanzania. However, as an illustration of how the huge world of foreign exchange and currency transactions can be invisible to some, including economists, the book does not mention the issue in any way.[77] Each transaction is like a particle of DDT which is undetectable to individual taste, but it adds up and large concentrations can be expensive.

For people purchasing foreign currency cash online through such companies as American Express, Oanda, and Wells Fargo, the percentage charges are typically between 4-7 percent, when purchases are less than 1,000 dollars.[78] When inputting information in March 2014 for a demonstration order for €1,000, the Wells Fargo utility used an exchange rate of $1.4591. On that day, the Bank of Canada quoted rate[79] was $1.3868, a rate which meant that Wells Fargo was charging me $.07 per euro, or 5.2 percent more than its cost when purchasing euros in large $1 million-plus blocks. These numbers meant that Wells Fargo would have charged me $1,459.10 for euros it would have cost the bank $1,386.80, which is a difference of $72.30. As this purchase would have been for more than the bank's threshold of $1,000 of foreign currency, the $15.00 shipping and handling fee would have been omitted. Added to the $72.30 cost would be the value of my time to shop for the best deal and then to complete the online form, and the charge from my credit card company to pay Wells Fargo, invisible to me though it may be. All together, let's assume the transaction cost for that one purchase was $100, or 6.85 percent of the $1,459.10 Wells Fargo would have charged me for €1,000. At that retail rate, the transaction cost of the $5.3 trillion traded daily worldwide would be $363 billion. Compared to the estimate in this book of $300 billion for the annual transactions costs, the $363 billion shows the dramatic difference between retail and wholesale and between small and large transactions.

Wells Fargo's utility has a "Frequently Asked Questions" section and the obvious question is asked and answered: "Why are rates quoted on the site different from those in the newspaper? Answer: Rates quoted in newspapers aren't available to the public. These rates are usually wholesale rates available on amounts of $1 million or more, transferred electronically between banks."[80]

In general, credit card companies charge one percent for consumer foreign exchange transactions and many banks add another one percent.[81] PayPal, now a division of E-Bay, "adds a 2.5 percent spread above" the Interbank rate, and it also charges one percent "cross-border fees" which may include foreign exchange charges.[82]

As most of the $5.3 trillion daily currency trading is in larger sized trades than my hypothetical Wells-Fargo $995.79 purchase of currency or my $28.93 purchase of *Le Chateau de Sable*, or $65.57 purchase of *Economics of Monetary Union*, the percentage cost of such trading is substantially lower for all trades on average. In fact, my currency trades were not even recorded in the foreign exchange markets as they were included in the vastly larger transactions by Wells-Fargo, the Montreal bookseller's bank, and Amazon.com.uk.

The European Council's 1990 pre-euro study, *One Market, One Money*, cited a 1988 Belgian experiment which involved a hypothetical person traveling through 10 European Community countries and converting all his/her cash at each border. Beginning with 40,000 Belgian francs, the traveler ended the hypothetical journey with 21,300 Belgian francs, showing a cost of 47 percent, for an average of 4.7 percent cost for each transaction.[83] If a similar traveler had traveled in 2006 from Belgium with €40,000 to all of the 146 other currency areas, with each charging 4.7 percent for currency exchanges on average, his or her funds would have diminished to less than €1,000 by the 78th currency, and dropped to €35.45 by the 146th. These high transaction cost hypotheticals were for cash, and the foreign exchange transaction charge percentages decline dramatically for large, non-cash transactions. Nonetheless, even small charges still add up. If the border exchanges charged only two percent, the worldwide "€40,000" traveler would have returned with only €2,094.

On 27 December 2006, I sold a Canadian twenty-dollar bill at a local Maine bank for $18.20, which translated into roughly a 6 percent transaction charge, compared to the Bank of Canada or Oanda quoted rates. At that rate, our traveler would have had to leave Belgium with €413,000 in order to ensure a return home with at least €1,000, perhaps to celebrate being a multicurrency foreign exchange system survivor.

Paraphrasing the late US Senator Everett Dirksen, if you take a bit of small change here and a bit of small change there, pretty soon we are talking real money.[84]

For the poor of the world, these percentages matter when they were applied to the $514 billion in remittances in 2012 received from relatives and friends who have migrated to employment elsewhere.[85] Jose de Luna Martinez of the World Bank has written that the exchange rate transaction charge is one of the three components of the 8.3-10 percent transaction fee which is applied to remittances.[86] If the exchange rate transaction charge was only one percentage point of that 8.3-10 percent range, that means that at least $5.14 billion was charged to the poor as their subsidy for the multicurrency foreign exchange system.

International Travelers

As noted with the Belgian study of a hypothetical traveler converting currency at each border, travelers pay dearly for the multicurrency foreign exchange system.

In addition to high transaction charges, they also leave unconverted their foreign currencies and accumulate bills and coins in pockets or purses and then in containers at home. While resting there, the contents of those containers change value according to the exchange markets, but they do not earn interest. Except for the value of the metal in the coins, the money has no intrinsic value and it's invested in nothing productive; and represents another inefficient and inconvenient aspect of the multicurrency foreign exchange system. One company, Travelex, addresses this need with an online utility, "Sell Us Your Currency" whereby customers print out a form and mail their foreign currency to the company, and home-currency cash or credit will be returned.[87]

International Investors

The fluctuations in currency values have significant effects on investors. In 2013, the USD price of a euro increased 3.8 percent from $1.32 to $1.37, which thus represented a 3.8 percent decline in the value of the US dollar as measured against the euro. In contrast, the USD price of 100 yen decreased 17.4 percent from $1.15 to $.95, and thus the value of the US dollar increased by 17.4 percent.[88] For example, for Europeans who invested in stocks paralleling the Standard and Poor Index which gained 25.5 percent, the currency fluctuation eliminated a small part of the gain, but for similar Japanese investors, the increase was nearly doubled by adding the 17.4 percent to the 28.5 percent for a total of 45.9 percent. All international investors know that currency risk is a major part of such investing, but the wide fluctuations of these three major anchor currencies to each other divert investor attention from the real value of their primary investments.

International Corporations

International corporations make investments and sell products and services around the world and must constantly be on the alert for currency risk. They must price their products and services in the currencies of their customers and always be alert that the exchange rates will not eliminate their profits. In addition to paying a percentage on all their foreign exchange transactions, international corporations have to cope with the fluctuations of foreign exchange values, in two areas: reporting and worldwide allocation of resources.

Reporting

Honda Motor Company is the eighth largest automobile manufacturer in the world as measured in 2011. It has been the world's largest motorcycle manufacturer since 1959, as well as the world's largest manufacturer of internal combustion engines measured by unit volume.[89] For the fiscal year ending 31 March 2013, Honda reported a 24.3 percent increase in net sales and operating revenue and attributed some of the increase to "favorable foreign currency effects."[90] As noted earlier, the yen declined in value 17.4 percent relative to the US dollar during calendar 2013. For the period of Honda's 2013 fiscal year, the decline was 12.3 percent.

In several instances, the Honda *Annual Report* clarified the statements of earnings of its divisions with comments about current fluctuations, e.g.

> "Total amount of finance subsidiaries-receivables and property on operating leases of finance subsidiaries increased by ¥955.3 billion, or 19.4%, to ¥5,874.2 billion from the previous fiscal year. Honda estimates that by applying Japanese yen exchange rates of the previous fiscal year to the current fiscal year, total amount of finance subsidiaries-receivables... would have increased by approximately ¥281.0 billion, or 5.7%, compared to the increase as reported of ¥955.3 billion which includes positive foreign currency translation effects."[91]

Thus, the reported increase was three times larger using the actual currency values during the current fiscal year, than if the currency values of the previous year had been used. Does this make cents/sense?

Vodafone is a multinational telecommunications company with operations in 70 countries and headquarters in London. It is the world's third-largest mobile telecommunications company measured by both subscribers and 2011 revenues, and is the third largest company traded on the London Stock Exchange.[92]

As with Honda a year later, Vodafone faced gains and losses in its fiscal year 2012 caused by foreign exchange valuation fluctuation in several of its operations, including sales and leasing. The company reported that the net foreign exchange gain in the consolidated income statement for the year ended 31 March 2012 was £702 million. The net consolidated income was £2.35 billion, which meant that the FX gains constituted almost 30 percent of net income.[93] Does this make cents/sense? Should almost one-third of the revenue of one of the world's largest corporations be determined not by the work or ideas of its employees, or the quality of its products, but by the skills of its FX managers who cope with the vagaries of the foreign exchange system? Its annual report mentioned "foreign exchange" 29 times. Here is one summary statement about "foreign exchange management," which could be from any of the world's multinational corporations.

> "As Vodafone's primary listing is on the London Stock Exchange its share price is quoted in sterling. Since the sterling share price represents the value of its future multi-currency cash flows, principally in euro, US dollars, South African rand, Indian rupee and sterling, the Group maintains the currency of debt and interest charges in proportion to its expected future principal multi-currency cash flows and has a policy to hedge external foreign exchange risks on transactions denominated in other currencies above certain de minimis levels."[94]

While the companies cited above are international, and the effects of currency fluctuation have been substantial, Mark Hulbert has written that international corporations are "immune from the effects of currency fluctuations," to the extent that their operations and risk are spread across currency areas.[95] However, that doesn't seem true in the two examples above, as currency fluctuation from year to year meant much to each company.

The problem is not so much profits and losses as it is uncertainty and risk—and both of which are anathema to corporations and their economies. In a standard text, *Corporate Risk-Strategies and Management*, currency risk is featured in seven of its thirty chapters.[96] All international corporations have people and departments to manage the foreign exchange risk. Joachim Herr is the CFO for BMW France, and was formerly the head of risk management at BMW International where he had approximately five people trading currencies with the goal of making "sure that the fluctuations of a currency do not impact our operating business, which is producing and selling cars."[97] He continued, "What we see ourselves as is hedgers...we have long-term strategic hedging, where we do very long, deep analysis on currency movements, and we have short-term technical hedging, where we decide how to cover the remaining open risk in the coming months...."[98] For each country where BMW operates, there is a Treasurer who is responsible for local currency exposure, and Herr estimated that such foreign exchange work takes about ten percent of such treasurers' time, which must be included as yet another cost of the multicurrency foreign exchange system.

Allocation of Resources

Richard Cooper noted that one of the widest fluctuations in currency values, the 70 percent change of the yen to the US dollar between 1995 and 1998, may have thrown many otherwise healthy firms into bankruptcy. Further, he surmises that the prolonged nature of the late 1990--2000s recession in Japan was partly caused by Japanese firms investing in other currency areas in order to hedge against losses in yen due to currency fluctuations.[99]

Many international corporations do more on the foreign exchange markets than hedge to control currency risk. One article notes, "Currency speculation has always had a vast influence on systems of flexible exchange rates. A large variety of empirical, experimental, computational, and theoretical investigations deal with this topic. But what determines the speculative decisions of a firm? Why do non-financial firms speculate [in the currency markets]? How do they deal with exchange rate uncertainty?"[100]

International Banks

For many banks, trading currencies for their customers represents a sizable portion of revenue. The European Commission's 1990 report found that such trading represented 5 percent of European banks' revenues.[101]

In 2004, the Bank of America was trading about $100 billion per day, according to Steve Nutland, Director of North American trading. Of the foreign exchange markets generally, he stated, "many people believe Forex is a necessary evil. On the institutional/hedge fund side of the business, many view it as the largest casino in the world. I like to see it that somewhere in between the two lies the truth."[102] As part of its trading business, and in order protect its own international operations, Nutland stated that the Bank of America "manages interest rate and foreign currency exchange rate sensitivity predominantly through the use of derivatives. Fair value hedges are used to limit the corporation's exposure to total changes in the fair value of its fixed interest-earning assets or interest-bearing liabilities that are due to interest rate or foreign exchange volatility. Cash flow hedges are used to minimize the variability in cash flows of interest-earning assets or interest-bearing liabilities or forecasted transactions caused by interest rate or foreign exchange fluctuation."[103] The Bank of America traded approximately $200 billion per day in 2013,[104] which is about $.03 per day for every human being.

Scotiabank is a leading Canadian Bank, and does extensive business in the United States, Mexico, South America and the Caribbean. Its 2013 *Annual Report* for the fiscal year ending 31 October 2013 reported that "Foreign currency translation had a positive impact on the Bank's earnings in 2013. On average, the Canadian dollar depreciated 1% against the US dollar and 5% against the Mexican peso."[105]

The oft-repeated phrase in the report is, "Before the impact of foreign currency translation...." and the term "currency translation" appears 27 times in the *Annual Report*. The effect is summarized, "As at October 31, 2013, a one per cent increase in the Canadian dollar against all currencies in which the Bank operates, decreases the Bank's before-tax annual earnings by approximately $47 million in the absence of hedging activity, primarily from exposure to US dollars. A similar change in the Canadian dollar would increase the unrealized foreign currency translation losses in the accumulated other comprehensive income section of shareholders' equity by approximately $224 million as at October 31, 2013, net of hedging."[106] Looking forward from 31 October 2013, the Canadian dollar (CAD) declined in value from $.96 to $.90 by 31 January 2014, a drop of six percent within three months. If that six percent drop of the value of the CAD against the USD, assuming here that the USD is equivalent to "all currencies," held steady for the entire fiscal year, that would mean a $282 million CAD increase in before-tax earnings and a decrease in accumulated comprehensive income of $1.344 billion CAD. Those are large changes which have nothing to do with the operating quality of the bank's work.

In addition to the effects of currency fluctuations on aspects of operations,
many banks are generating revenues and earning profits through their foreign exchange trading. In 1992, the foreign exchange trading profits of the top 8 US banks was $2.695 billion.[107] For the years 1984-1993, foreign exchange trading profits of seven of the largest FX trading US banks constituted 20 percent of those banks' total profits.[108]

Barclays Bank of England is one of the world's five largest foreign exchange trading banks with an approximately 10 percent market share of the world's daily $5.3 trillion trades. From that trading, in 2012 Barclays earned commissions of £176/$272 million.[109] This compares with the bank's total profits of £7/$10.8 billion. Two other top-eight banks, The Bank of New York Mellon and State Street Bank, each earned approximately $500 million from foreign exchange trading.[110]

Balance of Payments/Current Account
For all the countries/currency areas in the world, there must be a long term balance of payments for goods and services which are imported into a country/currency area and those which are exported, plus or minus capital flows. The term, "current account" is the same as "balance of payments," except that it excludes "capital transfers" or money used to buy/sell long term investments.

In theory, there are balancing factors which force countries into equilibrium, assuming a floating foreign exchange rate. For example, if a country is buying more than it is selling and its foreign reserves of other currencies necessarily decline in order to make those purchases, and the demand for its currency decreases; then the foreign exchange markets take notice. The result is that the value of the currency drops and the country's exports become cheaper, which leads to an increase in exports, which then leads to a surplus. Then, the value of the currency rises, and the cycle renews. Another remedy, for short term imbalances, is a loan from the IMF.

Considering the money supply of every country as a fuel tank, there must be a sufficient inflow of fuel to balance the consumption outflow. If an imbalance continues for too long, the tank will either overflow or run out. With a money supply, payments out of a currency must balance receipts into a currency. When receipts exceed payments, the reserves of a currency area's central bank increase; and the reverse causes depletion. While an overflow can be a problem, the much-feared danger for a money supply is extended outflow, causing a central bank's reserves to diminish so far as to reduce confidence in the value of the currency, possibly leading to a currency crisis. Thus, every central bank watches closely the balance of payments of its own currency.

The only country in the world which appears to be immune from the requirement that the current account be in balance is the United States, because the US dollar is recognized as the world's primary reserve currency and it is used throughout the world. More than one-half of the $1.2 trillion in US currency in circulation is circulating outside the United States.[111] There is no rush or panic to send those dollars home and use them to purchase US goods and services, because the dollars are useful in other countries as widely accepted money.

The major source for the US current account deficit is the trade deficit as more US citizens purchase foreign goods and services than foreigners purchase from the United States. In 2013 the trade in goods and services deficit was nearly $700 billion out of balance.[112] However, due to a surplus in other accounts, the overall current account deficit, defined by the US Dept. of Commerce as "the combined balances on trade in goods and services, income, and net unilateral current transfers," was running at the rate of approximately $380 billion annually, or approximately 2.2 percent of the US GDP.[113]

Except for a few years in the 1990's of balanced Federal Government budgets, the United States consistently has accumulated large annual deficits running into the hundreds of billions of dollars, and constituting three to ten percent of the annual Gross Domestic Product of the country. It has sold its bonds on the open market to finance its vast borrowing, and because the United States is viewed as a stable economy, foreigners purchase these debt securities in large amounts. Floyd Norris has noted in *The New York Times* that almost all of the increase in the US national debt incurred since 2000 has been purchased by foreigners.[114]

One may ask here why the US dollar cannot be regarded as the Single Global Currency, as some have suggested. The short answer is that while it's used in the retail marketplace around the world, it's not deemed as "legal tender" for all obligations including the payment of taxes in other countries. Also, its value is tied inextricably to the fortunes of one country, and its management is not shared with others as would be the case with a common currency in a monetary union. It is a national currency first, and a global currency second.

What Are The Real Costs to this Multicurrency Foreign Exchange System?

So far we have explored a system that is huge and has some pitfalls and risks and is largely invisible. How much does all this really cost, and how much might it cost if it breaks? The most easily quantifiable determination of cost is the total cost of foreign exchange transactions and then there are estimates of the cost of artificially low asset values due to currency risk, and then the potential cost of currency crises and, worst of all, a worldwide currency crisis.

Estimate of Total Worldwide Annual Transaction Costs--$300 Billion

In studies prepared during the run-up in the 1990s to the introduction of the euro, it was estimated that foreign exchange transaction costs were approximately .3 percent (.003] of the value of the currency being traded.[115] Applying that percentage to the daily $5.3 trillion now being traded daily, the daily transactions cost would be $15.9 billion and the annual cost to the world, using a 260 trading day year would be $4.1 trillion per year.

Since the European Commission studies were done, the automation of the currency markets has continued and the per-transaction costs of trading have dropped dramatically in the 24 years since 1990. In 2011, Joseph Gagnon, of the Peterson Institute of Economics, estimated that the annual global foreign exchange trading transaction costs probably did not exceed $325 billion.[116] That amount is rounded here to $300 billion, which translates to .022 percent per transaction. Again showing the high degree of automation since the 1990s, this represents 7.3 percent of the previous level of per transaction charges, i.e. the .3 percent.

Another such cost is the administrative burden of requiring some contracting parties to denominate a foreign currency as the currency of the contract. The European Commission's *One Market, One Money* study estimated that there would be a .05 percent GDP benefit to the European Community member countries when corporations and others engaging in international contracts could denominate their obligations in their home currency rather than in a foreign currency, such as the dollar.[117]

Another way to summarize the total cost of transactions is to express them as a percentage of GDP. "Focusing only on the transaction costs that are incurred in the Canadian foreign exchange market," John Murray found in 1999 those costs to be $3.0 billion (CAD) annually, or .4 percent of GDP.[118]

The *One Market, One Money* study found that "Overall, transaction costs can be conservatively estimated to amount to around 1/2 percent of GDP...."[119] In 1996, the IFO Institute of Munich found that "foreign exchange management costs within the EU amounted to almost 1 percent of the EU12 GDP in 1995," and explained that more up-to-date data accounted for the increased estimate.[120] Although trade and international financial transactions accounted for a larger percentage of the GDP for European countries than for others in 1990, the world has globalized significantly since then, so that the 1 percent estimate can be fairly applied to the rest of the world. Hugo Mendizabal found that the savings to the EMU from the elimination of intra-EMU transactions could be as much as .69 percent of EMU GDP, which accounted for one-half of members' international trade foreign exchange transactions.[121] For all transactions, including those with non-EMU countries, the percentage would be double, or 1.38 percent. However, that was then.

Using the rounded estimate of $300 billion for the annual transaction cost of all foreign exchange trading, the percentage of those costs to the estimated global GDP for 2013 of $73.9 trillion[122] of would be .41 percent.

We've seen how much $5.3 trillion per day might be. Although it is still nearly impossibly large to understand, it is easier than that amount annualized by multiplying by 260 trading days. (It's one quadrillion, 378 trillion.) We know that $300 billion is a much smaller number than $5.3 trillion. But how much is $300 billion, really?

Figure 1.1 How much is $300 billion? It's equivalent to:

$43	for every human being on earth;
177	times the annual budget of the United Nations;[123]
12	times the total value of worldwide microloans; and[124]
97	times the estimated annual global spending for family planning and reproductive health care support.[125]

The Cost of Low Asset Values Due to Currency Risk.

When calculating the value of an asset, an investor or owner must determine the likelihood of getting a real return on that investment; and such return will be adversely affected in inverse proportion to currency risk.

When the value of an asset is artificially low, compared to similar assets in other situations or places, the difference in value can be said to be a cost or opportunity cost. That is, owners of such undervalued assets are losing the opportunity to use that asset for other purposes that might be available if valuation were not artificially deflated by currency risk.

One down-to-earth illustration of the effect of high exchange risk on asset values is the status of the home mortgage market around the world. The issue in the United States or Europe is not whether there are mortgages available, but whether they are for ten, fifteen, twenty, or thirty years and whether they have a fixed rate or an adjustable rate, to be moved up or down with the linked prime rate. In contrast, in some parts of the world, mortgages are not available because of the high long term currency risk. John Edmonds pointed out to me in 2003 that mortgages with longer terms than a year were unavailable in Buenos Aires, due to Argentina's on-again, off-again currency problems. As mortgages were unavailable, demand for homes was crippled, and the resulting oversupply led to prices which were a small fraction of their equivalent value in a similar city and neighborhood in the United States or Europe. For example, a three-bedroom home in London might be worth €490,000, but the same home in Buenos Aires might be worth about €70,000 (252,700 Argentine pesos). The general situation in Buenos Aires continues in 2014 according to one observer, "There are currently no mortgage products available in Argentina for foreign investors, and even for resident Argentineans the conditions and interest rates on loans are prohibitive."[126]

Similarly, the values of financial assets in the less developed, or high currency risk or sovereign risk,[127] world, are undervalued because of that currency risk, i.e., the risk that a currency might severely inflate or collapse. Due to currency risk, the ability to earn reliable interest on an asset far into the future is in doubt, and therefore potential lenders are unwilling to lend. If they do decide to lend, they require much higher interest rates. Financial assets such as stocks and bonds are also undervalued due to the uncertainty of the currency value of future returns.

McKinsey Global Institute estimates that in 2013 the total value of the world's financial assets was $225 trillion[128], but if all currency risk were lowered to the same level as the developed world, and if the ratio of asset value to GDP were the same, it's estimated here that as much as $10 trillion (4.6 percent) additional value would be added. That opportunity cost amount could be called a cost of the existing multicurrency foreign exchange system.

Currency Crises

When confidence in a currency falls, then foreigners and citizens within a currency area accelerate their selling of the home currency and the purchase of other currencies. If confidence in the currency is not restored quickly, a classic market panic will set in and a currency crisis will begin, causing enormous loss of wealth and confidence in an economy. In the 1990s several currency crises shook the international financial system: Mexico (1994), Argentina (1995, and again in 2001), East Asia (1997), and Russia (1998). In 2008, Iceland's currency collapsed. In 2003-2009, Zimbabwe experienced hyper-inflation and then abandoned its own currency, forcing its citizens to use the US dollar, the South African rand and six other currencies, all of which were in short supply.[129] At the height of the Zimbabwe crisis, the country issued the largest known currency note in the global history of money, for 100 trillion Zimbabwean dollars.[130] In early 2014, Turkey, India, and Brazil experienced volatile currency problems, but not rising to the level of a currency crisis or collapse.

These crises caused significant economic damage to the affected countries and their peoples. Benn Still and Robert Litan reported that in Asia, "an estimated 22 million people were pushed into poverty by currency crises. In Thailand, where the crisis started, unemployment rose from 0.9 percent in 1997 to 5.3 percent in 1998, and measures of poverty rose significantly. Household expenditure on health care declined by 40 percent from 1996 levels.... But the hardest hit was Indonesia, which at one point saw its currency, the rupiah, fall to a mere 15 percent of its pre-crisis value. The country's 13.8 percent GDP decline in 1998 was comparable to the total decline over the worst of the Depression years (1929-32) in the United Kingdom."[131]

Argentina's GDP dropped 7 percent in 1989 and 10.9 percent in 2002.[132] Michael Hutchison and Ilan Neuberger estimated that currency crises in twenty-four emerging market economies during the years 1975-1997 suffered a 5-8 percent GDP output reduction over a typical two-to-three year period, before returning to a normal growth rate.[133]

The Iceland crisis began in 2008 as a banking crisis when all three of the country's commercial banks failed. As the banks had assets valued at 11 times the GDP of Iceland, with its population of 320,000, the problem dwarfed the ability of its central bank to save the krona, and the banking crisis became a currency crisis. An international consortium rescued the currency and the economy and the crisis officially ended in 2011.[134] However, the lives of many, if not most, of Iceland's citizens were forever damaged.

Several factors have been identified which facilitate and worsen a currency crisis such as an unrealistic fixed exchange rate, government instability, lack of capital controls and lack of central bank independence.[135] For example, if a currency with a fixed exchange rate to the euro is perceived by speculators and others to be artificially high, and thus likely to be lowered at some point, holders of that currency will move their assets into stronger currencies. Such sales will then reinforce the perception that a currency is overvalued and weak. Without capital controls, large amounts of money can be transferred quickly, and the selling can quickly become a rout, which a weak government may be unable to stop.

One irony about currency crises among smaller nations is that they have the perverse effect of boosting the value of the premier global currencies such as the USD, the euro and the Swiss franc as investors, citizens and corporations purchase assets in those currencies to escape those enduring currency problems in the weaker currencies.[136]

Note that there are three related types of financial crises: currency crises, banking crises where banks fail, and debt crises where individuals, corporations and nations default on their debts.[137] In this book, we focus on the first, the currency crisis. Each type of financial crisis may well lead to one or two of the others, but we are concerned here about those situations where there is a currency crisis.

Accumulated current account deficits are like accumulations of DDT in the bodies of animals, and up the food chain. At some point, the financial body cannot tolerate the imbalances and a crisis occurs. As with animals dying from DDT poisoning, it's hard to pinpoint the precipitant cause of death, but in a weakened financial system, a financial crisis can start when one individual or bank or government refuses to accept payment in a currency because a person has lost confidence in that currency's ability to hold its value for other transactions.

The emphasis in this book is not about trumpeting the fear of a regional or worldwide financial or currency crisis. There is enough fear in the world today. Nonetheless, it's important to note that there is considerable risk in the current foreign exchange system to cause concern, and many are sounding that alarm.

Former US Secretary of Commerce Peter G. Peterson wrote, "Many see a risk of a real crisis." He continued, "Former Federal Reserve Chairman Paul Volcker says the odds of this happening are around 75 percent within the next five years; former US Treasury Secretary Robert Rubin talks of 'a day of serious reckoning'."[138] Harvard University President, and former US Treasury Secretary and 2006 World Economic Forum Annual Davos Meeting Co-Chair, Larry Summers, stated in a pre-meeting interview, "There is the ever present risk that these balances will not prove sustainable and the adjustment process will be disrupted. If that happens there will be serious consequences for the US economy and the global economy."[139] What they foresaw may, or may not, have been the global financial crisis of 2007-2011. Or it may be the next.

As the next large currency crisis, with Iceland being a small crisis, has not occurred since the first edition of this book in 2006, a specific cost cannot be predicted in advance; but, by definition, a currency crisis affects all the users of a currency. Hundreds of billions of dollars are at risk, as are the livelihoods of millions, if not billions, of people. Every currency crisis that occurs until the implementation of a Single Global Currency will have been totally avoidable, and a vast waste.

Summary

The multicurrency foreign exchange trading world in 2014 is complex, expensive, unstable and hazardous. The economic well-being of every human being depends upon the international financial system, and therefore the system should be inexpensive, stable, safe and easy to understand.

The dangers and risks from the multicurrency system do not come from the lack of effort by many smart, well-intentioned people to make the multicurrency foreign exchange system work. Chapter 2 explores some of those efforts.

ENDNOTES

1. The rhythm for the title of this chapter may have come from reading aloud Judith Viorst's book, *Alexander and the Terrible, Horrible, No Good, Very Bad Day,* to granddaughters Madeline, Cameron and Sophie. New York, NY: Aladdin Paperbacks, Simon & Shuster, 1972.
2. The count of 140 comes from the listing on the Single Global Currency Association website, www.singleglobalcurrency.org/currencies_by_country.html.
   As with many count-em-ups, a lot depends upon definition, and the choice of the 193 UN members is a stake-in-the-ground starting point. There are actually many more currencies in the world. In addition to the "complementary" or "alternate" currencies which are discussed later in this book, there are a number of territories or countries with ambiguous political status which have convertible currencies, such as Netherlands Antilles, Aruba, Cayman Islands, Falkland Islands, Hong Kong, Macao, and Taiwan.
3. The term "currency area" became widely used upon the 1961 publication of Robert Mundell's "A Theory of Optimum Currency Areas,"*American Economic Review*, May 1961, pp. 657-65. The article is also contained in Robert Mundell's textbook, *International Economics*, as Chapter 12, pp. 177-86, and online at http://www.columbia.edu/~ram15/ie/ie-12.html. He originally defined "currency area" as a "domain within which exchange rates are fixed," at p. 662.
4. "Triennial Central Bank Survey: Foreign Exchange turnover in April 2013: preliminary global results," Bank for International Settlements, Sept. 2013, at https://www.bis.org/publ/rpfx13fx.pdf.
5. As reported for April, 2013, the daily total for the non-traditional "interest derivatives" was $2.3 trillion. At the end of June 2013, the notational value of "over the counter derivatives" was $693 trillion. See http://www.bis.org/publ/rpfx13.htm.

6. Shaohua Chen and Martin Ravallion, "The Developing World Is Poorer Than We Thought, But No Less Successful in the Fight against Poverty," The World Bank Development Research Group, Policy Research Working Paper 4703, August 2008, at http://www.wds.worldbank.org/external/default/WDSContentServer/IW3 P/IB/2010/01/21/000158349_20100121133109/Rendered/PDF/WPS470 3.pdf

7. Senator Everett Dirksen was a US Senator from Illinois and he used to tell a story to the same effect: "An old man once taught me what a million is. He said, look at your watch, and watch the second hand. You can see it every second, every minute, every day, every night, every week, every month, every year--and in three years it would go around 1,000,000 times." from http://en.thinkexist.com/quotes/everett_dirksen/. However, it would actually take a little less than two years as there are 525,600 minutes in a year.

8. "Gross world product," *Wikipedia*, http://en.wikipedia.org/wiki/Gross_world_product

9. This concept that foreign exchange represents the bartering of different goods, i.e., currencies, is, like some other ideas, an idea that I thought I developed on my own. As with most such ideas, there indeed was at least someone else. In this case, Richard Cooper had this to say, "Yet the exchange rate is technically not anchored by anything in the long run, being the barter price between two nominal variables (as Kareken and Wallace pointed out two decades ago)," in Richard Cooper, "Should Capital Controls Be Banished," in B.N. Ghosh, *Global Financial Crises and Reforms: Cases and Caveats*, page 401.

10. For an impassioned statement of the value of money, see "Francisco's Money Speech" in Ayn Rand's *Atlas Shrugged*, 1957, at http://capmag.com/article.asp?ID=1826. Francisco d'Anconia said, in part, "To trade by means of money is the code of the men of good will. Money rests on the axiom that every man is the owner of his mind and his effort. Money allows no power to prescribe the value of your effort except the voluntary choice of the man who is willing to trade you his effort in return. Money permits you to obtain for your goods and your labor that which they are worth to the men who buy them, but no more. Money permits no deals except those to mutual benefit by the unforced judgment of the traders."

11. World Trade Organization, *International Trade Statistics*, 2012, cover, http://www.wto.org/english/res_e/statis_e/its2012_e/its2012_e.pdf

12. "Gross World Product," *Wikipedia*, http://en.wikipedia.org/wiki/Gross_world_product with 2011 GDP calculated backwards from the 2012 GDP minus the 2011-2012 growth.

13. Dominick Salvatore, "The Euro-Dollar Exchange Rate Defies Prediction," *Journal of Policy Modeling*, June 2005, pp. 455-64, at http://www.sciencedirect.com/science/article/pii/S0161893805000451

14. During my research for this book, I found many such puzzles and may have discovered a new one which can be called the "currency pair sum puzzle." However, as with most ideas, it's likely that someone has already

identified this puzzle and solved it, or deemed it not a puzzle at all. I wondered about the sum of the two currency values in a traded pair, e.g., the euro/US dollar on 4 January 1999 of .8422/1.1874 summing to be 2.0296, and the significance of the changes in that sum over time. Looking at the daily sum of those pairs in 1999, the highest value for the sum was actually that first day of trading of the euro and it was also the high for the year for the euro (low for the US dollar). The sum never dropped below 2.0000, which point was reached on the same day as the euro low for the year on 3 December at $.9984, and on other days as well. On 30 December 2004, when the euro hit a high of $1.35, the sum was 2.0924.

To what extent should this sum be a "constant sum game," analogous to zero sum games? Readers who have comments on this puzzle, please send them to me at morrison@singleglobalcurrency.org. Better yet, and consistent with the general request in this book to economists, please devote whatever energy you might spend on the above and idly contemplated "puzzle" to the far more important issues of the Single Global Currency.

15. This point was made independently by Rainer Esslen in a letter to the *New York Times*, 18 June 1998, at http://www.nytimes.com/1998/06/18/opinion/18iht-edlet.t_30.html. He wrote "Money should, after all, be a steady measure of value, not a commodity in itself. How would international trade fare if the weight of the kilogram were different all over the world and changed drastically from day to day?

We Europeans are on the right track with the euro, but the world must go on to the uno, or whatever, if we are to overcome the vested interests in money manipulation and in currency trading and speculation."

16. Jose Luis Cordeiro, "Monetary Systems in Developing Countries: An Unorthodox View," IDE discussion paper #154, May, 2008 at http://ir.ide.go.jp/dspace/bitstream/2344/765/1/ARRIDE_Discussion_No.154_cordeiro.pdf. The Irving Fisher quote was from *The Purchasing Power of Money: Its Determination and Relation to Credit Interest and Crises*, 1911.

17. Rebecca Thurlow, "Australian Exporters Benefit From Currency Swing," *Wall Street Journal*, 13 March 2014, p. 21, at http://online.wsj.com/news/articles/SB10001424052702304834704579403281361891144

18. "Swiss Central Bank posts first quarter loss on exchange rates," *AFP*, 1 May 2008, at http://afp.google.com/article/ALeqM5gh8QulLdxuHmpBA1UrdGhMOxrM2A

19. "Homeowners Abroad Take Currency Gamble in Loans," Craig Karmin and Joellen Perry, *Wall Street Journal*, 29 May 2007.

20. Sarah Perry, Director of Visa's Strategic Investment Program, in *Efinance Insider*, Issue 3, 17 April 2001. The Single Global Currency Association followed up with a 5 August 2005 email to Ms. Perry about the mutual interest in a Single Global Currency.

21. Foreign Exchange Committee of the Federal Reserve Bank of New York, Foreign Exchange Trading report, January 2014, for the period of October 2013 at http://www.newyorkfed.org/fxc/2014/octfxsurvey2013.pdf

22. ibid. para 2f.

23. The Foreign Exchange Joint Standing Committee, "Results of the Semi-Annual FX Turnover Survey in October 2012," 29 January 2013, at http://www.bankofengland.co.uk/markets/Documents/forex/fxjsc/fxturnresults130129.pdf.

24. Michael Greenberg, "Aite Group 2010 volume report – makes no sense at all," blog posting, 24 March 2011, at http://forexmagnates.com/aite-group-2010-volume-report-makes-no-sense-at-all/.

25. Foreign Exchange Committee of the Federal Reserve Bank of New York, FX Volume Survey, Explanatory notes at http://www.newyorkfed.org/fxc/volumesurvey/explanatory_notes.html

26. "Derivative" as defined in Investopedia.com, "In finance, a security whose price is dependent upon or derived from one or more underlying assets. The derivative itself is merely a contract between two or more parties. Its value is determined by the fluctuations of the underlying asset. The most common underlying assets include: stocks, bonds, commodities, currencies, interest rates and market indexes. Most derivatives are characterized by high leverage.

"Futures contracts, forward contracts, options and swaps are the most common types of derivatives. Because derivatives are just contracts, just about anything can be used as an underlying asset. There are even derivatives based on weather data, such as the amount of rain or the number of sunny days in a particular region.

"Derivatives are generally used to hedge risk, but can also be used for speculative purposes. For example, a European investor purchasing shares of an American company on an American exchange (using American dollars to do so) would be exposed to exchange-rate risk while holding that stock. To hedge this risk, the investor could purchase currency futures to lock in a specified exchange rate for the future stock sale and currency conversion back into euros." At http://www.investopedia.com/terms/d/derivative.asp

27. Foreign Exchange Committee of the Federal Reserve Bank of New York, Foreign Exchange Trading report, October 2012, for period of April 2013 at http://www.newyorkfed.org/fxc/2014/octfxsurvey2013.pdf

28. Alan V. Deardorff, "Deardorff's Glossary of International Economics" at http://www-personal.umich.edu/~alandear/glossary/

29. "Dollar Rises Past 103 Yen, a 4-1/2 year high, on U.S. data.," *Reuters*, 17 May 2013, at http://www.reuters.com/article/2013/05/17/markets-forex-idUSL2N0DY1HG20130517

30. Martin Fackler, "Yen at 32-month Low as Japan's Small Investors Look Abroad," *The New York Times,* 5 December 2005, p. C3, at http://www.nytimes.com/2005/12/06/business/worldbusiness/06yen.html

31. Raul Lopez, "Currency Trading: Understanding the Basics of Currency Trading," at http://www.articlebiz.com/article/1626-1-currency-trading-

understanding-the-basics-of-currency-trading/ and also at
http://ezinearticles.com/?Currency-Trading:-Understanding-the-Basics-of-Currency-Trading&id=100502

32. "Forex Trading, or in other words, 'Currency Gambling'," 26 December 2007, at http://www.casinotimes.co.uk/casino-news/2007-12/forex-trading.htm

33. For a view of the requisite personality characteristics of foreign exchange traders, see "Perceptions of Successful Traders by Foreign Exchange Professionals," by Thomas Oberlechner, in *Journal of Behavioral Finance,* Vol 5, No. 1, 2004, pp. 23-31, at http://www.webster.ac.at/files/Perceptions_of_Successful_Traders_by_Foreign_Exchange_Professionals_0.pdf

34. Andrew Krieger, with Edward Claflin, *The Money Bazaar,* New York, NY: Times Books, a division of Random House, 1992, at p. 105.

35. Forex Capital Markets, at www.fxcm.com

36. Forex.com, a subsidiary of Gain Capital Group, www.forex.com.

37. Jack Egan, "Investing: Check the Currency Risk. Then Multiply by 100.," *The New York Times*, 19 June 2005, p. BU 8, at http://select.nytimes.com/gst/abstract.html?res=F40A17F83F5F0C7A8DDDAF0894DD404482.

38. Forex Capital Markets, at www.fxcm.com

39. https://www.interactivebrokers.com

40. http://www.markets.com/lp/campaigns/nb-25-bonus-sms-verification/it/index.html#

41. "Top Currency Traders 1 Jan 2000 - 31st Oct 2011 – IASG," at http://www.inschinvest.com/docs.php?id=8

42. "Gross World Product," *Wikipedia*, http://en.wikipedia.org/wiki/Gross_world_product.

43. BarclayHedge Currency Trader Index, at http://www.barclayhedge.com/research/indices/cta/sub/curr.html

44. Fidelity Investments, at https://www.fidelity.com/learning-center/investment-products/etf/using-etfs-invest-currencies

45. EverBank, headquartered in Jacksonville, Florida, and website at https://www.everbank.com/currencies.

46. A theme for this book is that economists should direct their research away from how the current multicurrency system works or doesn't work, and toward the questions of how a Single Global Currency will benefit the world and how it will be implemented and how it will function. Thus, while I'm curious about the extent that foreign exchange trading is a zero sum game, it's more important that economists focus their research in the direction of the 3-G world.

47. The "Treasury Amendment" was passed by Congress to ensure that the CFTC did not infringe upon the mandate of the Treasury Department, and was upheld by the US Supreme Court in Dunn v. Commodity Futures Trading Commission, 519 US 465 (1997) at http://law.onecle.com/ussc/519/519us465.html. Subsequently, Congress passed the Commodities Futures Modernization Act of 2000, at http://www.cftc.gov/opa/press00/opa4479-00.htm

48. William Nissen, "The Long and Tangled History of the CFTC's Jurisdiction in Foreign Exchange," in the *Futures Industry* magazine at the Futures Industry Association website at http://www.futuresindustry.org/fimagazi-1929.asp?a=962.

49. "Guidelines for Foreign Exchange Trading Activities," The Foreign Exchange Committee of the Federal Reserve Bank of New York, November 2010, at http://www.newyorkfed.org/FXC/2010/tradingguidelinesNov2010.pdf

50. Mark Snyder, "New Opportunities and Risks in Foreign Exchange: The Role of the Foreign Exchange Committee," speech presented at the Profit & Loss Forex Network Conference, 20 September 2005, Chicago, at http://www.newyorkfed.org/fxc/2005/fxc051117.pdf. He also said "I might also mention that I cannot see a day when a nation's central bank would cede its sovereign authority over the currency component of its monetary policy to any worldwide currency regulatory authority."

51. Jonathan Fuerbringer and William K. Rashbaum, "Currency Fraud Ran Deep, Officials Say," *The New York Times*, 20 November, 2003, page C1, at http://www.nytimes.com/2003/11/20/business/currency-fraud-ran-deep-officials-say.html

52. Brian Bowling, "Currency trader admits to fraud in Pittsburgh federal court," *Pittsburgh Tribune*, 23 September 2013. http://triblive.com/news/adminpage/4757164-74/lost-money-court#axzz2rAiEeaKz

53. "John Rusnak," *Wikipedia*, http://en.wikipedia.org/wiki/John_Rusnak

54. See the 31 January 2005 address to the Bank's stockholders by the new Chairman, Graeme Kraehe at http://www.nabgroup.com/vgnmedia/downld/AGM_Script_310105.pdf

55. "Dismissed Salesman Faces Fraud Charge," *The New York Times*, from *Reuters*, 7 February 2006, p. C7, at http://www.nytimes.com/2006/02/07/business/07currency.html

56. "Joel N. Ward, *Wikipedia*, at http://en.wikipedia.org/wiki/Joel_N._Ward

57. Craig Karmin, "How a Money Trader Went Bad – Bets on Currency Prices Become 'Fraud du Jour' Amid Regulatory Holes," 12 January 2008, *Wall Street Journal*, at http://online.wsj.com/news/articles/SB120010072930285383.

58. Dominic Rushe and Jill Treanor, "New York regulator demands bank documents as investigation widens," *The Guardian*, 5 February 2014, at http://www.theguardian.com/business/2014/feb/05/new-york-regulator-banks-trading-investigation

59. James McGeever, "BoE minutes reveal currency rigging fears first raised in 2006, *Reuters*, in *Chicago Tribune*, 5 March 2014, at http://www.chicagotribune.com/business/sns-rt-us-britain-boe-fx-20140305,0,6446745.story

60. Virginia Harrison, "Bigger than Libor? Forex probe hangs over banks," *CNN-Money*, at http://money.cnn.com/2013/11/20/investing/forex-probe-lawyers/

61. Kit Dawnay, "A history of sterling," the online *Telegraph* at
http://www.telegraph.co.uk/news/1399693/A-history-of-sterling.html
62. "World's Richest People," *Forbes* magazine's list, 2014, at
http://www.forbes.com/billionaires/
63. Warren Buffett subsequently explained his currency speculation in his
26 October 2003 *Fortune* magazine article, "Why I'm Not Buying the US
dollar" at
http://www.pbs.org/wsw/news/fortunearticle_20031026_03.html
64. David Leonhardt, "Gambling Against The Dollar," *New York Times*, 1
November 2006, at
http://www.nytimes.com/2006/11/01/business/01leonhardt.html?ex=13
20037200&en=036ab20bb5bb104a&ei=5088&partner=rssnyt&emc=rss
65. Floyd Norris, "Buffett's State of the World: There's Folly in Wonderland,"
New York Times, 1 March 2008, at
http://www.nytimes.com/2008/03/01/business/01berkshire.html?em&ex
=1204520400&en=b942a9727f3abf18&ei=5087 percent0A
66. The online blog FX Strategy, at
http://www.fxstrategy.com/articles/fundamental-articles/forex-trade-
netted-buffett-100m-36.html
67. David Leonhardt, op. cit.
68. James Hertling and Simon Clark, "Microsoft's Gates, World's Richest
Man, Bets Against the Dollar," *Bloomberg*, 29 January 2005, at
http://quote.bloomberg.com/apps/news?pid=10000006&sid=aAvDTJpsO1
Nk&refer=home.
69. Kenneth Raisler, "Giving Customers Trading Advice: Implications of the
de Kwiatkowski Decision," in the *Futures Industry Magazine*, "Outlook 03"
issue, January 2003, at the Futures Industry Association website at
http://www.futuresindustry.org/fimagazi-1929.asp?v=p&iss=150&a=998
70. Delphine Strauss, "Currency investors mourn loss of volatility,"
Financial Times, 13 March 2014, page 22, at
http://www.ft.com/intl/cms/s/0/237091ca-a98b-11e3-9b71-
00144feab7de.html.
71. "Deutsche Bank Guide to Currency Indices," October 2007, at
http://www.cbs.db.com/new/docs/DBGuideToFXIndices.pdf
72. Andres Schipani, "Caracas poised to ease access to dollars," *Financial
Times*, 13 March 2014, p. 6, at
http://www.ft.com/intl/cms/s/0/5b2bb890-aa00-11e3-8497-
00144feab7de.html
73. Mario Cerrato, Neil Kellard, and Nicholas Sarantis, "The Purchasing
Power Parity Persistence Paradigm: Evidence from Black Currency
Markets," November, 2004, Money Macro and Finance (MMF) Research
Group Conference 2005, at http://repec.org/mmfc05/paper34.pdf.
74. Willem Buiter, "Optimal Currency Areas: Why Does the Exchange Rate
Matter?" given at the Royal College of Physicians, Edinburgh, on 26 October
1999, at http://www.opengrey.eu/item/display/10068/564094, p. 2.
75. Every currency in the world is identified by a three-character code,
assigned by the ISO, International Standards Organization, according to its
4217 standard. Usually the first two characters of the code represent the

country and the third denominates the currency. For a list see http://www.xe.com/iso4217.htm

76. Pietra Rivoli, *The Travels of a T-Shirt in the Global Economy: An Economist Examines the Markets, Power and Politics of World Trade.* Hoboken, NJ: John Wiley & Sons, 2005. For the transcript of a panel discussion with Prof. Rivoli at the IMF on 19 October 2005, go to http://www.imf.org/external/np/tr/2005/tr051019.htm

77. One aspect of the Tanzanian foreign-exchange issue is that it's illegal to take Tanzanian currency out of the country. Many countries have such prohibitions which are intended to keep a close watch on the money supply so that their balance of payments is not rendered out of balance. For all countries except the United States, an imbalance in the balance of payments has serious consequences for the value of their money. In the US, when transporting or receiving more than $10,000 in cash or other monetary instruments, a CF-4790 form must be filed, but there are no US restrictions of such flows or of other capital flows. See http://www.cbp.gov/ImageCache/cgov/content/publications/currency_5fr eporting_2edoc/v1/currency_5freporting.doc

78. See the American Express online foreign exchange utility at https://travel.americanexpress.com/currency-center and the utility for Oanda.com at http://www.oanda.com/currency/ and the Wells Fargo utility at https://www.wellsfargo.com/foreign-exchange/.

79. The Bank of Canada, the Canadian central bank, has a "10-year Currency Converter" utility which can be used to determine exchange rates for a specific date, or over a period of time during the past ten years, at http://www.bankofcanada.ca/rates/exchange/10-year-converter/. The reported rates can be pre-selected as the "nominal" or Interbank rates at noon for the selected day or days, or the "cash" rate, which is four percent higher, as the bank states that transaction charges by financial institutions to their customers for currency conversions are typically at that rate.

80. Wells Fargo, San Francisco, California, at https://www.wellsfargo.com/foreign-exchange/

81. Frederick W. Stakelbeck, Jr., "Foreign Currency Conversion Fees and the Credit Card Industry," in *SRC Insights*, Federal Reserve Bank of Philadelphia, Third Quarter 2005. See also, David A. Kelly, "Overseas the Shock of the Surcharge," *The New York Times*, 19 February 2006, p. TR 6, at http://travel2.nytimes.com/2006/02/19/travel/19prac.html

82. PayPal, "Help Center—Where can I find PayPal's currency exchange rates?" at https://www.paypal.com/us/webapps/helpcenter/helphub/article/?soluti onId=12900&topicID=11500006&m=SRE and "Fees FAQ: What You Should Know" at https://www.paypal-community.com/t5/Fees-Archive/Fees-FAQ-What-You-Should-Know/m-p/276500/highlight/true#M2614

83. Michael Emerson, Daniel Gros, Alexander Italiener, Jean Pisani-Ferry, and Horst Reichenbach, *One Market, One Money-An Evaluation of the Potential Benefits and Costs of Forming an Economic and Monetary Union.* Oxford, UK, Oxford University Press, 1992, pp. 65-66.

84. Senator Dirksen's quotes and aphorisms were famous. The reference here is to: "A billion here, a billion there, and pretty soon you're talking about real money." The Dirksen Congressional Center in Illinois has an entire page about the quote on its website, and notes that Senator Dirksen may never actually have made the quoted statement. At bottom, the Center noted, "Update, May 25, 2004. A gentleman who called The Center with a reference question relayed that he sat by Dirksen on a flight once and asked him about the famous quote. Dirksen replied, 'Oh, I never said that. A newspaper fella misquoted me once, and I thought it sounded so good that I never bothered to deny it.' " At http://www.dirksencenter.org/print_emd_billionhere.htm

85. Saifur Rahman, "Global remittance flow grows 10.77% to $514 billion in 2012: World Bank," *Gulf News*, April 20, 2013, at http://gulfnews.com/business/economy/global-remittance-flow-grows-10-77-to-514-billion-in-2012-world-bank-1.1172693

86. Jose de Luna Martinez, "Workers' Remittances to Developing Countries: A Survey with Central Banks on Selected Public Policy Issues," World Bank Policy Working Paper 3638, June 2005, at http://documents.worldbank.org/curated/en/2005/06/5849590/workers-remittances-developing-countries-survey-central-banks-selected-public-policy-issues

87. See website of Travelex Worldwide Money, "The World's Foreign Exchange Company," at http://www.travelex.com/US/For-Individuals/Sell-Us-Your-Currency/

88. Bank of Canada, "10 year currency converter" at http://www.bankofcanada.ca/rates/exchange/10-year-converter/

89. "Honda Motor Company," *Wikipedia*, http://en.wikipedia.org/wiki/Honda

90. Honda, *Annual Report* for year ending 31 March 2013, page 7, at http://world.honda.com/investors/library/annual_report/2013/honda2013ar-all-e.pdf

91. ibid., page 23.

92. "Vodafone," *Wikipedia*, at http://en.wikipedia.org/wiki/Vodafone

93. Vodafone, *Annual Report* for the year ending 31 March 2012, page 103 at http://www.vodafone.com/content/annualreport/annual_report12/downloads/financials_vodafone_ar2012_sections/consolidated_financial_statements_including_notes_vodafone_ar2012.pdf

94. Ibid. at page 126.

95. Mark Hulbert, "The Dollar May Tumble, but It's OK to Shrug," *The New York Times,* 12 March 2006, p. BU6, at http://www.nytimes.com/2006/03/12/business/yourmoney/12stra.html

96. Gregory W. Brown and Donald H. Chew, Editors, "Table of Contents," *Corporate Risk-Strategies and Management.* London: 1999, Risk Books, at http://www.amazon.ca/Corporate-Risk-Strategies-Gregory-Brown/dp/toc/1904339980

97. Peter Rosenstreich, *FOREX Revolution-An Insider's Guide to the Real World of Foreign Exchange Trading.* Upper Saddle River, NJ: Prentice-Hall, 2005, p. 110. Interview with Joachim Herr at pp. 109-114.

98. ibid. at p. 114.

99. Richard Cooper, "Toward A Common Currency?" June 2000, presented at the conference on the Future of Monetary Policy and Banking, organized by the IMF and the World Bank, and published in *International Finance*, July 2000, pp. 287-308, at http://onlinelibrary.wiley.com/doi/10.1111/1468-2362.00053/full

100. Tom Aabo, "The impact of individual-owners on currency speculation: the case of Danish non-financial firms," *International Journal of Managerial Finance*, Vol 3, No. 1, pp. 92-107, 2007, at http://www.emeraldinsight.com/journals.htm?articleid=1589103&show=abstract.

101. Michael Emerson, and others, op. cit., p. 64.

102. Peter Rosenstreich, op. cit., p. 115. Interview with Steve Nutland, Director of Bank of America, North American spot and emerging markets trading, at pp. 114-23.

103. "Financial Review: Statement and Notes: Note 1, Summary of Significant Accounting Principles," 2004 *Annual Report*, Bank of America, at http://media.corporate-ir.net/media_files/irol/71/71595/reports/2004_ar.pdf

104. "Foreign Exchange Markets," *Wikipedia*, at http://en.wikipedia.org/wiki/Foreign_exchange_market

105. 2013 *Annual Report*, Scotiabank, Toronto, page 20, at http://www.scotiabank.com/ca/en/files/13/12/BNS_2013_Annual_Report.pdf

106. Ibid, p. 73.

107. Harri Ramcharran, "Sensitivity of Foreign Exchange Trading Income to Exchange Rate Changes: A Study of Large US Banks," *Multinational Business Review*, Spring 2000, at http://www.questia.com/library/journal/1P3-50116280/the-sensitivity-of-foreign-exhange-trading-income

108. "Are Banks Market Timers or Market Makers" by John Ammer and Allan Brunner, for the Federal Reserve Board of Governors, 1984, at http://www.federalreserve.gov/pubs/ifdp/1994/484/ifdp484.pdf

109. Barclays Bank, *Annual Report* 2012, at http://group.barclays.com/about-barclays/investor-relations/annual-reports

110. Jean Eaglesham, "Probes Nip Banks' Profits," *Wall Street Journal online*, 18 April 2012, at http://online.wsj.com/news/articles/SB10001424052702304331204577352213352352958

111. "How Currency gets into circulation?" Federal Reserve Bank of New York, 2014, at http://www.newyorkfed.org/aboutthefed/fedpoint/fed01.html

112. US Census, "US Trade in Goods with the World" at http://www.census.gov/foreign-trade/balance/c0015.html.

113. "U.S. International Transactions," US Dept. of Commerce, Press Release, 17 December 2013, at http://www.bea.gov/newsreleases/international/transactions/transnewsrelease.htm

114. Floyd Norris, "More Than Ever, the US Spends and the Foreigners Lend," *The New York Times*, p. B4, 1 October 2005.

115. T. K. Jayaraman, in his article, "A Single Currency for the Pacific Island Countries: a Stepwise Approach," in *Asia Pacific Development Journal*, June 2004, and at http://www.unescap.org/pdd/publications/apdj_11_1/jayaraman.pdf cited the 1990 European Commission report on the cost of currency transactions. He wrote, "The European Commission estimated the average currency transaction cost ranging from 0.3 per cent to 0.35 per cent of the value of the underlying transaction." At p. 107.
Charles Wyplosz wrote in 1997, "The European Commission report, (1990, p. 65) had publicized enormous costs for the retail market between 200 and 300 basis points." (i.e., .2-.3 percent, p. 9) Jayaraman also cited the 1999 article by M. Anthony and A. Hughes-Hallett, "Is the case for economic and monetary union in the Caribbean realistic?" which used the 0.3 per cent estimate. That paper was presented at the Annual Caribbean Centre for Monetary Studies Conference in Barbados, and sponsored by the Central Bank of Barbados. Also, it was published in *World Economics*, January 2000.

116. Email from Joseph Gagnon to author, 28 October 2011 with "upper bound" estimate of $325 billion annually. Also, see Chapter 4 of his book *Flexible Exchange Rates for a Stable World Economy*, available at http://bookstore.piie.com/book-store/6277.html

117. Michael Emerson, and others, op. cit., p. 25.

118. John Murray, "Why Canada Needs a Flexible Exchange Rate," July, 1999, for a conference at Western Washington University, 30 April 1999, at http://epe.lac-bac.gc.ca/100/200/301/bankofcanada/working_papers-ef/1999/99-12/wp99-12.pdf

119. Michael Emerson, and others, op. cit., p. 64.

120. "Box 5: The Cost of multicurrency management - A remaining barrier to trade and investment," *EUROPEAN ECONOMY,* a semi-annual publication of the European Commission, No. 63, 1997, at p. 85, at http://ec.europa.eu/economy_finance/publications/publication7875_en.pdf

121. Hugo R. Mendizabal, "Monetary Union and the Transaction Cost Savings of a Single Currency," *Review of International Economics*, Vol. 10, Issue 2, 2002, pp. 263-77, at http://www.blackwell-synergy.com/doi/abs/10.1111/1467-9396.00331

122. Using the Wikipedia number for global GDP of $71.8 trillion for 2012 multiplied by the estimated 2.9 percent growth rate, http://en.wikipedia.org/wiki/Gross_world_product

123. UN budget at http://www.un.org/en/hq/dm/pdfs/oppba/Regular%20Budget.pdf.

124. "Microfinance and financial inclusion," the World Bank, at http://web.worldbank.org/WBSITE/EXTERNAL/NEWS/0,,contentMDK:20 433592~menuPK:34480~pagePK:64257043~piPK:437376~theSitePK:4607, 00.htm.

125. "What Would It Cost to Meet Family Planning Needs in Developing Countries?" Population Reference Bureau, 2014, at http://www.prb.org/Publications/Articles/2010/addingupfpcosts.aspx

126. "How to Buy Property in Argentina," at http://www.wikihow.com/Buy-Property-in-Argentina

127. As countries have been the primary issuers of currency, "currency risk" is also called "sovereign risk." For a review of the impact of sovereign risk, see Bernardin Akitoby, "Pricing of Sovereign Risk in Emerging Markets," March 2006, *IMF Research*, pp 1, 4-5, at http://www.imf.org/External/Pubs/FT/irb/2006/eng/01/index.pdf.

128. McKinsey Global Institute, "Financial Globalization: Retreat or reset?" March, 2013, at p. 2, at http://www.mckinsey.com/insights/global_capital_markets/financial_glob alization

129. Brian Hungwe, "Zimbabwe's multi-currency confusion," *BBC*, at http://www.bbc.co.uk/news/world-africa-26034078

130. "Hyperinflation in Zimbabwe," *Wikipedia*, at http://en.wikipedia.org/wiki/Hyperinflation_in_Zimbabwe

131. Robert E. Litan and Benn Steil, *Financial Statecraft*. London and New Haven, CT: Yale University Press, 2006, p. 84, citing references.

132. Federico Marongiu, "Towards a New Set of Leading Indicators of Currency Crisis for Developing Countries: An Application to Argentina," p. 3, draft of March 2005, at http://128.118.178.162/eps/pe/papers/0512/0512011.pdf

133. Michael Hutchison and Ilan Neuberger, "Output Costs of Currency and Balance of Payments Crises in Emerging Markets, September 2001, at http://www.hnb.hr/dub-konf/7-konferencija-radovi/hutchison-output-costs-of-currency.pdf

134. "Icelandic Financial Crisis," *Wikipedia*, at http://en.wikipedia.org/wiki/2008%E2%80%9311_Icelandic_financial_crisi s

135. Pattama Shimpalee and Janice Boucher Breuer, "Currency Crises and Institutions," *Journal of International Money and Finance*, February 2006, pp. 125-45, at http://ideas.repec.org/a/eee/jimfin/v25y2006i1p125-145.html

136. Christopher Matthews, "Currency Crises Abroad Are Benefitting the U.S.," *TIME*, 30 January 2014, at http://business.time.com/2014/01/30/currency-crises-abroad-are-benefiting-the-u-s/

137. For this breakdown of the types of financial crises, see Jan Jacobs, Gerard Kuper, and Lestano, "Currency Crises in Asia: A Multivariate Logit Approach," Working Paper, July 2005, p. 2, Centre for Economic Research (CCS), University of Gronningen, at http://ccso.eldoc.ub.rug.nl/FILES/root/2005/200506/200506.pdf.

138. Peter G. Peterson, "Riding for a Fall," *Foreign Affairs*, September/October 2004, at http://tomweston.net/riding-for-a-fall.html
139. Interview with Larry Summers, 23 January 2006, at https://groups.yahoo.com/neo/groups/intldevelopmentnews/conversations/topics/541

Chapter 2. Coping with the Multicurrency Foreign Exchange System

Early History of Money and Foreign Exchange

Before there was money, the exchange mechanism for trade was barter. For each transaction, the parties needed to negotiate the relative worth of the goods and services they sought to trade and then execute. For example, how many apples can be traded for ten oranges? (If trading by unit, trading twenty apples for ten oranges might work in northeastern USA at roughly current prices. If trading by weight, twenty-two apples might buy eighteen oranges.)[1] Such a process can be very time consuming and imprecise, without, of course, having a market currency price to begin with. As metallurgy was developed and bartering value was assigned to weights of gold, silver, bronze, and other metals, the idea arose to establish uniform weights and shapes to pieces of metal.

Money was thus developed and it had the familiar three functions:
1. Medium of Exchange;
2. Store of Value; and
3. Unit of Account.

While the first metal coins may have been cast from bronze in China around 2000 B.C., it's believed that recognizable coinage in India and Turkey began around the seventh century B.C.[2] The silver drachma was coined in Athens around 580 B.C. and a Greek currency by that name continued, with minor interruptions, until replaced by the euro on 1 January 2002.

Specimens of the coins of China, India and Greece/Turkey have been unearthed archeologically in the other currency areas, but it's not clear how those coins were traded. They could have simply been used for their weight in precious metal and not in exchange with their counterpart coins of pre-determined value from another currency area.

In *The History of Foreign Exchange*,[3] Paul Einzig notes that foreign exchange trading really did not occur until people were exchanging standardized coins whose value was recognized and accepted without having to weigh them or otherwise assay them. It's not known when that moment first occurred. At that point, the art of barter passed from those trading with what could be called "primary goods" to those trading with "secondary goods," i.e., different types of money. They were then faced with the same kind of valuation problems as those bartering for "primary" goods.

With a goal of 2024 A.D. for a Single Global Currency, and thus the practical end of foreign exchange trading as we know it, let's arbitrarily designate the date of that first foreign exchange trade as 476 B.C., giving such trading, or Forex or FX, a round number run of 2,500 years (2024+476).

It was at that point of the first foreign exchange that the deficiencies of the new invention, money, became clearer. With the exposure to other currencies, people learned that they could not easily use *their* money to exchange it for goods or services from people who used *other* money. People could see that *their* money was not as secure as a store of value because the value of that money rose and fell in comparison to *other* money. Finally, people could see that the units of account of *their* money were not easily transferable and thus useless when dealing with people using *other* money.

At the time, however, there was no opportunity to choose between moving to a multicurrency foreign exchange world or persuading the world to utilize one currency. Even the concept of "the world" was beyond the reach of humans on the several continents.

The best known example of foreign exchange trading comes from the *Bible*, where the "money changers" were trading Roman currency for Hebrew currency and for currency of other currency areas. One impetus for the trading was the Hebrew requirement that the annual tax to the Temple be paid in only one currency, the half-shekel, and thus the burden of trading was upon the payers of the tax. Jesus found this currency trading in the Temple in Jerusalem sufficiently offensive to the belief that commerce and religion should be separate that he overturned their tables.[4]

During these 2,500 years, from the first coinage through today's digital signals, money was minted and printed by noblemen, traders, banks, corporations, nation states, and monetary unions.

Whether by ethnicity or geography, the nation state became the world's dominant political organization, throughout the nineteenth and twentieth centuries. One of the badges of nationhood was a national currency and due primarily to the end of European colonialism, there was a large increase in the 20th century of the number of countries and currencies in the world. In 1945, there were 51 countries which established the United Nations, and now there are 193 members.[5]

The history of the economies of the world is, in some substantial part, the history of money. As trade grew larger, more sophisticated and more international, the role of money also grew larger as did the potential damage it could cause. Kings, queens, and countries struggled with gold, silver, and paper money, and the establishment of national and central banks. Several of the depressions and crashes of the nineteenth and twentieth centuries were either caused or exacerbated by the inappropriate management of money by the managers of the money system, whether they were bankers or public officials. Those failures, in turn, were exacerbated and spread by the multicurrency system through a process now called "contagion." The Great Depression of the 1930s is the largest example of such contagion where countries constricted their money supplies precisely at the time when monetary expansion was needed to thwart the decline in investment. Industrialized countries sought to keep their currency exchange rates at a low value compared to others, in order to maintain or increase exports, but were thwarted by the misguided belief in the sanctity of the gold standard.

The 1944 Bretton Woods International Monetary Conference

In July 1944, the representatives of twenty-nine countries gathered at the rehabilitated Mt. Washington Hotel in Bretton Woods, New Hampshire, United States, where the town's human winter population the previous year was two: the caretaker of the hotel and his wife.[6] The goal of the conference was to establish a stable, internationally cooperative, post-war financial system that would avoid the perils of the Great Depression and would assist in the post-war recovery.

From the conference, and of primary interest here, came the International Monetary Fund and a gold/US-dollar-based exchange rate system. Also, the conference created the International Bank for Reconstruction and Development which was the predecessor to the World Bank. The conference's work on trade issues contributed to the later development of the World Trade Organization.

Later in this book will be discussed the idea of the worldwide reserve currency, the "bancor," which John Maynard Keynes brought to the conference.

The Bretton Woods Exchange Rate System

From 1946 to 1971, the IMF member countries pegged the values of their currencies to the US dollar and the value of the dollar was set as $35.00 per troy ounce[7] of gold.

A major problem was that even with a relatively minor US balance of payments deficit, as compared to the hundreds of billions in the early twenty-first century, foreigners with US dollars were redeeming them for gold. In 1950, the United States had gold reserves worth $23 billion, @$35 per troy ounce in its stockpile. At the 17 January 2014 gold price of $1,250 per troy ounce, those 657 million troy ounces would be worth $821 billion. Due to the redemptions of dollars for gold, the value of the stockpile had declined to $11 billion (using the $35.00 price) by 1970.[8] The problem was that the amount of US dollar currency circulating outside the United States had grown from a manageable $8 billion to $47 billion,[9] and every one of those dollars could legally be converted into US gold upon demand.

In 1971, the United States announced that it was abandoning its treaty requirements to back up its currency with gold, and without the anchor, the futures for all currencies became uncharted. The thirty-year trend toward nearly universal floating, or "treading water," of exchange rates on the open markets began in earnest. Actually, Canada began floating its dollar in 1950 until 1962, and then resumed floating again in 1970.[10] Other countries followed Canada and the United States.

In 1972, negotiations began for the modification of some of the Articles of Agreement of the International Monetary Fund, including the ratification of the US's departure from the gold standard, and an agreement was reached in 1976. The 1976 amendments legitimized the floating rate system, and eliminated the use of gold in the international monetary system except for settling accounts at the IMF. The amendments also established Special Drawing Rights (SDRs), with echoes of Keynes's "bancor," as the new reserve asset to be used by the IMF to assist countries with their balances of payments.

In 1977, further changes were made, including the important change to Article IV, that countries should refrain from manipulating their exchange rates in order to gain unfair advantage, but authorizing such intervention in the foreign exchange markets to counter excessive price volatility. When considering such intervention, countries should consider the interests of other countries, especially those whose currencies/reserves were to be used in the intervention.

However, the markets marched to their own drummers and caused concerns about international monetary stability. In September, 1985, The Group of Five (G-5), composed of the United States, United Kingdom, Japan, Germany, and France, met at the Plaza Hotel in New York and decided to collectively intervene in the foreign exchange markets to lower the value of the dollar which was viewed as overvalued at the time.

In 1986, the Group of Seven (G-5, plus Italy and Canada), met in Tokyo and issued the "Tokyo Economic Declaration," and in February, 1987, the Group of Seven met and then issued a G-6 Declaration (without Italy) at the Louvre in Paris. They agreed that the then-current exchange rates were satisfactory and that they would henceforth intervene only if the values of currencies varied excessively from their fundamental/real values. Of course, the key question was the perception of the real value of a currency. The economists' search for the Holy Grail of the true, real, fundamental value indicators of a currency continued.

From the G-6 "Louvre Declaration", we see the concerns of the participating Ministers of Finance and Central Bank Governors:

> "A high degree of price stability has been attained, and there have been substantial reductions in interest rates. Exchange rate adjustments have occurred which will contribute importantly in the period ahead to the restoration of a more sustainable pattern of current accounts.... the Ministers and Governors recognize that the large trade and current account imbalances of some countries pose serious economic and political risks.... The Ministers and Governors agreed that the substantial exchange rate changes since the Plaza Agreement will increasingly contribute to reducing external imbalances and have now brought their currencies within ranges broadly consistent with underlying economic fundamentals...." [11]

The underlying assumption of Bretton Woods persisted, that countries could somehow agree to fix, in both senses of the word, exchange rates. Central banks around the world were buying or selling dollars or their own currencies in order to keep the values of their currencies at some predetermined level. The lessons of the failed 1992 attempts by the Bank of England to intervene to maintain the value of the pound, despite market pressures, were not learned.

International Monetary Fund

The current purposes of the IMF presented below are stated in the "Articles of Agreement" and are consistent with the original documents. [12]

> The purposes of the International Monetary Fund are:
> i.   To promote international monetary cooperation through a permanent institution which provides the

machinery for consultation and collaboration on international monetary problems.

ii. To facilitate the expansion and balanced growth of international trade, and to contribute thereby to the promotion and maintenance of high levels of employment and real income and to the development of the productive resources of all members as primary objectives of economic policy.

iii. To promote exchange stability, to maintain orderly exchange arrangements among members, and to avoid competitive exchange depreciation.

iv. To assist in the establishment of a multilateral system of payments in respect of current transactions between members and in the elimination of foreign exchange restrictions which hamper the growth of world trade.

v. To give confidence to members by making the general resources of the Fund temporarily available to them under adequate safeguards, thus providing them with opportunity to correct maladjustments in their balance of payments without resorting to measures destructive of national or international prosperity.

vi. In accordance with the above, to shorten the duration and lessen the degree of disequilibrium in the international balances of payments of members.

Note that the last four purposes refer explicitly to exchange rates[13] or balances of payments, and the first to "international monetary problems." Even though the second is about trade, employment and "real income," the primary work of the fund since its creation in 1946 has been to assist member countries in the multicurrency foreign exchange world with the stability of their currencies as represented by their exchange rates and (im)balances of payments.

Exchange Rates and Inflation.
Among the variables in the international monetary system is the relationship between exchange rates and inflation. We know empirically and intuitively that when the US dollar declines in value, in relation to the yen, for example, that products made in Japan will become more expensive to US consumers. The reverse should also be true about prices when the dollar rises in value; but there may be an inherent inflationary bias which keeps prices from falling when the prices of foreign-made or foreign-resourced goods decline. Economists call this "price stickiness."

Inflation is more than an irritant to our society, and can be ruinous if not controlled. Of the destructive inflation in Germany after the First World War, John Maynard Keynes wrote in *The Economic Consequences of the Peace*, "There is no subtler, no surer means of overturning the existing basis of society than to debauch the currency."[14]

Exchange Rates and Interest Rates.

One of the primary tasks for central banks is to set base interest rates, primarily the rate at which client banks can loan money to each other. While there recently has been more emphasis on central bank transparency in the United States and elsewhere, the reasons for interest rate determinations and other decisions are never entirely clear. Generally, a central bank wants to keep interest rates low to encourage borrowing for investment and consumption. Pushing in the other direction is the need to raise interest rates sufficiently so as to encourage foreign and domestic investors and savers to keep money within the country. An illustration of that motivation was seen in January 2014 when the Turkish Central Bank raised interest rates to 10% to keep lira within the country, in the face of an accelerating run to other currencies.[15] Another reason to raise interest rates is to discourage loans in order to cool an overheated and inflationary economy.

Exchange Rate Regimes

Much has been written about the correct exchange rate for any one currency area. There is widespread agreement that such rates should reflect the "fundamentals" of a nation's or monetary union's economy, such as labor productivity, inflation, and balance of payments; but there the agreement stops--and becomes part of the larger question of why economists and others are not able to predict the changes in foreign exchange rates.

As with any large scale modern market, there is a context in which they operate, and a major consideration in the foreign exchange market is the degree of freedom which central banks permit to the values of their currencies relative to others.

Richard Cooper writes, "Yet, for most countries, all but the largest with the most developed capital markets, the choice of exchange rate policy is probably their single most important macro-economic policy decision, strongly influencing their freedom of action and effectiveness of other macro-economic policies, the evolution of their financial systems, and even the evolution of their economies."[16] A substantial proportion of the international economics books and academic articles about foreign exchange consider this question of which exchange rate regime is appropriate for a country or currency area.[17] However, in the euro and monetary union era, it's like asking which type of brake is best for a vehicle's fifth wheel: disc brakes or shoe brakes.

Exchange rate regimes vary from total float, where prices of currencies are established entirely by buyers and sellers, to total "peg" to another currency or currencies, and variations in between.

In 2006, the IMF classified by exchange rate regime 198 currencies issued by the then 192 UN members plus six from non-member countries.[18] The list below has been updated by moving the six new EMU countries from other categories into the first category.

     Exchange rates with no separate legal tender   58
     (i.e. those in Monetary Unions or "izing")
     Currency Board Arrangements   6

Other conventional Fixed Peg arrangements	52
Pegged Exch Rate within a Horizontal Band	3
Crawling Peg	5
Managed floating with no pre-determined path for the exchange rate	51
Independently floating	25
TOTAL	198

The largest category, the first above, is for those countries without their own national currencies, so their currencies should be categorized among the other categories. However, they are not so categorized because the list above is a list of countries rather than currencies. Below is a similarly structured table of the exchange rate regimes of the 140 currencies used by the current 193 UN members, and not including the six non-UN members from the table above. Illustrating the change, the currency of the 18 EMU countries, the euro, is included below within the "independently floating" currency category.

Currency Board Arrangements	5
Other conventional Fixed Peg arrangements	50
Pegged Exch Rate within a Horizontal Band	3
Crawling Peg	5
Managed floating with no pre-determined path for the exchange rate	51
Independently floating	26
TOTAL	140

For the purposes of this book, none of the exchange rate regimes is as useful to the people of participating countries as the monetary union, the most beneficial of which will be the Global Monetary Union.

What Can Go Wrong with the Current Multicurrency Foreign Exchange System?

In short, what can go wrong is a worldwide currency crisis, and worse. Wrote Paul Krugman, "There is no universally accepted definition of a currency crisis, but most would agree that they all involve one key element: investors selling a currency *en masse* out of fear that it might be devalued, in turn fueling the very devaluation they anticipated."[19]

<u>What can go wrong: Moving away from pricing of oil in US dollars, leading to currency crisis</u>

Oil from OPEC and most other countries is priced in dollars and payment must be made in US dollars. For customers in countries other than the United States, this means that they must purchase US dollars on the foreign exchange markets, or from their own central banks, and use those US dollars to purchase oil. Those customers can purchase dollars if they have other foreign exchange or if they can trade their own currency for dollars. This is where the need for a positive current account comes in--for all countries except the United States. Countries can only buy dollars if they have surpluses in their current accounts or from reserves or if they can float loans to borrow from the private market or, if in an emergency, from the International Monetary Fund.

Because its currency is the primary international reserve currency and because the oil prices and payment terms are denominated in dollars, the United States has less need to generate a positive current account and has not done so since the early 1980s. Instead, the United States "prints" dollars and spreads them around the world.[20] It can do that by selling US Treasury securities to foreigners for their US dollars either to finance a government fiscal deficit, or by refinancing existing debt and moving a larger proportion of that debt to foreigners.[21]

What could go wrong is that oil-producing countries could begin to insist that their oil be priced in another currency, such as euros. In fact, it is believed by some that one reason for the US invasion to overthrow Iraq's Saddam Hussein was his September 2000 decision to require payment in euros for Iraqi oil.[22] Wrote Clark Kee, "In a major challenge to 'dollar hegemony,' in October 2000, the government of Iraq discontinued using the dollar for its reserves and international transactions, in favor of the euro. The value of the euro relative to the dollar was declining at the time, and commentators predicted that the move would be costly to Iraq. Between 2001 and February 2003 almost all of Iraq's oil exports were paid for in euros, amounting to approximately $30 billion. Over the same period, the value of the euro relative to the dollar reversed course and increased by 30 percent."[23] Thus, Saddam Hussein had made a sound foreign exchange decision, which earned his country a higher price for his oil, in billions of euros, than if he had stuck with pricing it in US dollars. He could have achieved the same currency result by hedging in some way or by purchasing the equivalent amount of euros at the instance of every sale of oil in dollars, but denominating the price of his country's oil in euros was simpler. For that one country, the effect of invoicing in a non-dollar currency was largely symbolic, and more political than economic, even if it turned out to be profitable. When more oil-producing countries make the same decision, the results will be larger and more economic.

Further changes in oil pricing likely will come from Iran, which opened the Iran Oil Exchange, or Kish Oil Bourse in February 2008, with the intent to price oil in non-USD currencies. Since then, the new market has begun very slowly to support trading of oil-derived commodities.[24] The size of the problem to the United States, and hence the world, of a general shift of oil pricing to the euro or other currencies, could be large, given the hundreds of billions of dollars spent annually the world for oil from the Middle East.

What would be the problem? It's supply and demand, once again. With a large number of sizable countries purchasing euros and selling dollars, the value of a dollar would drop and perhaps contribute to a genuine worldwide currency crisis. This scenario is one reason why the oil producers are not pricing their oil in euros, at least not yet, because it's not in the interests of those holding huge reserves of dollars or dollar-denominated securities to drive the value of a dollar down.

<u>What can go wrong: Speculators drive the price down and panic selling of US dollars occurs, leading to currency crisis</u>

As has been noted, the currency markets are similar to every other market, in that there are buyers and sellers, and demand and supply. When there is less demand or fewer buyers, prices decline. Andy Krieger begins the Introduction to his book, *The Money Bazaar*, with "I have a nightmare," of the collapse of the yen, involving a large Japanese earthquake. "By the time the buying spree is over, trillions of yen have been ripped out of the market and bonds and money-market instruments around the world have been devastated, crumbling under the unprecedented selling pressure."[25] Later, Krieger describes a micro-nightmare, "The nightmare for any trader is a scenario in which he offers a currency and no bids come back. He offers the currency again at a lower level--and still there are no bids. As his 'offered' price falls lower, his view of the world changes. Instead of facing the possibility that he might lose 1 percent, 2 percent, or even 5 percent of his investment, he now faces the reality that he may lose 10 percent, 20 percent or conceivably 50 percent. 'Panic' becomes the operative word, because that is exactly what each trader begins to feel upon first confronting the possibility of such losses."[26]

Rarely does anyone know the precise origin of a panic, from that first seller who could not find a buyer.

<u>What can go wrong: Central banks begin to sell their US dollar reserves in favor of accumulating reserves of other currencies, leading to currency crisis</u>

There has been some diversification of the holdings of foreign exchange reserves, with some central banks moving slowly away from the US dollar. Near-panic developed in 2005 when a well-founded rumor spread that South Korea was planning to sell substantial amounts of its US Treasury notes in order to diversify its reserve holdings. The currency markets shuddered, "As Central Banks Shun the Dollar."[27] The South Korean central bank then backed away from its publicly announced plan. Similar concerns arose in January 2006 when the Chinese State Administration of Foreign Exchange (SAFE) announced that it wanted to "optimise the currency and asset structure," and subsequently announced that it was a misunderstanding to interpret that announcement as meaning it was planning to diminish its substantial dollar denominated reserves.[28] In 2005, Russia announced that it was changing the 10:90 euro/dollar ratio in its reserves to a 50:50 ratio.[29] In 2009, the euro share overtook the dollar, 53:47, in the Russian reserves.[30]

An economist at the Federal Reserve Bank of San Francisco takes the view that such selling could harm the sellers, as they would take losses due to the resulting decline in the value of the dollar. Also, such a decline would effectively raise the prices of their countries' exports, which is never a welcomed result.[31] Nonetheless, such movement away from the US dollar seems inevitable, and leaves the critical question of whether that movement will be measured or contain a measure of panic. When the selling begins and accelerates, who will be the buyers?

Central Banks and Foreign Reserves

The world's central banks store vast amounts of gold and foreign exchange reserves in order to protect the value of their currencies.[32] For internal purposes, reserves provide confidence in banks' liquidity and gives confidence to citizens and foreigners alike that the currency is backed by credible assets, even though there is no right of redemption. The more confidence in a currency, the less need there is for reserves.

The central banks can use the reserves to buy and sell currencies on the open market in order to maintain the value of their own currencies. Japan and China, for example, have purchased hundreds of $billions of US Treasury notes over the past several years to keep the relative value of their currencies low, by simultaneously working to elevate the value of the US dollar. China's and Japan's reserves in late 2013 stood at $1.7 trillion and $1.2 trillion, respectively.[33]

The total USD value of the foreign exchange reserves of all countries, including cash, debt obligations, gold and SDRS is approximately $13.2 trillion.[34] This represents a fivefold increase since 1999[35] and represents 18.4 percent of global GDP.

This dramatic growth of reserves led to a major IMF paper in 2010, "Reserve Accumulation and International Monetary Stability," which stated that "The risks associated with the recent reserve accumulation trends are potentially serious. Large reserve accumulation has significant opportunity costs for the accumulating countries, and in aggregate may have a systemic deflationary impact."[36]

In his *Making Globalization Work*, Nobel laureate Joseph Stiglitz, wrote of the real costs of the accumulation of foreign exchange currency reserves. He noted that countries lose by investing their wealth in low-interest bearing reserves when they could use that money in higher return investments, at home or abroad. "The difference between the interest rates can be viewed as the cost of the reserves. Economists call these costs - the difference between what could have been earned and what was actually earned - 'opportunity costs'."[37] He then estimated that gap to be 10 percent annually. Applying that logic to the entire world's $13.2 trillion in reserves, the annual global cost is $1.32 trillion. Even if Stiglitz's cost estimate was off by a factor of four, and the gap is only two percent annually, that still means an annual global cost of the maintenance of foreign exchange reserves at $330 billion.

Despite Stiglitz's analysis of the waste of accumulating foreign exchange reserves, economists continue to pursue the best formula for calculating what level of reserves[38] is "just right," to borrow from "Goldilocks and the Three Bears." Another major question is the best foreign exchange mix.[39]

At least one economist, Eduardo Yeyati, challenges as being overstated the estimates of Stiglitz and others of the real cost of foreign exchange reserves.[40]

The holding of reserves has ironic effects. As noted by Marion Williams, governor of the Central Bank of Barbados, such reserves are denominated in the hard currencies of developed countries, which means that the central banks of less-developed countries are financing investment and development in those other countries.[41] For the central banks of developing countries, that result seems bizarre.

Gold

These reserves are substantially wasted resources, including the stockpiling of gold.

Robert Mundell has observed, "the importance of gold in the international monetary system is reflected in the fact that it is today the only commodity held as reserve by the monetary authorities, and it constitutes the largest component after dollars in the total reserves of the international monetary system."[42]

As of June 2013, the top 100 central banks of the world possessed 31,320 tonnes (or metric tons) of gold, each with 1,000 kilograms, and 32,150 troy ounces. (Incidentally, that amounts to approximately 19 percent of the 165,000 metric tons of gold mined in all of human history.[43]) The value of this gold fluctuates like any other commodity, and currencies, too, but at a 17 January 2014 price of $1,250 per troy ounce per the London afternoon "fixing,"[44] the value of a tonne of gold was $40.2 million. At that price the total value of the 100 central bank reserves was $1.3 trillion. A year earlier on 15 January 2013, the price of gold was $1,680,[45] making the value of all the reserves $1.7 trillion. Thus in one year, the value of the central bank reserves lost approximately $400 billion in value due to the 26 percent drop, or $430 per troy ounce, in the price of gold as measured in USD.

If the value of any currency in the world were actually linked to the price of gold, this substantial change would have made a difference in the supply of money and in the prices of everything priced in that currency. However, the reality is that there is no currency in the world which currently pegs its value to the price of gold. Similarly, there is no currency in the world with a direct claim to any of that gold. It just sits in vaults and waits. Of gold and that status, Milton Friedman memorably wrote, "People must work hard to dig gold out of the ground in South Africa--in order to rebury it in Fort Knox or some similar place."[46] Does this make cents/sense?

The UK's former Chancellor of the Exchequer and later, Prime Minister, Gordon Brown, had championed, since 1999, the idea of selling gold from the IMF's and central banks' reserves in order to assist poor countries with relief of their crushing international debt, which stood at $220 billion in 1999.[47] In 2009, the IMF sold 403 tonnes of its gold in order to finance the new initiative, an endowment for the benefit of poor countries called the Poverty Reduction and Growth Trust. Since then, IMF members have pledged additional amounts based on "windfall profits" from the sale of gold at the recent higher prices.[48]

The IMF still holds 2,814 tonnes of gold, for a market value in January 2014 of $113 billion. Most of that gold was acquired at the inception of the IMF in 1946, and it constitutes the third largest gold holding, after the US and Germany. The IMF continues to view gold as "an important asset in the reserve holdings of a number of countries...."[49] The IMF accepts gold, at current market values, as a payment option of obligations by its 188 members.[50] It's the only place in the world where gold is actually exchanged as money, although there are near-money-like alternatives for gold in the marketplace.[51]

Such use may be one reason why central banks continue to acquire gold, even if such purchases are declining. In 2013, central banks purchased 368.6 tonnes of gold, with an approximate value, at $1,250 an ounce, of $14.8 billion.[52]

Capital Controls

The character of the flow of money across boundaries has changed dramatically since the early 1970s, when 90 percent of the currency trading was aimed at financing trade and 10 percent for purely financial transactions. By 2004, the mix was reversed with 90 percent of the $1.9 trillion foreign exchange daily trading being for non-trade-related finance, such as investments in public and private securities and other assets.[53] Since the 1970s, daily trading has increased from approximately $100 billion per day[54] to $5.3 trillion, an increase of 5,300 percent.

One way to prevent the havoc caused by large transfers of capital across currencies, called the "Achilles heel of globalisation,"[55] is to regulate capital transfers, but such controls have lost favor in recent years.[56] For example, South Africa's "40 years of experience with capital controls on residents and non-residents (1961-2001) reads like a collection of examples of perverse unanticipated effects of legislation and regulation."[57] One result is that investors and their lawyers and accountants spend considerable time calculating ways to achieve their investment goals by avoiding such government restrictions on international capital transfers. It's expensive and a waste of effort.

China's capital controls are strict, and no foreign investment is permitted in China without government approval. Also, the trading of its currency has been restricted to trades with the Chinese agency, SAFE (for State Administration of Foreign Exchange). However, in January 2006, the government opened up trading to thirteen international financial firms, including Citicorp, for interbank trading of yuan, which must be reported to SAFE.[58]

Summary: Coping with the Multicurrency Foreign Exchange System in 2014

By the end of 2013, it had been over ten years since the most recent currency crises involving a large country (e.g. Argentina) perhaps lulling the central bankers and the governments of the world into again believing that maybe the multicurrency system is safer against currency crises. The 2008-2011 crisis in Iceland and the ongoing currency crisis in Zimbabwe, beginning in 2003, were/are no threat to the global economy as those two countries are relatively small.

The US imbalance of payments has had such a long run that observers have become used to it. As stated US Federal Reserve Chair Alan Greenspan in December 2005, "... it is tempting to conclude that the US current account deficit is essentially a byproduct of long-term secular forces, and thus is largely benign. After all, we do seem to have been able to finance our international current account deficit with relative ease in recent years."[59]

On the other hand, as several people have said and written,[60] these imbalances cannot continue to grow forever, without correction. The existing multicurrency foreign exchange system simply cannot cope with them. Instead of ignoring the symptoms, it would be safer to rely upon Murphy's law: that what can go wrong, will go wrong.[61] However, if fixing this fifth wheel cannot be reliably and consistently done for all currencies, then the alternative of the Single Global Currency ought to be closely examined and implemented. In fact, the only way to permanently fix the US balance of payments problem is to develop a Single Global Currency.

Chapter 3 presents the perspectives of economists on the current multicurrency foreign exchange system.

ENDNOTES

1. In 2005, I purchased a package of 10 Navel oranges for $3.99 weighing 1.81 kilograms, and a package of 13 McIntosh apples weighing 1.36 kilograms for $2.59. The price per orange was $.40 and the price per apple was $.20, thus enabling an easy 1:2 trade. Note that this example is distorted because the parties already knew the currency price of each fruit. Without such pre-barter pricing or trading knowledge, the outcome of each barter trade for apples and oranges would have been far less predictable.
2. Robert Mundell, "The Birth of Coinage," at
 http://academiccommons.columbia.edu/catalog/ac%3A114141
3. Paul Einzig, *The History of Foreign Exchange*. London, UK: MacMillan/St. Martin's Press, 1962.
4. The *Bible*, Book of Mark, Chapter 11:15-17 Revised Standard Version. See also, Book of Matthew 21:12; Book of John 2:15.
5. See "Member States," United Nations website at
 http://www.un.org/en/members/index.shtml
6. Carol M. Highsmith and Ted Landhair, *The Mount Washington: A Century of Grandeur*. Washington, D.C.: Archetype Press, 2002, p. 93.
7. A troy ounce equals 1.097 ounces, or avoirdupois ounces. For the conversion of troy ounces and other measures, see utility, "Online Metrics Conversion--US Standard & Metric Unit Converter" by Science Made Simple, Inc., at http://www.sciencemadesimple.net/conversions.html.
8. Andrew Krieger, with Edward Claflin, *The Money Bazaar*. New York, NY: Times Books, 1992, at p. 122.
9. Andrew Krieger, ibid., at p. 122.
10. David Dodge, "Monetary Policy and the Exchange Rate in Canada," remarks by the Governor of the Bank of Canada to the Canada-China Business Council, Beijing, 2 June 2005, at
 http://www.bankofcanada.ca/wp-content/uploads/2010/02/sp05-8.pdf,
and Gordon Thiessen, previous Governor of the Bank of Canada, in speech before the Chamber of Commerce of Montreal, "Why a Floating Exchange Rate Regime Makes Sense for Canada," 4 December 2000, at
 http://www.bankofcanada.ca/wp-content/uploads/2010/01/sp00-7.pdf

11. Statement of the G-6 Finance Ministers and Central Bank Governors (Louvre Accord), 22 February 1987, from the University of Toronto Library at http://www.g8.utoronto.ca/finance/fm870222.htm.

12. International Monetary Fund, "Articles of Agreement, Article 1 - Purposes," as "Adopted at the United Nations Monetary and Financial Conference, Bretton Woods, New Hampshire, July 22, 1944. Entered into force December 27, 1945. Amended effective July 28, 1969, by the modifications approved by the Board of Governors in Resolution No. 23-5, adopted May 31, 1968; amended effective April 1, 1978, by the modifications approved by the Board of Governors in Resolution No. 31-4, adopted April 30, 1976; and amended effective November 11, 1992, by the modifications approved by the Board of Governors in Resolution No. 45-3, adopted June 28, 1990," at http://www.imf.org/external/pubs/ft/aa/

13. The term "exchange rates" is used throughout this book to mean the published values of one currency in terms of another, also called the "nominal exchange rate." Economists also use the terms "real exchange rate," which is a nominal exchange rate, adjusted for the price level/inflation for each country in the currency pair. See Alan V. Deardorff's "Glossary of International Economics" at http://www-personal.umich.edu/~alandear/glossary/ Also, Richard Cooper writes that the movements of nominal exchange rates and real exchange rates are highly correlated in the short and medium run, except where very high inflation is involved for either currency. In "Toward A Common Currency?" June 2000, presented at the conference on the Future of Monetary Policy and Banking, organized by the IMF and the World Bank, published in *International Finance*, July 2000, pp. 287-308, at http://onlinelibrary.wiley.com/doi/10.1111/1468-2362.00053/full

14. John Maynard Keynes, "Europe after the Treaty," *The Economic Consequences of the Peace* (1919), Chapter 6, at http://socserv2.socsci.mcmaster.ca/~econ/ugcm/3ll3/keynes/peace.htm

15. "Turkey's Central Bank Aggressively Raises Rates, *New York Times*, 28 January 2014, at http://www.nytimes.com/2014/01/29/business/international/stress-on-turkish-currency-eases-before-central-banks-emergency-session.html?_r=0

16. Richard Cooper, "Toward A Common Currency?" June 2000, op. cit.

17. See Yin-Wong Cheung, Menzie Chinn, and Antonio Garcia Pascual, "Empirical Exchange Rate Models of the Nineties: Are Any Fit to Survive?" IMF Working Paper WP/04/73, April 2004, at http://www.imf.org/external/pubs/ft/wp/2004/wp0473.pdf; and Selim Elekdag and Ivan Tchakarov, "Balance Sheets, Exchange Rate Policy, and Welfare," IMF working paper, WP 04/63, April 2004, at http://www.imf.org/external/pubs/ft/wp/2004/wp0463.pdf; and Thomas Willett, "The OCA Approach to Exchange Rate Regimes: A Perspective on Recent Developments," Claremont Colleges, Working paper 2001-04, April, 1999, at http://econ.claremontmckenna.edu/papers/2001-04.pdf. For an example of application of theory to the exchange rate regime choice for Kazakhstan and Pakistan, see Aasim Husain, "To Peg or Not to Peg: A

Template for Assessing the Nobler," IMF Working Paper 06/54, February 2006, at http://www.imf.org/external/pubs/ft/wp/2006/wp0654.pdf.

18. "De Facto Classification of Exchange Rate Regimes and Monetary Policy Framework," International Monetary Fund, with data as of July 31, 2006, at https://www.imf.org/external/np/mfd/er/2006/eng/0706.htm

19. Paul Krugman, editor, *Currency Crises*. Chicago, IL: National Bureau of Economic Research, by University of Chicago Press, 2000. Promotional paragraph, at
http://press.uchicago.edu/ucp/books/book/chicago/C/bo3632847.html

20. In 2000, it was estimated that 50-70 percent, or $250-350 billion, of the existing $500 billion in United States currency was held outside the United States. "Text: Report on Foreign Use, Counterfeiting of US Currency," Federation of American Scientists website at
http://www.fas.org/irp/news/2000/02/000228-bogus-usia1.htm. See also "Passing the Buck," Forbes.com, "As of April 2004, nearly $700 billion in US dollars was in circulation. Somewhere from one-half to two-thirds of it, mostly in $100 bills, was held overseas." At
http://www.forbes.com/2006/02/11/cx_dal_money06_0214moneyfactslide_21.html?thisSpeed=6000 As of 12 February 2014, the value of US currency in circulation around the world was $1.24 trillion, according to the Federal Reserve, at
http://www.federalreserve.gov/faqs/currency_12773.htm Most of it is estimated to be outside the US, according to the NY Federal Reserve, at http://www.newyorkfed.org/aboutthefed/fedpoint/fed01.html

21. For many years, foreigners have been purchasing more assets in the United States than its citizens have purchased abroad. However, due to uncertainties about the possible US default in 2013, it was reported that the percentage of foreign holdings of US debt dropped to a long term low of 48.7 percent in July 2013, *Bloomberg*, 21 October 2013, at
http://www.bloomberg.com/news/2013-10-20/treasuries-losing-cachet-with-weakest-foreign-demand-since-2001.html

22. William Clark, "Petrodollar Warfare: Dollars, Euros and the Upcoming Iranian Oil Bourse," *Energy Bulletin*, 2 August 2005, at
http://usa.mediamonitors.net/content/view/full/17450

23. Clark Kee, "Petroeuro Futures," *The Dubya Report*, 25 October 2003, at http://www.thedubyareport.com/econiraq.html.

24. "Iranian Oil Bourse" *Wikipedia*, at
http://en.wikipedia.org/wiki/Iranian_oil_bourse.

25. Andrew Krieger, op. cit., pp. 3-5.

26. Andrew Krieger, op. cit., pp. 213-14.

27. "As Central Banks Shun the Dollar," *Business Week* Online, 23 February 2005, at
http://www.businessweek.com/bwdaily/dnflash/feb2005/nf20050223_0503_db053.htm.

28. Richard McGregor and Andrew Yeh, "China Plays Down Idea of Selling Off Dollars," *Financial Times*, 11 January 2006, at
http://news.ft.com/cms/s/37fee9b4-8231-11da-aea0-0000779e2340.html.

29. Gunther Schnabl, "The Russian Currency Basket, The Rising Role of the Euro for Russia's Exchange Rate Policies," Econ Working Paper 0512, 12 December 2005, at
http://128.118.178.162/eps/if/papers/0512/0512005.pdf

30. "Russia Dumps US Dollar as basic reserve currency," Global Research, 20 May 2009, at http://www.globalresearch.ca/russia-dumps-us-dollar-as-basic-reserve-currency/13691

31. Diego Valderrama, "FRBSF Economic Letter: What If Foreign Governments Diversified Their Reserves?" Federal Reserve Bank of San Francisco, 29 July 2005, at
http://www.frbsf.org/publications/economics/letter/2005/el2005-17.html.

32. International Monetary Fund, "Annual Report of the Executive Board for the Financial Year Ended 30 April 2005," Appendix, Table 1, p. 108, at
http://www.imf.org/external/pubs/ft/ar/2005/eng/index.htm.

33. "List of countries by Foreign Exchange Reserves," *Wikipedia*, at
http://en.wikipedia.org/wiki/List_of_countries_by_foreign-exchange_reserves

34. ibid.

35. Patrick Carvalho and Renee A. Fry-McKibbin, "Foreign Reserve Accumulation and the Mercantilist Motive Hypothesis," February 2014, at
https://cama.crawford.anu.edu.au/sites/default/files/publication/cama_crawford_anu_edu_au/2014-02/18_2014_carvalho_fry-mckibbin.pdf

36. Several IMF Depts, and approved by Reza Moghadam, "Reserve Accumulation and International Monetary Stability," International Monetary Fund, 13 April 2010, page 8, at
http://www.imf.org/external/np/pp/eng/2010/041310.pdf.

37. Joseph Stiglitz, *Making Globalization Work*, op. cit., page 249.

38. See, e.g., Olivier Jeanne and Romain Ranciere, "The Optimal Level of International Reserves for Emerging Market Countries: Formulas and Applications," IMF Working paper 06/229, October 2006, at
http://www.imf.org/external/pubs/ft/wp/2006/wp06229.pdf

39. Elias Papaioannou and Richard Portes, "Optimal Currency Shares in International Reserves: The Impact of the Euro and the Prospects for the Dollar," CEPR Discussion Paper, No 5734, at
http://www.cepr.org/pubs/new-dps/dplist.asp?dpno=5734.asp

40. Eduardo Yeyati, "The Cost of Reserves," Universidad Torcuato Di Tella Working Paper 10, July 2006, at
http://www.utdt.edu/Upload/CIF_wp/wpcif-102006.pdf

41. Marion Williams, "Foreign Exchange Reserves: How much is enough?" speech delivered at the Central Bank of the Bahamas, 2 November 2005, at http://www.centralbank.org.bb/Publications/Adlith_Brown_Lec.pdf, and at http://www.bis.org/review/r060123c.pdf.

42. Robert A. Mundell, "The International Monetary System in the 21st Century: Could Gold Make a Comeback?" on his website at
http://www.columbia.edu/~ram15/LBE.htm

43. Alistair Bland, "The Environmental Disaster That is the Gold Industry," *Smithsonian Magazine*, 14 February 2014, at

http://www.smithsonianmag.com/science-nature/environmental-disaster-gold-industry-180949762/?no-ist

44. 2014 history of London PM Gold Price Fixing, at http://www.usagold.com/reference/prices/2014.html

45. 2013 history of London PM Gold Price Fixing, at http://www.usagold.com/reference/prices/2013.html

46. Milton Friedman, *Capitalism and Freedom*. Chicago, IL: University of Chicago Press, 1962, p. 40.

47. John Schmid, "G-7 Drafts Gold-Sale Plan To Cut Poor Nations' Debt," *New York Times*, 14 June 1999, at http://www.nytimes.com/1999/06/14/news/14iht-seven.2.t.htm. See also, for continued efforts to sell gold from reserves, Abid Aslam's 2005 article, "World Leaders Agree Poor Countries Need Debt Relief, But Can't Agree on Plan," from *One World*, 18 April 2005, at Global Policy Forum at http://www.globalpolicy.org/component/content/article/210/44779.html.

48. "IMF gold sales to fund lending to poor countries," Jubilee USA Network, 10 October 2013, at http://www.jubileeusa.org/press/press-item/article/imf-gold-sales-to-fund-lending-to-poor-countries.html

49. International Monetary Fund, "Fact Sheet, November 19, 2013--Gold in the IMF," at http://www.imf.org/external/np/exr/facts/gold.htm.

50. Of the 193 members of the United Nations, the following six are not members of the 188-member International Monetary Fund: Andorra, Cuba, Democratic Republic of North Korea, Liechtenstein, Monaco, and Nauru. Kosovo is the one IMF member which is not a UN member state. See the IMF list of members at https://www.imf.org/external/np/sec/memdir/memdate.htm, and the UN list of members at http://www.un.org/en/members/index.shtml

51. See www.goldmoney.com for a facility that keeps accounts as measured in grams of gold, and where customers can buy and sell gold and use it for payments to other customers.

52. Nicholas Larkin, "Gold Demand Dropped 15% as ETP [Exchange Traded Product] Sales Outpaced Record Purchases," *Bloomberg Businessweek*, 14 February 2014, at http://www.businessweek.com/news/2014-02-18/gold-demand-dropped-15-percent-as-etp-sales-outpaced-record-purchases

53. Robert E. Litan and Benn Steil, *Financial Statecraft*. London and New Haven, CT: Yale University Press, 2006, p. 3, citing Richard Cronin's, "Financial Crisis: An Analysis of US Foreign Policy Interests and Options," April 1998, *Congressional Research Report*, report for the United States Congress, at http://www.fas.org/man/crs/crs-asia.htm

54. Kavaljit Singh, *Taming Global Financial Flows*. New York, NY: Zed Books, 2000, p. 13. A lower estimate of $10-20 billion daily comes from Lionel Trilling, "Money in Crisis," at http://www.terratrc.org/PDF/Sup3-MoneyInCrisis.pdf.

55. Benn Steil, "The Developing world should abandon parochial currencies," *Financial Times*, 17 January 2006, at http://www.ft.com/intl/cms/s/0/1f48b4e6-86fe-11da-8521-0000779e2340.html#axzz2tKTSuLGH

56. For a review of literature on capital controls, see Nicholas Magud and Carmen Reinhart, "Capital Controls: An Evaluation," National Bureau of Economic Research, Working Paper 11973, January, 2006, at http://papers.nber.org/papers/w11973.

57. Eric Schaling, "Capital Controls, Two-Tiered Exchange Rate Systems and Exchange Rate Policy: The South African Experience," 2005, at http://ideas.repec.org/p/dgr/kubcen/2005110.html.

58. Keith Bradsher, "Speculators Turn Away from China, Making Revaluation Less Pressing," *The New York Times*, 5 January 2006, p. C3, at http://www.nytimes.com/2006/01/05/business/worldbusiness/05yuan.html

59. Alan Greenspan, "International Imbalances," remarks before the Advancing Enterprise Conference, London, 2 December 2005, at http://www.federalreserve.gov/boarddocs/speeches/2005/200512022/default.htm.

60. C. Fred Bergsten, "Rescuing the Doha Round," *Foreign Affairs*, WTO Special Edition., December 2005, at http://www.foreignaffairs.org/20051201faessay84702/c-fred-bergsten/rescuing-the-doha-round.html. Also, Edwin Truman, *Policy Analysis in International Economics 77--A Strategy for IMF Reform.*" Washington, D.C.: Institute for International Economics, 2006, at http://www.iie.com/publications/chapters_preview/3985/01iie3985.pdf. See also, speech by Tim Geithner, President of the Federal Reserve Bank of New York, (and, later, US Treasury Secretary, at the Financial Imbalances Conference in London, 23 January 2006, at http://www.bis.org/review/r060127a.pdf.

61. For the 1949 origin of Murphy's Law, as attributed to the US military engineer, Major Edward A Murphy, Jr., who was working on rocket-sled experiments to measure "g forces", i.e., the force of gravity, see http://en.wikipedia.org/wiki/Murphy's_law.

Chapter 3. Economists View the Pre-Euro Multicurrency System and its Exchange Rate Regimes

Most economists who research and write about the multicurrency foreign exchange system approach it from the view "inside the box,"[1] according to the ideas and theories developed to understand the pre-euro and pre-internet economies. The two major foreign exchange questions remain:

How to value one currency compared to another, and

Why do those values rise and fall?

The absence of answers is not for lack of analysis. In a widely used database of "International Economics" articles in 2013, there were more articles (3,507), about "Foreign Exchange" (F31) than for any other category.[2] Below are presented economists' views on the current multicurrency system and its benefits and costs.

Purchasing Power Parity

The purchasing power of money relates to two of the three parts of the definition of money: to act as a medium of exchange and as a unit of account. The "parity" concept comes when the purchasing power of one currency is compared to another by looking at prices of commonly available goods, as are listed in consumer price indices such as the US Consumer Price Index (CPI), or the European Monetary Union Index of Consumer Prices (MUICP).

The Economist magazine brought the concept to lay people with its 1986 "light hearted" publication of the "Big Mac Index" based on the price of McDonalds' "Big Mac" burger around the world.[3] Nominal exchange rates, as traded on the markets, should reflect the value of a currency, and should reflect, at some point, the Purchasing Power Parity of a currency. However, notes *The Economist*, "Economists lost some faith in PPP as a guide to exchange rates in the 1970s, after the world's currencies abandoned their anchors to the US dollar. By the end of the decade, exchange rates seemed to be drifting without chart or compass. Later studies showed that a currency's purchasing power does assert itself over the long run. But it might take three to five years for a misaligned exchange rate to move even halfway back into line,"[4] i.e., where the Purchasing Power Parity analysis indicates that it should be.

To help understand why Big Mac Purchasing Power Parity does not correlate well to nominal exchange rates, economists have further analyzed the Purchasing Power Parity of the prices of "tradable" ingredients in Big Macs, such as onions, beef, and rolls which can be shipped anywhere in the world, and the "non-tradable" ingredients such as rent and electricity.[5] The reason for the distinction is that exchange rates work best, in theory, to bring price levels of countries into Purchasing Power Parity to the extent that the goods of a country are traded with those of other countries. If prices are not in parity, and not obeying the "law of one price," then consumers in the high-priced country would purchase the same good in the lower-priced country, after an exchange rate conversion. Such purchases would, in turn, increase demand and the price in that country and decrease demand in the home country--all of which leads to the prices being brought into equilibrium.

At the extremes of the 23 January 2014 "Big Mac Index" for a Big Mac, for which *The Economist* calculated a cost of \$4.62[6] on average in the United States, were the purchases in India (low) and Norway (high), using the nominal, or generally published, exchange rates. The 95 rupee Indian price of a Big Mac in India, where they are made with chicken, converted to US \$1.54 using the 61.85:1 exchange rate. A key to making PPP comparisons is that the products being purchased must be as similar as possible, hence the use of a "Big Mac" by *The Economist*. We ignore here, the Indian substitution of chicken for beef. The next highest nominal price for a beef Big Mac was in Malaysia for \$2.23, but for the sake of this analysis, the Indian purchase is used here, just as it was in *The Economist*.

The 48 kroner Norwegian price, converted to the high nominal \$7.80 price, using the 6.16:1 published exchange rate.

If there had been "Big Mac" Purchasing Power Parity among the three currencies, i.e., that the same amount of money, whether measured in US dollars, Indian rupees or Norwegian kroner could purchase a Big Mac in any of the three countries, the nominal Big Mac exchange rates to the dollar would have been 20.54 rupee and 10.38 kroner to the dollar. Thus, using the Big-Mac Index, the krone would be said to be overvalued against the dollar, and the rupee undervalued.

Table 3.1 A Big Mac in India, Norway and \$4.62 in the US

	India	Norway
Local Price	95 rupees	48 kroner
Nominal Exchange Rate	61.85 rupee/\$	6.16 krone/\$
Nominal Dollar Price	\$ 1.54	\$ 7.80
PPP Exchange Rate	20.54 rupee/\$	10.38 krone/\$
PPP Dollar Price	\$ 4.62	\$ 4.62

Real Exchange Rates/Equilibrium Exchange Rates

Economists use the terms "real exchange rates" or "equilibrium exchange rates" or "fundamental equilibrium exchange rates" to measure what currencies *should* be worth, as compared to each other, after factoring in Purchasing Power Parity and inflation and other "fundamentals," such as the unemployment rate, GDP growth and money supply. The "real exchange rate" is actually unreal, as it's only a product of economists' analyses rather than coming from real, or actual, exchange markets. The nominal exchange rates are what we read in the newspapers and on the internet,[7] and economists believe that these rates tend to move toward their calculated equilibrium rates.

Beginning in 2008, the Peterson Institute of International Economics has published a semi-annual compilation and analysis of fundamental equilibrium exchange rates. The November 2013 report was particularly concerned with the "taper shock" effects of the reduction of the US Federal Reserve asset purchases. The report concluded:

> "Despite widespread concern that prospective tapering in
> US quantitative easing has wreaked havoc in
> international capital and currency markets, exchange
> rate misalignments have tended to narrow in the past six

months. Spurred by the taper shock, overvalued currencies have corrected downward in Turkey, South Africa, India, Indonesia, and even Australia. At the same time, medium-term surplus estimates have moderated in Taiwan, Sweden, Switzerland, and Japan, narrowing the extent of their undervaluations. Cases of large misalignments persist, however, with Singapore once again undervalued by 21 percent, New Zealand again overvalued by nearly 18 percent, and Turkey still overvalued by 18 percent despite some correction."[8]

Identifying undervaluations and overvaluations of currencies does not do much to correct the underlying problem, which is the residual continuation of the obsolete multicurrency foreign exchange system.

In an effort to bring order to the vast amount of exchange rate data, the Bank for International Settlements (BIS) produces two effective exchange rate (EER) indices for 52 major economies, including the Eurozone countries separately and together. Using data from 1994 forward, the indices are not based on any one currency, such as a US dollar or euro, but are set using the averages in 2000 at an arbitrary 100. The nominal EER's "are calculated as geometric weighted averages of bilateral exchange rates" and the real EER's are the nominal rates as adjusted by relative consumer prices.[9] Despite their apparent comprehensive authoritative nature, such indices give the illusion of precision to an unpredictable fluctuating system.

The Unpredictability and Volatility of the Ups and Downs of Exchange Rates

The other major focus of international economists has been to find answers to the second of the two questions about exchange rates: why they do they go up and down? The ultimate goal for these economists is to predict and control the fluctuations in order to achieve the currency stability that the people of the world require. Thousands of articles, and many books, have been written to explain the movements of exchange rates. Some economists focus on the "fundamentals" of a currency, such as productivity of the currency area or its cost of living or wealth.

While exchange rate fluctuations are probably not a completely "random walk," as some economists have found; they still defy analysis. On the connection between national productivity and exchange rates, Jaewoo Lee and Man-Keung Tang of the IMF found in 2007 when

> "Revisiting the time-honored link between productivity growth and the real exchange rate, ... higher labor productivity tends to appreciate the real exchange rate, consistent with the traditional view. Contrary to the traditional view, however, we find that the positive productivity effect is transmitted through the relative price between tradable goods, rather than through the relative price between tradables and nontradables. Moreover, higher total factor productivity is found to often depreciate the real exchange rate."[10]

In short, there is not much predictability for exchange rates.

Other economists focus on technical, and often mysterious, factors, as the abbreviated list below of articles indicates:

Communications: "The intra-day impact of communciation on euro-dollar volatility and jumps."[11]

Elections: "Election Cycle of Real Exchange Rate in Latin America and East Asia"[12]

Inflation Targeting: "Inflation Targeting and Real Exchange Rates in Emerging Markets "[13]

Interest Rates: "Interest Rates and the Exchange Rate: A Non-Monotonic Tale"[14] and " The impact of foreign interest rates on the economy: The role of the exchange rate regime"[15]

International Liquidity: "International Liquidity and Exchange Rate Dynamics"[16]

Level of Economic Growth: "The Real Exchange Rate and Economic Growth"[17]

Monetary Policy: "The impact of monetary policy on the exchange rate: a high frequency exchange rate puzzle in emerging economies"[18]

News: "Exchange Rate Response to Macro News: Through the Lens of Microstructure"[19]

Order Flow: "Order Flow and Exchange Rate Dynamics"[20]

Product Quality: "Quality, Trade, and Exchange Rate Pass-Through"[21]

Rational Bubbles or Traded Goods: "Are There Bubbles in the Sterling-dollar Exchange Rate? New Evidence from Sequential ADF Tests"[22]

Social Media Information: "Using Twitter to Model the EUR/USD Exchange Rate"[23]

Statistical Models: "Statistical and Economic Methods for Evaluating Exchange Rate Predictability"[24]

Stock Returns: "An Empirical Relationship between Exchange Rates, Interest Rates and Stock Returns"[25]

Technical Trading Systems: "Do Technical Trading Profits Remain in the Foreign Exchange Market? Evidence from Fourteen Currencies"[26]

Uncertainty and Technology: "Do Uncertainty and Technology Drive Exchange Rates?"[27]

Another explanation of the volatility of exchange rates comes from the nature of markets themselves. Ben Stein wrote about Alan Greenspan, "Mr. Greenspan understands that markets are like sensitive children,"[28] and thus not entirely efficient or rational.

When economists are honest enough to admit that they do not understand some aspects of exchange rate economics, they term the unknowns as puzzles.

Maurice Obstfeld and Kenneth Rogoff write of two exchange rate puzzles. The first is the Purchasing Power Parity puzzle which asks why the empirical data do not indicate a close relationship between changes in the exchange rates and changes in national price levels, as would be predicted by economic theory.[29] Also, part of the working definition of exchange rates is that they function to adjust the price levels of countries in the direction of the "law of one price," or Purchasing Power Parity. Again, however, the empirical data do not support a relationship.

The second multiple currency-related "puzzle is 'the exchange rate disconnect puzzle,' a name that alludes broadly to the exceedingly weak relationship (except, perhaps, in the longer run) between the exchange rate and virtually any macroeconomic aggregates."[30]

Obstfeld and Rogoff argue that including consideration of trade costs helps to explain the puzzles, but they urge more research.

Lucio Sarno addressed the above two puzzles and one additional, "the forward bias puzzle" whereby "high interest rate currencies appreciate when one might guess that investors would demand higher interest rates on currencies expected to fall in value."[31]

What is less well known is the harm caused by "wild gyrations of major exchange rates and the risk of instability of the dollar,"[32] as Robert Mundell puts it. He gives four examples of such harm:

"1. The debt crisis of the early 1980s was caused mainly by the swings of the dollar: negative interest rates in the late 1970s led to easy and lax borrowing, followed by soaring real interest rates and dollar depreciation in the early 1980s, pushing emerging market countries all over the world into default.

"2. The tripling of the value of the yen after the Plaza Accord between 1985 and April 1995 weakened balance sheets and clogged up the Japanese banking system with non-performing loans that persist to this day.

"3. The soaring dollar from 78 yen in April 1995 to 148 yen in June 1998 set in motion the Asian crisis, by cutting off FDI from Japan to SE Asia and undercutting the export markets of countries whose currencies were fixed to the dollar.

"4. Similar stories could be told about the Russian and Argentine crises."[33]

In 2013, Barbara Rossi sought to "provide an answer to the question: does anything forecast exchange rates, and if so, what variables?" Her essential answer was that " 'It depends' – on the choice of predictor, forecast horizon, sample period, model, and forecast evaluation method."[34]

The US Current Account and Fiscal Deficit Debate

Many economists say that the twin US deficits: current account deficit and the federal government deficit cannot continue forever. Raghuram Rajan, formerly of the IMF and now the Governor of the Reserve Bank of India, noted in 2006 that the US current account deficit approached 6 1/4 percent of the USA GDP, "and over 1.5 percent of world GDP. And to help finance it, the United States pulls in 70 percent of all global capital flows. Clearly, such a large deficit is unsustainable in the long run."[35] Since then, the current account deficit has declined relatively, and by the second quarter of 2013 it was running at the rate of 2.4 percent of GDP.[36]

Maurice Obstfeld and Kenneth Rogoff warn that such a day of reckoning may not be far off and it will be serious, as they refer to "the potential collapse of the dollar" and "the dollar decline that will almost inevitably occur in the wake of global current account adjustment."[37]   Paul Volcker wrote, "Under the placid surface, there are disturbing trends: huge imbalances, disequilibria, risks--call them what you will. Altogether, the circumstances seem to me as dangerous and intractable as any I can remember, and I can remember quite a lot."[38]

The Peterson Institute for International Economics proposes "a three-part package that includes credible, sizable reductions in the US budget deficit, expansion of domestic demand in major economies outside the United States, and a gradual but substantial realignment of exchange rates."[39]

Some do not agree there is a danger, and even if there is, how to fix it. Richard Cooper has written "that the startlingly large US current account deficit is not only sustainable but a natural feature of today's highly globalized economy."[40]

The former Chair of the Federal Reserve (2006-2014), Ben Bernanke, stated in 2005 that the US twin deficits are not a problem because they have served to soak up a worldwide "savings glut."[41] Others argue that the "savings glut" theory is not supported by the data.[42]

The Exchange Rate as Shock Absorber

Exchange rates and foreign exchange trading are believed to be useful to the international financial system as "shock absorbers." However, it could be argued that they only absorb the shocks, if at all, on the redundant fifth wheel. By "shock," economists mean something that seriously disrupts an economy such as a natural disaster or a labor strike or a financial bubble. With such negative shocks, the theory goes, the exchange rate for a currency would likely go down, making exports less expensive and therefore paving the way for their growth. The IMF established in 2008 an "Exogenous Shocks Facility" to assist member countries suffering from such shocks.[43] Interestingly, just as the freedom to control one's own monetary policy usually means in the economic literature the freedom to devalue, rather than revalue, the term "shocks" is usually used to mean negative shocks rather than positive shocks, such as the discovery of an oil field.

The large imbalance of trade between the United States and China might be considered such a negative "shock" to the United States, but positive to China, and classic exchange rate theory would predict the value of the US dollar to decline relative to the yuan. US exports to China would then increase and Chinese imports to the United States would decrease and the imbalance would disappear. However, the Chinese trade for all the countries in the world has been roughly in balance through 2014 so a large change in the dollar/yuan prices, which, in turn, would affect all the currencies of the world; would not help much. For February 2014, China actually reported trade deficit of $22.9 billion.[44] As Richard Cooper has pointed out, if the yuan increased in value sufficiently to reduce Chinese exports to the United States, there are several other Asian countries which could export similar goods at lower prices, and these countries manage their own exchange rates.[45]

However, the value of the yuan has risen gradually, and stood at 6.05 to the USD by the end of 2013.[46] That's an increase of about 27 percent from the longtime peg at 8.28 to the USD which continued until July 2005. Despite that rise, the trade deficit, in goods only, with the US has also increased. In 2005, the deficit was $202 billion, but it rose steadily to $315 billion in 2012 and will exceed that amount in 2013, having reached $293 billion by the end of November.[47] Despite continued pressure in the US to label China as a "currency manipulator" which produces large trade deficits with the US, China's trade with the rest of the world has been imbalanced in the other direction. For each of the four years 2009-2012, its total trade surplus has been less than $200 billion.[48] This means that China's trade with the rest of the world, minus the US, has been in deficit. Illustrating the perversity of national currencies and balances of payments, in 2011 China and the US both had trade deficits (goods) with Taiwan of $116 billion and $15 billion, respectively.[49] However, if Taiwan were to return fully to Chinese sovereignty, including a currency union, China's trade surplus with the US would increase by $15 billion to $310 billion. Similarly, China's surplus with the world would increase by $116 billion to $231 billion, because its $116 billion deficit with Taiwan would disappear. Thus re-incorporating Taiwan into China proper would increase China's trade surpluses and increase global pressure on China to accelerate the appreciation of the yuan against the USD.

In an impassioned 1999 article supporting the UK's joining the EMU, Willem Buiter argues that in a financially integrated economy, the value of an exchange rate shock absorber is minimal. He stated,

> "The 'one-size-fits-all,' 'asymmetric shocks,' and 'cyclical divergence' objections to UK membership are based on the misapprehension that independent national monetary policy, and the associated nominal exchange rate flexibility, can be used effectively to offset or even completely neutralise asymmetric shocks. This 'fine tuning delusion' is compounded by a failure to understand that, under a high degree of international financial integration, market-determined exchange rates are primarily a source of shocks and instability. Instead, opponents of UK membership in EMU view exchange rate flexibility as an effective buffer for adjusting to asymmetric shocks originating elsewhere. I know of no evidence that supports such an optimistic reading of what exchange rate flexibility can deliver under conditions of very high international financial capital mobility."[50]

The Exchange Rate Regime Debate

Since the collapse of the Bretton Woods system, central banks and economists have focused on the question of which exchange rate regime should a country use: fixed or floating or something in between. James W. Dean wrote that "the debate over ideal exchange rate regimes is the oldest and most central debate in open-economy finance."[51] Wrote 2008 Nobel laureate Paul Krugman, "I would suggest that the issue of optimum currency areas, or, more broadly, that of choosing an exchange rate regime, should be regarded as the central intellectual question of international economics."[52]

Much has been written simply to categorize the various exchange rate options. Mark Stone and Ashok Bhundia of the IMF list seven: "(i) monetary non-autonomy, (ii) weak anchor, (iii) money anchor, (iv) exchange rate peg, (v) full-fledged inflation targeting, (vi) implicit price stability anchor, and (vii) inflation targeting lite."[53]

The underlying assumption, which was not extensively questioned until the development of the euro, was that currencies should be issued by nations and managed by national central banks or related national institutions. Another specific assumption is that "No Single Currency Regime is Right for All Countries or at All Times," as the title of Jeffrey Frankel's 1999 article states.[54]

It's often forgotten that when an exchange rate declines, and when exports are expected to increase, there are losers, too. Arguably, there are an equal number of gains and losses during inflation and deflation. For example, during an exchange rate decline, importers must pay more for their goods and they pass those increases on to consumers. Thus, there is a risk of inflation, especially in a country which imports a substantial portion of its consumer goods, such as the United States. Other losers are foreign investors in the devaluing country.

Many countries have tried to fix or peg the values of their currencies to the US dollar or to other primary currencies. To support such a "fix" or "peg," central banks had to be prepared to intervene in the foreign exchange markets by either buying or selling their own currencies. However, due to the supply and demand dynamics of the foreign exchange market, and its huge size, central banks have found that their interventions could not withstand the power of the market, and sometimes that realization came with spectacular failure as with the 1992 Bank of England defense of the pound, as described earlier.

Economists have studied the benefits and costs of the different exchange rate regimes[55] and have gradually moved to the view that in the multicurrency world, floating rates are best for most countries. However, for small countries, it's recommended that they not have any independent monetary policy at all, and, instead, join a monetary union or ize to an anchor currency.[56]

The question of which exchange rate to adopt became sufficiently exasperating and puzzling that non-economic terms emerged to explain economic behavior. Guillermo Calvo and Carmen Reinhart suggested that "Fear of Floating," with an echo to Erica Jong's book, *Fear of Flying*, led countries to refrain from allowing their exchange rates to float.[57] Graham Bird and Dane Rowlands referred to the question of exchange rate regime choice as a "Bi-polar Disorder."[58]

While noting that "we are far from a consensus, however, on the relative merits of managing such regimes through managed floats or crawling bands," Thomas Willett makes the point that "this formal institutional distinction may well prove to be of considerably less importance than the specifics of how either type of regime is managed."[59] Similarly, Jesus Lopez and Hugo Mendizabal observe that most exchange rate regimes are actually intermediate regimes, somewhere in between pure floating and pure pegged, regardless of their nominal characterization.[60]

One exchange rate regime puzzle bedeviling economists is why the type of regime does not seem to make a macroeconomic performance difference among countries. Assaf Razin and Yona Rubinstein believe that there are discernible differences if one uses different data and measurements.[61] In any case, the performance differences are not large.

Currency Crises

Economists have written extensively about the currency crises of the 1990s and 2000s and focus on what caused them. One of the concepts developed by economists is "Original Sin," which describes the inability of developing countries to borrow in their own currencies, forcing them to borrow in hard currencies, such as the US dollar.[62] Such borrowing can contribute to subsequent currency crises when the hard currency increases in value relative to the borrower's currency. Whatever the original meaning of the term, "Original Sin," the real sin is that the existing multicurrency foreign exchange system continues to be tolerated, and those developing countries are forced into hazardous financial transactions.

Many articles describe "early warning systems" (EWS) which list the criteria, such as debt to GDP ratios, to watch in order to predict and avoid a currency crisis.[63]

These articles examine such criteria as the ratio of foreign exchange reserves to GDP, and the growth of M1 and M2 money supply. None, however, recommends the best way to eliminate a currency crisis, which is to replace a national currency with one that is more stable such as from a monetary union.

Summary

The previous three chapters show the cost, complexity and past and future potential crises of the existing multicurrency global monetary system. The theories and observations of economists to explain and guide that system are often obscure and hard to discern. Some understand that, at bottom, their work must make sense, and that they must write for the people of the world. They have to consider researching and writing "outside the box." This need to appeal to common sense was confirmed by Robert Mundell when he mapped the "Optimum Currency Area" in 1969. Arguing that there is a lower size floor for optimum currency areas, he noted that tiny economic pockets could not reasonably have their own currencies, writing, "Such an arrangement hardly appeals to common sense."[64] In contrast, the Single Global Currency does appeal to common cents/sense. Robert Mundell reconfirmed the message in 2013, "It is common sense to talk now about a new world currency."[65]

Further research should be directed away from the twin handles of the Holy Grail of the multicurrency foreign exchange system: the two questions of "What value?" and "Why fluctuate?" Instead, research should focus on the system which will eliminate the economists' Sisyphusian[66] pursuit: the Single Global Currency. A key puzzle for this book is why the community of international economists is not moving more rapidly toward a consensus that the Single Global Currency should be implemented.

At least, however, as Alberto Alesina and Robert Barro noted optimistically in 2001, the currency area discussion "has shifted toward one of desirable forms and sizes of currency unions,"[67] as we will see in Chapter 4.

ENDNOTES

1. Basil Moore has made this point, too. He wrote, "Economists must think outside the box," in his article, "A Global Currency for a Global Economy," *Journal of Post Keynesian Economics*, Summer, 2004, p. 637, at http://ideas.repec.org/a/mes/postke/v26y2004i4p631-653.html. "Thinking outside the box" is a phrase developed in the 1970s by management consultants and others to urge their clients to think of new solutions to old problems. The "box" consisted of three rows of three dots:

  . . .

  . . .

  . . .

and the challenge was to connect all nine dots with no more than four straight lines, drawn continuously without lifting the pencil from the paper. The key to the solution is that the straight lines must extend outside the imagined four walls of the box. See the solution in "Etymologies and word origins" at http://www.wordorigins.org/wordoro.htm.

2. Social Science Research Network, using the JEL (*Journal of Economic Literature*) category of "F3-International Economics." Category F31 is "Foreign Exchange," at http://papers.ssrn.com/sol3/displayjel.cfm. In 2014, the count for F31, "Foreign Exchange" was 3,507, and the next largest at 2,780, was F13, "Commercial Policy; Protection; Promotion; Trade Negotiations." In 2006 "Foreign Exchange" (F31) led with 1,308 matches compared to 576 for the next most frequent, F33, "International Monetary Arrangements and Institutions,"

3. "The Big Mac index: Global exchange rates, to go," *The Economist*, London, 23 January 2014, at http://www.economist.com/content/big-mac-index.

4. "The Economist's Big Mac Index: Fast Food and Strong Currencies," *The Economist*, London, 9 June 2005, at http://users.nber.org/~wei/data/parsley&wei2003/The%20Economist.pdf.

5. David Parsley and Shang-Jim Wei, "A Prism Into the PPP Puzzles: The Microfoundations of Big Mac Real Exchange Rates," December 2005 version available at http://users.nber.org/~wei/data/parsley&wei2003/Big%20Mac%2012-12-05.pdf

6. *The Economist* published the average price of $4.62 for a Big Mac in the US However, using input from www.humuch.com and personal friends, I calculated an average from 17 sites of $3.94. The low was in Falls Church, Virginia with $3.14 and the high was $4.75 in San Francisco, California. Not excluded were the sales taxes, which vary by locality. This example illustrates the difficulty in measuring representative prices for an average price even within a currency area.

7. See Currency conversion calculations at the Bank of Canada site at http://www.bankofcanada.ca/en/rates/exchform.html or the Oanda.com site at http://www.oanda.com/convert/classic/index.html.

8. William Cline, "Estimates of Fundamental Equilibrium Exchange Rates, November 2013," Policy Brief 13-29, Peterson Institute for International Economics, at http://www.iie.com/publications/pb/pb13-29.pdf

9. "BIS Effective Exchange Rate Indices," Bank for International Settlements, 15 January 2014, at http://www.bis.org/statistics/eer/index.htm

10. "Does Productivity Growth Appreciate the Real Exchange Rate?" Jaewoo Lee and Man-Keung Tang, *Review of International Economics*, Vol 15, Issue 1, page 164, February 2007, at http://www.blackwell-synergy.com/links/doi/10.1111/j.1467-9396.2006.00628.x/enhancedabs

11. Hans Dewachter, Deniz Erdemlioglu, Jean-Yves Cnabo, Christelle Lecourt, "The intra-day impact of communication on euro-dollar volatility and jumps," *Journal of International Money and Finance*, Volume 43, May 2014, pages 131-154, at http://www.sciencedirect.com/science/article/pii/S0261560614000072

12. Sainan Huang and Cristina Terra, "Election Cycle of Real Exchange Rate in Latin America and East Asia" at site of American Economic Assn. at http://www.aeaweb.org/search.php

13. Joshua Aizeman and Michael Hutchinson, "Inflation Targeting and Real Exchange Rates in Emerging Markets," *World Development*, May 2011 at http://www.sciencedirect.com/science/article/pii/S0305750X10002275

14. Viktoria Hnatkovska, Amartya Lahiri and Carlos A. Vegh, "Interest Rates and the Exchange Rate: A Non-Monotonic Tale," Working Paper, 13925, National Bureau of Economic Research, at http://www.nber.org/papers/w13925.pdf?new_window=1.

15. Julian di Giovanni, Jay C. Shambaugh, "The impact of foreign interest rates on the economy: The role of the exchange rate regime," *Journal of International Economics*, 2008, pp. 341-61, at http://julian.digiovanni.ca/Papers/diGiovanni_Shambaugh_JIE08.pdf

16. Xavier Gabaix and Matteo Maggiori, " International Liquidity and Exchange Rate Dynamics," National Bureau of Economic Research, Working Paper 19824, 2014, at http://www.nber.org/papers/w19854.pdf

17. Dani Rodrik, "The Real Exchange Rate and Economic Growth," October 2008, at http://www.hks.harvard.edu/fs/drodrik/Research%20papers/RER%20and%20growth.pdf

18. Emanuel Kohlscheen, "The impact of monetary policy on the exchange rate: a high frequency exchange rate puzzle in emerging economies," *Journal of International Money and Finance*, February 2014, at http://www.sciencedirect.com/science/article/pii/S0261560614000151

19. Tanseli Savaser, "Exchange Rate Response to Macro News: Through the Lens of Microstructure" Williams College, at http://web.williams.edu/Economics/wp/savaserMacronews.pdf

20. Martin D. D. Evans and Richard K. Lyons, "Order Flow and Exchange Rate Dynamics," *Journal of Political Economy*, February 2002, pp. 170-80, at http://faculty.haas.berkeley.edu/lyons/pubabs.html.

21. Natalie Chen and Luciana Juvenal, "Quality, Trade, and Exchange Rate Pass-Through," International Monetary Fund, Working paper 41, March 2014, at http://www.imf.org/external/pubs/ft/wp/2014/wp1442.pdf

22. Chen, Wenjuan and Bettendorf, Timo, "Are There Bubbles in the Sterling-dollar Exchange Rate? New Evidence from Sequential ADF Tests," 2013, at http://papers.ssrn.com/sol3/papers.cfm?abstract_id=2336043

23. Dietmar Janetzko, "Using Twitter to Model the EUR/USD Exchange Rate," 2014, at http://arxiv.org/pdf/1402.1624.pdf

24. Pasquale Della Corte, Ilias Tsiakas, "Statistical and Economic Methods for Evaluating Exchange Rate Predictability," at http://www.uoguelph.ca/~itsiakas/papers/FX_Predictability.pdf

25. Sudharshan Reddy Paramati and Rakesh Gupta, "An Empirical Relationship between Exchange Rates, Interest Rates and Stock Returns," October, 2013, at http://papers.ssrn.com/sol3/papers.cfm?abstract_id=2336043

26. Igor Cialenco and Aris Protopapadakis, "Do Technical Trading Profits Remain in the Foreign Exchange Market? Evidence from Fourteen Currencies," 2010, at https://msbfile03.usc.edu/digitalmeasures/aris/intellcont/Filter%20Rules%20%20FX_JIFMIM_06-21-1.pdf

27. Pablo A. Guerron-Quintana, "Do Uncertainty and Technology Drive Exchange Rates?" Federal Reserve Bank of Philadelphia, 16 September 2009 at http://www.philadelphiafed.org/research-and-data/publications/working-papers/2009/wp09-20.pdf

28. Ben Stein, "Everybody's Business: Master of the Art of Taming Inflation," *The New York Times*, 1 January 2006, p. BU4, at http://www.nytimes.com/2006/01/01/business/yourmoney/01every.html

29. Maurice Obstfeld and Kenneth Rogoff, "The Six Major Puzzles in International Macroeconomics: Is There a Common Cause?" NBER Macroeconomics Annual 2000, pp. 339-390, at http://www.nber.org/chapters/c11059.pdf.

30. Obstfeld and Rogoff, ibid.

31. Lucio Sarno, "Viewpoint: Towards a Solution to the Puzzles in Exchange Rate Economics: Where do we stand?" August 2005, *Canadian Journal of Economics*, pp. 673-708, at http://papers.ssrn.com/sol3/papers.cfm?abstract_id=772984.

32. Robert Mundell, "The case for a world currency," *Journal of Policy Modeling*, June 2005, pp. 465-75, at p. 470, at http://www.sciencedirect.com/science/article/pii/S0161893805000463.

33. Robert Mundell, ibid., p. 470.

34. Barbara Rossi, "Exchange Rate Predictability," *Journal of Economic Literature*, Vol 51, No. 4, pp. 1063-1119, at http://www.aeaweb.org/articles.php?doi=10.1257/jel.51.4.1063

35. Raghuram Rajan, "Financial System Reform and Global Current Account Imbalances," remarks to the American Economic Association, 8

January 2006, at
http://www.imf.org/external/np/speeches/2006/010806.htm.
36. "Current Account Deficit in US Narrowed 5.7% in Second Quarter," by Victoria Stilwell, 19 September 2013, Bloomberg News, at
http://www.bloomberg.com/news/2013-09-19/current-account-deficit-in-u-s-narrowed-5-7-in-second-quarter.html
37. Maurice Obstfeld and Kenneth Rogoff, "The Unsustainable US Current Account Position Revisited," Chapter in NBER book, *G7 Current Account Imbalances: Sustainability and Adjustment, 2007*, Richard H. Clarida, Editor at http://www.nber.org/chapters/c0127.
38. Paul Volcker, "An Economy on Thin Ice," *Washington Post*, 10 April 2005, p. B07, at http://www.washingtonpost.com/wp-dyn/articles/A38725-2005Apr8.html.
39. Peterson Institute for International Economics, "HOT TOPICS: US Current Account Deficit, The Issue," at
http://www.iie.com/research/topics/hottopic.cfm?HotTopicID=9.
40. Richard Cooper, "Living with Global Imbalances: A Contrarian View," Policy Briefs, No. PB0-5-3, November 2005, Institute for International Economics, Washington, DC: p. 1, at
http://www.iie.com/publications/pb/pb05-3.pdf.
41. Ben S. Bernanke, Sandridge Lecture, 10 March 2005, at
http://www.federalreserve.gov/boarddocs/speeches/2005/200503102/default.htm.
42. Menzie Chinn and Hiro Ito, "An Update on Medium-Term Determinants of Current Account Imbalances--The 'Savings Glut' Hypothesis Examined," 1 August 2005, at
http://www.ssc.wisc.edu/~mchinn/Chinn_Ito_CAmemo.pdf.
43. "IMF Establishes an Exogenous Shocks Facility," Public Information Notice No. 05/163, 8 December 2005, International Monetary Fund, Washington, DC: at
http://www.imf.org/external/np/sec/pn/2005/pn05163.htm.
44. William Kazer, "China February Exports Slide, Trade Balance Swings to Deficit," *Wall Street Journal*, 8 March 2014, at
http://online.wsj.com/news/articles/SB10001424052702304732804579426001879597542
45. Richard Cooper, "Living with Global Imbalances: A Contrarian View," op. cit., p. 7.
46. http://www.bankofcanada.ca/rates/exchange/10-year-converter/. However, the yuan dropped in March 2014 to a recent low of 6.1458 to the USD. See William Kazer, "China February Exports Slide, Trade Balance Swings to Deficit," op. cit.
47. "Trade in Goods with China," US Census Bureau, years 1985-2013, at http://www.census.gov/foreign-trade/balance/c5700.html
48. "European Union, Trade in goods with China," page 9 "China Trade with World," at
http://trade.ec.europa.eu/doclib/docs/2006/september/tradoc_113366.pdf

49. "US Taiwan Trade Facts," Office of the United States Trade Representative, http://www.ustr.gov/countries-regions/china/taiwan and "China, Taiwan hold historic talks in Nanjing," *Associated Press*, 11 February 2014, at http://www.washingtonpost.com/world/asia_pacific/china-taiwan-hold-historic-talks-in-nanjing/2014/02/11/2d493388-930a-11e3-b3f7-f5107432ca45_story.html

50. Willem Buiter, "Optimal Currency Areas: Why Does the Exchange Rate Matter?" speech at the Royal College of Physicians, Edinburgh, on 26 October 1999, at http://www.opengrey.eu/item/display/10068/564094, at p. 2.

51. James W. Dean, "Exchange Rate Regimes for the 21st Century: Asia, Europe, and the Americas," October 2003, prepared for a seminar at Carleton University, at http://carleton.ca/economics/wp-content/uploads/cep03-10.pdf.

52. Paul Krugman, "What Do We Need to Know about the International Monetary System?" p. 4, at http://www.princeton.edu/~ies/IES_Essays/E190.pdf

53. Mark R. Stone and Ashok J. Bhundia, "A New Taxonomy of Monetary Regimes," IMF Working Paper WP/04/191, October 2004, at http://www.imf.org/external/pubs/ft/wp/2004/wp04191.pdf. The last category, "Inflation Targeting Lite" echoes the description of diet foods, such as "lite butter" or "lite beer."

54. Jeffrey A. Frankel, "No Single Currency Regime is Right for All Countries or at All Times," September 1999, National Bureau of Economic Research, Working Paper 7338, at http://www.nber.org/papers/W7338. The paper is substantially similar to Prof. Frankel's 21 May 1999, testimony before the Committee on Banking and Financial Services at http://ksghome.harvard.edu/~jfrankel/TESTIMNY.HBC.PDF.

55. Vivek H. Dehejia, "Currency Options for Emerging Economies: Concepts and Arguments," Revised Version, 28 March 2004, at http://www.econbiz.de/Record/currency-options-for-emerging-economies-concepts-and-arguments-dehejia-vivek/10002141724.

56. See, for example, Robert E. Litan and Benn Steil, *Financial Statecraft*. London and New Haven, CT: Yale University Press, 2006.

57. Guillermo A. Calvo and Carmen M. Reinhart, "Fear of Floating," National Bureau of Economic Research, Working Paper No. W7993, November 2000, at http://papers.ssrn.com/sol3/papers.cfm?abstract_id=248599

58. Graham Bird and Dane Rowlands, "Bi-Polar Disorder: Exchange Rate Regimes, Economic Crises, and the IMF," 26 April 2005, at http://ideas.repec.org/p/sur/surrec/0705.html

59. Thomas D. Willett, "The Political Economy of Exchange Rate Regimes and Currency Crises," March 2004, background paper for the Claremont Conference on the Political Economy of Exchange Rates, 1 and 2 April 2004, at http://www.cgu.edu/include/spe_Willett5.pdf.

60. Jesus Rodriguez Lopez and Hugo Rodriguez Mendizabal, "How Tight Should One's Hands Be Tied? Fear of Floating and the Credibility of an

Exchange Rate Regime," Working Paper Series WP 06.03, Universidad Pablo de Olavide, Sevilla, Espana, 2 March 2006, at http://www.upo.es/serv/bib/wps/econ0603.pdf

61. Assaf Razin and Yona Rubinstein, "Evaluation of Currency Regimes: The Unique Role of Sudden Stops," *Economic Policy*, January 2006, pp. 119-52, at http://www.blackwell-synergy.com/doi/abs/10.1111/j.1468-0327.2006.00155.x

62. Ricardo Hausmann and Ugo Panizza, "The Mystery of Original Sin," 16 July 2002, at http://ksghome.harvard.edu/~rhausma/paper/mistery_march3.pdf

63. For a review of the EWS literature, see Jan Jacobs, Gerard Kuper, and Lestano, "Currency Crises in Asia: A Multivariate Logit Approach," Working Paper, July 2005, Centre for Economic Research (CCS), University of Gronningen, Netherlands, at http://ccso.eldoc.ub.rug.nl/FILES/root/2005/200506/200506.pdf.

64. Robert Mundell, "A Theory of Optimum Currency Areas," *American Economic Review*, May 1961, pp. 657-65, at p. 662, and as Chapter 12 in his book, *International Economics*, pp. 177-86, at http://www.columbia.edu/~ram15/ie/ie-12.html.

65. Shehab Al Makshleh, "Economist calls for a new world currency," *Gulf News*, 1 June 2013, at http://gulfnews.com/business/economy/economist-calls-for-a-new-global-currency-1.1191382

66. Albert Camus brought the tragedy of the mythical Greek character, Sisyphus, to the modern reader in *The Myth of Sisyphus*. See Camus' text at http://www.sccs.swarthmore.edu/users/00/pwillen1/lit/msysip.htm and see an analysis at http://www.nyu.edu/classes/keefer/hell/camus.html.

67. Alberto Alesina and Robert J. Barro, "Introduction," in *Currency Unions*. Stanford, CA: Edited by Alberto Alesina and Robert J. Barro, Hoover Institution Press, 2001, p. xv, at http://www.ebook3000.com/Currency-Unions--Hoover-Institution-Press-Publication--By-Alberto-Alesina_106810.html

Chapter 4. Monetary Unions

A monetary union, also called a "currency union," is created when two or more currency areas, usually countries, share a currency or currencies. To varying degrees the monetary unions move the responsibility for the currency away from the previous separate issuers and onto a union entity. In earlier monetary unions, there was agreement among political entities to accept the money of the other, essentially as legal tender. In the twentieth and twenty-first centuries, a monetary union is typically among countries which replaced their own currencies with the common currency, and the responsibility for the new currency is assumed by a monetary union central bank.

The Idea of Monetary Union

By 1582, the difficulties of valuing the coins of the various kingdoms, principalities, and republics of Europe led Gasparo Scaruffi of Viareggio on the coast of Toscana[1] (now a region of Italy), to propose the "alitinonfo" as a common currency, with every mint in Europe producing the same coins with the same characteristics, so as to create a standard currency. According to 1999 Nobel Prize winner, Robert Mundell, "alitinonfo" was derived from a Greek word meaning true light, and if all of Europe had a single currency, this would give true light to all transactions.[2]

Early Monetary Unions

There have been many efforts to overcome the difficulties of foreign exchange by forming monetary unions, and some of the better known are presented here.

Beginning in 1379 until the Napoleonic wars, cities along the Baltic Sea and North Atlantic Ocean joined together in the trading association known as the Hanseatic League, and cities and principalities inside Germany formed the Monetary Federation of the Rhine.[3] Within each group there was agreement upon the same gold and silver content for coinage.

From the 1600s until 1750, the British colonies of Connecticut, Massachusetts Bay, New Hampshire, and Rhode Island shared a paper currency unit and recognized each other's paper currency. Shmule Vaknin regards this union as the "first truly modern example" of a monetary union,[4] even though it lacked a central bank.

After the American Revolution, the thirteen states of the United States decided on a common unit of account, with little more than the name of the "dollar," but the value of paper money depended upon the credibility, i.e., reserves, of the issuing bank. Those thirteen states also formed a federal political union. Although the US dollar began more than 200 years ago as a common currency, the monetary role of the member states of the United States has disappeared, and the monetary role of the federal government has occupied the field. The US dollar is now as national a currency as can be.

In 1838 a German Monetary Union was established. "Baden, Bavaria, Frankfurt, Hesse, Nassau Saxe-Meiningen (joined later), Schwarzburg-Rudolstadt (joined later), and Wurttemberg agreed on a monetary union with the northern states adopting the thaler and the southern states, the florin with a fixed rate of exchange between them."[5] In 1857 the Austro-Hungarian Empire joined, but that union was dissolved by Bismark, the prime minister of Prussia, in 1867 after the Battle of Sadowa with the Austro-Hungarian Empire. The 1871 creation of the German Empire replaced the German monetary union with political and monetary union, which then used the mark as the national currency. The 1873 "gold mark" has been succeeded by its German progeny with the same root name, e.g., deutschmark, and then in 2002 by the euro.

In 1865, the Latin Monetary Union was established among Belgium, Bulgaria, France, Italy, and Switzerland, and in 1868, Greece and Romania joined. The monetary union continued until World War I, and the members shared coinage of the same values.

From 1873 through 1913, Denmark, Norway, and Sweden (the latter two being politically joined until 1905), comprised the Scandinavian Monetary Union which adopted the gold standard and the currency unit, the krona.[6]

As a political union is not required for a successful regional or Global Monetary Union; the examples of monetary unions within political unions are not discussed further in this book. One of the objections to the Single Global Currency is that it would require a world government, but that is not the case as the examples in this chapter will show. What is required is a high level of international cooperation, but not a world government in the feared sense of a government which governs and taxes its citizens directly.

20th Century Monetary Unions and Academic Background.

Princeton Economist Edwin Kemmerer became known as the "Money Doctor" as he advised numerous countries around the world on how to ensure a stable money system, including the roles of central banks. In 1916, he proposed the creation of a monetary union for all the Americas, with the unit to be called the "oro," the Spanish word for gold.[7]

Belgium and Luxembourg formed a monetary union in 1921 where each accepted the currency of the other, with monetary policy set by the Belgian Central Bank and "exchange regulations overseen by a joint agency."[8] This union was superseded by the European Monetary Union and the euro.

In 1930, a fundamental innovation was proposed for monetary unions: that the common currency be managed by a supranational central bank. This was the contribution of German banker Hans Furstenberg at the Congress of the Pan-European League in 1932.[9]

Henceforth, the money of most monetary unions was issued and managed by their central banks.

In 1950, the British Caribbean Currency Board was established among islands in the Caribbean. There have been subsequent inclusions and departures, and the successor Eastern Caribbean Currency Authority was formed in 1965. In 1981, the Treaty of Basseterre established the Organization of Eastern Caribbean States and in 1983, the Eastern Caribbean Central Bank and Monetary Authority was formed.[10] It now includes Anguilla, Antigua and Barbuda, Commonwealth of Dominica, Grenada, Montserrat, St Kitts and Nevis, St Lucia, and St Vincent and the Grenadines. The authority's central bank is located in Basseterre, St. Kitts, and its currency, the Eastern Caribbean dollar, is pegged at 2.7 to the US dollar, or at the value of $.37. [11] Other monetary union options are now being considered in the larger Caribbean area.

In 1957, J. E. Meade wrote approvingly of a common currency for areas where there was significant labor mobility, where workers could move freely to find work. [12]

In 1958, economist Tibor Scitovsky [13] published *Economic Theory and Western European Integration,* where he discussed monetary union and presented the view that countries within a monetary union tended to grow more alike. [14] Thus, monetary union was both a result of common economic interests and a cause of increased commonality. Both Meade and Scitovsky were cited by Robert Mundell in "A Theory of Optimum Currency Areas." He wrote, "In terms of the language of this paper, Meade favors national currency areas whereas Scitovsky gives qualified approval to the idea of a single currency area in Western Europe." [15]

Robert Mundell is called the "godfather of the euro," as the idea for a European Common Currency received a major boost with his 1961 article, "A Theory of Optimum Currency Areas." As he noted there, the idea of a European common currency had been "much discussed" before his article, [16] but he gave it the necessary theoretical backbone with that article and others over the next twelve years, including the 1973, "A Plan for a European Currency." [17]

Mundell's thinking came in the context of the drive toward Western European peace and unity after the devastation of World War II and the draping of the Iron Curtain. The movement toward openness in trade and finance was led by Jean Monnet. In 1952, six countries (Belgium, France, Germany, Italy, Luxembourg, the Netherlands moved dramatically toward the elimination of trade barriers, first for coal and steel, with establishment of the European Coal and Steel Community. It was expanded to include all goods and services with the 1957 establishment of the European Economic Community, known as the Common Market. That grouping led, in turn, to the formation of the European Union with the 1993 adoption of the Maastricht Treaty.

In his 1961 "Optimum Currency Areas," Mundell wrote, "Or, supposing that the Common Market countries proceed with their plans for economic union, should these countries allow each national currency to fluctuate, or would a single currency area be preferable? The problem can be posed in a general and more revealing way by defining a currency area as a domain within which exchange rates are fixed and asking: 'What is the appropriate domain of a currency area?'" [18] That, perhaps, is the twenty-first century's $multi-trillion question. [19]

In 1967, Brunei, Malaysia, and Singapore formed a monetary union, but Malaysia exited soon afterwards on 12 June 1967. Brunei, now known as Brunei Darussalam, and Singapore have 1:1 currency parity, meaning that the Brunei dollar and the Singapore dollar have the same value throughout the monetary union. They manage their exchange rate regime with a currency board which is required to have foreign exchange reserves equivalent to 70 percent of the outstanding internal currency, and internal liquidity reserves of 30 percent. [20]

Postwar independence for countries in French West Africa led to the transformation of the colonial currency arrangements to a loose monetary union linked to the French franc. The union split into two monetary unions in 1994: the West African Economic and Monetary Union (WAEMU) and the Central African Economic and Monetary Community (CAEMC). They both use what they call the CFA franc, but with slightly different values and names; it stands for the Communaute Financiere Africaine in the WAEMU and Cooperation Financiere en Afrique Centrale in the CAEMC.

The WAEMU has eight member countries: Benin, Burkima Faso, Ivory Coast, Guinea-Bissau (joined 1997), Mali (left in 1962 but rejoined in 1984), Niger, Senegal, and Togo. The CAEMC has six countries: Cameroon, the Central African Republic (C.A.R.), Chad, the Republic of Congo, Equatorial Guinea (joined in 1985 and is the only non-former-French colony), and Gabon. The WAEMU and CAEMC are also pursuing further trade integration through tariff reduction and other means. [21]

A list of existing monetary unions can be seen in the list of prices for this book in Appendix E.

A Variation of Monetary Union: "izing" and "ization"

The term "dollarization" was applied by economists in the 1990s to the practice of a country using the US dollar as its own currency. [22] Then the term was applied to the practice of countries using as an "anchor" another currency, such as the euro, and thus the term, "euroization." The generic process is called here "izing" or "ization." [23]

The use by one country of another's currency has been a long standing practice, because of military conquest, colonialism or voluntary cooperation. However, as the one-nation-one currency custom reached its peak after the independence of colonized countries in Africa, and from the former Soviet Union, ization was one of the processes reflecting the counter-trend toward monetary unions. This was especially true for small countries for which an independent monetary system was an expensive and even dangerous option.

The best known examples of izing to the US dollar are Ecuador and El Salvador, which separately adopted the US dollar as legal tender in 2000 and 2001, respectively. [24]

Ecuador had a GDP of $20 billion in the 1990s, but it had fallen to $13 billion by 2000 due in part to the border war with Peru and excess government deficit spending which brought high inflation. Ecuador's foreign debt was more than $16 billion. There were extensive negotiations with the International Monetary Fund about monetary assistance, but on 9 January 2000, President Mahuad abruptly announced the plan to ize to the US dollar, or dollarize. [25] Stanley Fischer, then the First Deputy managing director, and later the head of the Israel Central Bank and now the Vice-Chair of the US Federal Reserve, wrote, "If they had asked us, we would have said that the preconditions for making a success of dollarization were not in place. In particular, the banking system was unhealthy and the fiscal position was weak." [26] Mahuad was overthrown eleven days later, but his successor chose to continue the dollarization and the new system continues. Inflation and interest rates have dropped dramatically. This is perhaps another example of how economists advise against actions which are nevertheless taken and become successful.

A breakthrough occurred on 15 December 2008 when Ecuador defaulted on a $31 million foreign debt payment.[27] Within a few months, it restructured its foreign debt and paid creditors cash for bonds at the rate of 35 percent of nominal value.[28] This was not the first Latin American default in the 21st Century, as Argentina defaulted in 2001, but the difference between the two is that Ecuador had ized to the US dollar, so the default had zero effect on the value of its currency. In Argentina in 2001, the currency collapsed, as would happen to any national currency whose issuing government defaulted on debt, and therein is the answer to a Moody's analyst who wondered if Argentina and Venezuela will ask, "Well, Ecuador did it, why can't we?"[29] The answer is that if Argentina and Venezuela were to default today on their foreign debt, their currencies would collapse and that would cause much hardship for their citizens.

Despite President Correa's earlier opposition to dollarization, the Ecuadorean dollarization enabled his country to survive the 2008 default. There has been speculation in Ecuador that, despite the popularity of the dollarization and monetary stability with the general public, the policy may be abandoned.[30] However, as with a country leaving a full-fledged monetary union, it would be hard for Ecuador to establish a new and credible and stable currency if it were to cancel its dollarization policy. Perhaps the dollarization will remain until replaced by the better alternative of a regional monetary union.

Since the 1999 dollarization, the consensus in Ecuador seems to support the change, now 15 years old.[31] Benn Steil, of the Council on Foreign Relations, approvingly wrote in 2006 that Ecuador was Latin America's "star performer" in 2004 with 6.6 percent GDP growth with 2.7 percent inflation, and he urged other countries to follow, saying, "the best option for developing countries intent on globalising safely is simply to replace their currencies with internationally accepted ones, namely the dollar or the euro."[32] A 2011 academic study concluded that dollarization "improved the macroeconomic performance of Ecuador."[33] Still, there are some, including those who export goods to other countries, who seek the return of the sucre, which could be devalued from time to time to assist exports. However, Fernando Pozo, general manager of Banco Pichincha, Ecuador's largest private bank, correctly dismissed devaluations as a crutch, saying "The only way to sustain a process of exportation is through productivity."[34] Curiously, Ecuador still maintains a foreign exchange reserve valued at approximately $3 billion, perhaps as a hedge in case it de-dollarizes at some point.[35] At present, Ecuador doesn't need a foreign exchange reserve any more than does a state in the US, such as Maine.

El Salvador dollarized on 1 January 2001 pursuant to the "Monetary Integration Law." Despite initial confusion, the new monetary exchange rate regime seemed to be working as of 2005 as inflation was relatively low at 5 percent and GDP had almost doubled since 2001.[36] El Salvador's connection to the dollar is strengthened by the annual volume of expatriate remittances, $2.4 billion or 15.4 percent of GDP as of 2005, which are sent to the country in US dollars, without the need for expensive foreign exchange trading fees.[37] By 2012, remittances had risen by 50 percent to $3.6 billion, but constituted a slightly lower percentage of the growing GDP, 15.1 percent.[38] A 2011 IMF review of El Salvador's dollarization found continued positive effects, including a 4-5 percent reduction in interest rates due to the elimination of currency risk.[39]

Other countries which are ized to the US dollar, or dollarized, are the Marshall Islands, Micronesia, Panama, Timor-Leste, and Palau, the third smallest member nation of the United Nations. With a population of only 20,300, it makes no cents/sense for Palau to have an independent monetary policy or currency area. Of the 38 UN members with populations of less than 1 million, only 17 have their own currencies, and that number should drop to zero. For perspective, the 86 largest cities in the world all have populations over three million, and two have currencies, Hong Kong and Singapore.[40]

UN member countries which have euroized are Monaco, Andorra, Liechtenstein, Montenegro and San Marino.

Ized to the Australian dollar are Kiribati, Nauru, and Tuvalu.

A major concern about ization is that the chosen anchor country have stable monetary policies with stable exchange rates. Jeffrey Frankel and Andrew Rose note that the benefits of such ization depend upon the strength and stability of the anchor and not only whether the economies of the ized and anchor countries are integrated.[41]

In choosing an anchor currency, one would think that size equals stability, but the two largest currencies, the US dollar and the euro, have fluctuated widely against the other since the 1 January 2002 full implementation of the euro. Another major concern about ization is the lack of a vote at the monetary policy decision table, i.e., the US Federal Reserve Board or the European Central Bank Governing Council. Even if such a vote might not have much weight, it would preserve some measure of dignity for the residents of the ized country. This problem of ization without representation will be familiar to citizens of the US whose own revolution from 1775-83 was powered by the slogan, "No Taxation Without Representation."[42]

A related issue is the value of the seigniorage to the country issuing currency. Seigniorage is the profit accruing to the central bank issuers of currency which equals the nominal value of the currency minus the cost of production and reissuance. In the United States, for example, it costs 5.7 cents ($.057) to print a paper note, regardless of the denomination. Thus, the seigniorage is 94.3 cents ($.943) for a $1 bill, and $99.94 for a $100 bill.[43] The value of seigniorage to an issuing bank depends upon the relative usage of cash in an economy compared to other means of transacting business, but for most currency areas, the value is .5 percent of GDP or less.[44] A bill named "The International Monetary Stability Act" was introduced into the US Congress in 1999 to assist countries with the dollarization process. The bill provided for sharing seigniorage with countries which dollarized, but it didn't become law.[45] Its failure was a loss for the US and the world. Even though ization is an imperfect means of monetary union, it is better than an independent monetary policy for most small nations, and is a genuine step in the direction of the 3-G world. It was also a way for the US to acquire more partners in its efforts to promote the use of the USD.

Twenty-First Century Monetary Unions

The European Monetary Union and the Euro

Although the euro was established in the 1990s and was formally introduced on 1 January 1999 as a unit of account for banks and corporations, it's designated here as a twenty-first century monetary union because euro coins and bills became available to the people of the twelve member countries on 1 January 2002.

C. Fred Bergsten wrote in 2004 that the euro has been a "spectacular success" and that "countries throughout the world are expressing their admiration for the euro by seeking to join or emulate it."[46] Despite the difficulties for the euro stemming from the global financial crisis of 2007-2008, the success of the euro has continued. The 1 January 2014 accession of Latvia as the 18th member of the EMU confirms Bergsten's evaluation. Countries do not often climb aboard sinking monetary unions.

The vision for European monetary union took hold as political reality in 1971 when the Werner Commission recommended that Europe proceed with planning for a common currency.[47] In 1988, the Delors Commission continued those recommendations for a common currency.

In 1992, the Treaty on European Union was signed in Maastricht, the Netherlands, and when ratified in 1993, it was informally called the Maastricht Treaty.

Quite elegantly, the treaty RESOLVED, among other goals, "to achieve the strengthening and the convergence of their economies and to establish an economic and monetary union including, in accordance with the provisions of this Treaty, a single and stable currency."[48]

The initial twelve member countries were: Austria, Belgium, Finland, France, Germany, Greece, Ireland, Italy, Luxembourg, Netherlands, Portugal, and Spain.

Three other members of the European Union have thus far decided not to adopt the euro, as joining was optional for the original fifteen EU members. Denmark voted by referendum 53.1 percent to 46.9 percent against the euro in September, 2000. However, the Danish currency, the krone, "is still closely linked to the euro via the Exchange Rate Mechanism, ERM II. Danish monetary policy thus shadows the policy of the European Central Bank, ECB."[49] In practical terms, the value of the krone has not varied from the mid-point-value, 7.45 kroner to the euro, by more than .05 krone, i.e., from a low, from the perspective of the euro, of 7.5046 and a high of 7.4008. For euro members, the krone has varied by no more than €.0018, i.e., far less than a euro cent, from a low of €.1333 to a high of €.1351.[50] The ERM II mechanism is the same mechanism, or probationary phase, through which potential members of the Eurozone pass on their way to adopting the euro.

According to Danish public opinion polls, support for adopting the euro peaked in November, 2009 at 54% but dropped steadily to 29% by February, 2013 due to the general concern about the euro and the economy in EMU countries.[51] Another referendum may be scheduled during the current parliamentary term.

On 14 September 2003, almost two years after the euro had been circulated among the twelve member countries, Sweden voted by referendum 56 percent to 42 percent against adopting the euro. A December 2007 public opinion poll in Sweden showed 51 percent of Swedes opposed to adoption of the euro and 35 percent in favor. Said the *Thompson Financial* article, "The 'no' vote was seen as a reflection of deep-rooted opposition to moving power further away from the Swedish people to the European Central Bank in Frankfurt, which Swedes feared would not take the needs of their small country into account when shaping monetary policy."[52] However, Sweden is larger than Cyprus, Estonia, Latvia, Malta and Slovenia and geographically closer to Frankfurt than Eurozone member Finland. In 1999, the Swedes awarded a Nobel Prize to Robert Mundell for his work in monetary economics which led to the creation of the euro. Someday, the people of Sweden will catch up with its Nobel Prize committee.

The United Kingdom has not formally voted on the euro either in the Parliament or by referendum since the government has neither generated nor found sufficient popular support. The Conservative government of David Cameron has committed to a referendum, not on the euro, but on the larger question of UK membership in the European Union. In a January 2014 poll, the British public favored continued EU membership by a margin of 38 to 28 percent.[53]

In September 2007, the European Central Bank sponsored a Gallup Poll of attitudes toward the euro among the citizens of the 11 New Member States.[54] Eighty percent of those surveyed had seen the euro banknotes and coins and over half have actually used them, whether in their own countries or when traveling.

Across the 11 countries, 5 percent expected implementation of the euro in 2009-10, 34 percent in 2011-12, 27 percent in 2013-14 and 15 percent 2013 or later, and 2 percent, "never." Showing that polling is an inexact art or science, 6 percent of Cypriots believed that the euro would "never" be adopted there, even though the actual implementation of the euro on Cyprus was only four months away at the time of the polling.

In contrast to Denmark's link to the euro, Sweden and the United Kingdom allow their currencies to float on the currency markets. Over the past ten years, Sweden's krona has varied by 17.52 percent in both directions from the midpoint of 9.92 kroner to the euro, for a total swing of 35 percent. The UK pound has varied 19.8 percent from the midpoint of .817 pounds to the euro, for a total swing of 39.6 percent.[55] Such fluctuations have no real connection to the real health of the economies of the currency areas, and little correlation to Purchasing Power Parity; and that is a major problem with the multicurrency foreign exchange system-- its detachment from the reality of money and the people who use it.

A major concern for countries adopting the euro is how to block the immediate increases in prices which were claimed to have occurred in some parts of the EMU in 2002. Two economists in 2007 compared price changes in EMU and Non-EMU countries at the same time and concluded "that (a) there is no evidence of significant price increases associated with the adoption of the euro even for food items..."[56]

In May 2004, ten countries were admitted into the European Union, with the requirement that they all join the European Monetary Union. The ten Accession countries, or "New Member States" were: Cyprus, Czech Republic, Estonia, Hungary, Latvia, Lithuania, Malta, Poland, Slovakia, and Slovenia. Six of those ten, Slovenia (2007), Cyprus and Malta (2008), Slovakia (2009), Estonia (2011) and Latvia (2014) have officially adopted the euro and abandoned their former currencies, which brought the total number of Eurozone countries to 18. Lithuania is expected to join in January 2015.

On 1 January 2007, Romania and Bulgaria joined the European Union, followed by Croatia on 1 July 2013, bringing the total EU membership to 28, all of which are obligated by treaty to adopt the euro except Denmark and the United Kingdom.

The accession of the remaining seven countries (Bulgaria, Czech Republic, Croatia, Hungary, Poland, Romania, and Sweden) into the EMU has not been scheduled. The United Kingdom is unlikely to seek admission in the near future.[57] In fact, the UK is even considering a referendum on its overall membership in the larger European Union.

How the European Central Bank (ECB) Works

In 1999 Willem Buiter described the basic governing structure of the ECB:

> "Technically, the national central banks are the shareholders of the ECB. The Maastricht and Amsterdam[58] treaties distinguish between the ECB and the European System of Central Banks (ESCB), the collective of the ECB and the national central banks. In publications of the ECB and in public statements of its Executive Board members, there are frequent references to the 'Eurosystem.' Each national central bank provides one member of the decisionmaking Governing Council of the ECB (which consists of the eleven [now twelve] national central bank governors and six Executive Board members) and certain aspects of the implementation of the centrally determined monetary policy are administratively decentralized through the NCBs (national central banks). None of this detracts from the reality that the ECB/ESCB is a 'unitary' central bank. Monetary policy authority is unambiguously centralized in Frankfurt and the NCBs have effectively become the regional branch banks of the ECB."[59]

Like other central banks, the European Central Bank controls interest rates and the money supply within its currency area, the Eurozone. The bank has inevitably been compared to the US central bank, the Federal Reserve, which in a 2003 study by Paul De Grauwe and Claudia Storti, was found to be similarly effective.[60] From the beginning, the ECB has rigorously pursued its chartered goal of price stability,[61] to the apparent exclusion, according to critics, of other goals such as full employment. As inflation has stayed close to two percent, there have been few interest rate changes. In December 2005, the Governing Council raised a key interest rate to 2.25 percent, the first change in five years. The ECB then quickly reassured the markets that it had no plans for further increases, lest anticipation of such increases cut off planned investments.[62] Since then, the rate has dropped to its current historic low of .25%, as of November 2013, in response to the continued sluggishness of the European economy since the global "great recession."[63]

There is little question that the euro has been a remarkable achievement, and that the Eurozone is growing. There are questions, however, about how to make it better and how to make the European economy grow more rapidly. The three EU members who have thus far opted out, Denmark, Sweden and the UK, are continually evaluating their option to join; and they will ultimately join when their citizens and governments believe joining to be in their best interests. Already, there are studies about what might have been the economic results of joining. One 2005 study found that the UK would have benefitted.[64]

It remains to be seen how much financial integration will occur within the EMU, and to what extent it will be a direct or indirect result of the creation of the Eurozone. One area of progress is with non-cash payments across national borders, which still are managed by nation-centered banks. In March 2002, just after the introduction of the euro bills and coins to the public, the major banks of the EMU launched the plan for SEPA, the Single Euro Payments Area for the EU and affiliated countries. The SEPA goal is that "individuals and corporations are able to make cashless payments throughout the euro area from a single payment account anywhere in the euro area using a single set of payment instruments as easily, efficiently and safely as they can make them today at the national level."[65] SEPA was implemented by 1 February 2014, with ATM and debit cards being recognizable across the Eurozone. Such consolidation was expected to save consumers and corporations (and cost banks) approximately €13-29 billion through lower payments charges which were expected to drop 30-60 percent of pre-SEPA levels.[66]

The global financial crisis caused considerable stress within the EMU, and particularly in the member countries Cyprus, Greece, Ireland, Italy, Portugal and Spain. There were predictions by some economists[67] that one or more of those countries would have to leave the Eurozone, but through it all, the polls showed that their citizens wanted their euro to continue to be their currency. In May, 2012, a poll showed that 78 percent of Greeks wanted to keep the euro, while only 13 percent wanted to return to the drachma.[68] Another 2012 poll showed that 51 percent of Italians wanted to keep the euro.[69] What the people of the world, including Europeans, want is stable money, and the euro provides that stability – at least far more than their previous 18 currencies.

Among other reforms resulting from the crisis was the empowering of the European Central Bank with more supervisory authority over the banks within the EMU.[70]

In December 2013 the EU members approved a contingent bank bailout plan that will set up a common banking fund. This is one step toward what is called full "banking union" within the EMU.[71]

Future Twenty-First-Century Monetary Unions

Inspired by the success of the euro, countries around the world are exploring whether to join an existing monetary union or start a new one.[72] With each such option, there are studies of whether such a geographical grouping constitutes an "optimum currency area." Optimal or not, the people of the world are slowly asserting their interest in euro-like currencies, as they overcome some of the deficiencies of the multi-currency system, and they provide money which is more stable.

Arabian Gulf:[73] The six countries of the Gulf Cooperation Council-- Bahrain, Kuwait, Oman, Qatar, Saudi Arabia, and United Arab Emirates (UAE) --initiated in March, 2010 the formation of a monetary union with a single currency. The council is consulting with the European Central Bank which has recommended the establishment of a "supranational GCC monetary institution...to conduct a single monetary and exchange rate policy geared to economic, monetary, and financial conditions in the monetary union as a whole."[74]

Not surprisingly, the ECB-based authors recommended that fiscal policies of the six states be coordinated within a framework, echoing the EMU's Growth and Stability Pact.

The IMF has contributed to the project with a paper recommending the use of uniform economic statistics, and the creation of a GCC-wide statistical unit, "Gulfstat," which would do for the Gulf what Eurostat and Afristat do for Europe and Africa, respectively.[75]

Also not surprisingly, the difficulties with the EMU, and intra-GCC rivalries led to the slowing of the project and withdrawal by the UAE and Oman. The headquarters for the monetary union's central bank was determined to be Riyadh where the Gulf Monetary Council was established in the fall of 2013.[76] When implemented, the GMU will be the world's second largest monetary union, as measured by the GDP of member countries.

Europe/Asia: Since the breakup of the Soviet empire, several former satellites have considered monetary union with Russia. The most promising was with Belarus. The Tass News Agency quoted the Belarussian Central Bank Chairman Pyotr Prokopovich as saying, "The agreement signed in 2000 says that the Russian ruble shall become the legal tender in Belarus starting from 1 January 2005, and the Union will have a common currency starting from January 1, 2008."[77] However, these timetables have slipped. In September 2003, Belarus, Kazakhstan, Russia, and Ukraine signed an agreement to create a common market and a common currency within five to seven years.[78] The current status of all of these plans is currently uncertain, especially considering the 2014 tensions between Russia and Ukraine.

Africa: In addition to the two CFA zones, there are several other combinations of African countries which are considering monetary union.[79] Six countries: Ghana, the Gambia, Liberia, Sierra Leone, Guinea, and

Nigeria are forming the West African Monetary Zone which will issue the common currency, the "eco." While previous implementation goals have been missed, the current plan of the West African Monetary Institute is to introduce the "eco" by 1 January 2015.[80]

In southern Africa, the fifteen-member South African Development Community (SADC), led by South Africa, was planning a free trade area by 2008, a customs union by 2010, a common market by 2015, and a monetary union by 2016.[81] For most of the SADC members, the free trade area goal was achieved in 2008, with a few countries requesting slower implementation for some commodities. As of January 2014, the remaining respective goals have been advanced to 2013 (customs union), 2015 (common market) and 2018 (monetary union).[82]

In East Africa, the five countries of the East African Community: Burundi, Kenya, Rwanda, Tanzania, and Uganda have moved ahead with plans to have a common currency by 2024, beginning, like the SADC, with a common market and customs union.[83] The five members committed to achieving their "convergence criteria," including fiscal deficits at below three percent of GDP, by 2018.[84]

Most ambitiously, the African Union plans to implement a monetary union for the entire African continent by 2023.[85]

Australia and New Zealand: Many studies, with ambiguous results, have been done on the viability of New Zealand joining Australia in a two-country monetary union.[86] The most thorough is the 1999 study by Andrew Coleman, who was then working for the New Zealand Treasury. Noting that New Zealand is the smallest OECD country with an independent monetary policy, he recommended either izing to the US dollar or Australian dollar, or joining in a monetary union with Australia.[87] A boost for the idea came in December, 2013 from monetary economist Barry Eichengreen, who views monetary union as a way to resolve the problem of overvaluation of the existing currencies of the two countries.[88]

Pacific Islands: T. K. Jayaraman has concluded that the Pacific Island countries do not yet meet the OCA criteria for them to join in a monetary union, and urged further steps toward economic integration beforehand.[89] Options being considered are monetary union with Australia or with a future East Asian monetary union, or an izing relationship with the Australian or US dollar.[90]

South Asia: The South Asian Association for Regional Cooperation (SAARC), was established in 1985 and is now composed of eight countries: Afghanistan, Bangladesh, Bhutan, India, Maldives, Nepal, Pakistan and Sri Lanka. In January 2004 Indian Prime Minister Vajpayee urged a South Asian common currency, and a subcommittee of the association has recommended monetary union by 2020.[91] The SAARC has not officially endorsed that goal, but it has adopted a free trade area, and thus has taken one of the first steps toward monetary union.[92]

East Asia: The leading advocate for East Asian monetary union has been Haruhiko Kuroda, formerly the director of the Asian Development Bank and in 2013, the Governor of the Bank of Japan. He stated in October 2005, that "our long run objective should be the creation of an Asian monetary union with a single currency."[93] In spring 2006, the Asian Development

Bank planned to launch an "Asian Currency Unit" (ACU), which would consist of a specific mix in a basket of Asian currencies and be used as a monetary benchmark for the region.[94] It is modeled after the pre-euro European Currency Unit (ECU).

In November 2005 and using OCA criteria, Arief Ramayandi examined five ASEAN countries (Indonesia, Malaysia, the Phillipines, Singapore, and Thailand) and found that they "appear to be relatively suitable to form a monetary union."[95] The proposal for an ASEAN single currency resurfaced in 2011, but no consensus for further consideration has developed."[96]

South America: While ization to the US dollar, as implemented by Ecuador and El Salvador, seemed a valid option to some, no other South American country has followed their path. Panama was dollarized long before. Instead, the South American countries are pursuing the path to a common currency through trade integration, as did the European Community. In December 2004, twelve nations created the "South American Community of Nations" at a summit in Cuzco, Peru.[97] The name has been changed to the Union of South American Nations (USAN) and it has a broad goal of emulating the European Union, including the creation of a common currency.[98]

North America: Several economists and others have recommended monetary union among Canada, Mexico, and the US. Most of the impetus comes from Canadians, including Herbert Grubel, who coined the name "amero" for the proposed common currency. He wrote, "The Case for the Amero" in 1999.[99] Mexico's President Vicente Fox, inaugurated in 2000, urged the United States toward stronger trade ties, including a monetary union.[100] George von Furstenberg recommended ization for Mexico to the US dollar,[101] but as that is likely to be as politically unpalatable to Mexicans as immediate full monetary union would be to the US, perhaps some politically feasible middle ground can be developed.

In October 2007, J. Collin Dodds, the president of St. Mary's University in Nova Scotia wrote in an Op-Ed column, "Europe offers strong case for N. American currency," that "There is no doubt that a single currency would be more efficient for Canada, as we have close trade and investment relationships with the U.S.," and recommended the European model of the euro.[102]

As the people of the United Kingdom, Denmark and Sweden can attest, the politics of monetary union can sometimes work in odd ways. Canada's illustration of that premise came with the endorsement by a senior member of the separatist Bloc Quebecois party for a North American Monetary Union. Paul Crete, the lead Finance spokesperson for the party said, "Adoption of a common currency would make the life of our exporters a lot easier."[103] Another argument was that a common currency would free Quebec from the monetary policies of the Bank of Canada which the party sees as anti-Quebec.

Central America:

In 1964, five Central American countries formed a Monetary Council with the goal "to promote the coordination of credit and exchange policies which would progressively form the basis of a Central American Monetary Union."[104] The countries are Costa Rica, El Salvador, Guatemala,

Honduras, and Nicaragua, but there has been little subsequent interest in monetary union.

Caribbean Sea: In the *Jamaica Observer* in 2007, Sir Ronald Sanders supported monetary union for the 15 nation Caricom common market. He wrote,

> "Serious attention has to be given to the creation of a single currency by the countries of the Caribbean Community and Common Market (Caricom) that earlier this year signed an agreement to establish a single market...
>
>   A monetary union and a single currency in the countries of the Caribbean Community and Common Market (Caricom) would be a boon to commercial operations in the region from the smallest trader to the largest corporation.
>
>   It would also be a delight to multi-destination tourists and to the ordinary Caricom citizen travelling from one country to another.
>
>   Caricom countries need look no further than within their seven smaller member states, the countries that comprise the Organisation of Eastern Caribbean States (OECS), to witness some of the benefits of a currency union and single currency."[105]

Benefits and Costs of Monetary Unions--Benefits

Until a single Global Monetary Union is implemented, all monetary unions will still exist in a multicurrency foreign exchange world and will not fully realize the benefits of monetary union. Therefore, the extent of most of the benefits described below are proportional to the ratio of countries' economic activity and financial flows within the union and outside.

To the extent that a monetary union solves the problems of the existing multicurrency foreign exchange system for a country or countries, the benefits and costs are, in some ways, the flip side of the previously discussed benefits and the costs of the existing system. First are presented the benefits.

1. Stabilize the value of money.

In a multicurrency system, where there is substantial trade among currencies, there is inherent monetary instability due to fluctuating exchange rates. Thus, the larger the monetary union, the greater will be the monetary stability for member countries and their citizens.

The charters of nearly every central bank in the world, including those of monetary unions, have the primary goal of monetary stability, sometimes along with other goals such as economic growth and maximum employment. This monetary stability is what the people of the world want, and within a monetary union, money is inherently more stable than the money of individual countries.

2. Reduce the Total Cost of Foreign Exchange Transactions

When a country joins a monetary union, there are no longer any foreign exchange transactions among member countries. The transaction costs are reduced in the ratio of the value of intra-monetary union transactions to extra-monetary union transactions. For example, while there were foreign exchange transactions with deutschmarks and French franc pairs, both those currencies were also traded with non-European currencies as well. The former transactions have disappeared, and the latter have been replaced by foreign exchange trading with the euro.

Included in such savings will be the previously incurred costs of hedging against fluctuations of currencies now within a monetary union. Such hedging, which can be called "currency fluctuation insurance," might have included such foreign exchange transactions as buying and selling currencies for future delivery as described in Chapter 2.[106] Also diminished are the costs of translating foreign exchange values for corporations and individuals with assets and operations in the monetary union area. Gone, too, are the speculators in the currencies which have disappeared. In Europe, the legions of people who can describe how they made, or lost, their fortunes by speculating in lira or guilders are diminishing in number. It wasn't productive work.

3. Increase Asset Values

One of the most dramatic effects of monetary union is the increase in financial asset values which occurs when currency risk and interest rates decline relative to former risks and interest rates in the member nations. John Edmunds and John Marthinsen first described this dramatic effect in their book, *Wealth by Association, Global Prosperity through Market Unification.*[107]

Briefly, the effect is that a decline in interest rates increases the ability of people to borrow to finance investments and expansion, which increases the demand for such assets. That increased demand results in higher value for assets. This effect begins when the prospects for monetary unification become real to investors. Edmunds and Marthinsen wrote, "Adopting a stable foreign currency or creating an enduring currency union is an instantaneous way to reduce country risk, to stimulate economic growth, and to deliver a massive increase in a nation's wealth."[108]

In 2005, they used their analysis to show that the increase in asset values in the ten New Member States in the Eurozone in the years 1993-2003 was between €5 and €11 trillion, and the effect continues. They state, "After our analysis of the primary effects of currency unification, we describe dynamic processes of wealth creation that last beyond the initial quantum leap. The decline in a nation's currency risk unleashes an array of beneficial growth-generating forces, such as increased rate of output, intra-regional trade, specialization and logistic efficiencies."[109] One illustration of the phenomenon came in March 2006 when Moody's Investors Services increased the bond ratings for 7 EMU-bound countries because those countries "are set to benefit from participation in the EU's Exchange Rate Mechanism (ERM2)."[110]

They also applied their analysis to understand the possible effect on asset values in Italy if it seceded from the EMU, thereby increasing Italy's currency risk. They predicted that a loss in value of financial assets would be more than €4 trillion.[111] That's a substantial proportion of the value of all financial assets in Italy.

4. Reduce the Need to Maintain Foreign Exchange Reserves

Banks maintain reserves for several reasons. Internally, there must be sufficient reserves of coins and cash to supply banks within the country which may be subjected to large, or even panicked, demand. Also, reserve requirements can be used to affect the size of the money supply as they determine the percentage of deposits can then be loaned, which together with cash in circulation is known as the M1 money supply.[112]

In the US, pursuant to the Monetary Act of 1980, the Federal Reserve Board of Governors sets the reserve requirement for all banks and credit unions and other similar depository financial institutions. The reserve amounts must be in "vault cash" or demand deposits at a Federal Reserve Bank. For "transaction" accounts, i.e., checking and other very liquid accounts, the reserve requirement is three percent for banks with total deposits between $7 and $47.6 million and ten percent for larger banks.[113]

Foreign exchange, or international, reserves are maintained by central banks for similar, but external reasons. There is a stubborn belief that with more reserves, there will be more confidence in the quality of a currency, so central bankers are naturally inclined to accumulate foreign exchange reserves. The foreign exchange reserves can be used to intervene in the currency markets to buy and sell one's own currency, and to respond to a current account deficit.[114] An initial result of a monetary union is that the member countries no longer need to maintain foreign exchange reserves, but they would continue to support members' banks with their reserve requirements and other operational support. The central bank of the monetary union is the holder of the foreign exchange reserves.

5. Reduce the Balance of Payments/Current Account Problem for Every Country or Monetary Union

As the number of countries and trading partners in a monetary union increases, the proportion of intra-union trade to extra-union trade would increase. Correspondingly, the scope of concern for the balance of payments by the central bank of the monetary union would decrease, in relative terms. For example, if Germany was party to twenty percent of France's international trade before the euro and vice versa, then the international exposure to balance of payments problems for each country and the EMU, other things being equal, was reduced by twenty percent thanks to the implementation of the euro. Some European countries may have had large trade deficits with their future EMU partners, and smaller trade surpluses with the extra-European world. After the euro, their net contribution to the EMU current account would have been positive.

6. Reduce the Risks of Excessive Capital Flows among Currencies and Countries

Large capital flows can be a major problem for small and underdeveloped countries with fragile monetary systems. It's been known for some time that large capital flows among currencies can be disruptive to their values. At Bretton Woods, IMF Article of Agreement #6 reserved the right of member countries to use capital controls to limit capital flows.

Large capital flows caused or exacerbated all the recent currency crises. What's often overlooked in the discussion of capital flows is that they are a problem only when moving from one currency to another. Within a currency area, they may cause price fluctuations, but there is no risk of a currency crisis.

Within a currency area, there are surely large flows of capital back and forth, but to the extent that there are concerns at all, they are about differences in income among regions within that currency area and not about the risks of a flow-induced currency crisis. We do not hear currency concerns about capital flows between the Netherlands and Portugal, or between Grenada and St. Lucia, or between New Hampshire and California. To the extent that there are concerns about the availability of capital in specific geographic areas of a monetary union, they can be solved without affecting the value of the monetary union's currency.

7. Reduce the Cost of Operating an Entirely Separate Monetary System

Running a monetary system is complex work. To the extent that the foreign exchange work performed by multiple countries is replaced by the work of a single central bank, the total costs will be reduced. Since the adoption of the euro, the total number of people employed by the Eurozone's central banks, now including the European Central Bank, has declined. [115]

8. Separate the Value of Money from the Value of a Particular Country

The value of money in a monetary union is a function of confidence in the money and the custodian of the money, and not in any single country or its economy or its leaders. As Basil Moore has written, "Confidence is absolutely essential to the general acceptability of money." [116] Even in a two-country monetary union, such as the Brunei Darussalam-Singapore monetary union, the value of the money does not depend upon the perceptions of a single country, but of the joint custodians of the money. The larger the monetary union, the more secure is that perception that the value of one's money is protected by something larger than one's own elected officials.

9. Reduce National Currency Crises, e.g., Mexico, Argentina, East Asia, Russia, Iceland, and Zimbabwe

For some countries, this can be the most important effect of separating a national government from a currency. In each recent currency crisis, sellers of a currency doubted that the country issuing the currency was stable enough to ensure the stability of the currency. While a currency crisis in a currency union is not impossible, it's far less likely to occur for large monetary unions than small ones, and less likely for monetary unions than for national currencies. In short, it's less likely to occur when the people know that the currency is being managed by a central bank with the goal of monetary stability high on the list of priorities.

10. Reduce the Possibility of Currency Exchange Rate Manipulation by Countries

In 1988, the US Congress passed the Omnibus Trade and Competitiveness Act which requires the Secretary of the Treasury to report to the Congress semi-annually about countries which unfairly manipulate their currencies. Most of the annual reports since then have criticized China's pegging the yuan to the USD. The October 2013 CNN article stated that the Treasury report, "called China's currency, the yuan, 'significantly undervalued.' The report criticized the apparent resumption of large-scale purchases in the foreign exchange market that hold down the yuan's value against other currencies."[117] The problem is that the FX markets are driving up the price of the yuan because of its perception of the "fundamentals," while the Chinese are simply trying to keep the yuan close to its pegged relationship to the USD.

During the Great Depression, several countries devalued their currencies in order to increase their exports, but the net result was close to zero change in the trade balance and a great loss of income, as each devaluation canceled out the other. The IMF Articles of Agreement, crafted at Bretton Woods, explicitly discourage such exchange rate manipulation, directing members to "avoid manipulating exchange rates or the international monetary system in order to prevent effective balance of payments adjustment or to gain an unfair competitive advantage over other members."[118] The irony of the country with the largest current account problem, with its prospects for devaluation of its currency, complaining about the currency manipulations of other countries is surely not lost on those other countries.

C. Fred Bergsten and Joseph Gagnon argue for more surveillance of alleged currency manipulators and for trade sanctions against proven offenders.   Bergsten wrote that currency manipulation is "the largest gap by far in our international financial architecture," and that "The IMF and finance ministries have failed to resolve the currency issue for 70 years," i.e. since Bretton Woods.[119]   However neither economist supports the movement toward the Single Global Currency as a way, or as the way, to eliminate currency manipulation.

In any case, countries in a monetary union do not have the ability to manipulate their own currency. Thus, the economic nostalgia that exists for some in such countries as Italy, which almost made ongoing devaluation an element of trade policy, may be misplaced. Those practices violated the spirit of Article IV, and unfairly transferred onto other countries the burden of fixing local economic problems.

11. Reduce Inflation, Thereby Ensuring Low, Reasonable Interest Rates

Independent of the governments of the members of a monetary union, the central bank of a monetary union is chartered to promote monetary and price stability, which should lead to low inflation (but not too low, as to cause deflation.)

The generally accepted inflation target is about two percent, and central bankers have been criticized for allowing interest rates to fall too far below that target. In Europe, there have been calls for the ECB President, Mario Draghi, to do more to stimulate the Eurozone's economic recovery, given the ECB's prediction of inflations rates of 1.1 and 1.5 percent in 2014 and 2015, respectively.[120]

As predicted by the theory of "the Mundellian impossible trinity," or "trilemma,"[121] this benefit of ensuring low inflation is limited by the ability of the monetary union's central bank to control inflation while at the same time managing the value of the exchange rate. That exchange rate value, in turn, can affect inflation as the prices of imported goods rise and fall. The European Central Bank has made price stability its number one goal and has generally succeeded at that goal, even while contending with the wide fluctuations in value of the euro compared to the US dollar and other currencies. As a monetary union becomes larger, the targeting of inflation will be more effective as the percentage of trade with non-monetary union areas will be diminished, thereby reducing the risks of inflation due to exchange rate fluctuations.

12. Increase Trade Volume

There is considerable disagreement about the effect of a common currency on trade. Andrew Rose at the University of California at Berkeley has written extensively about how trade among countries increases dramatically within a currency union. At a May 2000 economic conference, Jeffrey Frankel and Andrew Rose stated, "We estimate that when one country adopts the currency of another, trade between them eventually triples in magnitude."[122] In an article presented to the American Economic Association in 2001, Rose and Eric van Wincoop of the Federal Reserve Bank of New York, concluded that trade within the European Monetary Union could increase over fifty percent.[123] In a subsequent study, Andrew Rose and T. D. Stanley found that a currency union led to increases in "bilateral trade by between 30 percent and 90 percent.[124] In 2002, Andrew Rose summarized the research on trade and monetary union and concluded, "my quantitative survey of the literature shows substantial evidence that currency union has a positive effect on trade."[125]

Then, skeptics did more research and questioned those results. John Helliwell and Lawrence Schembri found that, at least with respect to Canada, the potential impact on trade of a common currency with the US would not be significant.[126] That conclusion may, however, depend upon the specific idiosyncrasies of the US-Canada relationship.

Studies of real data from the EMU indicate that a common currency *does* improve trade, leaving only the question of how much. Alejandro Micco, Guillermo Orgonez, and Ernesto Stein found in their 2003 article that intra-EMU trade had increased, due to the common currency, 8-16 percent since the monetary union began. They even determined that trade between the Eurozone and the UK dramatically increased after the implementation of the euro.[127]

After summarizing the studies about trade and monetary unions, Paul De Grauwe concluded in 2005 that "monetary union in Europe could lead to an expansion of trade of 20 percent to 40 percent."[128]

Jeffrey Frankel concluded in a 2010 article that the creation of the EMU led to substantially increased trade during its first eight years, even if less than some predicted and even if less than has occurred after the creation of other monetary unions.[129]

In 2008 Giorgia Albertin confirmed previous studies when she found that joining a monetary union does increase trade for the accessioning country, but that increase is limited by the degree of dissimilarity of that country's economy with the economy of the existing monetary union.[130]

The percentage of increase does not matter if the question comes to a draw, or close to a draw, as there are so many other good reasons for a common currency. Still, it does seem that as a matter of common cents/sense, if a barrier to trade and travel, and a cost of doing business, is removed, trade will increase. The barrier is not just the cost. For travelers, it includes the time wasted in calculating costs of travel and in storing unused foreign currency following the completion of a trip. For trade, it's the avoided time and cost of deciding what currency to use in a trade transaction, and how to protect against a large, unpredictable change in the currency values during the time between the execution of a trade contract for the delivery and payment of the goods or services. Surely, with all those steps eliminated, trade among countries using a common currency would be facilitated. It's common cents/sense.

13. Increase Foreign Direct Investment (FDI)

Thierry Warin, Phanindra Wunnava and Hubert Janicki found that monetary union led to a doubling of FDI (Foreign Direct Investment). The purpose of the study was to assess "the endogenous optimum currency area theory...[as originally] developed by Mundell in 1973."[131] The question is whether the conditions for an Optimum Currency Area improve after a monetary union is actually created. When that happens, the validity of the originally high eligibility criteria should be questioned.

Benefits and Costs of Monetary Unions--Costs

The major monetary problems for a monetary union come not from within the monetary union, but from without. That is, until a Global Monetary Union is adopted, all monetary unions will continue to exist in a multicurrency foreign exchange world. For example, much of the debate about the success of the euro concerns whether the exchange rate has been too high, which throttles exports, or too low, which shows weakness. As that question is really about the functioning of the multicurrency foreign exchange system, and not about monetary unions, it's not discussed here. Below, other costs are discussed.

1. Sovereignty Theory of Money.

It is believed by many that citizens of nations prefer that their nation continue to use its own national currency out of loyalty to the nation. Robert Mundell wrote, "In the real world, of course, currencies are mainly an expression of national sovereignty, so that actual currency reorganization would be feasible only if it were accompanied by profound political changes."[132] Thus, money is a symbol of national pride, but such a preference is only as strong as the lack of evidence apparent to citizens about the actual costs of the national money, and the lack of awareness of a real alternative, such as monetary union. That's the major benefit of the euro; as people around the world now see that there is a realistic alternative to national unstable currencies.

To the extent that people wish to retain such a national symbol, then the cost of moving to a regional or Global Monetary Union might be the loss of public support for the government or loss of pride in a country; but no monetary value can be assigned to this cost.

Another way to look at this sovereignty value is that it's been a way for governments to communicate to the governed the power and history of the state or ruling family.[133] Every day, citizens using money see images reminding them of their country's heritage and pride, so the question arises about the extent to which citizens' loyalty to their nation's money was created by the state or arose from their hearts and minds.

Within a monetary union, the sense of sovereignty and political identity is transferred from a single nation to a group of neighboring countries, so there still can be personal identification with the money, albeit more remotely. Many parts of the world already use such remote monetary symbols. For example, countries of the British Commonwealth such as Australia and Canada, use the image of Queen Elizabeth II on their currencies. In the Eurozone, there are euro coins with unique national reverse sides for each of the EMU members with the front image being for all of Europe.[134] To the extent that citizens within a monetary union feel that they are members of a larger entity, such as "Europe" or "West Africa" or the "Caribbean," then citizens can still identify with their money. Someday, that entity will be the world.

2. Need for Independent Monetary Authority to Deal with Local Economic Needs, also Called Asymmetric Shocks

A major concern of economists is that nations need the flexibility to adjust interest rates to heat up or cool down an economy and to influence exchange rates to achieve those goals.

The larger the monetary union, the smaller is each country's ability to influence the crucial decisions about interest rates and exchange rates.

On the other hand, the economists are divided about whether the loss of monetary independence is really a loss at all. When preparing for the euro, the European Commission study found that the European Community would have better weathered the economic shocks of the 1970s and 1980s, especially the OPEC oil price shock, if a common currency had been in place.[135] Robert Mundell wrote that monetary independence "involves monetary independence to have monetary instability, and sometimes even hyperinflation. Monetary independence becomes valuable only when the rest of the world is unstable."[136] It also is valuable if the right decisions are made, and it's tempting for critics of monetary unions to argue that a particular country could have weathered a crisis better, or done better generally, if it had not been part of the monetary union. However, such "what ifs" almost always assume, from hindsight, that optimal monetary decisions were made by the national monetary authorities. There is plenty of evidence to show that such an assumption is often incorrect.

Many economists wrote that the EMU countries most affected by the 2008-2013 debt financial crises, e.g. Greece, would have worked their way out of their respective difficulties if they had the freedom to devalue their currencies. While emphasizing the benefits of increasing exports, such analyses ignored the costs of such devaluations and what could have gone wrong.

Charles Goodhart and D J Lee analyzed the adjustment mechanisms available to three states or countries which were hit by the real estate bubbles and shocks of 2007-2008: Arizona, Latvia and Spain. These three governments were in a fiscal and monetary union (Arizona), outside a monetary union (Latvia), and inside a monetary union (Spain). The authors concluded that a banking union would have helped Latvia, and especially Spain to come out of the crisis.[137]

Given the inability to manipulate the exchange rates of national moneys, several economists have developed the concept of "fiscal devaluation," which comprises a combination of taxes, e.g. VAT, which decreases the relative burdens on exporters.[138] Such measures can be implemented within monetary unions without violating monetary union rules, although there could be a "race to the bottom" if several competing countries all engaged in "fiscal devaluation."

3. Fiscal Interdependency.

Martin Feldstein continues to be a eurosceptic and viewed the increased spread of national bond yields as a harbinger of monetary union breakup. He wrote in 2008, "The current differences in the interest rates of euro-zone government bonds show that the financial markets regard a break-up as a real possibility. Ten-year government bonds in Greece and Ireland, for example, now pay nearly a full percentage point above the rate on comparable German bonds, and Italy's rate is almost as high."[139] Feldstein appears to be stuck in the view that the value of a monetary union currency depends upon the fiscal health of one or two or three member state governments, which is not the case. Instead the value depends upon the people's confidence in the monetary union and its central bank and its control of inflation.

Again focusing later on Greece for which he recommended secession from the EMU despite the hazards of such a step, Feldstein wrote in 2012, "The euro should now be recognized as an experiment that failed. This failure,... [is] the inevitable consequence of imposing a single currency on a very heterogeneous group of countries." However, recognizing that monetary union is about politics as much as economics, Feldstein acknowledged that "Looking ahead, the eurozone is likely to continue with almost all its current members."[140]

Others were not so optimistic. Megan Greene wrote, "Ultimately, the best solution for both the weaker and the stronger eurozone members may be to allow at least some of the former to abandon the common currency in an amicable divorce."[141]

Eligibility Criteria, when Considering a Monetary Union

In addition to the simple criteria of benefits and costs, there are other criteria to consider. Some people have the view that substantial trade is a pre-requisite for monetary union and that a monetary union will not work where the trade links are minor among members, or where there are trade barriers. One way to look at that argument is to ask what would happen within the European Monetary union today if each country began charging a tariff on wine coming into the country. The tariff would be paid in euros and the prices of wine from outside each country would become more expensive, but what effect would there be on the functioning of the union itself? Politically, there would be difficulties, since the wine-exporting countries would be hurt by lower sales, and the consumers of the net wine-importing countries would not be happy to pay more for their wine. But even if the economy of the Eurozone would be hurt by less trade, it's not clear that the tariff would have any bearing on the success of the monetary union. The issue would not be about the currency, but about free trade which is a related, but different issue.

Optimum Currency Area

The best known criteria for evaluating the suitability of an area for monetary union come from Robert Mundell's 1961 "Theory of Optimum Currency Areas." He wrote that "The optimum currency area is the region,"[142] and the region is defined by the similarity of three factors among the nations considering monetary union: the mobility of labor and capital, the extent of trade, and the congruence of economic cycles.

Mundell wrote that paper primarily as an argument against "a system of national currencies connected by flexible exchange rates."[143] While the three criteria are important, they have been considered by some economists to be three requirements for a minimally successful monetary union rather than, as the title of Mundell's article stated, criteria for "optimum" currency areas.

Even the United States is not clearly an "Optimum Currency Area."[144] A 1991 article "Is Europe an Optimum Currency Area?" found that "Europe remains further from the ideal of an optimum currency area than the currency unions of Canada and the United States, or China."[145] In a 2005 analysis, three economists from Lund University in Sweden concluded that China is "more of an optimum currency area than first expected," but they questioned whether Hong Kong and Macao would be appropriate additions pursuant to the criteria.[146] The political reality is that China has been a monetary union since the first emperor of a united China, Qin Shi Huang, implemented a single Chinese currency and other unified measurement systems in 221 B.C. Whether "optimum" or not, Hong Kong and Macao will soon be part of the Chinese monetary union, if not an East Asian or Asian monetary union. The optimum currency area analysis has been applied to many other geographies, too, and found to be insufficient, e.g., North America,[147] Asia,[148] East Africa,[149] and West Africa.[150]

Jeffrey Frankel and Andrew Rose enlarged the perspectives of those examining whether an area was "optimum" for a monetary union by examining whether preparations for joining a proposed or existing monetary union might, themselves, modify the economic landscape to transform the participating countries into a currency area more closely fitting the optimum currency area criteria.[151] They concluded that even for countries whose pre-monetary union trade relationships and correlation of business cycles did not appear to make those countries ideal candidates for optimum currency union, monetary union could be beneficial because of changes which would occur *after* such union. They wrote about the Eurozone, "EMU entry, *per se*, for whatever reason, may provide a substantial impetus for trade expansion; this in turn may result in more highly correlated business cycles. That is, a country is more likely to satisfy the criteria for entry into a currency union *ex post* than *ex ante*."[152] They called the effect, "endogeneity."[153] The result is like a company having application criteria for a job opening and then finding that people who didn't initially meet those criteria ultimately performed very well on the job. Thus, the use of the original Optimum Currency Area criteria as predictors of successful entry into a monetary union is of little or uncertain value.

In 2000, at the IMF Panel "One World, One Currency: Destination or Delusion?"[154] it was said of Mundell that, "He stated that the EMU had met the basic optimum currency area criteria of a monetary union:
"- common target or anchor for monetary policy;
 - common measures for inflation;
 - locked exchange rates;
 - implying a common monetary policy; and a
 - means for dividing up the seigniorage."[155]

On the other hand, the European Commission's 1992 report stated that "It became conventional wisdom to say that Europe was *not* an optimum currency area,"[156] and gave several reasons why EMU was still a good idea. The report concluded, "Summing up, the optimum currency area approach provides useful insights but cannot be considered a comprehensive framework in which the costs and benefits of EMU can be analyzed. Empirical applications of this approach are scarce and hardly conclusive."[157]

The Maastricht Criteria

Led in substantial part by concerns from Germany, the most prosperous European country with the strongest currency, the Maastricht Treaty established five criteria for entry into the monetary union:
1. Candidate country inflation is no more than 1.5 percent above the average of the lowest three inflation rates in the European Monetary System (EMS);
2. The long-term interest rate of the candidate country is no more than 2 percent higher than the average of the low inflation countries in the EMS;
3. The candidate country is a member of the exchange rate mechanism of the EMS and has not observed a

devaluation in the two years preceding entrance into the EMU;

4. The candidate country government budget deficit is no higher than 3 percent of GDP; and

5. The candidate country's government debt does not exceed 60 percent of GDP. [158]

There was initial difficulty by some of the EU members meeting the criteria, and there was even some concern that the numbers were distorted in some countries, e.g. Greece, to make them fit the criteria. With each passing year of successful use of the euro by all EMU countries, such concerns fade in importance, and bring into question their original utility.

British Five Criteria for Joining the EMU

The British government initially evaluated the utility of adopting the euro and established five criteria, in addition to the above criteria in the Maastricht Treaty, which the UK was acknowledged to have met.

"1. Are business cycles and economic structures compatible so that we and others could live comfortably with euro interest rates on a permanent basis?

2. If problems emerge, is there sufficient flexibility to deal with them?

3. Would joining EMU create better conditions for firms making long-term decisions to invest in Britain?

4. What impact would entry into EMU have on the competitive position of the UK's financial services industry, particularly the City's wholesale markets?

5. In summary, will joining EMU promote higher growth, stability, and a lasting increase in jobs?" [159]

The answers to these questions were not viewed sufficiently positively to give the government the political confidence to take the issue to the parliament or to the people in a referendum. Many pro-euro economists felt that either these criteria were not necessary or that the United Kingdom satisfied them, and thus that the issue of the UK entry into the EMU is far more a political than an economic question. The mixture of motivation is entirely legitimate as the motivations of the twelve countries which did join the EMU were also a political and economic combination. Someday, the UK's political assessment of the benefits and costs will turn positive and the UK will join the Eurozone.

General Criticism of Monetary Unions

Perhaps nobody has written as pessimistically about monetary unions as Benjamin Cohen in his 2004 book, *The Future of Money*. [160] His subsequent related books are *Global Monetary Governance* (2007) and *The Future of Global Currency* (2010). He labels the movement to a smaller number of currencies, through ization or monetary unions as the "Contraction Contention." [161] He believes that the power of nationalism, leading nations to establish and maintain their own currencies, will outweigh the public's desire for stable money. He writes, "...the Contraction Contention, I contend, is utterly wrong. The central argument of this book is that the population of the world's moneys is more likely to expand, not contract, both in number and diversity. The future of money will be one of persistently growing complexity, posing increasingly difficult challenges for state authorities."[162]

While noting the momentum of monetary union in Europe, Professor Cohen discounts the example of the EMU as "only one new monetary union."[163] Despite the evidence of the longevity of the euro and the accession of the ten New Member States, he believes that countries are simply not willing to give up their monetary sovereignty for the sake of monetary stability. His vision of nation states is that they are locked in a Darwinian struggle of currency competition on a zero-sum game basis, instead of being willing to join with others. Borrowing from the observation by George von Furstenberg, a monetary union supporter, that "like-minded countries" were best for monetary unions,[164] Cohen asks rhetorically, "Where in the quarrelsome family of nations can the requisite like-mindedness be found? The obstacles to finding willing partners are formidable and, in most instances, likely to turn out to be insurmountable."[165] In 2012, Cohen wrote, "The euro will neither succeed nor fail. Defective but defended, it will simply struggle on, repeatedly sustained by one shoddy compromise after another. The outlook is for survival, but not robust health."[166]

The answer is that the "quarrelsome family of nations" is seeing a better way of international relations and it's called working together, or soft power. That's the core of Mark Leonard's thesis in *Why Europe will Run the 21st Century*. He wrote, "By coming together and pooling their sovereignty to achieve common goals, the countries of the European Union have created new power out of nothing. The silent revolution they have unleashed will transform the world."[167]

Another critic of the euro is Bloomberg.com's Matthew Lynn who presented the view reminiscent of the US Army major during the Vietnam War who announced that he had to destroy a village in order to save it. Lynn wrote that the way to save the euro is to "try reissuing the twelve national currencies that were replaced with just one." Relying upon recommendations from John Gillingham, a historian from the US, Lynn argued that the euro is responsible for the sluggish EMU economy. He wrote, "What is important is that people recognize that the euro hasn't worked as planned..." and that member countries should have the option of bringing back their legacy currencies.[168] In an unintended rejoinder to this book, Lynn wrote that the recommendation was "just common sense."

We will see in the next few years whether the people of the world have common cents/sense and whether they really want stable money, or a risky, costly, worldwide currency competition. As Thomas Paine wrote, "Time makes more converts than reason."[169] With every passing day of stable money in Europe, and with every new country that joins the EMU, the world is seeing that monetary union works, and the "Contraction Contention" will itself contract out of contention as an explanation of actual events.

It is true that nearly all of the monetary unions of the past have ended, mostly due to political and economic changes. While the Maastricht Treaty contains no explicit provision for a member country's secession from the European Monetary Union, such a split is possible. Such secession was considered for each of the EMU countries suffering during the European 2008-2013 debt and financial crisis: Cyprus, Greece, Ireland, Italy, Portugal and Spain. George Provopoulos, Governor of the Bank of Greece since 2008, analyzed in 2014 the European crisis as "two separate crises - a sovereign-induced crisis and a banking-induced crisis."[170] However, in all those countries the calculation was made, and sometimes perilously narrowly, that whatever the fiscal and economic problems, it was better to move forward with a stable currency than to discard such a currency and start a new one. What the people and the organizations of the world want is stable money.

Starting a new currency was especially unpalatable to business interests (except exporters) and investors because a major goal of such a currency would be to devalue it in order to stimulate the economy. Excessive inflation, defined here as being more than two percent, is not a wise course for any economy.

Perhaps those who considered secession had second thoughts after hearing about Barry Eichengreen's summary of the plusses and minuses of leaving a monetary union. He wrote in 2007,

> "It is unlikely, I argue here, that one or more members of the euro area will leave in the next ten years; total disintegration of the euro area is even more unlikely. While other authors have minimized the technical difficulties of reintroducing a national currency, I suggest that those technical difficulties would be quite formidable. Nor is it certain that the economic problems of the participating member states would be significantly ameliorated by abandoning the euro. And even if there are immediate economic benefits, there would be longer-term political costs."[171]

As a sign of the health of the EMU, the end of consideration of EMU secession confirms what the bond markets were saying in early 2014, as the yields on bonds from the endangered countries, e.g. Greece, declined.[172]

A major difference between such secession discussions, with the EMU and with previous monetary unions, is that the European Monetary Union is growing and the only limit is that members be a member of the EU, which requires that its members be a "European State."[173] However, the definition of "European State" is flexible and includes political heritage, which is why Iceland's application to the EU is being seriously considered. Growth of any organization has a way of becoming empowering and self-fulfilling. As will become clear in subsequent chapters, the ultimate end of such growth will be the Global Monetary Union, where the advantages of monetary unions are compounded annually.

Summary

The monetary unions of the twenty-first century, and those which survived the twentieth, are the milestones on the path to the future, and to the Global Monetary Union. It ought to be the policy of every country of the world to join an existing or new monetary union if the money managed by that union's central bank is likely to be more stable than the current money of that country. Thus, every country should join a monetary union.

Many economists now recommend this course of action for small countries.[174] William White, economist and head of monetary policy at the Bank for International Settlements from 1995-2008, recommended that the world move to "a small number of more formally based currency blocks."[175]

As a monetary union's central bank is far more focused on its goal of stable money than are the governments of any of its member nations, the probability is high that joining is better than not joining.

Until the rise of the international monetary unions, central banks were considered to be best oriented to a single nation, but that alignment made money a symbol of a nation, instead of being a symbol and unit of value. Once that critical distinction was discovered or re-discovered, the road to Global Monetary Union was opened.

As the euro is now securely established as a stable international reserve currency, it is more attractive to potential members than it was in 1999 when joining meant an uncertain future.[176] It has emerged from the 2008-2013 difficulties stronger and with a clear "blueprint" for a stronger economic and monetary union in the future.[177] The larger the Eurozone gets, the more stable it will be, and the closer the world will be to the "tipping point" toward the Single Global Currency.

Chapter 5 explores the logical final step for any discussion about monetary union: a Global Monetary Union.

ENDNOTES

1. The Toscana region translates as Tuscany in English. I've tried in this book to use the rule that localities should be known as they are known by the local inhabitants, rather than just to speakers of English. It's easier to apply that rule for non-state localities as Toscana and the Arabian Gulf, than for countries such as Italy and Germany, which are known as Italia and Deutschland to their citizens.

2. Scaruffi, Gasparo, *L'Alitinonfo. Reggio Emilia.* Italy:1582, as cited by Robert Mundell, at IMF Economic Forum "One World, One Currency: Destination or Delusion?" 8 November 2000, with Alexander Swoboda, Maurice Obstfeld and Paul Masson, at http://www.imf.org/external/np/tr/2000/tr001108.htm. Not having read the original text, it's assumed that even if Count Scaruffi used the term "world," he was really thinking of Europe at the time, and there was no consideration of including China, India, or Japan, of which little was known in Europe.

3. Luca Einaudi, "'The Generous Utopia of Yesterday can become the Practical Achievement of Tomorrow': 1000 Years of Monetary Union in

Europe," *National Institute of Economic Review [Italy]*, 1 April 2000, p. 2, at http://ner.sagepub.com/content/172/1/90.abstract.

4. Sam Vaknin, "The History of Previous Currency Unions," at http://samvak.tripod.com/nm032.html.

5. John Hawkins and Paul Masson, "Introduction" to "Regional Currencies and the Use of Foreign Currencies," Annex A, May 2003, Bank for International Settlements, p. 27, at http://www.bis.org/publ/bppdf/bispap17.pdf.

6. For more details, see Benjamin J. Cohen, "Monetary Unions," at *EH.net, Economic History Net Online Encyclopedia* at http://eh.net/?s=monetary+union.

7. Eric Helleiner, "Dollarization Diplomacy: US Policy Toward Latin America Coming Full Circle?" TIPEC Working Paper 02/8, Trent International Political Economy Centre, Ontario, 2002, at http://www.trentu.ca/tipec/2helleiner8.pdf.

8. Sam Vaknin, "The History of Previous Currency Unions," op. cit.

9. Luca Einaudi, "'The Generous Utopia of Yesterday can become the Practical Achievement of Tomorrow': 1000 years of Monetary Union in Europe," *National Institute Economic Review (Italy)*, 1 April 2000. op. cit.

10. "Finance Ministers Express Confidence in Strength, Stability of EC Currency," Press Release from the Office of the Prime Minister, St. Kitts & Nevis, 22 February 2006, at http://www.cuopm.com/?p=840

11. See website of Eastern Caribbean Monetary Union, at http://www.eccb-centralbank.org/About/index.asp.

12. J. E. Meade, "The Balance of Payments Problems of a Free Trade Area," *Economics Journal*, Sept. 1957, pp. 379-96, at http://www.jstor.org/discover/10.2307/2227357?uid=2129&uid=2&uid=70&uid=4&sid=21103455286617

13. Tibor Scitovsky, *Economic Theory and Western European Integration*. London: Allen and Unwin, 1958, cited by Robert Mundell at http://www.columbia.edu/~ram15/ie/ie-12.html.

14. T. K. Jayaraman, "Prospects for a Currency Union in the South Pacific," 31 December 2001, p. 12.

15. Robert Mundell, "A Theory of Optimum Currency Areas," *American Economic Review*, May 1961, pp 657-65, at p. 661. The article is also contained in Mundell's textbook, *International Economics*, as chapter 12, pp. 177-86, and online at http://www.columbia.edu/~ram15/ie/ie-12.html.

16. Ibid., at p. 661.

17. Robert Mundell, "A Plan for a European Currency" and "Uncommon Arguments for Common Currencies," both in H. G. Johnson and A. K. Swoboda, *The Economics of Common Currencies*. London, UK: Allen and Unwin, 1973, pp. 143-72. Mundell gave an unpublished presentation, "A Plan for a European Currency," at a 10 December 1969 American Management Assn. seminar on the International Monetary System, at "The Works of Robert Mundell," at http://robertmundell.net/. See also "Capital Mobility and Stablilization Policy under Fixed and Flexible Exchange Rates," in *Canadian Journal of Economics and Political Science*,

Vol. 29, November 1963, pp. 475-85. Citations from Ronald McKinnon's, "Optimum Currency Areas and the European Experience," 16 October 2001, at http://www.stanford.edu/~mckinnon/papers/optimumreveur.pdf.

18. Robert Mundell, 1961, "A Theory of Optimum Currency Areas," op. cit., p. 657.

19. The reference to a "$multi-trillion question" refers to a US television quiz show in the 1950s called the "$64,000 question." On the show that question was *the* question, as is the question now of planning and implementing a Single Global Currency. See "The $64,000 Question and the $64,000 Challenge" at http://www.museum.tv/eotv/quizandgame.htm.

20. "APEC Study Report: Brunei Darussalam," for 2009 conference, p. 8, at http://mddb.apec.org/Documents/2009/SOM/SOM1/09_som1_006anx2.pdf.

21. Lubin Kobla Doe, "Reforming External Tariffs in Central and Western African Countries," IMF Working Paper, No. 06/12, 1 January 2006, at http://www.imf.org/external/pubs/cat/longres.cfm?sk=18617.0.

22. See the major analysis of dollarization, *The Dollarization Debate*, edited by Dominick Salvatore, James W. Dean, and Thomas D. Willett. Oxford, UK: Oxford University Press, 2003. See also, for an analysis of dollarization in the Americas, Harvey Arbelaez, "The Political Economy of the Dollarization Debate in the Americas: Pros and Cons, Myths and Realities, Issues and Implications," from a First Paper Development Workshop in Stockholm, July 2004, at http://citeseerx.ist.psu.edu/viewdoc/summary?doi=10.1.1.200.8018.

23. The term "ization" has no etymological relation to Alain Ize, who is an economist at the International Monetary and who has written about dollarization. See his " Financial Dollarization Equilibria: A Framework for Policy Analysis," IMF Working Paper 186, 2005, at https://www.imf.org/external/pubs/ft/wp/2005/wp05186.pdf.

24. For an analysis of the dollarizations in Ecuador and El Salvador, see Jose Luis Cordeiro's *La Segunda Muerte de Sucre*. Guayaquil, Ecuador: Instituto Ecuatoriano de Economia Politica, 1999, at http://www.amazon.com/Segunda-Muerte-Sucre-Renacer-Ecuador/dp/980607341X. The title translates as *The Second Death of Sucre*. Sucre was the name of Ecuador's pre-dollarization currency, named after the South American liberation hero, Antonio Jose de Sucre. The book's text is in Spanish.

25. Stanley Fischer, "Ecuador and the International Monetary Fund" in *Currency Unions*. Stanford, California: edited by Alberto Alesina and Robert J. Barro, Hoover Institution Press, 2001, pp. 2-10, at http://www.amazon.com/Currency-Unions-HOOVER-PRESS-PUBLICATION/dp/0817928421

26. Stanley Fischer, ibid., pp 2-10.

27. "Ecuador defaults on foreign debt," *BBC News*, 13 December 2008, at http://news.bbc.co.uk/2/hi/business/7780984.stm

28. Felix Salmon, "Lessons from Ecuador's bond default," *Reuters*, 29 May 2009, at http://blogs.reuters.com/felix-salmon/2009/05/29/lessons-from-ecuadors-bond-default/

29. "Calling Foreign Debt 'Immoral,' Leader Allows Ecuador to Default," by Anthony Faiola, *Washington Post,* 13 December 2008, at http://www.washingtonpost.com/wp-dyn/content/article/2008/12/12/AR2008121204105.html

30. "Ecuador May Be Forced to Scrap Dollar After Default," by Lester Pimentel and Matthew Walter, *Bloomberg*, 17 December 2008, at http://www.bloomberg.com/apps/news?pid=20601086&sid=aVwE0KXFzY3A&refer=latin_america

31. "On A Roll: Ecuador's gamble with the U.S. Dollar," by Lance Brashear, *Ecuador Herald*, 12 March 2013, at http://www.todayinecuador.com/noticias-ecuador/on-a-roll-ecuador-s-gamble-with-the-u-s-dollar-576256.html

32. Benn Steil, "The Developing World Should Abandon Parochial Currencies," *Financial Times*, 17 January 2006, at http://www.ft.com/intl/cms/s/0/1f48b4e6-86fe-11da-8521-0000779e2340.html#axzz2tKTSuLGH.

33. Bedri Kamil Onur Tas and Selahattin Togay, "Effect of Official Dollarization on a Small Open Economy: Ecuador," 7 November 2011, at http://papers.ssrn.com/sol3/papers.cfm?abstract_id=1955949

34. "On A Roll: Ecuador's gamble with the U.S. Dollar," Op. cit.

35. Ibid.

36. "IMF Executive Board Concludes 2004 Article IV Consultation with El Salvador," Public Information Notice, No. 05/21, International Monetary Fund, 14 February 2005, at http://www.imf.org/external/np/sec/pn/2005/pn0521.htm.

37. US Department of State, "2005 Investment Climate Statement--El Salvador," at http://www.state.gov/e/eb/ifd/2005/43026.htm.

38. "El Salvador," World Bank data, at http://data.worldbank.org/country/el-salvador, and "Remittances to Latin America," Pew Research Center, 15 November 2013, at http://www.pewhispanic.org/2013/11/15/remittances-to-latin-america-recover-but-not-to-mexico/

39. Andrew Swiston, "Official Dollarization as a Monetary Regime: Its Effects on El Salvador," IMF Working Paper 11/129, at http://www.imf.org/external/pubs/ft/wp/2011/wp11129.pdf

40. "List of Cities Proper by Population," *Wikipedia*, at http://en.wikipedia.org/wiki/List_of_cities_proper_by_population

41. Jeffrey A. Frankel and Andrew K. Rose, "An Estimate of the Effect of Currency Unions on Trade and Growth" in *Currency Unions*. Stanford, CA: Edited by Alberto Alesina and Robert J. Barro, op. cit., p. 37.

42. This expression originated in the British colonies in America when taxes were imposed by the British Parliament, in which the colonies had no elected representatives. See the Wikipedia entry, including the reference to today's license plates in Washington, DC, the US capital where citizens do

not have elected representatives in the US Congress. At
http://en.wikipedia.org/wiki/No_taxation_without_representation

43. "Dollars and Cents" in "Twenty-five things you didn't know about money," Forbes.com, at
http://www.forbes.com/2006/02/11/cx_dal_money06_0214moneyfactslide_8.html?thisSpeed=6000. Complicating the seigniorage value is the life expectancy of paper money. See "R.I.P." ibid, "One-dollar bills have an average lifespan of 22 months, while ten-dollar notes live for only 18 months. Twenties can circulate for 25 months, and $100 notes last about five years," See also "New Money," ibid., "The US Bureau of Engraving and Printing produces 35 million notes a day with a face value of approximately $635 million. Ninety-five percent of the notes printed each year are used to replace notes already in circulation, and 45% of the notes printed are $1 notes."

44. "Measuring Profits from Currency Issue," *Reserve Bank of Australia Bulletin*, July 1997, pp. 1-4, Reserve Bank of Australia, at
http://www.rba.gov.au/publications/bulletin/1997/jul/1.html.

45. Kurt Schuler and Robert Stein, "The International Monetary Stability Act: An Analysis." Paper for North-South Institute Conference "To Dollarize or Not to Dollarize?" in Ottowa, 5 October 2000. The bill was primarily about dollarization. See the hearings before the Senate Banking Committee, Subcommittee on International Trade and Finance on 22 April 1999, 15 July 1999, and 8 February 2000, at
http://banking.senate.gov/99_04hrg/042299/index.htm,
http://banking.senate.gov/99_07hrg/071599/index.htm, and
http://banking.senate.gov/00_02hrg/020800/index.htm.

46. Adam S. Posen, editor, *The Euro at Five: Ready for a Global Role?* Washington, DC: Institute for International Economics, 2005, at pp. 28-29. See online version of C. Fred Bergsten's chapter "The Euro and the Dollar: Toward a Finance G-2?" 26 February 2004, at
http://www.iie.com/publications/papers/bergsten0204-2.pdf

47. For an excellent summary of the progress toward European Monetary Union, see Chapter 4, "European Monetary Unification" in John Edmunds' and John Marthinsen's *Wealth by Association, Global Prosperity through Market Unification.* Westport, CT: Praeger Publishers, 2003, pp. 43-77.

48. Treaty on European Union, popularly known as the Maastricht Treaty, on the website of the European Central Bank at
http://www.ecb.int/ecb/legal/pdf/maastricht_en.pdf.

49. Denmark National Bank, "euro referendum," at
http://www.nationalbanken.dk/dnuk/eurohist.nsf/side/Euro_referendum_.

50. Bank of Canada "10-year Currency Converter" utility, using dates from 1 January 1999 through 10 December 2005, at
http://www.bankofcanada.ca/en/rates/exchform.html.

51. "Denmark and the euro," *Wikipedia*, at
http://en.wikipedia.org/wiki/Denmark_and_the_euro

52. "Swedes remain opposed to euro four years after referendum," *Thompson Financial*, 18 December 2007, at

http://www.finanznachrichten.de/nachrichten-2007-12/9719530-swedes-remain-opposed-to-euro-four-years-after-referendum-020.htm

53. "Poll Finds British Public Want to Stay in EU," *Huffington Post,* 12 January 2014, at http://www.huffingtonpost.co.uk/2014/01/11/polls-find-public-want-to-stay-in-eu-reduce-powers_n_4581786.html

54. "Flash Eurobarometer - Introduction of the Euro New Member States," by the Gallup Organization for the European Commission, 2007, at http://ec.europa.eu/public_opinion/flash/fl_214_sum_en.pdf.

55. Op. cit., Bank of Canada 10-year Currency Converter.

56. "In Search of a Euro Effect: Big Lessons from a Big Mac Meal?" David Parsley and Shang-jin Wei, Munich Personal RePEc Archive (MRPA) paper 6041, September 2007, at http://mpra.ub.uni-muenchen.de/6041/

57. "Enlargement of the Eurozone," *Wikipedia,* at http://en.wikipedia.org/wiki/Enlargement_of_the_eurozone

58. The 1997 Treaty of Amsterdam modified the Maastricht Treaty. Among other changes affecting the euro, it modified the first phrase of the enabling "Article B" from "to promote economic and social progress, which is balanced and sustainable" to "to promote economic and social progress and a high level of employment and to achieve balanced and sustainable development," (changes are underlined in the original) at http://www.ecb.int/ecb/legal/pdf/amsterdam_en.pdf.

59. Willem H. Buiter, "The EMU and the NAMU: What Is the Case for North American Monetary Union?" September 1999, *Canadian Public Policy,* pp. 285-306, at p. 302, at http://qed.econ.queensu.ca/pub/cpp/sept1999/Buiter.pdf.

60. Paul De Grauwe and Claudia Costa Storti, "Is Monetary Policy in the Eurozone Less Effective than in the US?" CESifo Working Paper No. 1606, November 2005, at http://papers.ssrn.com/sol3/papers.cfm?abstract_id=870394.

61. States the ECB's website, "The primary objective of the ECB's monetary policy is to maintain price stability. The ECB aims at inflation rates of below, but close to, 2% over the medium term." "Monetary Policy" at http://www.ecb.int/mopo/html/index.en.html.

62. Andrew Stead, "ECB raises interest rates, says no more hikes for now," 2 December 2005, ABCmoney.co.uk, at http://www.abcmoney.co.uk/news/0220051461.htm.

63. "European Central Bank," *Wikipedia* at http://en.wikipedia.org/wiki/European_Central_Bank

64. M. Hashem Pesaran, L. Vanessa Smith, and Ron P. Smith, "What if the UK Had Joined the Euro in 1999? An Empirical Evaluation Using a Global VAR," June 2005, CESifo Working Paper 1477, at http://papers.ssrn.com/sol3/papers.cfm?abstract_id=740424.

65. "Toward a Single Euro Payments Area, Objectives and Deadlines (4th Progress Report)," European Central Bank, 17 February 2006, at http://www.ecb.int/pub/pdf/other/singleeuropaymentsarea200602en.pdf.

66. "Single Euro Payments Area," *Wikipedia,* at http://en.wikipedia.org/wiki/Single_Euro_Payments_Area

67. Nouriel Roubini, and others listed in the article, "Davos: How Nouriel Roubini got it wrong on Greece," *Financial Post*, 21 January 2013, at http://business.financialpost.com/2013/01/21/how-roubini-got-it-wrong-on-a-greece-eurozone-exit/. See also "Rogoff predicts wave of sovereign defaults," in which article Kenneth Rogoff said of the EMU in general, "I don't think Europe's going to succeed," in Central Banking, 23 February 2010, at http://www.centralbanking.com/central-banking/news/1593243/rogoff-predicts-wave-sovereign-defaults

68. Greek Opinion Poll Shows 78% Want Greece to Remain in Euro Area," *Newsmax*, 13 May 2012, at http://www.newsmax.com/Economy/Greek-Opinion-Poll-euro/2012/05/13/id/438880

69. Paul Getner, "Euro Isn't Loved, but Few Want to Drop It, Poll Says," *New York Times*, 26 May 2012, at http://www.nytimes.com/2012/05/29/business/global/euro-isnt-loved-but-poll-shows-little-desire-to-drop-it.html?_r=0

70. *Central Banking* Staff "Governor of the Year: Mario Draghi," Central Banking.com, 13 January 2014, at http://www.centralbanking.com/central-banking-journal/feature/2321730/governor-of-the-year-mario-draghi

71. "EU leaders approve euozone banking reform deal," 20 December 2013, *BBC*, at http://www.bbc.co.uk/news/world-europe-25419119 . See also "Why the Economic and Monetary Union needs a banking union," speech by Christian Noyer, 31 January 2014, at http://www.bis.org/review/r140205e.htm. See also Angel Ubide, "How to Form a More Perfect European Banking Union," Peterson Institute for International Economics, Policy Brief 13-23, October 2013, at http://www.piie.com/publications/pb/pb13-23.pdf

72. For a review of current monetary union efforts, through 2009, see "Current and future monetary cooperation with a focus on the possible monetary union of Gulf Cooperation Council," by Magdaléna Drastichová at http://www.academia.edu/3824224/Current_and_future_monetary_cooperation_with_a_focus_on_the_possible_monetary_union_of_Gulf_Cooperation_Council

73. The Arabian Gulf is known by that term, albeit not in English, to the people living in that region. The term Persian Gulf is used by non-Arabs. Using the rule that geographical places, cities, and countries should be known to the world as they are known to the local inhabitants, the term "Arabian Gulf" is used here.

74. Michael Sturm and Nikolaus Siegfried, "Regional Monetary Integration in the Member States of the Gulf Cooperation Council," European Central Bank, June 2005, at http://www.ecb.int/pub/pdf/scpops/ecbocp31.pdf

75. Abdulrahman K. L. Al-Mansouri and Claudia Dziobek, "Providing Official Statistics for the Common Market and Monetary Union in the Gulf Cooperation Council (GCC) Countries: A Case for 'Gulfstat'," IMF Working Paper 06/38, at http://www.imf.org/external/pubs/ft/wp/2006/wp0638.pdf

76. "Make haste slowly on GCC monetary union," *Gulf Times*, 12 October 2013, at http://gulfnews.com/business/opinion/make-haste-slowly-on-gcc-monetary-union-1.1242333

77. "Russia-Belarus Union to Have Common Currency Starting from 2008," ITAR-TASS news agency, 27 January 2006, at http://www.freerepublic.com/focus/f-news/1566723/posts.

78. Vladimir Chaplygin, Andrew Hughes Hallet, and Christian Richter, "Monetary Integration in the Ex-Soviet Union: A 'Union of Four'?" *Economics of Transition*, March 2006, and at http://ideas.repec.org/a/bla/etrans/v14y2006i1p47-68.html

79. For an economic analysis of the West African prospects, see Xavier DeBrun, Paul Masson, and Catherine Pattillo, "Monetary Union in West Africa: Who Might Gain, Who Might Lose, and Why?" IMF Working Paper 02/226, December 2002, at http://www.imf.org/external/pubs/ft/wp/2002/wp02226.pdf.

80. "Welcome to West African Monetary Institute," at http://wormholedev.net/qwamz/?q=menuhome

81. Bester Gabotlale, "Links with Madagascar Could Benefit Botswana," 23 February 2006, at http://allafrica.com/stories/200602240394.html.

82. "Integration Milestones," South African Development Community, at http://www.sadc.int/about-sadc/integration-milestones/

83. Elias Biryabarema, "East African trade bloc approves monetary union deal," 30 November 2014, Reuters at http://www.reuters.com/article/2013/11/30/us-africa-monetaryunion-idUSBRE9AT08O20131130

84. George Omondi, "IMF boss cautions East Africa on monetary union," *The East African*, 7 January 2014, at http://www.theeastafrican.co.ke/news/IMF-East-Africa-on-monetary-union/-/2558/2138592/-/57801jz/-/index.html

85. "African Monetary Union," *Wikipedia*, at http://en.wikipedia.org/wiki/African_Monetary_Union

86. See, for example, Arthur Grimes, "Regional and Industry Cycles in Australasia: Implications for a Common Currency," Motu Working Paper 05-04, May, 2005, at http://www.motu.org.nz/publications/detail/regional_and_industry_cycles_in_australasia_implications_for_a_common_curre

87. Andrew Coleman, "Economic Integration and Monetary Union," Treasury Working Paper 99/6, 1999, p. 32, at http://www.treasury.govt.nz/publications/research-policy/wp/1999/99-06

88. Matthew Brockett, "Australia-N.Z. Currency Union Worth Examining, Eichengreen Says," *Bloomberg*, 6 December 2013, at http://www.bloomberg.com/news/2013-12-06/australia-n-z-currency-union-worth-examining-eichengreen-says.html http://www.radionz.co.nz/news/bulletins/radionz/200602090733/32ea38f7

89. T.K. Jayaraman, and Chee-Keong Choong, "A Single Currency for Pacific Island Countries: a Revisit," *Journal of Economic Integration*, 2009,

at http://econpapers.repec.org/article/risintegr/0476.htm which updated article by T. K. Jayaraman, "Prospects for a Currency Union in the South Pacific," December 2001, p. 12.

90. See Willie Lahari, "Shocks and Prospects for a Pacific Islands Currency Union," *Modern Economy*, September, 2012 at http://www.scirp.org/journal/PaperInformation.aspx?PaperID=23316

91. Sweta Chaman Saxena, "Can South Asia Adopt a Common Currency?" *Journal of Asian Economics*, August 2005, pp. 635-62, at http://ideas.repec.org/p/wpa/wuwpif/0508001.html.

92. "Agreement on South Asian Free Trade Area," SAARC, 2004, at http://wits.worldbank.org/GPTAD/PDF/archive/SAFTA.pdf

93. Haruhiko Kuroda, "Single Currency Will Climax Asia's Economic Integration," *Shanghai Daily, The Daily Star,* 7 November 2005, at http://archive.thedailystar.net/2005/10/27/d51027050456.htm

94. "Asian Common Currency Not to Come in Short Term!" VNECONOMY, *Viet Nam Economic Times*, 25 February 2006, at http://www.elitetrader.com/vb/showthread.php?s=264147f9c8cf06007b1bef8bf6719064&threadid=68732&perpage=6&pagenumber=2.

95. Arief Ramayandi, "ASEAN Monetary Cooperation: Issues and Prospects," Pacific Economic Paper No. 349, Australia-Japan Research Centre, Asia Pacific School of Economics and Management, p. 15, at http://www.eaber.org/node/22028

96. Joseph Allchin, "ASEAN mulls single currency," *Democratic Voice Burma*, 11 May 2011, at http://www.dvb.no/news/asean-mulls-single-currency/15562

97. "S. America Launches Trading Bloc," *BBC News*, 9 December 2004, at http://news.bbc.co.uk/1/hi/business/4079505.stm. See also the "Cusco Declaration," in Spanish, at http://www.comunidadandina.org/documentos/dec_int/cusco_sudamerica.htm

98. "Union of South American Nations," *Wikipedia*, at http://en.wikipedia.org/wiki/Union_of_South_American_Nations

99. Herbert Grubel, "The Case for the Amero--The Economics and Politics of a North American Monetary Union," The Fraser Institute, 1999, at http://www.fraserinstitute.org/publicationdisplay.aspx?id=13493&terms=amero.

100. Thomas J. Courchene, "A Canadian Perspective on North American Monetary Union," 5 January 2001, p. 23, at http://www.irpp.org/newsroom/archive/2001/0105pape.pdf.

101. George von Furstenberg, "Mexico versus Canada: Stability benefits from making common currency with USD?" at http://marriottschool.net/jefonline/articles/JEF_200510_v10_i02_p15.pdf.

102. J. Collin Dodds, "Europe offers strong case for N. American currency," *Halifax News*, 11 August 2007.

103. "Bloc Quebecois advocates common currency with U.S," *Reuters*, 7 November 2007, at http://ca.news.yahoo.com/s/reuters/071108/canada/canada_dollar_bloc_col

104. The Central American Monetary Union Council was succeeded in 1974 by the Central American Monetary Agreement, which has a website, in Spanish, at http://www.secmca.org/.

105. "Time for a Single Caribbean dollar," Sir Ronald Sanders, *Jamaica Observer*, 25 June 2007, at http://www.jamaicaobserver.com/columns/html/20070623T210000-0500_124605_OBS_TIME_FOR_A_SINGLE_CARIBBEAN_DOLLAR_.asp

106. For further information about currency hedging, see Alan Deardorff's definition, "To offset risk. In the foreign exchange market, hedgers use the forward market to cover a transaction or open position and thereby reduce exchange risk. The term applies most commonly to trade," at http://www-personal.umich.edu/~alandear/glossary/. See also, Rui Albuquerque, "Optimal Currency Hedging," 11 April 2003, at http://ideas.repec.org/p/wpa/wuwpfi/0405010.html.

107. John Edmunds and John Marthinsen, *Wealth by Association, Global Prosperity Through Market Unification*. Westport, CT: Praeger Publishers, 2003.

108. Ibid., p. 181.

109. Ibid., p. 6.

110. "Moody's Issues Positive Rating Revisions to 7 States Posed [sic] to Join EMU," Forbes.com from AFX News Limited, 9 March 2006, at http://www.forbes.com/work/feeds/afx/2006/03/09/afx2582548.html.

111. John Edmunds and John Marthinsen, "Wealth Creation via Currency Unification & Mama Mia! Here We Go Again!" presentation at the Second Annual Single Global Currency Conference, Bretton Woods, New Hampshire, July 2005, at http://www.singleglobalcurrency.org/documents/WealthCreationviaCurrencyUnificationbyEdmundsandMarthinsenExecutiveSummary050714.doc.

112. The money supply in the United States is defined as M1, M2, and M3. The Federal Reserve defines M1 as "(1) Currency outside the US Treasury, Federal Reserve Banks, and the vaults of depository institutions; (2) Travelers checks of non-bank issuers; (3) Demand deposits at commercial banks (excluding those amounts held by depository institutions, the US government, and foreign banks and official institutions) less cash items in the process of collection and Federal Reserve float; and (4) Other checkable deposits (OCDs), consisting of negotiable order of withdrawal (NOW) and automatic transfer service (ATS) accounts at depository institutions, credit union share draft accounts, and demand deposits at thrift institutions." See "Money Stock Measures: Federal Reserve Statistical Release," 19 January 2006, at http://www.federalreserve.gov/releases/h6/current/.

113. Federal Reserve Board, "Reserve Requirements," at http://www.federalreserve.gov/monetarypolicy/reservereq.htm and Federal Reserve Bank of New York, "Reserve Requirements," at http://www.federalreserve.gov/boarddocs/press/bcreg/2003/20031001/attachment.pdf.

114. Marion Williams, Governor, Central Bank of Barbados, "Foreign Exchange Reserves: How Much Is Enough?" delivered at the twentieth Adlith Brown Memorial Lecture at the Central Bank of the Bahamas, 2

November 2005, at
http://www.centralbank.org.bb/Publications/Adlith_Brown_Lec.pdf.
115. Kathryn M.E. Dominguez, "The European Central Bank, the Euro, and Global Financial Markets," *Journal of Economic Perspectives*, Volume 20, Number 4, Fall 2006, pages 67-68, at http://www-personal.umich.edu/~kathrynd/JEP.ECB%26Euro.Fall06pdf.pdf
116. Basil Moore, *Shaking the Invisible Hand: Complexity, Endogenous Money and Exogenous Interest Rates*. London, UK: Palgrave MacMillan, 2006, Chapter 19, p. 1 of chapter, at
http://us.macmillan.com/shakingtheinvisiblehand/BasilMoore
117. "Report to Congress on International Economic and Exchange Rate Policies, October, 2013," US Dept. of the Treasury, at
http://www.treasury.gov/resource-center/international/exchange-rate-policies/Pages/index.aspx.
118. Article 4 (Obligations Regarding Exchange Arrangements), Section 1 (General Obligations of Members), iii, of the Articles of Agreement, International Monetary Fund, as signed at Bretton Woods in 1944, at
http://www.imf.org/external/pubs/ft/aa/aa04.htm#1.
119. C. Fred Bergsten, "Our Chance to Slash the High Costs of Currency Manipulation," *Financial Times*, 16 December 2013, at
http://www.piie.com/publications/opeds/print.cfm?ResearchId=2535&doc=pub, which, in turn cited the article by Bergsten and Joseph Gagnon, "Currency Manipulation, and the Global Economic Order," Peterson Institute for International Economics, Policy Brief 12-25, December 2012, at http://www.piie.com/publications/interstitial.cfm?ResearchID=2302
120. Brian Blackstone and Todd Buell, "Europe Central Bank Ready for New Stimulus," *Wall Street Journal*, 6 February 2014, at
http://online.wsj.com/news/articles/SB10001424052702304680904579366481785544034
121. For discussion of the "impossible trinity," see Joshua Aizeman, "The Impossible Trinity – from the Policy Trilemma to the Policy Quadrilemma." March 2011 at
http://economics.ucsc.edu/research/downloads/quadrilemma-aizenman-11.pdf
122. Jeffrey A. Frankel and Andrew K. Rose, "An Estimate of the Effect of Currency Unions on Trade and Growth" in *Currency Unions*, Stanford, CA: edited by Alberto Alesina and Robert J. Barro, Hoover Institution Press, 2001, p. 32 at http://www.amazon.com/Currency-Unions-HOOVER-PRESS-PUBLICATION/dp/0817928421
123. Andrew K. Rose and Eric van Wincoop, "National Money as a Barrier to International Trade: The Real Case for Currency Union." Presented at American Economic Association Meeting on "Currency Unions" on 6 January 2001, at http://faculty.haas.berkeley.edu/arose/RvW.pdf.
124. Andrew Rose and T. D. Stanley, "A Meta-Analysis of the Effect of Common Currencies on International Trade," *Journal of Economic Surveys*, July 2005, p. 347, at http://faculty.haas.berkeley.edu/arose/MetaR.pdf.

125. Andrew K. Rose, "The effect of Common Currencies on International Trade: Where Do We Stand?" (draft), 7 August 2002, at http://faculty.haas.berkeley.edu/arose/MASOP02.pdf.

126. John F. Helliwell, and Lawrence l. Schembri, "Borders, Common Currencies, Trade and Welfare: What Can We Learn from the Evidence?" *Bank of Canada Review*, Spring 2005, pp 19-35, at http://www.bankofcanada.ca/wp-content/uploads/2010/06/helliwell.pdf.

127. Alejandro Micco, Guillermo Orgonez, and Ernesto Stein. "The EMU Effect on Trade: What's in it for the UK?" as Chapter 7 of *Prospects for Monetary Unions after the Euro*. Cambridge, MA: MIT Press, 2005, p. 4, Paul De Grauwe and Jacques Melitz, editors, and at http://www.eea-esem.com/papers/eea-esem/2003/2397/UK-EMU%20July14b.pdf.

128. Paul De Grauwe, *Economics of Monetary Union*. Oxford, UK: Oxford University Press, 2005, 6th edition, p. 28.

129. Jeffrey Frankel, "The Estimated Trade Effects of the Euro: Why Are They Below Those from Historical Monetary Unions among Smaller Countries?" pp. 169-212 in book, *Europe and the Euro*, National Bureau of Economic Research, at http://www.nber.org/chapters/c11658.pdf

130. Giordia Albertin, "Trade Effects of Currency Unions: Do Economic Dissimilarities Matter?" IMF Working Paper, WP 08/249, October 2008, at http://www.imf.org/external/pubs/ft/wp/2008/wp08249.pdf

131. "Thierry Warin, Phanindra Wunnava and Hubert Janicki, "Testing Mundell's Intuition of Engodenous OCA Theory IZA Discussion Paper 3739, September 2008, at http://ftp.iza.org/dp3739.pdf

132. Robert Mundell, "A Theory of Optimum Currency Areas," 1961, op. cit., p. 660.

133. "Money and Sovereignty--Money Talks, But What Does It Say?" Brochure from the IMF Center, Washington, DC, 2006.

134. For further information about euro coins, see the European Central Bank website at http://www.ecb.europa.eu/euro/coins/html/index.en.html.

135. Michael Emerson, Daniel Gros, Alexander Italiener, Jean Pisani-Ferry, Horst Reichenbach, *One Market, One Money--An Evaluation of the Potential Benefits and Costs of Forming an Economic and Monetary Union*. Oxford, UK: Oxford University Press, 1992, p. 11.

136. Robert Mundell, "The Case for a World Currency," 2005, op. cit., p. 467.

137. Charles Goodhart and D.J. Lee, "Adjustment Mechanisms in a Currency Area," Centre for Economic Policy Research, No. DP9226, November 2012, at http://www.cepr.org/pubs/dps/DP9226.asp

138. Philipp Engler, Giovanni Ganelli, Juha Tervala, and Simon Voigts, "Fiscal Devaluation in a Monetary Union," SFB 649 Discussion Paper 2014-011, at http://sfb649.wiwi.hu-berlin.de/papers/pdf/SFB649DP2014-011.pdf

139. Martin Feldstein, "Will the euro survive the current crisis?" *Daily Times*, Pakistan, 25 November 2008, at http://www.dailytimes.com.pk/default.asp?page=2008_percent5C11_percent5C25_percent5Cstory_25-11-2008_pg5_23

140. Martin Feldstein, "The Failure of the Euro – The Little Currency That Couldn't," *Foreign Affairs*, January/February, 2012, at http://www.foreignaffairs.com/articles/136752/martin-feldstein/the-failure-of-the-euro

141. Megan Greene, "Chapter 5: The Future of the Eurozone: An amicable divorce is better than an unhappy marriage," page 158, in *Currencies After the Crash*, edited by Sara Eisen, McGraw Hill, New York, 2013,

142. Robert Mundell, "A Theory of Optimum Currency Areas," 1961, op. cit., p. 660.

143. Ibid., p. 661.

144. Michael A. Kouparitsas, "Is the United States an Optimum Currency Area? An Empirical Analysis of Regional Business Cycles," December 2001, Federal Reserve Bank of Chicago, at http://ideas.repec.org/p/fip/fedhwp/wp-01-22.html

145. Barry Eichengreen, "Is Europe an Optimum Currency Area?" National Bureau of Economic Research, Working Paper W3579, January 1991, abstract at http://ssrn.com/abstract=226815. See also, Paul De Grauwe and Wim Vanhaverbeke, "Is Europe an Optimum Currency Area? Evidence from Regional Data," *International Macroeconomics*, May 1991, at http://ideas.repec.org/p/cpr/ceprdp/555.html, and Peter Bofinger, "Is Europe an Optimum Currency Area?" CEPR Discussion Paper 915, 1994 at http://ideas.repec.org/p/cpr/ceprdp/915.html. The question is so popular among students that essays are available for sale online with the subject, "Is Europe an Optimum Currency Area?" at http://www.essaysadepts.com/paper/Is-Europe-an-Optimum-Currency-Area-148661.html.

146. Hans N. E. Bystrom, Karin Olofsdotter, and Lars Soderstrom, "Is China an optimum currency area?" *Journal of Asian Economics*, August 2005, pp. 612-34, at http://www.sciencedirect.com/science/article/B6W53-4GMJ958-1/2/1b13be7ee1c23c16bc6a05ca6e9589bc.

147. Jack L. Carr and John E. Floyd, "Real and Monetary Shocks to the Canadian Dollar: Do Canada and the US Form an Optimal Currency Area?" Working Paper, University of Toronto #UT-ECIPA-Floyd-01-02, at http://ideas.repec.org/p/tor/tecipa/floyd-01-02.html.

148. Barry Eichengreen and Tamim Bayoumi, "Is Asia an Optimum Currency Area? Can It Become One? Regional, Global, and Historical Perspectives on Asian Monetary Relations," Center for International and Development Economics Research, University of California, 1996, at http://emlab.berkeley.edu/~eichengr/research/c96-81.pdf.

149. Beatrice K. Mkenda, "Is East Africa an Optimum Currency Area?" Working Papers in Economics, Goteborg University, Number 41, April 2001, at http://ideas.repec.org/p/hhs/gunwpe/0041.html

150. Cecile Couharde, Issiaka Coulibaly, David Guerreiro and Valerie Mignon, "Revisiting the theory of optimum currency areas: Is the CFA franc zone sustainable?" University of Paris, 2012, at http://economix.fr/pdf/dt/2012/WP_EcoX_2012-34.pdf

151. Jeffrey A. Frankel and Andrew K. Rose, "The Endogeneity of the Optimum Currency Area Criteria," National Bureau of Economic Research, Revised Draft, 25 September 1997, pp. 1-30, at http://faculty.haas.berkeley.edu/arose/ocaej.pdf.

152. Ibid., p. 22.

153. For a review of the "endogeneity" literature, see Paul DeGrauwe and Francesco Paolo Mongelli, "Endogeneities of Optimum Currency Areas-- What Brings Countries Sharing a Single Currency Together?" European Central Bank Working Paper No. 468, April 2005, at http://www.ecb.int/pub/pdf/scpwps/ecbwp468.pdf.

154. IMF Economic Forum "One World, One Currency: Destination or Delusion?" 8 November 2000, with Paul Masson, Robert Mundell, Maurice Obstfeld, and Alexander Swoboda. Transcript is at http://www.imf.org/external/np/tr/2000/tr001108.htm, and see *IMF Survey* article, "Economic Forum-Despite Trend Toward Fewer Currencies, a Single World Currency Seems Unlikely in Near Future," 11 December 2000, p. 391, at http://www.imf.org/external/pubs/ft/survey/2000/121100.pdf.

155. *IMF Survey*, ibid.

156. Michael Emerson, Daniel Gros, Alexander Italiener, Jean Pisani-Ferry, Horst Reichenbach, *One Market, One Money-An Evaluation of the Potential Benefits and Costs of Forming an Economic and Monetary Union.* Oxford, UK: Oxford University Press, 1992, p. 46.

157. Michael Emerson, ibid., p. 46.

158. Hubert P. Janicki, Thierry Warin, and Phanindra Wunnava, "Endogenous OCA Theory: Using the Gravity Model to Test Mundell's Intuition," 15 June 2005, Center for European Studies, Working Paper No. 125 at http://aei.pitt.edu/9032/.

159. "UK Membership of the Single Currency: An Assessment of the Five Economic Tests: EXECUTIVE SUMMARY," Her Majesty's Treasury, June 2003, at http://www.archive2.official-documents.co.uk/document/cm57/5776/5776-03.html.

160. Benjamin J. Cohen, *The Future of Money.* Princeton, NJ: Princeton University Press, 2004. It must be noted, that despite Professor Cohen's strong belief that the Single Global Currency is neither useful nor feasible, his correspondence with the Single Global Currency Association has been warm, respectful, and helpful.

161. Ibid., p. xiv.

162. Ibid., p. 1.

163. Ibid., p. 156.

164. George von Furstenberg, "A Case Against US Dollarization," *Challenge* 43, no. 4, July-August 2000, as cited by Cohen, *op.cit.*, p. 158, at http://www.jstor.org/discover/10.2307/40722023?uid=2129&uid=2&uid=70&uid=4&sid=21103460190047.

165. Benjamin J. Cohen, *The Future of Money*, op. cit., p. 158.

166. Benjamin J. Cohen, "The Future of the Euro: Let's Get Real," Review of International Political Economy, October 2012, as he quoted at a 2013 conference, "The Future of the Euro: Lessons from History," at

http://eurofuture2013.files.wordpress.com/2013/03/bcohen-talking-points.pdf

167. Mark Leonard, *Why Europe Will Run the 21st Century*. New York, NY: Public Affairs, 2005.

168. Matthew Lynn, "Want to Save the Euro? Bring Back 12 Currencies," Bloomberg.com, 27 February 2006, at http://quote.bloomberg.com/apps/news?pid=10000039&refer=columnist_lynn&sid=aPtIvYsjheK0

169. Thomas Paine, *Common Sense, Rights of Man, and other essential writings of Thomas Paine*. New York, NY: New American Library, 2003, p. 3, "Introduction."

170. George Provopoulos, "From Financial Crisis to Financial Stability: A European Odyssey," Speech at the Bank of Poland, 14 February 2014, at http://www.bis.org/review/r140224b.htm.

171. "The Breakup of the Euro Area," Barry Eichengreen, NBER Working Paper 13393, September 2007, at http://www.nber.org/papers/w13393.pdf

172. Lukanyo Mnyanda and Anchalee Worrachate, "Greek Yields Fall Below 7% as Crisis Source Regains Confidence," Bloomberg Businessweek, 28 February 2014, at http://www.businessweek.com/news/2014-02-28/greek-10-year-bond-yields-fall-below-7-percent-amid-euro-debt-optimism

173. Article 49 of the Consolidated Version of the Treaty on European Union, at http://eur-lex.europa.eu/LexUriServ/LexUriServ.do?uri=OJ:C:2010:083:0013:0046:en:PDF

174. George M. von Furstenberg, "Should Small Countries Join an Existing Monetary Union?" *Journal of Economic Integration*, March 2002, pp. 104-32, at http://papers.ssrn.com/sol3/papers.cfm?abstract_id=472262.

175. Edmund Conway, "UK Policy Blamed for Soaring Debt Levels," *Business Telegraph*, 20 February 2006, at http://www.telegraph.co.uk/finance/2932605/UK-policy-blamed-for-soaring-debt-levels.html

176. Ronald McKinnon, "Optimum Currency Areas and the European Experience," October 2001, at http://www.stanford.edu/~mckinnon/papers/optimumreveur.pdf.

177. "The Commission presents a blueprint for a deep and genuine economic and monetary union," Press Announcement, 28 November 2012, at http://ec.europa.eu/commission_2010-2014/president/news/archives/2012/11/20121128_2_en.htm

Chapter 5. The Single Global Currency: Origin, Benefits and Costs

What is meant by a Single Global Currency? The easiest way to answer is to present the typical responses of people to whom the idea is presented. Many ask, "Do you mean - like the euro?" Yes, indeed. Like the euro, except that it's for the entire world. Our definition of a Single Global Currency is:

> A common currency, managed by a Global Central Bank within a Global Monetary Union, that people can use within member countries as legal tender and for international transactions.

In short: A euro-like currency for the world.

This doesn't necessarily mean that the Single Global Currency must be the only currency in the countries that utilize it. There can be others, too, whether national or local, alternate currencies, but the common cents/sense, inherently simple, goal is for one global currency. Almost all of the economic analysis below assumes that "single" equals "one."

Some people would say that the US dollar already functions as a global currency, but it is proprietary to the United States which, so far, has shown no inclination to share governance of its currency. The US dollar is not considered legal tender except in the US and dollarized countries. People cannot, for example, pay their taxes in Egypt with US dollars.

When the world eventually commits itself to a Single Global Currency, more precise criteria will be established to determine when the goal is reached. It might be when the currency is used as legal tender by countries with a specified percentage of the people of the world, or in countries with a percentage of the world GDP. Fifty-one percent would work in both instances, but it could also be forty percent. Another measure might be when a common currency is involved in a specified percentage of foreign exchange trades, or when the total volume of trading declines to a specified percentage of its current $5.3 trillion daily. On the other hand, and paraphrasing the late US Supreme Court Justice Potter Stewart, perhaps we will know it when we see it,[1] as for example, when a future international monetary conference creates a 3-G world, with a Global Central Bank and a Global Monetary Union and a Single Global Currency.

The Origin of the Idea: John Stuart Mill

There is a fine line between the idea of a regional monetary union and a Global Monetary Union. It's the difference between "all" and "some." It's the difference between a one-, two-, or three-wheeled vehicle and a four-wheeled vehicle. The implicit origin of the idea of a Global Monetary Union can be said to have been John Stuart Mill's observation in 1848, "Let us suppose that all countries had the same currency, as in the progress of political improvement they one day will have...." He went on to say, "So much of barbarism still remains in the transactions of the most civilized nations that almost all independent countries choose to assert their

113

nationality by having, to their own inconvenience and that of their neighbours, a peculiar currency of their own."[2]

Of Mill and Walter Bagehot, an early editor of *The Economist* magazine, Robert Mundell wrote in 2005, "...they wanted to go further and fine-tune the system to eliminate or reduce unnecessary information and transaction costs associated with international trade. This concern, which was shared by Bagehot and other far-sighted economists, derived from the common sense of saving on information and transactions costs, before the development of erudite mathematical models of information theory."[3]

These statements were not idle observations by the versatile Mill who had also written about feminism, slavery, and other subjects. The comments came in Chapter XX, "Of the Foreign Exchanges," of Book III, "Exchange," of his five-book 1848 volume, *Principles of Political Economy*. Other chapters in Book III have titles showing considerable thought about economics and money: "Of Value," "Of Money," "Of the Value of Money as Dependent on Demand and Supply," "Of International Trade," and "Of Money, Considered as an Imported Commodity."[4]

In sum, while most ideas have many sources, John Stuart Mill's role in the origin of the idea of a modern Single Global Currency seems substantial, as he used common cents/sense in 1848.

Over the next century there were several International Monetary Conferences, beginning with the 1867 Conference in Paris. Although termed "international," its primary focus was Europe, and proponents tried to achieve a larger monetary union than the existing Latin Monetary Union. The United States participated and even minted samples of appropriate coins, including a 5 dollar/25 franc coin, but the differences in metallic content among the coins of the participating countries contributed to the failure of the idea.[5] There was no significant participation from non-Western countries.

Much of the discussion centered about mutually acceptable coinage and standardizing the values of currency, gold, and silver. Robert Mundell observed that the goals of the Paris conference were thwarted primarily by the United Kingdom which was then the world's financial superpower.[6] Part of the lesson here is that the country at the top of the world financial system gets benefits from that status, and is usually reluctant to be dislodged, especially by another country.

In 1930, the Bank for International Settlements was established and "is the world's oldest international financial institution and remains the principal centre for international central bank cooperation."[7] In the succeeding years, the bank has fulfilled several temporary roles such as the development of the Basel Capital Accords in 1988, and acting as "agent" for the European Exchange Rate System (ERM) immediately prior to the establishment of the euro and the European Central Bank.

The first explicit proposal for a proto-global currency came at the 1944 Bretton Woods international monetary conference, with John Maynard Keynes' proposal for a new global currency clearing system, to be called the "Bancor." The US proposal for a world currency was developed primarily by Harry Dexter White of the US Treasury, and given the name, "Unitas."[8] It was withdrawn before the conference, perhaps, as suggested by Robert Mundell, because of the upcoming 1944 elections. The US reluctance, as the reigning financial superpower, to relinquish that position, even to a non-national world currency, fit the earlier-noted pattern established by the United Kingdom in the nineteenth century. Although the conference ultimately established the US dollar as the pre-eminent national currency, and fixed its value to gold at $35.00 per troy ounce, a kernel of the Bancor proposal was resurrected with the establishment of Special Drawing Rights (SDRs) in 1969, as administered by the International Monetary Fund. "Originally intended within the IMF as a sort of international money for use among central banks pegging their exchange rates, the SDR is a transferable right to acquire another country's currency. Defined in terms of a basket of currencies, today it functions as a unit of international account."[9] The basket originally consisted of more than ten currencies, but has been reduced to only four, thanks to the consolidation of currencies in the European Monetary Union. The four are the US dollar, euro, UK pound, and yen.[10] Each IMF member is allocated amounts of SDRs which can be used to acquire other members' currencies to restore balances of payments. For example, the IMF loaned SDRs to Argentina during its currency crises of 1997-99 and thereafter. Those SDR loans were repaid in full by January 3, 2006.[11] Someday, the four currencies in the basket will be collapsed into one, the Single Global Currency, and SDRs will disappear.

In addition to solving the exchange rate problem, the Bretton Woods conference also permitted, if not encouraged, the use by member nations of capital controls, again at the behest of John Maynard Keynes. He viewed the flow of international capital in support of trade and commerce as essential, but deplored the free movement of speculative funds as "the major cause of instability.... Nothing is more certain than that the movement of capital funds must be regulated."[12] The use of capital controls subsequently diminished as part of the general opening of international trade and commerce. The elimination of capital controls was considered to be part of the economic prescription in the 1980s called "the Washington Consensus."[13]

Robert Mundell briefly touched on the idea of a world currency in "A Theory of Optimum Currency Areas" when he wrote, "The 'optimum' currency area is not the world. Optimality is here defined in terms of the ability to stabilize national employment and price levels."[14] However, in the same article he noted that when considering that the role of money is to make transactions more convenient, "Money is a convenience and this restricts the optimum number of currencies. In terms of this argument alone, the optimum currency area is the world, regardless of the number of regions of which it is composed."[15]

Thus, in 1961 the verdict was mixed on whether the world could be considered an optimum currency area, at least according to the criteria stated in that innovative article. However, as has been noted by many, Europe did not satisfy all the criteria either, at least not before the establishment of the euro.[16]

In 1968 Mundell presented his "Plan for a World Currency" to the Joint Economic Committee of the US Congress.[17] He wrote, "It is clear in what direction we need to move. We need to construct, out of all the assets currently used by the monetary authorities, a new world currency," and then he quoted a former central banker of the Bank of France, Charles Rist, who wrote in 1952, "What international commerce needs is a common and unquestioned money to which all the international prices can be pegged."[18] Rist's belief that the backing should be gold does not detract from the point of the statement. The world currency would be open to any country in the world, although Mundell clarified that its success would depend upon adoption by the large economic powers, who would contribute assets into a monetary fund, like a world central bank.[19]

Mundell was not alone in his vision for a new world financial architecture. Retired US Federal Reserve Chair William McChesney Martin recommended a "strong world central bank" in his 1970 book, *Toward a World Central Bank?*[20]

In 1972, Nobel Prize Winner James Tobin proposed an international tax to reduce the increasingly worrisome cross-currency capital flows, with the observation that the tax was the second best alternative after a Single Global Currency which he viewed as infeasible for several decades. Nonetheless, he continued to believe it to be the best solution, and guardedly repeated the suggestion in 1998 at a World Bank "Conference on Developmental Economics."[21] Note that the daily volume of foreign exchange trading in the 1970s was less than $100 billion, or only 1.9 percent of the $5.3 trillion volume in 2013.

In 1979, *The New York Times* first used the phrase, "Single Global Currency," in the sense used here, in a column by Robert Magnuson. He noted that Charles Kindleberger had urged economists to

"become more 'artistic' than technical if they are to solve the world's monetary woes. On the other hand, artistic solutions often tend to be unrealistic. They envision the evolution of a monetary system with a Single Global Currency and overseen by a world bank."[22]

The previous use of the phrase by *The New York Times* was to describe the US dollar, in a 20 November 1967 article by Edwin Dale about the devaluation of the pound.[23]

In 1981, Charles Kindleberger published his book, *International Money: A collection of essays*, in which he wrote,

"...start with the best and worst of international monetary systems. The first-best, in my judgment, is a world money with a world monetary authority. The authorities should be charged with regulating the world money supply so as to maintain its value stable, or perhaps declining very slightly each year to stimulate employment."[24]

In 1984, Richard Cooper of Harvard wrote "A Monetary System for the Future," which was considered by many as a clarion call for a Single Global Currency. He wrote, "I suggest a radical alternative scheme for the next century: the creation of a common currency for all of the industrial democracies, with a common monetary policy and a joint Bank of Issue to determine that monetary policy." The term "industrial democracies" is viewed by Cooper as being restrictive.[25] However, as illustrated by the success of the Eastern Caribbean Monetary Union and others, monetary unions can be useful to all peoples and nations, regardless of the level of their economic development.

In his 1987 book, *The Alchemy of Finance*, George Soros called for the creation of a Single Global Currency, together with an international central bank.[26] Even by that time, he was one of the best known currency speculators in the world, so his recommendation might have been considered ironic, but who would better understand the failings of a system than someone who has mastered its intricacies? Subsequently, he is understood to have earned over $1 billion by betting that the United Kingdom's pound sterling would be pounded down from its pegged position in 1992, and it was.

Soros is not the only currency speculator to understand what is needed for world financial stability. Andrew Krieger, a currency trader, wrote in 1992 in *The Money Bazaar*, "Ever since John Maynard Keynes' finest hour at Bretton Woods, there have been strong advocates of a single world currency. In fact, at this point it is a concept with so many benefits that it requires little advocacy."[27]

In 1988, *The Economist* published a cover story, "Get Ready for a World Currency," which it called the "Phoenix." The article begins,

> "THIRTY years from now, Americans, Japanese, Europeans, and people in many other rich countries, and some relatively poor ones, will probably be paying for their shopping with the same currency. Prices will be quoted not in dollars, yen, or D-marks but in, let's say, the phoenix. The phoenix will be favoured by companies and shoppers because it will be more convenient than today's national currencies, which by then will seem a quaint cause of much disruption to economic life in the late twentieth century."[28]

Ten years later, in 1998, *The Economist* followed up with "One World, One Money," which presented the option of a "global currency union," four months before the 1999 introduction of the euro on the books of the Eurozone's financial institutions. The article concluded, "Fine, you say, but how would the world ever get from here to there?"[29] (See Chapter 6).

In 2000, Robert Mundell participated in a panel discussion at the International Monetary Fund, "One World, One Currency: Destination or Delusion," where he said, "But I don't know anyone who has actually advocated a single currency for the world," and " 'One World, One Currency' could exist in a dictatorship or a world empire, but I couldn't imagine a world democracy with a single currency. I couldn't imagine that system."[30] It appears, however, that he was addressing the question of whether a Single Global Currency was required to be the *only* currency around the world and the answer is no. Also, he seems to have believed that a Single

Global Currency required a higher degree of world government than is necessary. A monetary union requires only an agreement among peoples or nations to vest responsibility for the issuance and stability of their money in a non-national entity, usually a central bank. Other governmental agreements may be helpful, but are not required, as can be seen with the range of integration among current monetary unions.

As could have happened with the euro, which was considered at one point to be utilized in parallel to the retained national currencies, it may be that nations or cities or corporations want to issue or retain their own currencies in parallel with the Single Global Currency, and that will be up to the issuers. Panama uses two currencies: the US dollar and the Panamanian balboa. During the 1999-2002 implementation of the euro, it was used in parallel to the legacy currencies. Bank statements were issued to customers in both currencies, and customers could write checks and make other payments in euros, but not with cash. Perhaps that experience with parallel currencies strengthened the resolve to discard the legacy currencies upon the issuance of cash in January 2002. Barry Eichengreen recommended in 2006 a parallel currency approach for Asia, with an AMU (Asian Currency Unit) which would be similar to Europe's pre-euro ECU.[31]

Cramped by the pre-euro views of the inviolability of the sovereignty value of money, Mundell didn't believe many countries would willingly abdicate their monetary control.

Mundell fine-tuned his expectations by saying that what he was really hoping for was "one world, one currency area" with a system of fixed exchange rates, beginning with the G-3: the United States, United Kingdom, and Japan.[32]

At a 2001 OECD conference in Luxembourg, Charles Goldfinger gave a name to a prospective "Single Global Currency," the "geo," calling it "a logical consequence of a broad globalisation trend, a monetary translation of deepening economic integration." He continued, "...over the next ten to twenty years, the question of a global currency is more than likely to return to the top of the public policy agenda."[33]

Also in 2001, Mundell, then widely recognized as the 1999 Nobel Prize laureate for his work on exchange rates and common currencies, returned to the IMF to give a lecture, "The International Monetary System: Quo Vadis?"[34] and renewed the call for G-3 monetary union, saying that such a monetary union would set the stage for the implementation of a Single Global Currency. The *IMF Survey* article reported,

> "Such an IMF currency would need a new name, he said, 'because who wants a currency called *special drawing rights*.'[?] The currency would be perfectly convertible into the currencies of the group of three, and the IMF Board of Governors could then designate the group of three area as the agent for managing the world currency. The establishment of a world currency along the lines of the original 1944 proposals would insulate it from the criticism that the IMF was being transformed into a central bank, he said, or that the world currency would

be 'run by a bunch of international bureaucrats.' A world with a single currency, he said, 'would be a tremendous inducement to trade and to a great opening up of trade. It would make for transparency. There'd be no currency crises in the world, by definition. There'd also be no hedge funds to make $20-30 trillion on derivatives now floating around the world--hedge funds trying to overcome the inefficiency that's created by this absurd currency system.' "[35]

Mundell's term for this G-3 currency is the "dey" for dollar-euro-yen, and his term for the world currency would be "intor," with "int" for international, and "or" for the word for gold in French.[36]

Globalization and the Single Global Currency

The term "globalization" means many things to many people. To supporters of the trend, it may mean greater international trade with the rising tide of international prosperity lifting all boats. To opponents, it may mean the destruction of local customs and natural resources without just compensation.

The flip side of globalization is the reduced role of national governments and national economies in the lives of its citizens. Stephan Schulmeister made the point in 2000 in "Globalization without Global Money," that it was an anomaly for globalization to accelerate while the global monetary system was glued to national monies.[37] Despite the growth of monetary unions, they provide only four of the world's 140 currencies and provide money to only 44 of the UN's 193 members. Thus, Schulmeister's characterization remains correct: that national currencies are still the anomalous norm in an increasingly globalized world.

The Single Global Currency is obviously a part of globalization, but will play a nominally neutral role in the struggle to promote equality and fair utilization of the world's resources. The SGC is part of what can be called "good globalization" and should be included with other global standardizations, such as the metric system, the calendar and the internet, each of which has had different side effects on the world.

Perhaps a Single Global Currency could be considered the eleventh "flattener" by Thomas Friedman in subsequent editions of his book, *The World is Flat*. In his flattened world, people everywhere have a chance to compete in the international marketplace. Paul Volcker's article in 2000, "Toward a Single World Currency to Level the Playing Field," can be considered an endorsement of such an additional flattener or leveler.[38]

Benefits and Costs of the Global Monetary Union/Single Global Currency--Benefits

The overall benefit of the Single Global Currency will be to promote international financial stability, the essential basis of commerce and economic growth. All of the foreign exchange systems which have been developed since approximately 276 B.C. have failed in this essential goal. In fact, some exchange rate regimes have rendered the international financial system less stable. As noted earlier, Robert Mundell has labeled it, "an absurd currency system."[39]

In the lists below of benefits and costs, there are close similarities to the benefits and costs of monetary unions, as listed in Chapter 4. As Ramkishen Rajan wrote in 2000, "...the conceptual framework with which the costs and benefits of the EMU have been discussed would be just as pertinent in analyzing the feasibility of an AMU [Asian monetary union], or even Global Monetary Union."[40] However, there is a quantum leap from a world of several monetary unions, which still must relate to each other in the existing multicurrency foreign exchange system, to a world with one Global Monetary Union.

For some benefits, it's the leap from "reduce" to "eliminate." For others, it's more complicated.

The analysis of benefits and costs is about the utility of the Single Global Currency and not its political feasibility which is covered in Chapter 7.

1. Eliminate the Costs of Foreign Exchange Transactions

It was estimated earlier in this book that the annual cost of the multicurrency foreign exchange system is $300 billion, and that some saved reduction of that cost will come to every country which joins a monetary union. However, each such reduction still leaves the large overhead infrastructure in place in banks, corporations, and international organizations. Upon the implementation of a Single Global Currency, and the gradual disappearance of the foreign exchange market, the infrastructure can be dismantled and utilized for other purposes. It's the difference between seeing several foreign exchange booths at airports with many employees, then seeing fewer and fewer upon the implementation of several monetary unions, and then seeing none.

Included in the $300 billion are the barely quantifiable costs of writing and utilizing all the contract provisions for hedging and for denominating a currency for payment, and the legal time spent in preparing and negotiating such contracts.

2. Increase the Value of the World's Assets by $10 Trillion, and Trigger Additional $3 Trillion GDP activity.

The phenomenon explored by John Edmunds and John Marthinsen, and described in the previous chapter--an increase in asset values caused by the reduction of currency risk through the formation of a monetary union-- would continue with the implementation of the Global Monetary Union. The amount of the increase will be approximately inversely proportional to the level of previous currency risk. The one-time increase in global asset values will occur most dramatically in those remaining countries where there is significant currency risk and/or high inflation, such as in Africa and South America.

The total worldwide increase in financial asset values, attributable to the elimination of currency risk due to the adoption of the Single Global Currency, was estimated in Chapter 1 to be $10 trillion, with an estimated currency risk of 4.6 percent. Looking at the effect of a Single Global Currency from another direction, the IMF reported in 2005 that the ratio of financial assets to GDP was approximately 3.5 for the whole world and 4.0 for the developed world.[41] With the elimination of worldwide currency risk, the world's 3.5 asset/GDP multiple will move closer to the 4.0 asset/GDP multiple in the developed world. Applying an estimated 3.7 multiple (midway between 3.5 and 4.0) to the world's financial assets in 2013 of $225 trillion to GDP would bring the value of financial assets to $235 trillion, an increase of $10 trillion.

Using the same multiplier in reverse, the increased annual GDP activity to be expected from the $10 trillion increase in asset values is approximately $3 trillion. Subsequently, annual percentage increases in GDP, using an estimate of three percent, will bring continued benefits from that one-time increase in asset values, and GDP at the initial rate of three percent. Without compounding that annual GDP increase arising from the one-time increase in asset values of $3 trillion would be estimated

Such amounts of money boggle the mind, and readers are invited to do further research and calculations. What is a better estimate of the one-time gain and further annual GDP gains to come from the lowering of inflation and the elimination of currency risk, worldwide?

3. Eliminate the Need to Maintain Foreign Exchange Reserves

With no need to defend an exchange rate and no need to thwart an externally sourced currency crisis and no need to defend against speculators, there would be no need for the Global Central Bank to maintain foreign exchange reserves. By definition, in a 3-G world there will cease to be international reserves, as there would be no substantial international currency exchange. In 1999, US Federal Reserve Chair Alan Greenspan made a similar observation, saying, "One way to address the issue of the management of foreign exchange reserves is to start with an economic system in which no reserves are required. There are two. The first is the obvious case of a single world currency."[42]

In 1992 the European Commission estimated that by joining together, the future Eurozone members might be able to reduce their total international reserves by one-half or $200 billion.[43]

When developing countries acquire foreign exchange reserves in the form of low-interest bearing bonds from other countries, they often have to borrow at higher interest rates to finance such borrowing. Professor Dani Rodrik estimated in 2006 that such a cost could amount to one percent of GDP of such countries.[44] That's a substantial cost, and it will be eliminated upon the adoption of a Single Global Currency by such countries. For example, one percent of Angola's $84.4 billion GDP[45] is $844 million, which is more than four times the $200 million foreign aid received by Angola in 2011.[46] In a 3-G world without the need for foreign exchange reserves, such costs no longer will be borne by developing countries.

With the elimination of foreign exchange reserves would go also all the analyses by economists of such reserves, and all the reporting and tracking of the values of those reserves and their composition.[47] This is another reason to discard the fifth wheel.

However, to the extent that some international currencies will remain in use alongside the Single Global Currency, some foreign exchange reserves would be needed by the countries still using their own currency, perhaps as a second currency. Even facing such an option might encourage some planners to reconsider the need for those extra currencies and seek to remove them, for the same reasons that the legacy currencies in the Eurozone were removed.

The Global Central Bank would still maintain domestic reserves of units of the Single Global Currency to protect banking liquidity, as would the central bank of any currency area.

When the conversion is made to a Single Global Currency, decision makers would need to develop a plan of how to deal with the existing reserves of international currency, including the gold in the vaults. At the end of September, 2013 the central banks of the world had international reserves worth $11.4 trillion which includes "foreign banknotes, bank deposits, treasury bill, short and long-term government securities" but not gold.[48]

A major question for the establishment of the Global Central Bank will be the future role for gold, whether as money or as a reserve commodity or simply as a prized metal.[49] Its use will be a political question, rather than economic, and gold has many vocal advocates.[50]

4. Eliminate the Risks of Excessive Capital Flows Among Currencies and Countries

Kavaljit Singh argues in *Taming Global Financial Flows-A Citizen's Guide* that "it is increasingly being accepted that capital controls are necessary and desirable."[51] However, in that book he didn't consider the large benefits and small costs of a Single Global Currency as the preferred method of coping with capital flows, compared to the small benefits and large costs of capital controls.

In a 3-G world, there will be no need for capital controls among nations, just as there is no need for capital controls among members of monetary unions, except during financial crises. Such controls were applied in Cyprus in 2013, but were expected to be lifted in early 2014.[52]

5. Reduce the Cost of Operating an Entirely Separate Monetary System

Thanks to economies of scale, it costs less per capita to administer foreign exchange monetary policy for a monetary union than for its individual country members, and the economies of scale increase as the monetary union expands. As the number of currencies decreases, the cost of administering the multicurrency foreign exchange system also will decrease until it reaches the logical end point of zero--with a fully implemented Single Global Currency.

6. Eliminate the Balance of Payments/Current Account Problem for Every Country or Monetary Union

The balance of payments is the sword of Damocles[53] hanging over every central bank because a lingering current account imbalance threatens a lowering of the value of a currency, and even possibly a currency crisis. Rodrigo de Rato, formerly the Managing Director of the IMF, 2004-2007, made the point that current account imbalances are not only a problem for the United States and China. He said, "Many countries need to share the burden of reducing global imbalances and sustaining growth. Furthermore, since these imbalances will eventually be corrected, one way or another, it is worth bearing in mind that a disorderly adjustment of global imbalances would harm all countries."[54] Conversely, an orderly adjustment or transition to a Single Global Currency will help all countries.

Regarding balances of trade, there still will be some concern in a 3-G world about whether countries are frequent net importers of goods and services, as that imbalance may lead to a general decline in a country's overall wealth. No one in net exporting countries will worry. However, even for the trade deficit countries, citizens can find some security that such imbalances will not lead to devaluation of the currency, or to a currency crisis.

There will continue to be concerns about the quality of trade and such issues as whether a country is exporting raw materials and importing high technology products, or the reverse. In any case, the balance of payments aspect of such considerations will disappear for countries participating in the Global Monetary Union. A trade deficit is not a serious problem unless there is foreign exchange involved and thus becomes a currency problem. As Benn Steil and Robert Litan wryly observed, "It's the Currency, Stupid,"[55] paraphrasing the political mantra of the political campaigns for US President Bill Clinton in 1992 and 1996, "It's the economy, stupid."[56]

7. Separate the Value of Money from the Value of a Particular Country

Since the establishment of modern states, their citizens have struggled to determine what functions ought to be performed by directly elected government bodies and what functions by semi-public and private organizations. Laws are created by elected officials, but they are enforced by judges who are usually appointed. Airports are often run by appointed authorities. Local banks are typically owned by their shareholders.

The concept of the state controlling the peoples' money[57] is relatively new, as currencies previously were issued by private banks or other organizations.

Increasingly, and fortunately, central banks have become more independent of their respective governments, so they are not perceived as being appendages of those governments. The movement of the responsibility for money away from national central banks and toward monetary union central banks represents a further shift. Even in those countries with independent national central banks, they are still perceived as being part of the governments, due to the numerous links between them. In the United States, the seven members of the Board of Governors of the Federal Reserve are all appointed by the President, and then confirmed by the Senate. Another indication of the close relationship of the central bank to the US Government is the multi-billion dollar Exchange Stabilization Fund (ESF) which is managed by the US Treasury to intervene in the foreign exchange markets to support the US dollar or support currency stabilization efforts by other countries.[58] The Federal Reserve Board also intervenes in the foreign exchange markets.

Having one country manage what is widely accepted as the world's primary currency, the US dollar is the ultimate example of what can go wrong when such a primary currency is run by one country. In order to pull the US out of the Great Recession, the US Federal Reserve launched in 2008 the purchases of vast amounts of financial assets in order to depress interest rates in order to stimulate borrowing and investment. The world adjusted its interest and exchange rates accordingly. However, when the Fed began to taper off its purchasing in late 2013, which had accumulated to a total of $3+ trillion,[59] and US interest rates began to rise, or were expected to rise, several "emerging market" countries were exposed to runs on their currency, including Turkey and India.[60] These capital movements occurred because money moves to places where it can earn higher and safe returns. Nobel Laureate Paul Krugman wrote in 2011, "...it's not the business of the Fed to save other countries from the necessity of making choices."[61] In other words, the USD is a national currency first, and global currency second.

The failure of the US Federal Reserve and the United States government in general to manage the US dollar for the benefit of the world is especially galling when considering that it was the fiscal and monetary recklessness of the US that caused the 2007-2009 global financial crisis and "Great Recession." The US government watched the abuses of Lehman Brothers and similar investment companies, and their large international role, and then allowed Lehman Brothers to go bankrupt with substantial disruption to the global financial system.

It is not enough for US defenders to say that such financial crises are the price that we pay for a free enterprise system. Canada has a free enterprise system, and it has a similar North American 19th century western expansion story, but it doesn't have the history of bank failures, for example, as in the US. During the Great Depression of the 1930's the US had approximately 9,000 bank failures, and Canada had zero. In the Savings and Loan debacle in the US in the 1970s and 80s, the US had 3,000 bank failures and Canada had two. The US saw no need to change substantially its system and when the 2007-2009 financial crisis came, there were another 196 bank failures in the US and none in Canada.[62] A country with the responsibility for the world's dominant currency should be more concerned about the health of its banks and national financial stability.

Governments come and go, as does the confidence held in those governments. Governments are responsible for fiscal policy, and they assess taxes and spend funds on education, defense, and health care. Sometimes their budgets are balanced and sometimes they are not. Sometimes those countries are hit by natural disasters or their boundaries change. Such volatility is not appropriate for the valuation of the peoples' money, just as it should not affect the length of a meter or the weight of a gram or the temperature of a degree centigrade.

Moving responsibility for the value of money to a regional monetary union achieves some separation from national governments, and the logical end of that movement is to the Global Monetary Union, the primary goal of which will be to manage stable money for the people of the world.

8. Eliminate National Currency Crises for Member Countries of the Global Monetary Union

A currency crisis occurs when holders of a currency, or securities or contracts denominated in a currency, move their money away from that currency to refuge in another currency. With a Single Global Currency, there would be no realistic "other currency."

While there has been considerable debate about the precise causes of the currency crises of the 1990s, two general causes emerge: expectations and currency mismatches. Kenneth Kasa wrote, "a consensus has emerged that expectations are at the heart of the matter."[63] Some economists look at expectations about monetary and fiscal policies and others at what is happening in the overall economy, but the overall expectation is that a currency crisis is a possibility in every existing currency in the multicurrency foreign exchange system. In a Single Global Currency world, such a crisis will not be the expectation.

Benn Steil and Robert Litan noted that a currency mismatch is at the root of every recent currency crisis, and they arise in part because 97 percent of all securities sold in the international markets are denominated in only five currencies: US dollar, euro, yen, UK pound, and Swiss franc. When the securities of those five currency areas are excluded, the percentage is still a high 85 percent.[64] A typical currency mismatch might occur as in Russia in 1998, where large loans were denominated in dollars and payment became difficult when the ruble lost value. There were insufficient dollar reserves in the central bank to repay all the loans denominated in dollars, and then panic selling of the ruble occurred. With a Single Global Currency, there can be no currency mismatch because there would be no other large currency, and loans will be denominated in the Single Global Currency.

One outcome of currency crises, and even for those facing the risk of currency crises, is that people with the ability to send money or wealth out of the country at risk will do so. The middle class and the poor do not have that option, and will suffer the consequences of that risk. While there still will be other types of risk in member countries of a Global Monetary Union, currency risk will no longer be a factor to consider. This change will hopefully contribute to keeping funds in developing countries at home where they can be invested, rather than being sent to Geneva, London, Miami, or Singapore.

While it's possible for confidence to decline in a global currency if it's mismanaged, it would not occur for the reasons we currently attribute to the causes of recent international currency crises, i.e., because speculators and others are converting vast amounts of the Single Global Currency into other currencies. By definition, there would be no other currency which could absorb such transfers. Also, what would such a decline in confidence mean in a Global Monetary Union? Every member country government would be accepting, and usually requiring, the Single Global Currency as the means of payment of taxes and other debts. Thus, the effect of declining confidence might translate into inflationary expectations where prices would be raised through fear that a currency would be less valuable. Nonetheless, there would be no currency crisis.

9. Eliminate the Possibility of Currency Exchange Rate Manipulation and Intervention by Countries

A significant source of tension among countries has been the concern that other countries manipulate the exchange rates of their currencies to their own advantage by buying and selling massive amounts of currency in the foreign exchange markets. Curiously, this concern always has seemed to mean that a country would intervene to devalue its currency rather than revalue; but this is something that economists will no longer need to study upon the adoption of a Single Global Currency.

Despite its record-setting trade and budget deficits, the US government continues to point fingers at others, particularly China, for such currency manipulation.

Not all agree that China has been manipulating its currency by pegging it constantly for about ten years to the US dollar. Junning Cai argues that countries that intentionally do not prudently manage their current account balances are guilty of trade manipulation, which is just as serious as direct currency manipulation.[65]

While acknowledging the responsibility of the United States for most of the world's financial imbalances, a former US Treasury Under-Secretary for International Affairs, Tim Adams, viewed the exchange rate as a major means to the end of eliminating those imbalances. He urged the IMF in 2006 to strengthen its surveillance of exchange rates to ensure that the "right" exchange rate equilibrium is reached.[66]

However, such a "right" exchange rate, like "manipulation," and art can only exist in the eyes of the beholder, since there will never be an acceptable objective validation of exchange rates in the multicurrency foreign exchange world. Even if the United States were more successful in jawboning China to increase the exchange rate of the yuan to the US dollar, it's not clear that such a strategy will be in China's or the US's interest. Ronald McKinnon writes that the overvaluation of the yen in the 1990s, resulting from US pressure, contributed to the destablization of the Japanese financial system and subsequent economic problems though the 2000s.[67]

A large example of central bank intervention was by the central bank of Japan in the years 2003-04 when it sold trillions of yen, and purchased billions of US dollars in order to keep the value of the yen down against the dollar. On thirty-four trading days in the first six months of 2003, the Bank of Japan sold about 9 trillion yen and purchased about $75 billion, but the yen still rose in value.[68] A more successful and continuing intervention began in early 2013 when a US dollar would purchase about 92 yen. In April 2013, the Bank of Japan began a $630 billion intervention which has decreased the value of the yen about 10 percent, to 102 yen to the USD in early February 2014.[69]

10. Eliminate the Fluctuations of Currency Values

It is a truism that stability is a cornerstone of a sound, worldwide financial system. While the necessary partner to investment is risk, it is safe to say that investors seek to minimize risk for the respective gain sought. Currency fluctuations are risky. No one wants to work hard for a year and hope for a return on an investment of work or money and find that currency fluctuation eliminated the return, or, worse, created a loss.

With a Single Global Currency, there will be no currency fluctuations, without regard to the fundamentals of that currency, i.e., what it could actually purchase. Such fluctuations in values make uncertain the decisions of billions of people who trade their goods and services every day. There will be no such fluctuations with a Single Global Currency.

11. Eliminate Currency Speculation

The value of money should not be subject to the needs and greed of speculators. There are no speculators in the future length of a meter or the weight of a gram and there should be none for currencies. However, the way to eliminate speculation is not to ban it, but to eliminate the basis for its existence. Banning opportunities to make money, such as prohibiting the sale of alcohol in the US from 1920-1933, are usually doomed and they can have unwanted unintended consequences such as an increase in crime.

To eliminate illicit gambling, many governments have established legal opportunities for wagering, such as lotteries and bingo, and most people who choose to gamble can do so legally and safely. The Single Global Currency will present a different choice for speculators: if they wish to speculate, they will need to choose another commodity, as the peoples' money will no longer be for sale. It will no longer rise or fall in value as now happens with each currency for mysterious reasons in the world's current multicurrency system.

12. Reduce Worldwide Inflation, Thereby Ensuring Low, Reasonable and Stable Interest Rates

Thanks to better techniques of central banks' management of money, including the more widely used strategy of "inflation targeting," worldwide inflation has declined over the past several years.

With a Single Global Currency, and no need to modify interest rates in order to cope with an outflow of money due to an unfavorable exchange rate, interest rates are likely to be even more stable and lower within a Global Monetary Union.

The European Central Bank has made stable prices a major--and public--goal and has kept its interest rates low and stable. Whether such interest rate stability is an inherent aspect of a large monetary union or whether for other reasons, the euro's stability has been impressive. As noted in Chapter 4, inflation that is too far below a target rate may lead to harmful deflation.

13. Increase Trade

In the previous chapter of this book, the positive effects of monetary union on trade were discussed. In a Global Monetary Union, the effect would be continued. As Robert Mundell has written,

> "The benefits from a world currency would be enormous. Prices all over the world would be denominated in the same unit and would be kept equal in different parts of the world to the extent that the law of one price was allowed to work itself out. Apart from tariffs and controls, trade between countries would be as easy as it is between states of the United States. It would lead to an enormous increase in the gains from trade and real incomes of all countries including the United States."[70]

The Single Global Currency would stimulate trade the most in those developing countries where inflation and currency risk have been high. As with other aspects of the 3-G world, the subject of worldwide trade growth has seen little research. In an article about the effect of the EMU on Swedish trade, Andrew Rose did note in 2001 that international trade would increase by 10 percent with a Global Monetary Union, but that estimate is surely understated.[71]

14. Actualize a Fundamental Human Right to a Stable Currency

The world has made considerable progress in identifying fundamental human rights, such as the right to own property. Article 17, of the Universal Declaration of Human Rights, adopted in 1948, states:

(1) Everyone has the right to own property alone as well as in association with others.
(2) No one shall be arbitrarily deprived of his property.[72]

This right to property should be interpreted to include a fundamental human right to a stable currency, where people have the ability to earn, save, invest, and spend stable money. With respect to money, the right to be free from arbitrary deprivation of property includes the right to be free from state-induced inflation and devaluations, and from fluctuations in the multicurrency foreign exchange system that the world has deliberately left in place.

Former German Prime Minister Ludwig Erhard declared that monetary stability was a basic human right.[73]

This human right would not require government expenditures to protect, but it would require government and central bank practices which keep inflation to a low level, such as two percent. Allowing inflation to rise above four percent could be said to violate the human right to a stable currency, as it deprives many people of their property without just compensation.

Of course, declaring a human right is not the same as enforcing it, but it's a start. Zimbabwe is the latest example of a mismanaged monetary system, leading to hyperinflation, through no fault of its 12.7 million citizens who struggle with low per capita incomes. In a 3-G world, such destruction of property would not occur.

Establishing a Single Global Currency, with a Global Central Bank with a representative governing structure, within a Global Monetary Union is the only way to ensure the people's fundamental human right to a stable currency.

15. Make the International Financial System More Fair Among Nations and People

Since Bretton Woods, the US dollar has been designated, formally and in practice, as the primary international reserve currency. This status survived the 1971 collapse of the gold-reserve basis for the dollar. Such a status may have its costs, such as the international pressure on what might be said to be internal monetary policy, but its major benefit to the United States is that it gets, in the words of Basil Moore "a perpetual free lunch."[74] Moore continues,

> "The US has been the sole country that was not seriously forced to compromise its internal balance considerations for the sake of maintaining external balance. It alone has been able to lower its domestic short term rate towards zero in response to increases in unemployment rates with no concern for the ensuing current account deficit. It has felt sufficiently confident in the position of the US dollar as a 'safe haven' as to actively encourage a fall in the external value of the dollar, in order to reduce its current account deficit. In contrast, most countries must attempt to stabilize their dollar exchange rate, by holding their domestic bank rate significantly above the level of the US federal funds rate."[75]

The issuer of the world's primary reserve currency benefits from the seigniorage, i.e., the value of the issued cash minus the costs of production, and such benefit should be shared with the world. The US Federal Reserve has received such a seigniorage benefit from all the cash which is now in circulation in the United States, and the hundreds of billions throughout the world.

Such a one nation/world reserve currency system is simply not fair, as any school child would recognize. As the euro, and perhaps other monetary union currencies, gain in stature and are counted among the international reserves of central banks, the world will become less tolerant of a single national currency which benefits from its exalted status, but whose sponsoring nation ignores its part of the bargain, which is to maintain monetary and fiscal stability. For the US dollar, it is the credibility of the US government which provides confidence and stability, while for the euro, it's the credibility of the European Central Bank. Monetary stability is the primary mission of a monetary union's central bank, whereas such stability is only one of many goals of a national government.

By analogy, the United States took a lead role in developing the Internet, but as it has become a worldwide phenomenon, other countries are no longer content that it be managed entirely by the United States. The US was not elected to be the world's electronic overseer, and the world is taking notice.[76] Soon, the governance of the internet will become more globally representative, as it must. It's common cents/sense.

Similarly, the responsibility for money must become more representative. With a Single Global Currency, the seigniorage would accrue to the Global Central Bank and would likely be used to fund its operations. If there is an excess seigniorage benefit, it could go to fund global social and economic programs to be determined by the bank's representative governing council. The European Commission study *One Market, One Currency* estimated that the one-time gains to the European Community from having its currency circulated in the world as one of the major international currencies, "would develop, gradually accumulating perhaps to around $35 billion."[77]

In addition to eliminating the need for a single pre-eminent country to be the issuer of the international reserve currency, a Single Global Currency will also be fairer among the second and third-tier countries. This was one of the three criteria by which the European Commission measured the value of the euro, "Equity as between countries and regions: opportunities and risks for all regions, and not a priority balance of relative advantage for the original or newer Member States. The least-favoured regions have a real opportunity for rapid catch-up."[78] The other criteria were microeconomic efficiency and macroeconomic stability.

The problem of fairness extends to individual people as well. A friend once described to me how he had purchased a home in France when the euro was valued at $.87 and a few years later, and for non-speculative reasons, he chose to sell it for the same number of euros, but when a euro was worth $1.26, an increase of 44.8 percent. Assuming that his home cost him €300,000, his cost in US dollars would have been $261,000 and when returning to the United States with the proceeds of his sale, he would have converted that into $378,000, a windfall gain of $117,000. Such an undeserved gain is unfair, although my friend is blameless for his good fortune. It must be remembered that for every such person for whom the timing was exquisitely lucky, there is another person for whom the timing is exquisitely poor and who lost the same amounts. Just because such windfalls and losses have been occurring daily for 2,500 years doesn't make them fair or right.

There are macro-ethics concerns to consider regarding the Single Global Currency, as well as micro-ethics. Peter Singer, in his book, *One World*, urges that all decisions be viewed with one reality in mind: "the idea that we all live in one world."[79] It is unethical and even unconscionable to continue to tolerate the multicurrency foreign exchange system, while knowing its costs and risks, and the potential benefit to treating the world of money as "one world." Such a one-world view is made more realistic by human space travel, accelerated by President John Kennedy's ambitious goal to put a man on the moon in the 1960s, whereby the earth is put into real perspective. Gaining further perspective, the US rover, "Curiosity," took the first nighttime photo of earth and its moon from Mars on 1 February 2014.[80]

16. The World's Private, Business and Public Economic Data Would Be More Accurate.

All business and trade transactions depend upon the accuracy of information. In the multicurrency foreign exchange world, every analysis of an international economic problem, and every annual report of an international corporation must adjust for exchange rate variations. Soon after printing, every adjustment became outdated and uncertain.

The International Accounting Standards Board, based in London, "is committed to developing a single set of high quality, understandable and enforceable global accounting standards...."[81] However, in a world where the values of money fluctuate from minute to minute and day to day, the accounting goals of precision and stability are frustrated. With a Single Global Currency, a reliable global accounting standard can be developed. A 2006 paper by Ratnam Alagiah, "A Single Global Currency and its Impact on Accounting" presents the view that "*Only* on this basis will comparable financial reports be attained."[82]

With every analysis of the inequality among the people of the world, there is an inherent fuzziness when exchange rates are factored into the numbers. One can write, as Branko Milanovic and Peter Singer do, that the world contains unacceptable inequality,[83] but when poverty in China is measured in yuan and poverty in Tanzania is measured in Tanzanian shillings, there is an element of disbelief, after foreign exchange conversion, that the poverty could be so extreme. There are many ways that one can present the gross inequalities. Here are two:
-The richest 50 individuals in the world have a combined income greater than that of the poorest 416 million.
-The 2.5 billion people living on less than $2 a day—40 percent of the world's population—receive only 5 percent of global income, while 54 percent of global income goes to the richest 10 percent of the world's population.[84]

Those numbers are staggering, but within a multicurrency foreign exchange world, we always have the emotional escape that it cannot be that grossly bad; so, we reason or feel, the exchange rates must explain some of the discrepancy.

With a Single Global Currency, such a psychological escape would no longer be possible. Would it really matter? That's hard to say. In the United States, it did make a difference in 1962 when Michael Harrington published *The Other America* and showed Americans that there was inexcusable poverty within their own country. Whether the world would respond sufficiently to a similar exposure of the true facts of the world's inequalities is unknown.

Not only would the world's financial data be more accurate, but there would be enormous savings from the reduction of data to be reported. In a world of exploding amounts of information, this is one area where there will be a reduction. Saved will be the vast amount of reporting to governments of foreign exchange trading which then is used in reports of national current accounts, international reserves, and of foreign exchange trading itself. For a sampling of such reports see the US Treasury's "Treasury International Capital System."[85]

17. Eliminate the Illogical Results of the Existing System

Why should the value of money change when the fortunes of a government change, or even the fortunes of an economy? Here are excerpts from a typical news report about foreign exchange from the Reuters news service:

"FOREX-Hawkish policy stance lifts Australian dollar

"Tuesday, Feb 4, 2014 (Reuters) - The Australian dollar rose more than 2 percent on Tuesday after the country's central bank dropped its easing bias toward interest rates and toned down its long-term call for the currency to weaken.... The Aussie has fallen by almost a fifth in the past 12 months as a commodities boom expired, growth in China began to slow and the central bank campaigned for a weaker currency to help stir economic growth."[86]

Why should the unit of account change when other factors change? Is it logical that an Australian worker should be paid tomorrow in a currency that is worth two percent more than yesterday on the international markets because the central bank toned down its call for a weaker currency? It is not, and it does not make cents/sense.

With 260 trading days a year, a two percent change in a single day in the value of a currency translates into 10 percent a week, 43 percent a month and 520 percent change in a year. That is, of course, absurd, but why is even the two percent in a single day tolerable?

Another illustration of the illogical multicurrency foreign exchange system is that the importance of a national currency in the world system has little to do with the country's importance or the size of its economy. For example, with .8 percent of the world's GDP and .12 percent of the population, Switzerland's franc is usually among the ten most traded currencies in the foreign exchange markets. The Swiss franc is more important to world trade and finances than the currencies of such countries as Brazil, China, Korea, Russia, or South Africa. Such a disproportional use of a small country's currency can be called one of the imbalances in the current multicurrency foreign exchange system.

As a small country, large inflows of money can easily affect the exchange rate, by raising the value of the Swiss franc as occurred during the Eurozone crisis of 2009-2013. The value rose so fast through late 2011, that Swiss exporters, including the tourism industry, forced the Swiss National Bank to intervene to prevent the Swiss franc from becoming more expensive than 1.2 to the euro. Prior to 6 September 2011, it had "risen" as "high" as 1.04 to the euro, but after the central bank intervention began on that date, it hasn't risen "above" 1.20 to the euro.[87] Someday, of course, the Swiss will join the European Union and the Eurozone and eventually, the Global Monetary Union.

Similarly, the US dollar declined 6.5 percent against the euro during the six month period from 2 July 2013 to 2 January 2014.[88] That's an annual rate of decline of 13 percent for the world's largest currency, as compared to the second largest, which doesn't seem logical, either.

Such changes can wreak havoc with monetary statistics and valuations. An American student might have measured the GDP of the Eurozone on 2 July 2013 and found it to be $12 trillion. Assuming that the GDP did not change one cent, that same student might have taken the same measurement on 2 January 2014 and found a 5.025 percent increase to $12,602,950,215,120. A $602 billion change is considered by most people to be a lot of money. On the other hand, a European student might have looked at exactly the same European GDP in July 2013 and found it to be equal to €9,219,422,249,539 and then measured it again in January 2014 and found it be exactly the same. Of course, the American student would have been required to give his/her results in USD at the beginning of the six month period or at the end. Thus, s/he could have reported that in July 2013 dollars, the Eurozone GDP was $12 trillion in July and in the following January, or that it was $12,602,950,215,120 in July 2013 and January 2014, in January 2014 dollars.

During that same period a European investor might have invested €10,000/$13,016 in the US stock market in a mutual fund indexed to the Standard & Poor 500 index. During that last six months of 2013, the S&P 500 increased by .089 percent. Without the currency fluctuation, the European's gain would have been a mere €8.90/$11.59. That return would have been discouraging, but if s/he exchanged the $13,027.59 back into euros, and had not been charged for the foreign exchange trade or for any trading fees, s/he would have received €9,530.06 for a loss of €469.94. Such is the power of foreign exchange fluctuations. If a foreign exchange trading transaction fee had been charged for the initial July 2013 investment, and the rate of the charge had been calculated as the ratio of all estimated FX transaction costs divided by the value of all the estimated 2013 FX transactions, i.e. $300 billion/($5.3 trillion X 260 trading days), or .0185 percent, the charge would have been €1.85/$2.4077. The charge to trade the $13,027.59 back into euros on 2 January 2014 would have been €1.76/$2.4098. Subtracting the total of the two FX transactions charges of €3.61, the investor would have received €9,526.45, for a loss of €473.55.

Consistent with the themes of this book, such results for Australia, Switzerland, the US and Europe indicate that the value of money is not necessarily related to the size or economic power of the issuing country. It should not be related to either. Instead, the value of money is more logically related to the soundness of the management of the money, and some reasonable relationship to purchasing power parity, and that's what the Global Central Bank will do well for the Single Global Currency.

These enormous shifts in wealth could have occurred because traders of dollars and euros on the foreign exchange markets had moved the price of euros down by 5 percent according to the law of supply and demand. It defies common cents/sense. The same valuation reasoning can be applied to any United States or European asset over the same period, thus making a very real difference in the investment calculations of people in both countries.

Aligning currencies with national borders is illogical for many reasons, including the fact that the world's economic stage has many players which are larger than most countries. In May 2013, *Forbes* listed the Chinese bank, ICBC as the largest corporation in the world.[89] Its assets of $2.8 trillion exceeded the GDPs of 189 of the 193 UN member states. Only the US, China, Japan and Germany had larger GDPs. ICBC's sales of $134 billion exceeded the GDPs of 136 members and even the company's profits of $37.8 billion exceeded the GDPs of 104 countries.[90]

Further, there are many individuals with a personal wealth larger than the GDP of several countries. According to the *Forbes* 2013 ranking of the world's richest people, the richest is Carlos Slim Helu of Mexico with a personal worth of $73 billion.[91] That's larger than the GDPs of 127 countries.[92] In January 2014, Oxfam reported that the richest 85 individuals in the world possessed more wealth than the poorer one-half of humanity, i.e. 3.5 billion people.[93]

In this context, organizing currencies by countries does not make cents/sense.

18. The Single Global Currency Has the Prospect of Being a Permanent Solution

Previous solutions to the multicurrency foreign exchange trading system have been short term solutions. For all the nostalgic respect for the Bretton Woods currency solution, it lasted only twenty-six years, from 1945 to 1971. Bretton Woods still deserves considerable deference, however, because it's where the World Bank and International Monetary Fund were established.

Monetary unions can have staying power, especially when they are combined with a measure of political union. The best example is the European Monetary Union, the relatively young age of which is balanced by its prospects for significant growth over the next several years, and beyond.

The Central and West African Monetary unions have continued since 1994, and were preceded by currency boards inherited from the French African Empire. The Singapore-Brunei monetary union has continued since 1967. The Eastern Caribbean Currency Authority was formed in 1965.

Once a Single Global Currency is created or affirmed or otherwise recognized, it will last a long time, and the 2,500 period with a multicurrency system will be regarded as a minor interlude in the progress of history.

19. The Value of Money Should Be an International Standard and Not Determined By the Supply and Demand of the Marketplace

Increasingly, the world is standardizing its measurements and identifications to assist international trade and reporting. The world uses the same calendar, the same measure of a day, week, and month and the same computer protocols. Most of the world uses the metric system, and nearly all international trade uses it. Even US citizens take their medicines in grams and their soft drinks in liter bottles. Why should money be different? Perhaps the value of currency should become part of the work of the International Standards Organization (ISO) and related organizations. The ISO "is the world's largest developer of voluntary International Standards. International Standards give state of the art specifications for products, services and good practice, helping to make industry more efficient and effective. Developed through global consensus, they help to break down barriers to international trade."[94]

Another potential vehicle for standardizing the values of money is the Statistics Division of the United Nations Department of Economic and Social Affairs which maintains the international standards for reporting gross economic statistics.[95] First developed in 1953, the System of National Accounts (SNA) "consists of a coherent, consistent, and integrated set of macroeconomic accounts, balance sheets, and tables based on a set of internationally agreed concepts, definitions, classifications, and accounting rules."[96] It's time for the standardization of financial reporting around the world, now fifty years old, to be supplemented by standard values of money.

Looking at standards from another viewpoint, and the view by some economists that countries should retain the ability to devalue/revalue their currencies, what sense would it make to reduce the length of a meter in order to boost the annual statistics on sales of meters of rope? Why not reduce the weight of a kilogram to increase the statistics on steel production? The ideas are absurd, as is the idea that money should be devalued in order to increase exports. Ingemar Bengtsson has written, "Just like it is inconvenient that some countries have not fully adopted the meter system, it is inconvenient that we do not have a single measure for value."[97]

Money should have a predictable standard value around the world. That doesn't mean that prices will be the same everywhere, just as they are not uniform within large currency areas. Nonetheless, there will be some stability of knowing what the Single Global Currency will buy around the world, and thus, there will still be a place for a Big Mac Index, but it will compare actual prices and not prices filtered through the fog of the multicurrency foreign exchange system.

Remembering the three-part definition of money as a medium of exchange, a unit of account and a store of value, the marketplace is not the place to ensure adherence to the definition. The price that a Brazilian pays to purchase Vietnamese shoes should not depend upon foreign exchange brokers in Sydney, Singapore, London, or New York.

20. The idea of the Single Global Currency Has an Elegant and Understandable Simplicity to It

There is one earth, and one human race. As Paul Volcker has written, "A global economy requires a global currency."[98] Similarly, "One market requires one money."[99]

Foreign exchange trading began 2,500 years ago as metal coins became standardized in the Indian, Turkish, and Chinese currency areas. Now most money changes hands electronically through wires, cables, laser beams, and electronic waves in the air. "To put it in succinct and current terms, money's destiny is to become digital."[100] As money is becoming increasingly digital, then it makes little cents/sense for the electrons to continue to be scrambled as they cross the boundaries of currency areas.

There is no magic to money, and there should be less mystery than there is now with the multicurrency foreign exchange system. Money is made by human beings and used by all of them and should, therefore, be understood by everyone.

Benefits and Costs of the Single Global Currency--Costs

If there were no perceived costs or disadvantages to the implementation of a Single Global Currency, it could have occurred long ago. Below are described these perceived costs.

1. Sovereignty Theory of Money

Before the rise of nation states and before the time when coins and bills featured national themes and the images of national heroes, the users of money felt no loyalty to money, except the desire that it not lose value. When nation states began issuing of money, the bills and coins became symbols of their history and power. Some people are tempted to view such symbols as they do their flags and national constitutional documents, and the loss of such symbols can be considered a national loss. However, money is different from flags.

Given the extent and growth of monetary unions, it is now apparent that people care more about the value and stability of their money than they do about whose image is stamped and printed on their coins and bills. Stated Jose Cordeiro of Venezuela, "In Africa, Latin America, and parts of Asia— which is to say, most of the world—people would love to give up their national currency and replace it with the dollar, or the euro, or the yen, because they don't trust their own national currency."[101]

Is it always a cost when a country abandons the ability to act or pursue a goal? Was it a cost when most of the UN members abandoned the use of anti-personnel land mines?[102] Was it a cost when most of the UN members abandoned the ability to develop nuclear weapons?[103] In each case, the signing countries perceived that abandonment was less costly than pursuit of a heretofore sovereign right.

Still, the feelings for nationalism remain very strong in the world, even if slowly declining; and they are hard to overcome.

2. Need for Independent Monetary Authority to Deal with Local Economic Needs Which May Require Adjustments of Interest Rates or Money Supply or Exchange Rates

As previously discussed, a major concern of many international economists is their view that nations need the flexibility to be able to adjust interest rates to heat up or cool down an economy and to influence exchange rates to achieve the same goals. It is very difficult to evaluate the true value of the cost of losing that ability, if it is a cost at all. One 2005 study, "And If One Size Fits All, After All?" concluded "that the ECB did a far better stabilization job for Eurozone countries than national central banks would have done."[104] When some people or economists look wistfully at how past devaluations helped bring countries out of a recession, they conveniently ignore the costs of those devaluations and they ignore the concept of unintended consequences. That is, not all central bank efforts to pull countries out of recession end well.

As Robert Mundell has stated, "another dimension of the benefits from a world currency would be a great improvement in the internal monetary policies of perhaps two-thirds of the countries of the world. The benefits to each country from a stable currency that is also a universal currency would be enormous."[105]

Without the ability to tailor monetary policy to the separate needs of nations, then other politically acceptable means of ameliorating regional economic differences can be developed. Germany has the strongest system of regional "Revenue Equalization," according to a formula based on tax revenues.[106] Worldwide, but on a smaller per capita scale, there are foreign aid programs.

In a world where inflation and interest rates are low, the loss of the ability to lower interest rates in order to stimulate investment is not as powerful tool as in high-interest rate economies.

3. Employment for Those Maintaining the Current Multicurrency Foreign Exchange System

There are approximately 200,000 full-time foreign exchange traders in the world, and they are all very bright people. With the movement to a Single Global Currency, they will either move to trade other commodities or stocks and bonds or retire or move into some other kind of work.

From 2002 to 2008, the number of people employed in the central banks of the ESCB (European System of Central Banks), including the ECB, declined 21 percent from 85,538 to 67,281.[107] In addition to automation, some of the decline must be attributed to the elimination of the need at each National Central Bank (NCB) to maintain a separate national currency.

The Single Global Currency in Culture: Religion, Literature, Movies, and Museums

Money or currency is part of the larger culture which interprets its other meanings and utility. While money, wealth, and poverty are the subjects of countless songs, books, and movies, the subject of the governance of money is less prevalent. As the number of countries within monetary unions increases, perhaps we will see more such references.

Religion: The concept of a Single Global Currency has aroused the suspicion of some Christian groups who associate it with the end of the world as prophesied in the *Bible*.[108]

On the other hand, the Baha'i religion embraces the concept of a Single Global Currency as an indication of strengthening world human values. In one article, "One World, One Currency," it was stated, "A global currency would also be an important step in promoting economic justice in the world, removing the advantage of a few favored countries whose currency is seen as stronger or more secure, and preventing the poor from being hurt by the impacts of currency fluctuations.... Ultimately, technical solutions to economic problems will only work effectively if a new spirit permeates economic life and a new economic system is evolved based on the application of spiritual principles."[109]

Literature: One of the most popular current science fiction series in the United States is the *Left Behind* saga. The Single Global Currency plays a role in this long-running, eleven-volume science fiction saga by Tim LeHaye and Jerry Jenkins. A 2003 review of one book in the series, *Armageddon*, stated "Meanwhile, the rising Antichrist is Nicolae Carpathia, a handsome, urbane and lethally devious Romanian national who started his ascent to power as Secretary General of the United Nations (a longstanding object of fundamentalist wrath). Before long, Carpathia establishes himself as a global dictator and foists onto a gullible population a totalitarian, one-world government, a Single Global Currency and a syncretic universal religion that combines Catholic-style pomp with New Age rhetoric."[110]

In Curtis Sittenfeld's *Prep*, protagonist Lee Fiora muses about life after her prep school years at Ault School, "I've never since Ault been in a place where everyone wants the same things; minus a universal currency, it's not always clear to me what I myself want."[111]

Movies: Called a "religious thriller," the 1999 film, "The Omega Code" was surprisingly popular. In a review, Steve Rhodes wrote, "Described as a Buddha-like figure, Chairman Stone Alexander (Michael York) presents himself as a world savior. Responsible for world peace and for skyrocketing stock markets due to his revolutionary idea of a Single Global Currency, Chairman Alexander will, nevertheless, prove to have some serious character flaws. As a clue to his true identity perhaps I should mention that strange bombings, food shortages, and epidemics have recently been striking the planet...."[112]

Museums: There are a number of money museums in the world, which feature exhibits of the coins and bills of the past.[113] Someday, there will be a section for exchange rates, because visitors will have long since forgotten what they were.

Summary

The entire world, with 7+ billion people is THE Optimum Currency Area, but not only as measured by the pioneering criteria of Robert Mundell's articles. The world is the optimum currency area for ALL the reasons listed above which can be summarized as follows: A stable Single Global Currency will benefit the people of the world--period. It will give them what they have wanted since the beginnings of the use of money--monetary stability. One is optimal, and one size does fit all.

However, it cannot be expected that the Single Global Currency will solve all the world's financial problems, as disappointment would be certain. Where there is discontent with the euro, it may be that excessive expectations were more responsible than its actual performance. This brings to mind the social equation: H = E - R, or Happiness Equals Expectations Minus Reality.[114]

Banding together to solve the exchange rate problem is not the same as having countries join together to solve some other kind of problem, such as world hunger or global warming. With all its wealth, or former wealth, the US has not successfully eradicated hunger even within its borders. It was not the national boundaries which caused the hunger, nor the climate change, but agricultural, industrial and government tax practices within and among countries. In the case of the multicurrency foreign exchange rate problem, the borders are the problem. If a Single Global Currency can be developed which can cross all borders and be legal tender within each, then at least that problem is solved.

John Stuart Mill and Robert Mundell both noted above that money should be convenient, and it can be added that people will pay for convenience, as they do in other contexts such as express shipping. However, we are all now paying for INconvenience. The world pays at least $300 billion annually to maintain a system that makes international trade and travel INconvenient. It's argued above that the benefits of a 3-G world would greatly outweigh the costs, but even if a 3-G world brought a net cost, it's likely that the people of the world would still be willing to implement it, due to the obvious convenience.

Implementing the Single Global Currency shows common cents/sense, but most international economists do not yet agree that the 3-Gs will be useful to the world, and even if useful, that they will be feasible to implement within a reasonable time. Chapter 6 presents some of those views.

ENDNOTES

1. Justice Potter Stewart, in concurring opinion in the United States Supreme Court case, Jacobellis v. Ohio, 378 US 184 (1964). The Court reversed Ohio's conviction of a theater manager who showed a film the state claimed violated its obscenity laws. Justice Stewart wrote, "I shall not today attempt further to define the kinds of material I understand to be embraced within that shorthand description; and perhaps I could never succeed in intelligibly doing so. But I know it when I see it, and the motion picture involved in this case is not that." The case is online at http://caselaw.lp.findlaw.com/scripts/getcase.pl?court=US&vol=378&invol=184.
2. John Stuart Mill, Principles of Political Economy with Some of Their Applications to Social Philosophy. London: 7th Edition, with introduction by W.J. Ashley, 1909, first edition published 1848, full text at http://www.econlib.org/library/Mill/mlP36.html. The view that Mill can be credited as being the originator of the concept of the single global currency was shared by Myron Frankman of McGill University in his article, "Beyond the Tobin Tax: Global Democracy and a Global Currency," in Annals,

Volume 581, May 2002, pp. 62-73, at p. 63, at
http://ann.sagepub.com/content/581/1/62.
3. Robert Mundell, "The Case for a World Currency," *Journal of Policy Modeling*, June 2005, pp. 465-475, p. 468, at
http://ideas.repec.org/a/eee/jpolmo/v34y2012i4p568-578.html
4. John Stuart Mill, *Principles of Political Economy with some of their Applications to Social Philosophy*, op. cit.
5. "Patterns for an International Coinage," Society of United States Pattern Collectors, (numismatics), at
http://www.uspatterns.com/uspatterns/patforincoin.html.
6. Robert Mundell, "The Case for a World Currency," op. cit., p. 468.
7. Bank for International Settlements, "BIS History," at
http://www.bis.org/about/history.htm.
8. James M. Boughton, "America in the Shadows: Harry Dexter White and the Design of the International Monetary Fund," January 2006, IMF Working Paper, 06/6, at
http://www.imf.org/external/pubs/ft/wp/2006/wp0606.pdf.
9. Deardorff's Glossary of International Economics, at http://www-personal.umich.edu/~alandear/glossary/.
10. For more information about SDRs, see the IMF's FACT sheet at
http://www.imf.org/external/np/exr/facts/sdr.htm.
11. "Argentine Debt Restructuring", *Wikipedia*, at
http://en.wikipedia.org/wiki/Argentine_debt_restructuring.
12. "Post-War Currency Policy," a British Treasury memorandum dated September 1941, reprinted in Donald Moggridge, editor, *The Collected Writings of John Maynard Keynes*, Vol. 25, *Activities*, 1940-1944; *Shaping the Post-war World, the Clearing Union*, Cambridge, UK: Cambridge University Press, p. 31, as quoted in Benjamin J. Cohen, *The Future of Money*. Princeton, NJ: Princeton University Press, p. 107.
13. John Williamson, "Did the Washington Consensus Fail?" Outline of speech at the Center for Strategic & International Studies, Washington, DC, 6 November 2002, Institute for International Economics, at
http://www.iie.com/publications/papers/paper.cfm?ResearchID=488.
Williamson is recognized as the originator of the term "Washington Consensus" and its criteria for international finance, but he states that capital controls were not part of his proposal.
14. Robert Mundell, "A Theory of Optimum Currency Areas," 1961, op. cit., p. 659,
15. Robert Mundell, ibid., p. 662.
16. Lars Jonung, "Euro: The Great Experiment," CNN.com.
17. Robert Mundell, "Plan for a World Currency," prepared for hearings on 9 September 1968 before the Subcommittee on International Exchange and Payments of the Joint Economic Committee, being a paper prepared for a conference at Ditchley Park, England, 10-13 September 1968, at pp. 14-28 of the Committee's report entitled, "Next Steps In International Monetary Reform."
18. Robert Mundell, ibid., at p. 19, and quoting from Charles Rist, *The Triumph of Gold*. New York, NY: 1961, p. 205.

19. Robert Mundell, ibid., at p. 25.

20. William McChesney Martin, *Toward a World Central Bank?* 1970, the Per Jacobsson Foundation, an organization within the IMF.

21. International Monetary Fund, *IMF Survey*, 11 May 1998, p. 146. at http://www.imf.org/external/pubs/ft/survey/pdf/051198.pdf.

22. Robert Magnuson, "Currency: Why Blocs Can't Work," *The New York Times*, 22 July 1979, p. F14, at http://query.nytimes.com/mem/archive/pdf?res=FB0E14F83F5A12728D DDAB0A94DF405B898BF1D3

23. Edwin Dale, "The Pound Experiment--Global Financial System Could Gain If a Small Devaluation Is Successful," *The New York Times*, 20 November 1967, p. 74, at http://select.nytimes.com/gst/abstract.html?res=F00C17FF3F59137A93C 2AB178AD95F438685F9

24. Charles P. Kindleberger, *International Money: A collection of essays, Routledge Press*, 1981, republished in 2006, page 178.

25. Richard Cooper, in email to author, "...I do not support a global currency. I cannot think of a way to manage it that would command legitimacy." 18 July 2003.

26. George Soros, *The Alchemy of Finance*. New York, NY: John Wiley & Sons, 1987. Chapter 18 is "Toward An International Central Bank" with a sub-chapter, "An International Currency," pp. 324-344.

27. Andrew Krieger, with Edward Claflin, *The Money Bazaar*. New York, NY: Times Books, 1992, p. 215.

28. *The Economist*, 9 January 1988, "Get Ready for the Phoenix," pp. 9-10, London.

29. *The Economist*, 26 September 1998, "One World, One Money," p. 80, London.

30. IMF Economic Forum "One World, One Currency: Destination or Delusion?" 8 November 2000, with Alexander Swoboda, Maurice Obstfeld, and Paul Masson, transcript at http://www.imf.org/external/np/tr/2000/tr001108.htm. See also the article about the forum in the IMF periodical, the *IMF Survey*, "Economic Forum-Despite Trend Toward Fewer Currencies, A Single World Currency Seems Unlikely in Near Future," 11 December 2000, pp. 75-76, at http://www.imf.org/external/pubs/ft/survey/2000/121100.pdf.

31. Barry Eichengreen, "The Parallel Currency Approach to Asian Monetary Integration," prepared for the American Economics Association annual meeting, January 2006, at http://www.aeaweb.org/annual_mtg_papers/2006/0107_1015_1303.pdf

32. International Monetary Fund, *IMF Survey*, "Economic Forum--Despite Trend Toward Fewer Currencies, a Single World Currency Seems Unlikely in Near Future," op. cit., pp. 75-76.

33. Charles Goldfinger, "Intangible Economy and Electronic Money," in *The Future of Money*. Paris: Organization for Economic Co-Operation and Development, 2002 p. 113.

34. International Monetary Fund, *IMF Survey,* "Mundell Calls for a Closer Monetary Union as Step toward Single World Currency," 5 March 2001, pp. 75-76, at http://www.imf.org/external/pubs/ft/survey/2001/030501.pdf.

35. International Monetary Fund, *IMF Survey,* ibid., p. 76.

36. Robert Mundell, "Currency Areas, Exchange Rate Systems and International Monetary Reform," paper delivered in Buenos Aires on 17 April 2000, p. 25, at http://www.columbia.edu/~ram15/cema2000.html.

37. Stephan Schulmeister, "Globalization without Global Money: the double role of the dollar as national currency and world currency," 2000, at http://stephan.schulmeister.wifo.ac.at/fileadmin/homepage_schulmeister/files/GlobalizationWithoutGlobalMoney.pdf

38. Paul Volcker, "Toward a Single World Currency to Level the Playing Field," 31 January 2000, *International Herald Tribune,* at http://www.nytimes.com/2000/01/31/opinion/31iht-edpaul.2.t_0.html.

39. International Monetary Fund, IMF Survey, "Mundell Calls for a closer Monetary Union as Step toward Single World Currency," 5 March 2001, pp. 75-76, at p. 76, op cit.

40. Ramkishen Rajan, "Counterbalance: The Euro in Asia," *Harvard Asia Pacific Review,* Winter 2000, at http://hcs.harvard.edu/~hapr/winter00_millenium/Euro.html.

41. "Global Financial Stability Report," International Monetary Fund, Table 3 in Statistical Appendix, 2005, at p. 171, at http://www.imf.org/External/Pubs/FT/GFSR/2005/02/pdf/statappx.pdf

42. Alan Greenspan, "Currency Reserves and Debt," speech before the World Bank Conference on Recent Trends in Reserves Management, Washington, DC, 29 April 1999, at http://www.federalreserve.gov/BoardDocs/Speeches/1999/19990429.htm.

43. Michael Emerson, Daniel Gros, Alexander Italiener, Jean Pisani-Ferry, Horst Reichenbach, *One Market, One Money--An Evaluation of the Potential Benefits and Costs of Forming an Economic and Monetary Union.* Oxford, UK: Oxford University Press, 1992, p. 25. It's difficult in 2014 to evaluate the prediction, as the Eurozone now has 18 members, and its foreign exchange reserves in 2013 totaled $748 billion, according to the Wikipedia entry at http://en.wikipedia.org/wiki/List_of_countries_by_foreign-exchange_reserves

44. Dani Rodrik, "The Social Cost of Foreign Exchange Reserves," National Bureau of Economic Research Working Paper No. 11952, January 2006, at http://papers.nber.org/papers/W11952

45. See World Bank, "Gross Domestic Product 2010," by country at http://siteresources.worldbank.org/DATASTATISTICS/Resources/GDP.pdf

46. "List of Countries by Foreign Aid Received," *Wikipedia,* at http://en.wikipedia.org/wiki/List_of_countries_by_foreign_aid_received

47. See "US International Reserve Position," United States Treasury, 31 January 2014, at http://www.treasury.gov/resource-center/data-chart-center/IR-Position/Pages/01312014.aspx.

48. "Currency Composition of Official Foreign Exchange Reserves (COFER)," International Monetary Fund, as of end of Q3, 2013 at
http://www.imf.org/external/np/sta/cofer/eng/glossary.htm#fer
49. The Single Global Currency Association takes no position on the future role of gold in the international financial system, as it focuses on its 3-G goals: Single Global Currency managed by a Global Central Bank, within a Global Monetary Union. In the interest of full disclosure, one of the attendees at the first Annual Single Global Currency Conference in 2004, and an early financial contributor, was James Turk, founder of www.goldmoney.com and a supporter of a larger role of gold in the world's financial system. For another view of gold see Alex Wallerwein's, "A Single GLOBAL CURRENCY? Sure, Why Not. But, Only if It's Gold and Silver Bullion!" at http://www.gold-eagle.com/article/single-global-currency
50. The Single Global Currency Association has received many emails from advocates of gold. A typical email came on 25 February 2006 from "Ruler100," and said simply, "I find this very interesting. Just wanted to point out to you that we already have a single global currency. It's called Gold."
51. Kavaljit Singh, *Taming Global Financial Flows*. New York, NY: Zed Books, 2000, p. 147.
52. Martin Santa and John O'Donnell, "Cyprus to fully lift capital controls within months," *Reuters*, 15 November 2013, at
http://uk.reuters.com/article/2013/11/15/uk-eurozone-cyprus-idUKBRE9AE0M120131115
53. In Greek legend, but not Greek mythology, a sword hung over Damocles head by threads of horsehair as he traded places for a day with King Dionysius II of Syracusa, Sicilia. Wikipedia, at
http://en.wikipedia.org/wiki/Damocles.
54. Rodrigo de Rato, "It's Not Just Up to Washington to Correct Global Imbalances," *European Affairs*, a publication of the European Institute, Vol. 6 No. 4, 31 December 2005, at
http://www.imf.org/external/np/vc/2005/123105a.htm.
55. Benn Steil and Robert E. Litan, *Financial Statecraft*. London and New Haven, CT: Yale University Press, 2006, at p. 98.
56. "It's the economy, stupid." See Wikipedia, at
http://en.wikipedia.org/wiki/It's_the_economy,_stupid
57. The term "peoples' money" is used here with a nod to former British Prime Minister Tony Blair who referred to Princess Diana as the "peoples' princess." See "Blair pays tribute to Diana." BBC, 31 August 1997, at
http://www.bbc.co.uk/news/special/politics97/diana/blairreact.html
58. See "Exchange Stabilization Fund," at the website of the United States Treasury, at http://www.treasury.gov/resource-center/international/ESF/Pages/esf-index.aspx. This fund was used, for example, to support the peso during the Mexican currency crisis which began in 1994.
59. Annalyn Kurtz, "This could be the largest Fed stimulus yet," *CNN Money*, 28 October 2013, at

http://money.cnn.com/2013/10/28/news/economy/federal-reserve-qe-stimulus/

60. Barry Eichengreen and Poonam Gupta, "Tapering Talk: The Impact of Expectations of Reduced Federal Reserve Security Purchases on Emerging Markets," 19 January 2014, *Munich Archive*, at http://mpra.ub.uni-muenchen.de/53040/

61. Paul Krugman, "Currency Wars and the Impossible Trinity," New York Times, 9 May 2011, at
http://krugman.blogs.nytimes.com/2011/05/09/currency-wars-and-the-impossible-trinity-wonkish/

62. Mark Perry, "Bank Failures: 12,000 in the U.S. vs. 2 in Canada," Blog, 26 February 2010, at http://mjperry.blogspot.it/2010/02/bank-failures-12000-in-us-vs-2-in.html

63. Kenneth Kasa, "Learning, Large Deviations, and Recurrent Currency Crises," February 2004, *International Economic Review*, pp. 141-73 at p. 141.

64. Benn Steil and Robert E. Litan, *Financial Statecraft*. London and New Haven, CT: Yale University Press, 2006, at p. 99 and pp. 110-11.

65. Junning Cai, "Currency Manipulation versus Current Account Manipulation," October 2005, at
http://papers.ssrn.com/sol3/papers.cfm?abstract_id=834487.

66. Tim Adams, "Working with the IMF to Strengthen Exchange Rate Surveillance," speech to a seminar at the American Enterprise Institute, 2 February 2006, summarized at http://www.treasury.gov/resource-center/international/exchange-rate-policies/Documents/Appendix_2.pdf.

67. Ronald McKinnon, "China's Exchange Rate Trap: Japan Redux?" presented at the American Economic Association meeting, Boston, MA, 7 January 2006, at
http://www.aeaweb.org/annual_mtg_papers/2006/0107_1015_1302.pdf

68. Jonathan Feurbringer, "Japan Is Spending Heavily to Pursue a Weak-Yen Policy," *The New York Times*, 27 August 2003, p. B1, at
http://www.nytimes.com/2003/08/27/business/japan-is-spending-heavily-to-pursue-a-weak-yen-policy.html

69. David Jolly, "Japan's Moves to Weaken the Yen Have a Global Effect," *New York Times*, 8 April 2013, at
http://www.nytimes.com/2013/04/09/business/global/yen-slides-close-to-level-of-100-to-the-dollar.html and Bank of Canada 10-year Currency Converter at http://www.bankofcanada.ca/rates/exchange/10-year-converter/

70. Robert A. Mundell, "The Works of Robert A. Mundell--World Currency," at his website, at http://robertmundell.net/economic-policies/world-currency/.

71. Andrew Rose, "EMU and Swedish Trade," 2001, Confederation of Swedish Enterprise, at
http://faculty.haas.berkeley.edu/arose/SEMUdec.pdf.

72. "Universal Declaration of Human Rights," United Nations, Adopted and proclaimed by General Assembly Resolution 217 A (III) of 10 December 1948, at http://www.un.org/Overview/rights.html.

73. Jose Luis Cordeiro, "Different Monetary Systems, Costs and Benefits to Whom?" November 2002, p. 3, at http://www.hacer.org/pdf/Cordeiro00.pdf.

74. Basil Moore, *Shaking the Invisible Hand: Complexity, Endogenous Money and Exogenous Interest Rates.* London, UK: Palgrave MacMillan, 2006, p. 2 of Chapter 18.

75. Basil Moore, ibid., p. 2 of Chapter 18.

76. "US Retains Working Control of Internet," 16 November 2005, *The New York Times*, p. C2.

77. Michael Emerson, Daniel Gros, Alexander Italiener, Jean Pisani-Ferry, Horst Reichenbach, *One Market, One Money - An Evaluation of the Potential Benefits and Costs of Forming an Economic and Monetary Union.* Oxford, UK: Oxford University Press, 1992, p. 25.

78. Michael Emerson, and others, ibid., p. 9.

79 . Peter Singer, *One World.* London and New Haven, CT: Yale University Press, 2002, at p. 13.

80. Greg Botehlo, "Curiosity rover takes snapshot of Earth – from 100 million miles away on Mars." *CNN*, 6 February 2014 at http://www.cnn.com/2014/02/06/tech/innovation/mars-curiosity-earth-image/

81. International Financial Reporting Standards Foundation and International Accounting Standards Board, website at http://www.ifrs.org/Pages/default.aspx.

82. Ratnam Alagiah, "A Single Global Currency and its Impact on Accounting," Working Paper, Griffith University, 2006. This paper addresses the issue of the implementation of a single global currency (SGC) by analysing the top 1000, of the *Fortune* 500 companies and the change in the reporting practices of multinational companies, given the evidence that the capital market values foreign currency gains and losses. Alagiah expanded upon this work for global standardization of accounting with his article, "The econometrics of a uniform and universal system of currency in accounting," 2011, at http://ura.unisa.edu.au/R/?func=dbin-jump-full&object_id=64622

83. See *Worlds Apart*, Princeton, NJ: by Branko Milanovic of the World Bank and the Carnegie Endowment for International Peace, Princeton University Press, 2005, and Peter Singer, *One World*, London and New Haven, CT: Yale University Press, 2002. Especially in Chapter 3, "One Economy," pp. 51-105.

84. Jens Martin, "A Compendium of Inequality," Global Policy Forum, October 2005, relying upon the *2005 United Nations Human Development Report*, (http://hdr.undp.org/en/content/human-development-report-2005) at http://www.globalpolicy.org/images/pdfs/10compendium.pdf.

85. United States Treasury, "Treasury International Capital System," at http://www.treasury.gov/resource-center/data-chart-center/tic/Pages/index.aspx

86. Daniel Bases, "FOREX-Hawkish policy stance lifts Australian dollar," *Reuters*, 4 February 2014, at

http://www.reuters.com/article/2014/02/04/markets-forex-idUSL2N0L91WG20140204

87. Joe Weisenthal, "THEY DID IT: Swiss National Bank Makes Epic Intervention Move, Sending The Swiss Franc Plunging," *Business Insider*, 6 September 2011, at http://www.businessinsider.com/wow-swiss-national-bank-takes-intervention-to-a-new-level-franc-plunges and the Bank of Canada 10-year Currency Converter at http://www.bankofcanada.ca/rates/exchange/10-year-converter/

88. Ibid. Bank of Canada Currency Converter.

89. "The World's Biggest Public Companies," *Forbes*, as of 14 February 2014, with values calculated in May 2013, at http://www.forbes.com/global2000/list/

90. "List of Countries by GDP," *Wikipedia* at http://en.wikipedia.org/wiki/List_of_countries_by_GDP_(nominal)

91. "The World's Billionaires," *Forbes*, as of 14 February 2014, at http://www.forbes.com/billionaires/

92. "List of Countries by GDP," op. cit.

93. Graeme Wearden, "Oxfam: 85 richest people as wealthy as poorest half of the world," *The Guardian*, 20 January 2014, at http://www.theguardian.com/business/2014/jan/20/oxfam-85-richest-people-half-of-the-world

94. International Organization for Standards (ISO), "World Trade Report 2005 Highlights ISO's Key Role," at http://www.iso.org/iso/en/commcentre/pressreleases/2005/Ref965.html.

95. United Nations Statistics Division, at https://unstats.un.org/unsd/default.htm

96. "Introduction: The SNA as a System," United Nations Statistics Division, United Nations, at http://unstats.un.org/unsd/nationalaccount/glossresults.asp?gID=674.

97. Ingemar Bengtsson in email to author, 27 June 2005.

98. A call to the office of Mr. Volcker in 2004 confirmed that he stands behind this statement, even if the exact quote does not have a definite initial attribution of publication. The statement, "A global economy requires a global currency" is similar to his statement in 2004 that "in a globalized world, we should have an international currency," as reported in "Calling for a Global Currency" by Joan Veon at http://www.wnd.com/2005/07/31116/ on 1 July 2005. Similarly, on 31 January 2000, Volcker wrote the column, "Toward a Single World Currency to Level the Playing Field" in the *International Herald Tribune* where he stated, "...if we are to have a truly globalized economy, a single world currency makes sense," at http://www.nytimes.com/2000/01/31/opinion/31iht-edpaul.2.t_0.html

99. Willem Buiter, Richard Layard, Christopher Huhne, Will Hutton, Peter Kenen, and Adair Turner, with a foreword by Paul Volcker, "Why Britain Should Join the Euro," 1 August 2002, p. 8, at http://cep.lse.ac.uk/layard/RL334D.pdf.

100. "Executive Summary," *The Future of Money*. Paris: Organization for Economic Co-Operation and Development, 2002, p. 7.

101. Marco Visscher, "Everyone Should Pay in Mondos," *ODE Magazine*, Netherlands, November 2005, an interview with Jose Cordeiro, an economist in Venezuela.

102. See International Campaign to Ban Landmines, with headquarters in Belgium, at http://www.icbl.org/. The full name of the 1997 treaty is the "Convention on the Prohibition of the Use, Stockpiling, Production and Transfer of Anti-Personnel Mines and on Their Destruction."

103. See "Treaty on the Non-Proliferation of Nuclear Weapons," at http://www.un.org/disarmament/WMD/Nuclear/NPT.shtml. As of 2002, 187 countries had signed that treaty.

104. Jerome Hericourt, "And If One Size Fits All, After All?--A Counterfactual Examination of the ECB--Monetary Policy under Duisenberg Presidency," November 2005 version, at http://ideas.repec.org/p/mse/wpsorb/bla04004a.html. The title functions as a response to a previous paper by Otmar Issing, "The Single Monetary Policy of the European Central Bank: One Size Fits All," *International Finance*, March 2001, at http://ideas.repec.org/a/bla/intfin/v4y2001i3p441-62.html and referenced by Issing in his May, 2004 lecture, "The ECB and the Euro - the First Five Years" at the City University Business School, London, at http://www.ecb.int/press/key/date/2004/html/sp040512_1.en.html

105. Robert A. Mundell, "The Works of Robert A. Mundell--World Currency" at his website, op. cit.

106. See 1999 changes to 1999 Revenue Equalization Implementation Act, at http://www.sachsen-anhalt.de/LPSA/index.php?id=pgoqpyujbgr0.

107. "Activities and Structure of European Central Banks," Report of Standing Committee of European Central Bank Unions, June 2008, page 12, at http://bo.scecbu.org/fileuploads/GKaskarelisActivitiesandstructureofNCBs.pdf

108. The Book of Revelation in the <u>Bible</u> is cited thusly, "Setting The Stage for the Prophesied Global Currency and Economy--In Revelation 13:16-17, we see that the economy of the world must have become global, with unprecedented dictatorial control, and that the money must have become cashless. Listen to the prophecy. 'And he causeth all, both small and great, rich and poor, free and bond, to receive a mark in their right hand, or in their foreheads: And that no man might buy or sell, save he that had the mark, or the name of the beast, or the number of his name,' " and "Bible scholars have long maintained that the only way in which verses 16-17 could be fulfilled was for three distinct events to have occurred...

1. The individual economies of the world had to have become global by this point in world history,...

2. The currency in this new global system had to have become global as well....

3. The currency had to have become cashless by this point in history...."

Cutting Edge Ministries, Lexington, South Carolina, at http://www.cuttingedge.org/news/n1169.cfm

109 . "Perspective: One World, One Currency," *One Country*, the Online Newsletter of the Baha'i Community, Volume 10, Issue 4, January-March 1999, at http://www.onecountry.org/e104/e10402as.htm.

110. Melani McAlister, "An Empire of Their Own," in *The Nation*, 22 September 2003, at http://www.thenation.com/doc/20030922/mcalister. See also Craig Unger, "American Rapture," December, 2005, *Vanity Fair*, about the United States evangelical movement and politics in the United States, at http://www.vanityfair.com/politics/features/2005/12/rapture200512.

111. Curtis Sittenfeld, *Prep.* New York, NY: Random House, 2005, p. 400.

112. Steve Rhodes, review of "The Omega Code," 1999, at http://www.imdb.com/reviews/216/21625.html.

113. See the money museum in Zurich, Switzerland, at http://sunflower.ch/en/moneymuseum/museum and the American Numismatic Association Money Museum, Colorado Springs, Colorado, United States, at http://www.money.org.

114. As my friends and relatives know, and sometimes to their consternation, I've been using this expression, H = E - R for about twenty-five years. The expression is also given as "Happiness equals Reality minus Expectations."

Chapter 6. Economists View The Single Global Currency

There are thousands of economists in the world who specialize in "international economics," but few of them have explored the costs and benefits of the Single Global Currency. Some books which purport to explore the future for the world economy say nothing about the Single Global Currency.[1] There are some economists who support the idea, and their work has been represented earlier in this book. Others are skeptical of its utility and even more are doubtful of its political feasibility, and their views are presented in this chapter.

Schools of Economic Thought

Among economists, ideas ripple through the discipline and some center around a university or major economist and become known as a "school" or group. There is the "Chicago school" which became known in the late twentieth century for its free market beliefs, and there are the "Keynesians" and "post-Keynesians," who continue to research and promote the work of John Maynard Keynes.

There is yet no "school" of economists who are promoting or even researching the Single Global Currency. There is not yet an identifiable school nor center even for the more general concept of monetary unions. As John Edmunds of Babson College has pointed out, it takes time for economists' views and focus to change, like the proverbial supertanker changing course.

So many books and articles have been written, and so many Ph.D.s have trained to master the uncertainties of foreign exchange, that moving forward to analyze and support a world financial system completely without exchange rates is understandably difficult. It requires thinking outside the box or what Charles Kindleberger referred to as "artistic" thinking.

Many economists seem glued to the analysis of what IS and what WAS rather than what WILL BE. Of the 87 doctoral dissertations granted by US universities between July 2012 and June 2013 (down from 106 in 2004-05) in the category of *International Economics*, eight had titles which were explicitly about exchange rates (compared to 20 in 2004-05), and several others were about currency crises, currency boards, and other subjects related to the multicurrency foreign exchange world. None was explicitly, by their titles, about monetary unions, the euro, the US dollar, nor any aspect of the 3-G world. The 87 constituted only 12.4 percent of the 700 total number of dissertations.[2]

At the January 2013, annual meeting of the American Economic Association there were no presentations about the Single Global Currency, and the only presentation about monetary union was in economic history, "Politics on the Road to US Monetary Union." Of those relating to currency, eight were about exchange rates, and one about the proposed ASEAN currency basket.[3]

At the January 2014 annual meeting, there were no papers presented about exchange rates or monetary union and only one about currency, which was a paper about an alternative currency used in Brighton, England.[4]

Even for experts on monetary unions, most still do not explore the connection between monetary unions and the prospect of a Global Monetary Union. In 2005, MIT Press published the book, *Prospects for Monetary Unions after the Euro*,[5] edited by Paul De Grauwe and Jacques Melitz, and one would have expected some exploration of the obvious next step after the euro, or the step after that. They only wrote, "One outstanding result of monetary union in Europe is a fresh impetus to thinking about monetary unions in other parts of the world."[6] In DeGrauwe's *Economics of Monetary Union*, also published in 2005, he wrote, "Where should the process of monetary integration stop? Should there be one currency for just twelve countries of the present EMU, or for the EU, or for the whole of Europe, or maybe for the whole world?"[7] However, there was no further discussion in either book of the 3-Gs: a Global Monetary Union with a Single Global Currency and a Global Central Bank. In the Introduction to *Prospects*, the editors correctly noted, "The introduction of the euro is a milestone in the history of international monetary relations."[8] But they did not pursue the question: a milestone on the journey to where?

They continued, "One of the more remarkable aspects of the process of monetary integration in Europe is that it started at the end of the 1980s at a time of widespread skepticism, if not hostility, about the project among economists."[9] It is the hope of *this* book that the widespread skepticism, if not opposition, by economists to the Single Global Currency will someday be regarded as similarly "remarkable"--and wrong.

Robert Wade announced "The case for a global currency" in the *International Herald Tribune* on 4 August 2006, pointing out that having a national currency, the US dollar, as the primary international currency did not make sense as the goals for a national currency and an international currency are different. He supported the creation of the ACU (Asian Currency Unit), but said that it "and other regional currencies, however, are only partial solutions. Because they could still be subject to destabilizing speculation and revaluation against the US dollar, they do not solve the problem of US incentives to be irresponsible in fiscal and monetary policies. What we need is a global currency."[10]

In the 3 October 2006 *New York Times*, Joseph Stiglitz addressed global imbalances, which "simply can't go on forever," and concluded, "Underlying the current imbalances are fundamental structural problems with the global reserve system. John Maynard Keynes called attention to these problems three-quarters of a century ago. His ideas on how to reform the global monetary system, including creating a new reserve system based on a new international currency, can, with a little work, be adapted to today's economy. Until we attack the structural problems, the world is likely to continue to be plagued by imbalances that threaten the financial stability and economic well-being of us all."[11]

Utility and Feasibility of the Single Global Currency

After its formation, the Single Global Currency Association (SGCA) began sending emails to economists who research and write about subjects related to the multicurrency foreign exchange world to ask them about their views of the utility and feasibility of the Single Global Currency. The results are on the SGCA website, by the name of each respondent.[12] The distinction is echoed in Martin Wolf's 3 August 2004, column, "We Need A Global Currency," in the *Financial Times*, when he wrote "I am well aware of the economic and political objections to this idea,"[13] (a.k.a. utility and feasibility).

In some responses from the economists, it was not clear whether the support or non-support is about the utility or feasibility or both, as with Andrew Rose's response to an SGCA inquiry, "I'm afraid I'm not in favor of a Single Global Currency...."[14] This response came despite his findings of the substantial increase in trade for countries joining a monetary union.

Attached to the SGCA emails, and appearing on the SGCA website, are the two scales below for Utility, with a range from -5 ("very harmful") to +5 ("very useful"), and for Feasibility, with a range from 0 ("will never happen") to 5 ("2024"--the SGCA goal).

Figure 6.1
UTILITY

```
  5     4     3     2     1     0    -1    -2    -3    -4    -5
|------|------|------|------|------|------|------|------|------|------|
 Very        Useful              No    Harmful              Very
 Useful                          Utility                    Harmful
```

FEASIBILITY - Start Planning now for the Single Global Currency in....

```
  5         4         3         2         1         0
|----------|----------|----------|----------|----------|
 2024      2044      2074      2104      2124      Will never
                                                   Happen
```

Of the 1,430 economists to whom such emails have been sent through 10 November 2005, 88 responded with a comment, most of which are positive. We have numerical ratings for only 28, and even a few of those are assumed, given their other responses. The low response rate can be attributed to many factors, including
-the rush of working in a world with too many emails and too much information;
-the unwillingness to respond to questionnaires generally;
-the unfamiliarity with the source, i.e., the SGCA;
-the unwillingness to say something negative; and
-the unwillingness to make a commitment to evaluate the SGC.
For a discipline that has been able to quantify a substantial amount of human behavior, the reluctance to assign numerical ratings to the Single Global Currency seems ironic. As the waves of research and public interest encounter the supertanker, *3-G*, it is hoped that the thinking about the

Single Global Currency will shift and more economists can be expected to respond in the future, and respond positively.

On the positive side, Matt Polasek of Flinders University in Australia wrote, "I do not think that any economist who has given the matter any thought would deny that on your Utility Scale of Rating the project merits a +4 or +5, for the simple reason that the benefits of a common currency area are in direct proportion to its size, and hence the optimum of any such system is an arrangement that comprises the whole world."[15] His rating of the SGC was 4-5 ("very helpful") for Utility and 1-2 (between 2104 and 2124, i.e., at least one hundred years) for Feasibility.

Similarly, Basil Moore of South Africa forwarded a draft of several chapters in his upcoming book, where he wrote, "Most economists would agree that a world central bank and a world currency are the logical final future solution to the problems of the global trading system, and at some distant date will probably materialize."[16]

The discussion below is broken into those two categories: utility and feasibility. Sometimes the distinction is unclear, as some economists addressed both issues. Economists are most qualified to address the utility issue, and feasibility is a political question best addressed by others.

Utility of the Single Global Currency

By virtue of the title of his 2001 article, "On Why Not a Global Currency."[17] and by virtue of his former position as chief economist at the IMF, Harvard Professor Kenneth Rogoff has posed the most visible academic challenge to the idea of a Single Global Currency.

As with Richard Cooper and Robert Mundell, Rogoff focused on what he called the "core currencies" of the major economic powers.

He begins by agreeing that it's likely that the number of currencies in the world will "decline sharply" over the next two decades and that exchange rates will fluctuate "almost as wildly as stock prices," although the effect of such gyrations to the overall economies is not clear. "Thus, the mere fact that exchange rates between the yen, the euro, and the dollar fluctuate wildly does not provide a *prima facie* case that we should permanently fix them." He continues that the increase in trade within the Eurozone since the euro may not indicate a causal relationship, as other changes within the European Union have been made as well.

Professor Rogoff uses an analogy:

> "There is a good analogy in the old fable of nail soup: A beggar, trying to talk his way in out of the cold, claims that he can make a most delicious soup with only a nail. The farmer lets him in, and the beggar stirs the soup, saying how good it will taste, but how it would be even better if he could add a leek. After similarly convincing his host to contribute a chicken and all sorts of other good things, the beggar pulls out the magic nail and, indeed, the soup is delicious. The euro is the nail."[18]

If the soup could be considered as the broth of financial stability into which is stirred all the $300 billion transactions savings and asset value increases plus the sweetness of life without currency crises, together with the iron-rich Single Global Currency nail, the world would gladly drink it-- indefinitely.

Professor Rogoff wrote that "One could bypass many of the objections I have raised by adopting a world currency pegged to a commodity basket (or just, say, to gold)." However, none of the major currencies, including the common currency euro, is now pegged to any commodity nor gold, nor to each other, so a monetary union of the G-3, 4, 5, or 6 or whatever, would not need such support either.

He concluded his brief article, "I have argued here that, into the foreseeable future, it would not be desirable to aim for a single world currency, and that from an economic point of view, it would be preferable to retain at least, say, three to four currencies if not *n* currencies."[19]

If Professor Rogoff sees utility for a common currency within each of three or four or *n* currency areas, then there is surely utility for everyone being in a single currency. If, for example, if we had a three-currency world today, there could be approximately 2.2 billion people in each of the currency areas. That's more people than the entire population of the world in 1940. Thus, a single currency could have supported all the people of the world in 1940. Why not all the people of the world in 2014? Is there a qualitative difference between a common currency for 2.2 billion people and 7+ billion people?

In a 1999 *Slate* article, "Monomoney Mania," Paul Krugman describes the "current enthusiasm for currency unification" as "an intellectual fad, not a deep insight. I say let a hundred currencies bloom. Well, maybe 20 or 30."[20]

It is hard to see a reason for efficiencies which justify consolidating currencies from 193 to 140 to 100 to 50 to 40 to Paul Krugman's 30 to 20, and then stopping at Kenneth Rogoff's 4 to 3 or *n* (presumably 2). Whatever merit can be found in the competition among currencies, it cannot possibly justify the huge transaction and currency risk costs of having more than one global currency. If the world can progress to such a small number of currencies, why stop at four, three or *n*?[21] Why doesn't *n* = 1, and only 1? Moving to one is common cents/sense.

Professor Rogoff refers to several "puzzles" in international economics which have befuddled economists, such as the Purchasing Power Parity Puzzle which explores why price fluctuations correlate to exchange rate changes more weakly than economic theory predicts. While he notes that solutions to those puzzles might come if one incorporates the costs of trade, which seems to illustrate common sense, he does not examine those puzzles in the context of a Single Global Currency. Indeed, several of the puzzles would disappear entirely or require substantial redefinition in a 3-G world.[22]

Together with Maurice Obstfeld, Kenneth Rogoff examined in 2000 the value of cooperation among central banks in such areas as the setting of interest rates, and found that cooperation had no empirical advantage over non-cooperation. Thus, the existing system has their support, and they wrote that it "should give pause to the many economists who presume that the current monetary system is vastly suboptimal and must someday give way to something like a world euro standard."[23]

<u>"Impossible Trinity"</u> Economists cite the "Impossible Trinity" as a reason why a Single Global Currency will not work. It is "the impossibility of combining all three of the following: monetary independence, exchange rate stability, and full financial market integration."[24] Richard Cooper defines "incompatible triangle" as "fixed exchange rates, independent monetary policy, and freedom of capital movements."[25] Benn Steil and Robert Litan state the problem even more strongly for two of the three legs of the trinity, "It is not possible simultaneously to target the inflation rate and the exchange rate."[26]

This doctrinal certainty has been cited as the reason why the Single Global Currency will not work, but the "Impossible Trinity" does not apply in a Global Monetary Union because there will be zero percent "monetary independence" as there will be only one monetary authority, the Global Central Bank. Also, there will be 100 percent "exchange rate stability" because there are no exchange rates, although some economists would argue that within a monetary union, exchange rates are fixed. Without the other two legs of the trinity, it follows that "full financial market integration" is not limited by either of the other legs and is therefore neither required, nor impossible, in a Global Monetary Union.

In 2013 Michael Klein and Jay Shambaugh stated the trilemma this way, "A central result in international macroeconomics is that a government cannot simultaneously opt for open financial markets, fixed exchange rates, and monetary autonomy;..."[27] However, as the success of the euro has shown, monetary autonomy is not necessarily a good in itself and fixed exchange rates are fully compatible with open financial markets. Perhaps, by definition, the reference to "a government" excludes monetary unions from the operation of the trilemma.

Related to the "Impossible Trinity" is the "Unholy Trinity" about rapid spreads of currency or financial crises: "(i) they follow a large surge in capital flows; (ii) they come as a surprise; and (iii) they involve a leveraged common creditor."[28] With a Single Global Currency, there would be little risk of a surge in capital flows, currently thought of as being risky cross-currency capital flows, leading to a currency crisis. Within a Global Monetary Union, a surge in capital going *from* one region would be equal to a surge *into* other regions and thus balance out. Steil and Litan make the point strongly, "We know of no economist who questions the wisdom of free capital flows between the continental United States and the commonwealth of Puerto Rico; or dollarized Panama, Ecuador, and El Salvador, for that matter."[29]

At a conference at the IMF in April 2007, the author asked a question of the three panelists, Guillermo Calvo, Jeffrey Frankel, and Kenneth Rogoff: "If the world political leaders were to ignore the conventional wisdom that a Single Global Currency should not be implemented, and they, the political leaders, were to implement a Single Global Currency tomorrow, how would that change your analysis of financial globalization?"[30]

Only Guillermo Calvo, to his credit, responded to the question, and he said,
"On the issue of the currency union or one currency, I think the big problem there is the lender of last resort. I think that is an issue we should come and rethink all the time seriously....

Of course we think it [the Single Global Currency] does not work and so strongly we think that it does not work that I have never seen in my years at the IMF that being an issue for discussion. So I think we have to put that together. My short answer, because this is a really big issue, is that we are going to have trouble setting up a lender of last resort which is effective at the global level, so it is a political issue more than an economic issue. But once we agree why it would not work as it does for an individual country, and even a large individual country like the U.S."

The issue of the "lender of last resort" is an interesting issue for monetary unions. The question is: will the monetary union central bank come to the rescue of a national bank of a member country in the event of a crisis? For the EMU, now fifteen years old, the question has never been fully tested, but the responses of the ECB to the 2008-2013 economic crisis shows that the ECB is quite willing to take necessary steps to ensure the stability of the euro. When the Global Central Bank is established, eventually, within a Global Monetary Union, this "lender of last resort" issue should be clearly addressed in the Bank's charter. That is, the Global Central Bank should be the lender of last resort, and it should be given the resources and tools to accomplish that mission, if necessary.

The *Asia Times* carried on 10 June 2008 the only article that year by an International Monetary Fund economist about a Single Global Currency, when it published, "Time Overdue for a World Currency" by the IMF's Noureddine Krichene and Professor Hossein Askari of George Washington University. They wrote,

> "A world central bank is becoming a necessity in a global economy. Such an independent central bank, not subject to the political whims of a particular government, would be more likely to apply orthodox and safe central banking. Contrary to any country's central bank, a world central bank would have no obligation to accommodate budgetary deficits, war spending, domestic wage and price rigidities, speculative asset bubbles, or rescue ailing domestic banks. Its law should be as meticulously applied as any constitutional law of a Western democracy....
>
>   The world currency note will circulate along with national currencies, serve as a reserve asset, and become part of the international payments system.
> By becoming a full-fledged reserve asset, a world currency would cushion the real value of international reserves against inflationary policies of reserve currency centers and wide fluctuations in exchange rates...."[31]

Feasibility of the Single Global Currency

It appears that economists permit their doubts about the political feasibility to cloud their views about the utility. Ralph Bryant wrote in *Turbulent Waters--Cross Border Finance and International Governance* that "Our grandchildren's grandchildren, for example, might well be discussing the possible evolution of a world central bank and the political independence of that bank from supranational federalist institutions and from national governments."[32] Former Assistant Secretary of the US Treasury Edwin Truman said in 1999, "Although I can imagine convergence toward such a monetary regime at some point in the 21st century, I doubt it is a realistic possibility in the next few decades."[33]

Even Robert Mundell has occassionaly seemed to retreat from the full potential of his earlier writings, i.e., a Single Global Currency for everyone. Instead, he has sometimes focused on interim steps, such as monetary union, or pegged exchange rates, among Europe, Japan, and the United States.

Professor Mundell wrote, "...nor would I propose scrapping all national currencies in favor of the dollar or world currency."[34] Here, he was concerned not about the economic utility of scrapping obsolete currencies, but expressing his belief that such a requirement would not be politically feasible. Such scrapping of vestigial currencies is not required in the proposal of the Single Global Currency Association, but is an option. If a country participating in the Global Monetary Union seeks to retain a local or national currency, that might well be that country's option, just as it was the option for the EMU members. For reasons of efficiency, the EMU countries chose to abandon their old currencies, and such scrapping of the legacy currencies is required to be part of the adoption of the euro by the ten New Member States.

The focus of "A Theory of Optimum Currency Areas" was to explore the maximum effectiveness of flexible exchange rates, and not a Single Global Currency for the world. Mundell wrote,

> "The second question concerns how the world should be divided into currency areas. We have argued that the stabilization argument for flexible exchange rates is valid only if it is based on regional currency areas. If the world can be divided into regions within each of which there is factor mobility and between which there is factor immobility, then each of these regions should have a separate currency which fluctuates relative to all other currencies. This carries the argument for flexible exchange rates to its logical conclusion."[35]

He did not speculate on the possible number of such optimum currency areas, but said there was an upper limit.

When discussing the idea of a Single Global Currency, Nobel Laureate James Tobin believed that it would need to be accompanied by worldwide fiscal coordination, thus making it impracticable, at least in the foreseeable future from his vantage point of the 1970s. So he pressed on with his second recommendation, the "Tobin Tax" on currency transactions.[36] He wrote,

"There are two ways to go. One is toward a common currency, common monetary and fiscal policy, and economic integration. The other is toward greater financial segmentation between nations or currency areas, permitting their central banks and governments greater autonomy in policies tailored to their specific economic institutions and objectives. The first direction, however appealing, is clearly not a viable option in the foreseeable future, i.e., the twentieth century. I therefore regretfully recommend the second, and my proposal is to throw some sand in the wheels of our excessively efficient international money markets."[37]

The "Tobin Tax" was to be the "sand."

Richard Cooper proposed a single currency for the industrialized democracies in the fall 1984 issue of *Foreign Affairs*. While that broke new ground, he had no illusions about how long it might take. "The idea of a single currency is so far from being politically feasible at present--in its call for a pooling of monetary sovereignty--that it will require many years of consideration before people become accustomed to the idea."[38] Note that only eight years later, the fifteen member European Union's Maastricht Treaty was signed and twelve of the fifteen subsequently abandoned their monetary sovereignty. Thirty years later, 18 European countries had abandoned their currencies.

Cooper wrote, "But there is serious question about whether one world money is either necessary or desirable. And it is certainly not feasible, even within our generous 25-year timeframe."[39]

Cooper is quite definite on distinguishing between a Single Global Currency and a common currency among the major democracies. He wrote to the Association in 2003, "...since I do not support a global currency, I cannot think of a way to manage it that would command legitimacy. My proposal of some years ago, which I have repeated more recently in the August 2000 issue of *International Finance*, is for a common currency among the major industrial democracies, i.e., Europe, USA, and Japan."[40]

Professor Rogoff also addressed the feasibility question in his "On Why Not a Global Currency" article in the section, "Other Reasons to be Cautious About Adopting a Single World Currency." He stated that it is unlikely that a central bank could be established for the world with as much credibility as the US Federal Reserve or the European Central Bank. Also, "political problems could make it difficult to choose top-notch central bankers."[41] However, with a Single Global Currency, the work of the central bankers at the Global Central Bank and the work of the national and monetary union central banks would be easier. Presently, most of them have to face the "Impossible Trinity" and juggle exchange rates AND internal interest rates. There often occurs the impossible challenge of needing to raise interest rates in order to keep currency within the currency area boundaries, but needing to keep interest rates low in order to encourage economic growth. Finally, Professor Rogoff argued that "through a number of channels, global currency competition provides a check on inflation," and cited his own 1985 article to support that proposition.[42] This was seventeen years before a common currency was introduced to the people of the Eurozone who can now easily compare prices across 18 nations. This ability to compare prices, along with the ECB's careful inflation targeting, has helped to dampen inflation. A similar effect will be seen with a Single Global Currency. We do not need currency competition to achieve low global inflation. we need a Single Global Currency.

Having one Global Central Bank, with open governance, and whose every decision is exposed to the internet eyes of billions of people, does not mean that it will exhibit the price-raising characteristics of monopolistic corporations. Having one standard-setter often enhances competition at a different level, such as the standardizing work of the World Trade Organization. It will "level the playing field," which is now contoured and subject to earth-splitting earthquakes. With one worldwide interest rate, national banks would be forced to compete more on the basis of service than is currently the case. Nations would compete for investment dollars without the complicating factor of exchange rates, which presently clouds such competition.

One overly cautious assumption made by economists is that a Single Global Currency will not work unless there is a global government or global trading system, or both. Even supporters of the Single Global Currency can take this view as they consider the feasibility of the SGC. Wrote SGC supporter, Basil Moore, "Unfortunately in the foreseeable future it is inconceivable that the world could unite into a single global trading federation, with a single central bank and a single currency." Similarly, regarding a central bank, he wrote,

> "...it is unfortunately inconceivable that such an entity
> could be created in the foreseeable future. If by some
> fortuitous miracle it were somehow imposed it would
> soon dissolve in widespread alienation, dissatisfaction,
> and policy failure. There is a very serious question
> whether a world government and world central bank will
> ever become feasible."[43]

While a common currency is obviously more feasible and easier to administer within a political entity with free trade among its regions, there is no requirement for either a common government or a free trade zone for a successful common currency. Fariborz Moshirian wrote of the need for a Single Global Currency in the context of a "New International Financial Architecture,"[44] but a common government is not a requirement. There is no common government among the countries of the Eastern Caribbean Monetary Union, nor among the countries of the Central African Monetary Community and West African Monetary Union. Within the European Union, there is a European Parliament and Commission, but their powers are limited and their boundaries are not the same as the European Monetary Union.

However, as the Eurozone is within the European Union, it might appear that an economic union or common market is a requirement, but suppose France were to announce trade quotas or tariffs on some goods within the

EU. Apart from EU trade agreements, could France do that and remain a part of the Eurozone? Suppose France merely established a tax of one euro per person or per 100 kilograms on all people and goods traveling into the country. It would surely be harmful to France, but not to its participation as a member of the Eurozone, or European Monetary Union.

Richard Cooper wrote that the link between free trade and a common currency was not required, "Free trade is a natural but not entirely necessary complement to these macroeconomic arrangements."[45]

In January 2001, several prominent international economists gathered at the World Economic Forum to respond to the question, "Does the Global Economy Need a Global Currency?" The answer was summarized, "As attractive as the idea may sound...a Single Global Currency is not a viable alternative to the world's existing mix of fixed and floating exchange rates."[46] That is, it's useful for the world but not yet politically feasible.

Volker Nitsch analyzed about 245 examples of dissolutions of monetary unions, for such reasons as differential inflation and the end of a colonial regime.[47] However, he did not conclude from his study that monetary unions were impossible or doomed. Indeed, his research reminds one of the legendary Thomas Edison who experimented with thousands of filaments in 1878 and 1879 before perfecting the longer-life electric light bulb. The EMU *is* the light bulb lighting the way to Global Monetary Union.

Benjamin Cohen's criticisms of monetary unions naturally lead to his view of the Single Global Currency. He wrote, "...neither is it likely that competition will drive the number (of currencies) down toward the 'odd figure less than three' favored by Robert Mundell."[48] Of the Global Central Bank, he writes, "As a response to the challenge of money's new geography, the approach has the merit of being parsimonious and even elegant. Regrettably, it is also flawed and hopelessly unrealistic."[49] Cohen dismisses a Single Global Currency as "utopian."[50] However, as Paul De Grauwe has observed, most economists felt the same way about the European Central Bank and the euro.

Instead of a movement toward a Single Global Currency, Cohen's forecast for the global monetary system is

> "for a more fragmented currency system, with three or four monies in direct competition in different parts of the world.... Once again, as during the long interregnum following the start of sterling's decline, it could be decades before the final outcome becomes clear."[51]

Less forcefully, Eswar Prasad notes the benefits of a Single Global Currency, but wrote that the "concept raises a whole host of thorny operational questions."[52]

The strongest written statement against the Single Global Currency is by Professor Nouriel Roubini of the Stern School of Business at New York University, New York. He wrote on his website on 23 August 2004, the article, "A Single Global Currency? Not Any Time Soon Nor in the Long Run in Which We Are All Dead."[53] He addresses the utility and the feasibility of the Single Global Currency and his comments are presented below in their entirety. Some of the endnoted references were weblinked in the original online essay.

Roubini writes, "The usually sharp Martin Wolf of the FT has recently come out in favor of a Single Global Currency for all countries:

'Martin Wolf 'We Need a Global Currency

Last month was the 60th anniversary of the conference at Bretton Woods, New Hampshire, that inaugurated the post-second world war international economic order. The flood of analysis that this occasion brought forth has concentrated on that meeting's institutional progeny: the International Monetary Fund and the World Bank. But a bigger question needs to be addressed. It is whether floating exchange rates have proved to be the ideal replacement for the unsustainable adjustable exchange-rate pegs of the Bretton Woods monetary regime. The answer is: no....

A world in which borrowing abroad is hugely dangerous for most relatively poor countries is undesirable. A world that compels the anchor currency country to run huge current account deficits looks unstable. We should seek to lift these constraints. The simplest way to do so would be to add a global currency to a global economy. For emerging market economies, at least, this would be a huge boon.

I am well aware of the economic and political objections to this idea. But if the global market economy is to thrive over the decades ahead, a global currency seems the logical concomitant. In its absence, the world of free capital flows will never work as well as it might. This is a world I am unlikely ever to see. But maybe my children or grandchildren will do so.' [54]

Roubini continued,

"His case in favor of a global currency is a combination of different arguments.

First, he is concerned about the United States running large current account deficits and accumulating debt.

Second, he is concerned about emerging market economies having to borrow in foreign currency (as they suffer of "original sin" or "liability dollarization"[55] as in the celebrated arguments of Hausman and Eichengreen)[56] and thus being vulnerable to highly disruptive financial crises when capital reversals and sudden stops occur and currencies collapse.

Third, he is concerned about the excessive and inefficient accumulation of forex reserves by Asian and other emerging market economies. All these phenomena, he argues, are explained by currency instability that would be eliminated by a Single Global Currency.

These arguments, however, do not make a compelling case for a Single Global Currency. Spending time with Robert Mundell--a great supporter of a global currency--in the Tuscany hills may impair one's better judgment about the benefits of a Single Global Currency. There are many arguments against such Single Global Currency.

First, as forcefully argued in a recent monograph by Goldstein and Turner,[57] liability dollarization is not as widespread as claimed by Hausman & Co.; also, countries are not bound to remain in "liability dollarization" hell forever; "original sin" may not be really eternal and may rather be a purgatory from which you can graduate (and start issuing local currency debt) if you follow sound economic policies for a while.

Second, even if emerging markets were to suffer of "original sin" it is not obvious that they are good candidates for formal dollarization. As has been discussed in previous papers of mine, the conditions for a country being a good candidate for adopting a foreign currency (formal dollarization) are very stringent and very few do satisfy them. Even an originally gung-ho[58] supporter of dollarization for many emerging market economies such as Hausmann has recently come around in favor of flexible exchange rates and in favor of resolving "original sin" via institutional changes in international financial markets so as to allow emerging market economies to borrow abroad in their own currency.

Third, a Single Global Currency would prevent currency crises but would not necessarily prevent debt and financial crises. Take the case of Panama: it dollarized a century ago but it has been in a fiscal mess for the last three decades, has been the most prolonged user of IMF resources and it defaulted on its external debt in the 1980s and eventually reduced it with a Brady bond deal. So, eliminating currency risk does not lead to economic virtue, as the recent case of Ecuador also suggests. Liquidity runs can still occur (and they are even more dangerous as domestic lender of last resort support tools are much more limited with a Single Global Currency) and debt crises can also occur with grave severity.

Fourth, would a Single Global Currency prevent large global current account imbalances such as those currently observed? Not necessarily as currency misalignment is only one of the ways that such imbalances are created and persist over time. Since the current account balance is equal to savings-investment balance, the recent large US current account deficit--

driven by fiscal deficits--would have been almost as large as it is now even with a Single Global Currency. Indeed, the US fiscal deficit would have led to a current account deficit (twin deficits) even in the absence of currency movements: real appreciation and depreciation can occur via changes in nominal prices rather than currency values when domestic currencies are pegged or non-existent. Yes, saving-investment imbalances driven by factors such as fiscal imbalances may be exacerbated by the currency misalignments that such imbalances create; but eliminating currency movements does not prevent large current account imbalances from emerging in the first place. If anything, lack of currency risk may make the financing of such large imbalances easier, as there is not risk of capital losses on US dollar assets held abroad if the dollar does not exist and cannot depreciate. Thus, lack of currency volatility may cause imbalances to persist longer and thus cause a more severe--and in long run unsustainable--accumulation of external debt.

Fifth, if we had a Single Global Currency, we would need a single Global Central Bank that would set the single global short term policy interest rate (the global Fed Funds rate). But, if business cycles of major regions--US, Europe, Japan/Asia and other emerging markets--are not highly synchronized to begin with, a common world interest rate would not be optimal; it could be outright dangerous and destabilizing instead.

Sixth, if there was a Single Global Currency someone would have to provide lender of last resort support in the case of bank runs and banking crises. But how would a Global Central Bank decide whether to "bail out" or provide liquidity to a particular country banking system but not to another one? Which criteria would be used? A Single Global Currency requires also a single global supervisor and regulator of the banking and financial system; otherwise moral hazard distortions from potential lender of last support could be severe. But are we ready to accept a single global financial regulator?

Seventh, the reason why Asian and other emerging market economies are accumulating foreign reserves is not anymore their concern about the risk of a liquidity run (as in 1997-98); in fact, the accumulation of such a war chest of reserves is now well in excess of what is required to avoid a liquidity run. The Asians are accumulating reserves because they want to prevent an appreciation of their currencies relative to the US dollar (a variant of this argument is the Garber, Folkerts-Landau, and Dooley argument of the restoration of a Bretton Woods 2 regime of global fixed exchange rates).

But we are really not in a new BW2 regime (as argued in a forthcoming paper of mine with Brad Setser). Also, Asian countries' desire to follow a low-consumption, high-savings, high export and large current account surplus growth model could be partially achieved even in a world of a single currency. If your economic policies repress consumption and stimulate savings, your excess of national saving relative to investment will lead to current account surpluses and export-led growth. Yes, maintaining an artificially cheap currency can help but such global current account imbalances depend more on saving and investment imbalances than on exogenous currency misalignments that may cause such imbalances. After all, currency misalignment is in large part a product of such macro savings-investment imbalances in the first place.

Finally, monetary unions have been historically associated with political unions; and, indeed, EMU emerged as a stage of a drive towards political union in Europe. Monetary Unions without political unions have historically failed, as the Latin Monetary Union of the nineteenth century. So, a Single Global Currency will require something closer to a single political union in the world. And chances of having a single global government are nil, to say the least.

In summary, not only is the likelihood that we will see a Single Global Currency in our lifetimes slim; it is also a bad idea to begin with. It is still possible that, in 20 to 30 years, the number of national currencies may be significant smaller. If, and that is a big if, the Euro/EMU experiment is successful, most of an integrated greater Europe would eventually be under a single currency. In the Americas, a few more countries (on top of the recently dollarized Ecuador and El Salvador) may also decide to unilaterally dollarize. A NAMU (North American Monetary Union) including the USA, Canada, and Mexico would make some economic sense but it is politically unlikely to come alive. So, the process of monetary unification in the Americas will be slow at best and based on unilateral dollarizations rather than formal Monetary Unions as in the EMU.

Finally in the Asian region the desire for some currency stability may lead to more formal currency arrangements. At first, like in Europe, the Asians could go for a loose form of ERM/EMS (or better, AMS) with wide but narrowing bands. A formal AMU (Asian Monetary Union) is quite unlikely for two main reasons: 1) in Europe EMS led to EMU because Europe was integrating politically, not just economically; 2) any monetary union requires an

163

implicit strong anchor currency as an intermediate step to a MU (the US dollar for the Americas' unilateral dollarizations; the German Mark for the Europe and the EMS to EMU process). But in Asia, it is not clear which currency would be the anchor of such AMU. Japan, and its currency the Yen, used to be the leading economic power. But now, the emergence of China as the major regional economy implies that Asians' currency policies and managed floats are driven more by China's currency policy than by Japan's. But China and its currency do not have yet the economic/financial and political status to become the true anchors of an AMU.

Thus, while it is not far fetched to believe that in 30 plus or so years, there may be three broad currency blocs with the world, one in the Americas anchored around the US dollar, one in Eurasia anchored around the Euro and one on Asia anchored around the Yen or the Yuan, we could expect, at most three global currencies in our lifetimes, certainly not a Single Global Currency. And even this process towards three main global currencies is likely to be bumpy and highly uncertain: unilateral dollarizations in the Americas may have little appeal to most Latin economies if they do not imply a road to a symmetric monetary union, an idea that is a politically toxic in the US. In Europe, the EMU has still to prove itself before it can become the currency of all the EU fifteen, now twenty-five, and soon thirty to forty-plus members. And in Asia, monetary and currency stability may depend on the resolution of the question of who will be the political and economic hegemon of the region: Japan, now China, or maybe India in some future?

So, for the time being a Single Global Currency in the next two decades? Not a fat chance of that happening and/or being desirable!"[59]

Roubini wrote that analysis in 2004, and his "two decades" will arrive in 2024, which is coincidentally the year of the goal for the Single Global Currency Assn. for a Single Global Currency.

Strong opposition to an SGC came in a paper by Michael Bordo and Harold James at a conference in Vienna in February 2006, "Regional and International Currency Arrangements." Their paper, "One World Money, Then and Now," used many examples from the past to show how a future world currency would not work.[60] Citing the Eurozone as a unique political effort, they minimized the future of other monetary unions in the section, "The fading attractions of monetary union." They stated that several claimed benefits of a Single Global Currency, such as international financial stability, are now being met by reforms in the existing multicurrency system.

They wrote, "It is striking how the most widely touted proposals for world money do not attempt to deal with the issue of who is making policy and in whose interest," and then focused on Robert Mundell's proposal for a G-3 monetary union. As discussed broadly here and in the 06 Edition, the monetary policy would be established by a Global Central Bank in the interest of the people of the world and their various organizations. The political details of the makeup of their constituencies will be established by international agreement through international monetary conferences or other representative framework.

Sergio Schmukler, of the World Bank responded directly to the Bordo and James article and to Richard Cooper's article favoring a common currency among the industrial democracies. Schmukler wrote "Based on the recent experience and discussions, one could argue that a world currency is unlikely to materialize soon, and even in the long run...To conclude, it is difficult to conceive a world with one currency."[61]

The prevailing view of economists appears to be that the Single Global Currency is utopian and economists are not trained to prepare for utopias. Respected academics, though not economists, join the mantra, without further analysis. In a blog Q & A session relating to his 2008 book, *The Ascent of Money*, Niall Ferguson was asked, "Can you envision a single global currency in the future, and could it serve to stabilize international relations or prevent runaway inflation in some state economies?" Ferguson responded, "I doubt it, though world money is quite an old idea. For a big nation state, there are strong arguments for retaining an independent monetary policy — that's why Britain has resisted joining the Eurozone. The argument is less strong for small economies, which is why regional currencies are easier to imagine."[62] For a person of Ferguson's vision and insight, it's hard to see why a Single Global Currency is hard to imagine. Ironically, the reasons for Britain to join a Single Global Currency are far stronger than for joining the EMU.

In 2011, Peter Kenen began a paper, "Let me be bold and look many years ahead. What currency, if any, might challenge the role of the dollar as the dominant international currency, assuming that no great economic or political calamity befalls the United States? There is, I submit, no plausible candidate."[63] He then examined the prospects for the euro, SDR, or the yuan to replace the dollar and found each unlikely.

China has been a source of some impetus toward a new monetary system, without the domination by the currency of one nation's currency, i.e. the USD.

In March 2009, China's central bank governor, Zhou Xiaochuan, called for a new international reserve currency to replace the USD. He wrote,

> The outbreak of the current crisis and its spillover in the world have confronted us with a long-existing but still unanswered question, i.e., what kind of international reserve currency do we need to secure global financial stability and facilitate world economic growth, which was one of the purposes for establishing the IMF?[64]

In October 2013, during the struggle in the US to avoid defaulting on payments on its debt, Xiaochuan stated one of the obvious reasons for moving away from the USD, "It is perhaps a good time for the befuddled world to start considering building a de-Americanized world."[65]

In January Jan 2014, a Chinese former World Bank economist, Justin Yifu Lin, called for a "super-currency." The English language *China Daily* reported,

> "The World Bank's former chief economist wants to replace the US dollar with a single global super-currency, saying it will create a more stable global financial system.
> 'The dominance of the greenback is the root cause of global financial and economic crises,' Justin Yifu Lin told Bruegel, a Brussels-based policy-research think tank.
> 'The solution to this is to replace the national currency with a global currency.' "[66]

Justin Lin's proposal was a followup to his discussion of a "composite currency or a purely international currency," in his 2013 book, *Against the Consensus*.[67]

Such calls are likely to increase, especially when the US shows that its primary interests are in its own economy and not in maintaining a stable currency for the rest of the world to use. For most of the period of the US dollar's global dominance, those interests have been perceived as being in unison. For example, the US government's nearly continuous deficits helped supply the world with liquidity for economic growth. However, in our electronically connected world, the world watches closely when the US dances perilously closely to default, as if the concerns about monetary stability for the rest of the world mean nothing.

In a paper aiming to persuade the largest 20 countries to act together for world reform, Barry Carin and Gordon Smith wrote in 2005,

> "What are the prospects for a global currency – say in 2040? The benefits of a hypothetical single global currency are undeniable. The factor of foreign exchange rate risk would be eliminated. Asset values in all participating countries would increase in value due to the decrease in foreign exchange risk. Billions of dollars, yen and euros of exchange transaction costs would be eliminated. While there would be very substantial benefits for OECD countries, there would be extraordinary benefits for the developing world. Political and intellectual energy would not be invested defending the illusion of independent monetary policy. Interest rates would simply reflect the real credit risk of borrowers. Authorities would not have interest rates held hostage to defend exchange rates. No longer would entire economies have to be damaged by high interest rates in order to save them. The net benefits of the hypothetical world currency are unquestioned. The problem is 'you cannot get there from here.' "[68]

Fariborz Moshirian concluded in 2008,

> "Indeed, it is easier to envisage an interdependent world, with technology that did not exist in the 19th or even the

20th century and capital mobility that has the potential to connect nations together and transfer technology, without creating unemployment in developed countries, with global institutions such as a world government, a world parliament, an international tribunal, a world central bank and a global single currency. This could happen without any requirement of workers from poor countries migrating to rich countries and change the composition of populations and the cohesiveness that exists amongst nations. Despite the fact that the concept of a world government may sound either too idealistic or too costly, the process suggested here could have fewer complications and challenges than what Americans went through in the 19th century and what the Europeans experienced in the 20th century. The urgent tasks of dealing with global environmental issues, international security and peace, stable global financial markets and the eradication of poverty should make us think about the most effective way to address these and other pressing global issues."[69]

The Single Global Currency and Financial Globalization

Philip Arestis, Santonu Basu and Sushanta Mallick wrote in 2005 that "the term *financial globalization* refers to the process by which financial markets of various countries of the globe are integrated as one." Further, they argued, "The necessary condition for a complete process of financial globalization is the need to introduce a worldwide single currency for settling all transactions. The currency should be managed and regulated by a single international monetary authority."[70]

The authors stated "The above analysis highlights the argument that the existence of different currencies, with their differing degrees of convertibility, stands as a serious impediment to the integration of the different financial markets into one. It also segregates the market in such a way that in an unregulated environment, it disproportionately favors developed countries at the expense of the developing world."[71]

The current multicurrency system is unfair because, they continued, it "enables developed countries to issue international debts in their own domestic currency, with their own central bank acting as a lender of last resort, so that they can ignore the IMF, in a way the rest of the world is not in a position to do. Thus, it appears that the above problem principally emerged due to the absence of a single currency. The absence of a single currency is not only the principal barrier to financial globalization or integration, but it also segregates the market thereby causing unequal treatment.

"The above analysis suggests that there is a need to introduce a single currency, and to establish an international financial institution with sufficient power to be able to play the leadership role required to alleviate these problems. The current international institutional arrangements do not appear to provide a global financial institution, which is prepared to play such a central coordinating role."[72]

Later, they continued, "Thus, the issue is not just unequal access to the international financial market, but more importantly, possible changes in the degree of convertibility introduce the possibility of a developing country falling into the debt trap. This problem can only be solved provided we eliminate the differential and change the degree of convertibility of each currency, which is only possible if we introduce a single [global] currency.... In short, the introduction of a single [global] currency will unify the borrowing terms and conditions for all the countries across the globe, and may tie their borrowing ability together with their economic performance."[73]

A key element of their proposed single global currency was that "it does not depend on any national currency."[74]

SUMMARY

The interplay between utility/economics and feasibility/politics has been a constant dynamic in the consideration of changes to the economic system. Commenting on the euro, Ben Bernanke noted that "Robert Mundell argued that, ideally, economic similarity, not political boundaries, should define the geographical area spanned by a common currency" and also wrote that "political factors, rather than economic ones have played the dominant role" in the establishment of the euro.[75] So it may be for the Single Global Currency.

Right up to the day that the Single Global Currency is implemented, there will be economists who will argue that it will not work, or that implementation is premature. Even afterwards, there will be some who forecast its demise. For those who have opposed it so far, one wonders whose statement will be remembered in the same vein as those who have, in the past, made sweeping negative predictions about the future, e.g., an 1876 Western Union internal memo: "This 'telephone' has too many shortcomings to be seriously considered as a means of communication. The device is inherently of no value to us."[76]

The 3-G world will come with the support of some economists, and they will either join with, or be led by, the people of the world who want convenient, stable money.

We must move ahead, despite the reservations of many economists. Next are considered, in Chapter 7, the means to the ends of a 3-G world.

ENDNOTES

1. See, e.g., C. Fred Bergsten and the Institute for International Economics, *The United States and the World Economy: Foreign Economic Policy for the Next Decade*, Washington, DC: Institute for International Economics, 2005. The book's final chapter, "The International Financial Architecture" by Morris Goldstein, makes no mention of the Single Global Currency nor Robert Mundell nor the euro nor monetary unions.
2. "Doctoral Dissertations in Economics," *Journal of Economic Literature*, American Economic Association, December 2013, Vol. 51, Number 4, pp.

1326-1355 at
http://www.aeaweb.org/articles.php?doi=10.1257/jel.51.4.1326
3. "AEA 2013 Annual Meeting Papers" Annual meeting of the American Economic Association, January 2013, San Diego, California, at
http://www.aeaweb.org/aea/2013conference/program/meetingpapers.php
4. "AEA 2014 Annual Meeting Papers" Annual meeting of the American Economic Association, January 2014, Philadelphia, Pennsylvania at
http://www.aeaweb.org/aea/2014conference/program/preliminary.php
5. Paul De Grauwe and Jacques Melitz, editors, *Prospects for Monetary Unions after the Euro*. Cambridge, MA: MIT Press, 2005.
6. Paul De Grauwe and Jacques Melitz, editors, ibid., p. 4.
7. Paul De Grauwe, *Economics of Monetary Union*. Oxford, UK: Oxford University Press, 2005, 6th edition, p. 1.
8. Paul De Grauwe and Jacques Melitz, editors, op. cit., p. 1.
9. Paul De Grauwe and Jacques Melitz, editors, ibid.
10. Robert Wade, "The Case for a Global Currency," *International Herald Tribune*, 4 August 2006, at
http://www.nytimes.com/2006/08/03/opinion/03iht-edwade.2375020.html
11. Joseph Stiglitz, "How to Fix the Global Economy," *The New York Times*, Op-Ed, 3 October 2006, page 27, at
http://select.nytimes.com/search/restricted/article?res=F20E1FFA3F540C708CDDA90994DE404482
12. See the economists' comments and ratings for the Utility and Feasibility of the Single Global Currency at
http://www.singleglobalcurrency.org/economists_ratings_system.html
13. Martin Wolf, "We Need a Global Currency," *Financial Times*, 3 August 2004, at http://courses.wcupa.edu/rbove/eco338/040Trade-debt/Currency/040804global.txt.
14. Email from Professor Andrew Rose to the author, 15 August 2004.
15. Matt Polasek, Honorary Fellow, Flinders University, Adelaide, Australia, in email to the author, 11 November 2005.
16. Basil Moore, "Using a Common Currency in International Transactions: The Post Keynesian Case for No Exchange Rates," p. 8 of Chapter 19 of book, *Shaking the Invisible Hand: Complexity, Endogenous Money and Exogenous Interest Rates*. London, UK: Palgrave MacMillan, 2006.
17. Kenneth Rogoff, "On Why Not a Global Currency," 8 January 2001, presented to the American Economic Association Meeting on "Exchange Rates and Choice of Monetary Regimes," published in the *American Economic Review*, Vol. 91(2), 2001, pp. 243-47 and on the web at
http://scholar.harvard.edu/rogoff/publications/why-not-global-currency.
18. Ibid., at p. 6.
19. Ibid., at p. 9.
20. Paul Krugman, "Monomoney Mania," *Slate Magazine*, 16 April 1999, at
http://www.slate.com/articles/business/the_dismal_science/1999/04/monomoney_mania.html.
21. In the tradition of polite expressions of disagreement, Professor Rogoff wrote to the author upon the establishment of the Single Global Currency

Association, "Congratulations on your ambitious enterprise." Email, 28 July 2003.

22. See also, Maurice Obstfeld and Kenneth Rogoff, "The Six Major Puzzles in International Macroeconomics: Is There a Common Cause?" 2000. Posted at the National Bureau of Economic Research, at http://www.nber.org/chapters/c11059.pdf.

23. Maurice Obstfeld and Kenneth Rogoff, "Do We Really Need a New Global Monetary Compact?" in *Currency Unions*, Edited by Alberto Alesina and Robert J. Barro. Stanford, CA: Hoover Institution Press, 2001, p. 81.

24. Deardorff's Glossary of International Economics, at http://www-personal.umich.edu/~alandear/glossary/.

25. Richard Cooper, "Toward A Common Currency?" June 2000, p. 17, presented at the conference on the Future of Monetary Policy and Banking, organized by the IMF and the World Bank, at http://onlinelibrary.wiley.com/doi/10.1111/1468-2362.00053/abstract.

26. Benn Steil and Robert E. Litan, *Financial Statecraft*. London and New Haven, CT: Yale University Press, 2006, p. 104.

27. Michael Klein and Jay Shambaugh, "Rounding the Corners of the Policy Trilemma: Sources of Monetary Policy Autonomy," NBER Working Paper No. 19461, September 2013, at http://www.nber.org/papers/w19461?utm_campaign=ntw&utm_medium=email&utm_source=ntw

28. Graciella Kaminsky, Carmen Reinhart, and Carlos A. Vegh, "The Unholy Trinity of Financial Contagion," *Journal of Economic Perspectives*, 2003, v17(4, Fall), pp. 51-74. at http://www.nber.org/papers/W10061.

29. Benn Steil and Robert E. Litan, *Financial Statecraft*. London and New Haven, CT: Yale University Press, 2006, p. 108.

30. "Transcript of an IMF Economic Forum: "New Perspectives on Financial Globalization," 27 April 2007, at http://www.imf.org/external/np/tr/2007/tr070427.htm

31. Hossein Askari and Noureddine Krichene, "Time overdue for a world currency" *Asia Times*, 10 June 2008, at http://www.atimes.com/atimes/Global_Economy/JF06Dj04.html

32. Ralph Bryant, *Turbulent Waters--Cross Border Finance and International Governance.* Washington, DC: Brookings Institution Press, 2003 at p. 414.

33. Edwin Truman, "The Evolution of the International Financial System," remarks at the Institute for International Monetary Affairs Eighth Symposium, Tokyo, 6 December 1999, at http://www.iima.or.jp/Docs/symposium/19991206/Mr.Truman.pdf

34. Milton Friedman and Robert Mundell, "One World, One Money? A Debate," *Policy Options/Options Politiques* (May): 10-30, as quoted in Benjamin J. Cohen, *The Future of Money*. Princeton, NJ: Princeton University Press, 2004, p. 214.

35. Robert Mundell, "A Theory of Optimum Currency Areas," *American Economic Review*, May 1961, pp. 657-65 at p. 663, and as Chapter 12 in his book, *International Economics*, pp. 177-86, at http://www.columbia.edu/~ram15/ie/ie-12.html.

36. Recognizing the vast amounts of money which might be generated, a loose worldwide network of Tobin Tax supporters (and spenders!) has arisen. See "Tobin Tax Initiative" at http://www.ceedweb.org/iirp/.

37. James Tobin, "A Proposal for Monetary Reform," *Eastern Economic Journal*, July/October 1978, pp. 153-59, at http://www.globalpolicy.org/socecon/glotax/currtax/original.htm.

38. Richard Cooper, "A Monetary System for the Future," *Foreign Affairs*, Fall 1984, pp. 182, at http://www.jstor.org/discover/10.2307/20042091?uid=2129&uid=2&uid=70&uid=4&sid=21103474241607

39. Richard Cooper, ibid., p. 184.

40. Richard Cooper, email to the author, 18 July 2003. The referenced article is in the July 2000 issue of *International Finance*, "Toward A Common Currency?" at pp. 287-308, at http://onlinelibrary.wiley.com/doi/10.1111/1468-2362.00053/abstract.

41. Kenneth Rogoff, "On Why Not a Global Currency," 8 January 2001, op cit.

42. Ibid. The 1985 article he referenced was his "Can International Monetary Policy be Counterproductive?" in *Journal of International Economics*, May 1985, pp. 199-217.

43. Basil Moore, "Using a Common Currency in International Transactions: The Post Keynesian Case for No Exchange Rates," pp. 8-9 of Chapter 19 of book, *Shaking the Invisible Hand: Complexity, Endogenous Money and Exogenous Interest Rates*, London, UK: Palgrave MacMillan, 2006.

44. Fariborz Moshirian, "New International Financial Architecture," presented at First Single Global Currency Conference, Bretton Woods, July 2004 at http://www.singleglobalcurrency.org/documents/Newinternationalfinancia larchitecturebyFariborzMoshirian.doc. Also published in *the Journal of Multinational Financial Management*, October-December 2002, at http://www.econbiz.de/Record/special-issue-new-international-financial-architecture-moshirian-fariborz/10001708120.

45. Richard Cooper, "A Monetary System for the Future," *Foreign Affairs*, Fall 1984, pp. 166, at http://www.jstor.org/discover/10.2307/20042091?uid=2129&uid=2&uid=70&uid=4&sid=21103470935907

46. Annual Meeting, World Economic Forum, with contributors: Martin Feldstein, Jeffrey Frankel, Jacob Frenkel, Otmar Issing, Haruhiko Kuroda, Robert Mundell, Jean-Pierre Roth, and Federico Sturzenegger, "Does the Global Economy Need a Global Currency?" 26 January 2001.

47. Volker Nitsch, "Have a Break, Have a . . . National Currency: When Do Monetary Unions Fall Apart?" Chapter 12, in Paul De Grauwe and Jacques Melitz, editors, *Prospects for Monetary Unions after the Euro*. Cambridge, MA: MIT Press, 2005.

48. Benjamin J. Cohen, *The Future of Money*. op.cit., p. 192. Note that Cohen observed that Mundell's characterization of the number 1 was said in jest, at p. 213. See also, International Monetary Fund, *IMF Survey*, "Conference Examines US Economic Uncertainties, Exchange Rate Choices,

and Globalization," 22 January 2001, p. 27, "Mundell recommended a move toward a single world currency area in the future; he said the optimum number of currencies for the world, like the optimum number of gods, 'should be an odd number, preferably less than three.' " At http://www.imf.org/external/pubs/ft/survey/2001/012201.pdf.

49. Benjamin J. Cohen, *The Future of Money*, op.cit., p. 211.

50. Benjamin J. Cohen, *The Future of Money*, ibid., p. 214. There are many references to global currency and money in classic utopian novels. In particular, Edward Bellamy's 1888 *Looking Backward*, presented a 2000 world "in which money was unknown and without conceivable use," Chapter 28, online at http://xroads.virginia.edu/~HYPER/BELLAMY/ch28.html.

Myron Frankman wrote in 1990 "A Vision of the New Order," which was a look at the 1999 economy by a 1999 observer, who told of its "single world currency--not a centrally created reserve asset like the SDR, but a circulating currency which would replace all national monies," at *The Trumpeter, Journal of Ecosophy*, Volume 7.3, 1990, at http://trumpeter.athabascau.ca/index.php/trumpet/article/view/486/815.

51. Benjamin J. Cohen, *The Future of Global Currency – The Euro vs. The Dollar*, Routledge, Taylor and French Group, 2011, p. 166.

52. Eswar Prasad, *The Dollar Trap – How the U.S. Dollar Tightened Its Grip on Global Finance*, Princeton University Press, 2014, p. 267.

53. This phrase comes from the oft-quoted statement from John Maynard Keynes, "In the long run we are all dead." Wikiquote gives context to his meaning: "The long run is a misleading guide to current affairs. In the long run we are all dead. Economists set themselves too easy, too useless a task if in tempestuous seasons they can only tell us that when the storm is past the ocean is flat again." John Maynard Keynes, *A Tract on Monetary Reform*, 1923, Ch. 3.

From Wikiquote comes this observation: "Many thought this meant Keynes supported short terms gains against long term economic performance. Keynes on the other hand wanted to criticize those who believed that inflation will control itself without government intervention," at http://en.wikiquote.org/wiki/John_Maynard_Keynes.

54. Martin Wolf, "We Need a Global Currency," *Financial Times*, 3 August 2004, at http://courses.wcupa.edu/rbove/eco338/040Trade-debt/Currency/040804global.txt.

55. As noted in Chapter 3, "original sin" refers to the practical requirement that when countries with risky or soft currencies borrow money internationally, that repayment be denominated in hard currencies such as the US dollar. "Liability dollarization" describes the status of having debt or liabilities denominated in those hard currencies. See Ricardo Hausmann and Ugo Panizza, "The Mystery of Original Sin," 16 July 2002, at http://ksghome.harvard.edu/~rhausma/paper/mistery_march3.pdf

56. Barry Eichengreen, Ricardo Hausmann, and Ugo Panizza, "The Mystery of Original Sin," August 2003 at

http://emlab.berkeley.edu/users/eichengr/research/osmysteryaug21-03.pdf.

57. Morris Goldstein and Philip Turner, "Currency Mismatches at Center of Financial Crises in Emerging Economies," 22 April 2004, Institute for International Economics, Washington, DC, at http://www.iie.com/publications/newsreleases/newsrelease.cfm?id=99.

58. The term "gung-ho" is slang in English for "enthusiastic," and also used as the title of a 1986 US movie directed by Ron Howard. See Wikipedia at http://en.wikipedia.org/wiki/Gung-ho.

59. Nouriel Roubini, "A Single Global Currency? Not Any Time Soon Nor in the Long Run in Which We Are All Dead." Blog at http://www.economonitor.com/nouriel/2004/08/23/a-single-global-currency-not-any-time-soon-nor-in-the-long-run-in-which-we-are-all-dead/.

60. Michael Bordo and Harold James, "One World Money, Then and Now," Cambridge, February, 2006, National Bureau of Economic Research, at http://www.nber.org/papers/w12189 and also presented at the 24-25 February 2006 conference in Vienna.

61. Sergio Schmukler, "Discussion: Exchange Rate Arrangements and Disarrangements" Prospects for a World Currency," March 2006, at page 43 of Oesterreichische Nationalbank Working Paper 127, http://www.oenb.at/dms/oenb/Publikationen/Volkswirtschaft/Working-Papers/2006/Working-Paper-127/fullversion/wp127_tcm16-42690.pdf

62. "Book World Live: Niall Ferguson, Author of 'The Ascent of Money,' " 25 November 2008, at http://wootters.wordpress.com/2009/01/11/book-world-live-niall-ferguson-author-of-the-ascent-of-money/

63. Peter B. Kenen, "Beyond the Dollar," Paper presented at the 2011 American Economic Association annual conference, at http://www.aeaweb.org/aea/2011conference/program/meetingpapers.php

64. Zhou Xiaochuan, "Reform the international monetary system," Central Bank Speeches, Bank for International Settlements, 23 March 2009, at http://www.bis.org/review/r090402c.pdf

65. Dexter Roberts, "China's State Press Calls for 'Building a de-Americanized World', Business Week, 14 October 2013, at http://www.businessweek.com/articles/2013-10-14/chinas-state-press-calls-for-building-a-de-americanized-world

66. Michael Barris, Fu Jing and Chen Jia, "Replace dollar with super currency: economist," USA China Daily, 29 January 2013, at http://usa.chinadaily.com.cn/world/2014-01/29/content_17264069.htm

67. Justin Wifu Lin, Against the Consensus – Reflections on the Great Recession, Cambridge University Press, 2013, page 190.

68. Barry Carin and Gordon Smith, "Making Change Happen at the Global Level," Chapter 1 in John English, editor, et al., Reforming from the Top - a Leaders' 20 Summit, New York, United Nations University Press, October 2005, at http://www.globalcentres.org/html/pdf/G20%20pdf/Making%20Change%20Happen%20at%20the%20Global%20Level.pdf.

69. Fariborz Moshirian, "The significance of a world government in the process of globalization in the 21st century," *Journal of Banking and Finance*, August 2008, page 1439, at
http://www.sciencedirect.com/science?_ob=ArticleURL&_udi=B6VCY-4S4JYPT-1&_user=2721828&_coverDate=08/31/2008&_rdoc=1&_fmt=&_orig=search&_sort=d&view=c&_acct=C000050221&_version=1&_urlVersion=0&_userid=2721828&md5=b6a381829e547fe61b99ceebd3ed2ccd

70. Philip Arestis, Santonu Basu, and Sushanta Mallick, "Financial Globalization: the need for a single currency and global central bank," *Journal of Post Keynesian Economics*, Spring 2005, pp 507-531, at page 508, at
http://mesharpe.metapress.com/(pkospvf3wjgs55qbdbcsnhra)/app/home/contribution.asp?backto=issue,11,13;journal,7,17;linkingpublicationresults,1:109348,1

71. ibid, page 522.

72. ibid, page 523.

73. ibid , page 526-27.

74. ibid, page 529.

75. Adam S. Posen, Editor, *The Euro at Five: Ready for a Global Role?* Washington, DC: 2005, Institute for International Economics, Chapter 8 by Ben S. Bernanke, "The Euro at Five: An Assessment," at p. 179.

76. Western Union internal memo, 1876, as quoted in "Some interesting and bad predictions, courtesy of Susan Nicholas...." at
http://www.cfcl.com/~vlb/Cuute/Quotes/famous.words.txt.

Chapter 7. How to Get There from Here[1]

Thanks to the success of the European and other monetary unions, we now know how to create and maintain the 3-Gs: a Global Monetary Union, with a Global Central Bank and a Single Global Currency. Given the preponderance of benefits over the costs of that solution, the costs of continuing the current system, and the risk of a serious world financial crisis if the problem is not fixed, the world must move forward and start planning now.

Some writers are hopeful that the movement toward a 3-G world is accelerating and further along than it is. Wrote Sisira Mishra optimistically, "For decades there has been a groundswell of opinion developing in support of a single global currency."[2] Ambrose Evans-Pritchard sees the world moving faster toward the goal than it is, per his 2009 article in the UK's *Telegraph* about the G-20 request to the IMF to release $250 billion in SDRs, where he wrote, "The G20 moves the world a step closer to a global currency – ... backed by a global central bank, running monetary policy for all humanity."[3] Paraphrasing Mark Twain, reports of the birth of the Single Global Currency are exaggerated,[4] even if promising.

The task can be stated quite simply: how to move from the current 140 currencies down to one. Developing the political will to overcome the residual strength of nationalism is the major challenge for the movement to a 3-G world. As with the implementation of the euro, the economics and politics of monetary union are inextricably bound together; and the logic of both point toward the 3-G world. For perspective, consider that 53 countries (193-140) now use currencies other than their own national currency, and that's two more than the original 51 members of the United Nations in 1945.

The question now is not whether the world will adopt a Single Global Currency but When? and How smooth, inexpensive, and planful OR rough, costly and chaotic will the journey be? Former US Assistant Secretary of Commerce Jeffrey Garten wrote in 2009,

> "The issue is no longer whether the dollar is in long-term decline but which of two options will be taken. Should Washington and other capitals calmly and deliberately manage the transition to a new era, or, by default, should they let the market do it, with the risk of massive financial disturbances. Today, governments have a choice. Soon they may not."[5]

When?

Some of the earlier predictions now seem timely. *The Economist* magazine's 1988 prediction for implementation of a global currency in 2018, to be called the "Phoenix,"[6] is only four years away. Richard Cooper's 1984 proposal for a common currency among the industrialized democracies anticipated implementation by 2009, now four years past. However, it can be said that the euro is the common currency of his prediction, even if the US is not yet included and even if Professor Cooper probably doesn't view the current EMU members as the "industrialized democracies" he had in mind. What takes time is the work required for the establishment of the goal and the date for implementation. By comparison, actual implementation will take little time.

The twenty-first century began with 159 currencies among 189 UN members. By 2005, the number of currencies had declined to 147,[7] a drop of 12 over 5 years of 7.5 percent. At that rate of 12 every 5 years, the journey to the Single Global Currency will take 62 years until 2067, the 200th anniversary of the 1867 Paris International Monetary Conference.

By 1 January 2014, the number of currencies had dropped to 140, even though the number of UN members had grown to 193. If the rate of the drop since 2000, of 19 (159-140) in 14 years, could be continued every 14 years, the journey to the Single Global Currency will be completed by approximately 2150. If the "tipping point" is 70, then the implementation of the Single Global Currency will reach that point at approximately 2080.

If the several planned regional monetary unions around the world are implemented as scheduled, and if existing monetary unions expand as planned, the arrival of the Single Global Currency would come much sooner.

If the political decisions were made by just a few major countries to move toward a Single Global Currency, the implementation could be accomplished in less than five years. Bryan Taylor wrote in 1998,

"Once the transition to a single currency for Europe and the United States was made, the transition to a single currency for the entire world could come with a speed that might surprise many. The world might easily move from having almost 200 currencies today to having one within a decade, and twenty-five years from now, historians would wonder why it took so long to eliminate the Babel of currencies which existed in the twentieth century."[8]

Paul De Grauwe and Jacques Melitz wrote of the shift of view during the runup to the euro, "However, at some point monetary union began to be seen as something inevitable, as something that was written in the stars. At that point, professional opinion largely rallied in its favor. There can be no doubt that the mere existence of European Monetary Union has changed economists' outlook about monetary union."[9]

The remaining questions are only when the political decisions will be made and the level of commitment which will be given to the project.

Even if there is no formal decision to plan for a 3-G world, we are moving toward a smaller number of currencies, to achieve related goals. Benn Steil and Robert Litan urge that the IMF promote the "ridding of the world of nontradable currencies" and promote "currency consolidation."[10] As noted earlier, Benjamin J. Cohen called the process, even while criticizing it, the "Contraction Contention."

In this chapter are described steps to move the world more rapidly toward the 3-G goals. Unless the calls for the Single Global Currency take serious root, the pace may remain dangerously glacial. Robert Mundell wrote, "It looks as if we are a long way from that position [a world currency]

now. Yet it is surprising how quickly moods can change and producers of statecraft can escape the old modes of thought."[11]

If, however, there is a currency crisis, and especially if such a crisis involves the US dollar, pressure for reform likely will increase dramatically. The world is unlikely to tolerate continued dependence upon one nation for worldwide financial liquidity and stability. Robert Mundell also wrote, "The next big crisis might be the occasion for a reconvening of a Bretton Woods type conference to establish the conditions for a new international monetary system."[12]

By 2019, the GDP of China is predicted by *the Economist* to overtake that of the United States, and such a moment will dramatize the relative decline of the US dollar and its role in the multicurrency foreign exchange system, which will have already occurred.[13] By that time, perhaps the world will have decided whether to anoint another currency as the primary, but still a national, international reserve currency or whether to cancel the competition and join together with others to form a Single Global Currency.

The annual benefit from the implementation of a Single Global Currency has been estimated conservatively here to be $300 billion in saved transaction costs. Also predicted is a one-time $10 trillion increase in worldwide asset values, together with an associated GDP increase of $3 trillion, and the annual increase compounded from that $3 trillion boost. Every year of delay will postpone those savings, plus the achievement of the other substantial benefits of a Single Global Currency.

How Smooth, Inexpensive and Planful OR Rough, Costly and Chaotic Will the Journey Be?

Whether or not the world chooses to begin planning for the inevitable Single Global Currency, large and risky changes are very likely to occur in the foreign exchange markets. Planning now for a Single Global Currency would help assure a soft landing. If currency traders and all their customers knew that the future will bring a Single Global Currency, and not a chaotic struggle for currency supremacy by an uncertain victor, the journey might be smoother.

A major and unknown consideration is the potential cost of future currency and financial crises which will likely occur in the obsolete multicurrency foreign exchange world if no change in direction is made. That cost could be trillions of dollars or euros and untold harm to the people of the world.

What Can Be Done?

There is no single required path to the Single Global Currency. The goal will likely be achieved through some combination of the feasible steps described below, and not necessarily in the order presented. There are other possible interim steps to achieve some of the goals of the Single Global Currency, such as the Tobin Tax, but the effort required to implement and continually maintain such a tax could exceed the effort required to simply implement the Single Global Currency itself. Similarly, Robert Guttmann's 1994 suggestion that a new kind of money, "supranational credit money (SNCM)," be created and circulated domestically, would require as much effort as the implementation of the Single Global Currency.

He wrote,

> "Rather than reaching for the most difficult and utopian version, the introduction of a single currency for the entire world economy, it would be much more realistic to conceive of this new form of world money [the SNCM] as used only in international transactions between countries. This kind of arrangement allows national currencies to exist but confines them to strictly domestic circulation for transactions within their countries of issue. This was precisely the basic idea behind the plan Keynes put forward at the Bretton Woods Conference. But, unlike his Bancor proposal, the supranational credit-money (SNCM) of the future should function fully as money."[14]

This also sounds similar to current calls for increasing the use of the IMF Special Drawing Rights (SDRs), even if they are not to be used by the people of the world as regular money.

Taking the steps proposed below will all lead toward the best solution: the 3-G world.

-Increase Public and Governmental Awareness of the Need for a Single Global Currency, and Encourage Political Support;
-Conduct Public/Private Large-Scale Research into the Single Global Currency;
-Establish a Single Global Currency Institute;
-Establish the Goal and Date, and Give the New Currency a Name;
-Ize to Anchor Currencies;
-Expand Existing Monetary Unions;
-Establish New Monetary Unions;
-Establish a Global Central Bank and a Global Monetary Union;
-Establish a prototype Global Central Bank;
-Expand the use of SDR's and/or Issue "Global Greenbacks"
-Ensure that Currency Area Competition is Constructive;
-Convene International Monetary Convention(s);
-Build Political Support; and
-Mobilize Stakeholders to Encourage the Tasks Above and the Implementation of the Single Global Currency.

Increase Public and Governmental Awareness of the Need for a Single Global Currency, and Encourage Political Support

The 3-G world will come when the people of the world either lead their leaders in that direction or indicate their willingness to be led. It takes time to mobilize support for an idea that affects every human being on the earth. The Kyoto Protocol,[15] and its followup meetings, regarding air pollution is an example of the large-scale efforts that are needed to achieve global political change.

Public support of the 3-G world is critical, just as it was critical for the implementation of the euro. Robert Mundell implicitly noted the need for public support of a monetary system when he cited Sir Roy Harrod as observing that the nineteenth-century "bimetallism was a 'high-brow' standard, too complicated for the average person to understand...."[16]

As noted earlier, it has been the combination of politics and economics that led to the creation of the European Monetary Union. Whatever the economists said and wrote, and they were never united on the subject, the politicians have seen that the people and their corporations want stable money.

One political leader explicitly indicated support in 2008 for a Single Global Currency. It was reported that Indonesia's President Susilo Bambang Yudhoyono

> "proposed the use of one single global currency to
> prevent pressures on currencies, in particularly the
> rupiah, when economic crisis hits. This can at least
> maintain the stability of currency rates in each country
> and protect it against pressures of other currencies.
>
> The president maintains that with a single global
> currency rate, there would no longer be a currency
> exchange crisis and money would not be commercialized.
> With a single currency, the function of money as a
> trading value will not change. 'It could be done in stages,
> starting with the dollar, euro, or Asian currency,' said the
> president at the Bogor Institute of Agriculture (IPB)
> yesterday."[17]

Chukwuma Charles Soludo, the Governor of the Central Bank of Nigeria, called for the creation of a Single Global Currency in his inaugural address in November, 2008. About the risks of global imbalances, he said, "In the current order, there is no mechanism to correct the imbalances except by talking about it, or advising the deficit countries to live within their means and the surplus countries to revalue their currencies."[18]

Jose Antonio Campo, former Finance Minister for Columbia proposed in 2008 several reforms to respond to the current financial turmoil, and the

> "first is the need for a truly global reserve currency,
> perhaps based on the IMF Special Drawing Rights
> (SDRs). This would overcome both the inequities and the
> instability that is inherent in a global reserve system
> based on a national currency. Today's system is plagued
> by cycles of confidence in the dollar and by periodic
> shocks due to American policies that are adopted
> independently of their global impact and thus imposed
> on the rest of the world."[19]

A global reserve currency is not the same as a Single Global Currency in the hands and pockets of the people of the world, but it's a step in the right direction.

The Economy Minister of Italy, Giulio Tremonti, said in October, 2008, "Today the dollar is the currency of Bretton Woods, but now it could be that there will be other combinations. The debate on foreign exchange is being reopened,"[20] While he didn't commit to a plan for a Single Global Currency, he at least opened the door to consideration of an alternative to the multicurrency system which has been accepted as permanent for too long.

Also in 2008, the Brookings Institution published a report on the "Top Ten Global Economic Challenges facing America's 44th President," and the first of the ten was:

"1. <u>Restoring financial stability</u>: With our financial
troubles at the center of the current global vortex, the US
has important obligations to strengthen the global
financial system, including by strengthening our own
financial regulation and diminishing our reliance on
foreign credit. The next US president should work with
the international community to develop a common
agenda for managing capital flows, including increasing
flexibility in exchange rates to facilitate the adjustment of
persistent imbalances, developing global codes for
improved transparency of new players such as sovereign
wealth funds, and updating the mission and governance
of the international financial institutions to address
today's challenges and engage today's players."[21]

Every listed part of "restoring financial stability" could be solved, or substantially solved, by moving the world to a Single Global Currency, managed by a Global Central Bank, within a Global Monetary Union. However, there is no discussion of the multicurrency financial system being the problem, and no discussion of the best long term solution. The challenges facing President Obama, therefore, include the correct recognition of the international financial problems and then the identification of the Single Global Currency as being a substantial part of the solution.

Mr. Campo's comments were similar to those made in March 2009 by Zhou Xiaochuan, of the Chinese Central Bank, as noted in Chapter 6. However, because of China's role in the global economy and its vast accumulation of USD reserves, Mr. Xiaochuan's comments received more attention.

At President Obama's news conference on March 24, there was this exchange:

QUESTION: Good evening, Mr. President. Thank you.
Taking this economic debate a bit globally, senior
Chinese officials have publicly expressed an interest in
an international currency. This is described by Chinese
specialists as a sign that they are less confident than
they used to be in the value and the reliability of the U.S.
dollar....
PRESIDENT OBAMA: ...As far as confidence in the U.S.
economy or the dollar, I would just point out that the
dollar is extraordinarily strong right now. And the reason

180

the dollar is strong right now is because investors
consider the United States the strongest economy in the
world, with the most stable political system in the
world....
QUESTION: Is there a need for a global currency?
PRESIDENT OBAMA: I don't believe that there's a need
for a global currency.[22]

President Obama surely meant that he saw no need for a new global currency to replace the dollar. Nonetheless, his answer squarely faced a question which has clearly arrived on the US political agenda: what should the US do to ensure a smooth transition to the next primary global currency and with minimal harm to US interests?

On 25 March 2009 US Secretary of Treasury Tim Geithner was asked about Zhou Xiaochuan's comments and Mr. Geithner said he that he understood the proposal as "designed to increase the use of the IMF's special drawing rights. And we're actually quite open to that." The USD quickly declined on the currency markets, but the losses stopped when Geithner subsequently clarified his response to say that the US stands for a "strong dollar."[23]

The very sensitive issue is that some part of the value of the USD arises from the self-fulfilling view that it is the primary global currency and thus there is considerable demand for it on the global currency markets. When the idea arises that the USD might be displaced by another currency, the currency market is quick to lower its valuation of the USD. This is one reason why the Federal Reserve should ensure that the USD is part of the future Global Monetary Union, so that the USD is not displaced by the future Single Global Currency, but that it is included in the new currency of a Global Monetary Union, just as the deutschmark was included in the euro of the European Monetary Union.

The value of the US dollar is a sensitive political issue in the US as it's a visible symbol of what many Americans believe is US "exceptionalism," the idea that the US is somehow better than all other countries. These nationalistic feelings are deeper than the usual nostalgic feelings about one's national money. As citizens of the UK can attest, it takes some time to adjust to being dethroned from the "No. 1" position.

Conduct Public/Private Large-Scale Research into the Single Global Currency

This is one step that does not require government action, but as the governments of the world have access to large resources, government involvement would be helpful. In the meantime, however, foundations, universities, and individuals can initiate this step.

Thousands of economists continue to study the ups and downs of the multicurrency foreign exchange trading world, perhaps looking for the Holy Grail explanation, but it is not to be found. Even within the European Central Bank, where the concern about exchange rates was reduced for member countries by the euro, economists are still studying what is--rather than what can be.[24]

Instead, economists could self-impose a moratorium on the Sisyphusian search for the explanation of exchange rate ups and downs the mythical hill, and turn their energies to explore the 3-G world. Continuing the extensive exploration of the existing multicurrency foreign exchange world is like devoting large research efforts to exploring how to make carburetors work better in the age of fuel-injection, or how to improve the performance of vacuum tubes in the age of semi-conductors.

Economists could study economic phenomena that heretofore have been considered to be complicated by exchange rate movements; and consider those same phenomena in a 3-G world. For example, economists have studied the "Dutch Disease,"[25] which describes how the discovery of abundant natural resources in a country may actually decrease economic growth. As the Dutch Disease, and the resulting inflation, have previously been studied in affected countries with their own currencies, economists could study the effects of exploitation of new natural resources in prospective countries within the Global Monetary Union. It's predicted here that the Dutch Disease should not exist in the 3-G world, or at least that its effect will be substantially reduced. However, it's more important that the world learn what does the IMF think about how the Dutch Disease would fare in the 3-G world.

Other questions and issues which economists at the IMF, BIS, World Bank and hundreds of academic economics departments and think tanks might ask include:

- What are the actual costs and benefits of a Single Global Currency as claimed in this book, e.g. the benefit of elimination of the costs of maintaining foreign exchange reserves?
- What will be the meaning of Purchasing Power Parity in a 3-G world?
- What will be the effect on developing nations of the elimination of "Original Sin?"
- How many of the six Obstfeld and Rogoff international economics puzzles[26] will be solved or simply rendered moot in a 3-G world?
- What are the costs and benefits of keeping their own currencies for domestic use for countries considering joining the Global Monetary Union?
- What will be the role of alternative currencies in a 3-G world?
- What should be done with the foreign exchange reserves, including gold, now being held by central banks?
- What level of inflation should the Global Central Bank target for the world, if any?
- How transparent should be the operations of the Global Central Bank, given that there will be no currency competition?
- What should be the initial value of a single unit of the SGC, i.e. should it be set at some symbolic value such what is needed to purchase a kilogram of bread in three or four cities in the world?

Finally,

- As a matter of economic history, why did it take so long for the world to move to a Single Global Currency after John Stuart Mill's and Robert Mundell's explicit observations of the absurdity of the existing multi-currency system?

Among the thousands of economists working at the World Bank, International Monetary Fund, Bank for International Settlements, and all the central banks and universities, none is known to be working full-time on 3-G issues.

Establish a Single Global Currency Institute

There are many international economics institutes,[27] such as the Peterson Institute for International Economics in Washington, DC, the Institute for International Economic Studies in Stockholm, the Kiel Institute for World Economics, and the Vienna Institute for International Economic Studies. However, none is yet dedicated to exploring the issues surrounding the Single Global Currency. None has published an article specifically about the costs and benefits of a Single Global Currency. Perhaps what is needed is a separate think-tank for the Single Global Currency issues, only. One model for such a goal-directed Single Global Currency Institute could be the US National Cancer Institute, which is dedicated to solving the puzzles of cancer.

With such an institute, attention could be focused on the 3-G goals. There would not be a monopoly of such research at that institute, but it would increase recognition for the issue.

A Single Global Currency Institute could have an advisory board or board of directors who are the leaders of international monetary thinking. Such a group could also constitute an "International Macroeconomic Advisory Council" as was recommended by Robert Mundell in 2009.[28]

A Single Global Currency Institute could be located within a foundation, a government, a non-governmental organization, an international organization such as the IMF or Bank for International Settlements, a university, or it could stand alone. In this cyber age, it could be located anywhere in the world. Wherever located, it will bring credit unto itself and its associated organization; and will help the world focus on the work that needs to be done.

Establish the Goal and Date, and Give the New Currency a Name

Goal. The G-7 or G-8 countries meet regularly and they issue statements about their views of the needs of the world and their role in their solution. In June 2005, the *Financial Times'* Martin Wolf asked his readers for recommendations that might be passed on to the G-8 meeting in July in Scotland, and the Single Global Currency Association recommended that he urge the G-8 to begin planning for the Single Global Currency.[29] Such planning would effectively be the statement, if not otherwise stated: "We seek a Single Global Currency," or even "We are exploring whether we should seek a Single Global Currency."

To date, two members of the G-8, China and Russia, have made similar individual announcements, but it needs to be accepted by the G-8 as a global goal and not a part of national competition with the United States.

In June 2001, Malaysian Prime Minister Mahathir Mohamad "proposed the creation of a single international currency that would anchor global trade. The currency, in which banking reserves would be held, should belong 'to no one country.'" He also stated that currencies "must never be traded as commodities."[30] Such vision from a single controversial national leader is not enough, but it was a start.

Setting a goal has a way of focusing people's attention on what really matters, and all existing work can be reviewed as to whether it supports that goal. For example, the IMF still conducts Article IV consultations with the Eurozone countries even though the purposes of the IMF are about foreign exchange rates. See, for example, the August 2013 report of consultation with Germany[31] where the IMF continued to measure Germany's balance of payments, even though Germany has no currency of its own, and therefore it does not have a currency-relevant issue with a current account or balance of payments. To the extent that there are imbalances within the EMU, that should be an EMU or ECB issue, rather than the IMF.

Another example of residual measurement of monetary factors is the May 2013 Article IV consultation with El Salvador where the IMF tracked the "real effective exchange rate" and the balance of payments for the years after El Salvador ized to the US dollar.[32] Such analyses are not necessary where they do not affect the primary interests of the IMF, i.e. currencies, not nations.

As the goal of a 3-G world is extremely measurable and highly visible to the people, it will be a more specific motivator than a goal more generally stated. For example, the goal of placing a man on the moon by the end of the 1960s was similarly visible and it was explicitly achieved, as was the elimination of smallpox. In contrast, some goals are more general and less measurable, and therefore less motivating, such as reducing poverty.

Date. Setting a date also would be an important step, and it will raise the expectations of the people of the world that the efforts toward implementation are serious. The example used in this book is President John Kennedy's 1962 goal of landing a man on the moon before 1970. In January 1994, the Europeans established January 1999 as the inauguration date for the euro, with bill and coins to be distributed three or four years later.[33] Both goals were dramatic and fortunately, both were successfully achieved.

Name. In 1995, the European Council gave the name "euro" to the planned currency, and that was surely influential in assuring people of the reality of the planned change.

One way to increase public support, and to raise expectations for the Single Global Currency, is to conduct a multi-stage worldwide internet-based polling effort to determine the name of the new currency. The selection process would begin with nominations from around the world, primarily on the internet. A nominations committee, with representatives from around the world, would select the best of them, perhaps 100 possible names, according to pre-established criteria. Such criteria would include the need to be pronounceable in as many languages as possible, and the need to ensure that for all major languages, no offensive words or sounds are used. Then the nomination committee's selections would be presented to voters around the world, and the field could be narrowed to the top 25 or 10. Then the second round of voting could select the top three, and then a final election would be held to select a winner. This process could take several years. A similar process was used by the New Open World Foundation in 2007 to select the modern "Seven Wonders of the World."[34]

Perhaps the representatives of the 193 UN members could have a role in the decision process, but the foundation principle for the poll should be maximum public participation, according to the principle of one person-one vote.

While it's possible that the world will select the word "dollar" to denote the Single Global Currency, it's unlikely. The word "dollar" is unalterably now linked to the currency of the United States, even if used by other countries such as Australia and Canada. The term "dollar" is weighted too heavily with the politics and the reputation of the United States.[35] A fresh start with a fresh non-national name is likely to be preferred. The EMU founding members understood that euro would have faced difficulty if it had been named the "mark" or the "lira," or if the new currency's name had included those words.

Apparently, the term "euro" has escaped the European heritage of colonialism, warfare, and the Holocaust. Instead, Europe now stands for cooperation and negotiation, and countries are joining the European Union and the European Monetary Union because they want to be part of the New Europe.[36]

Ize to Anchor Currencies

In 1999 Willem Buiter defined "dollarization" as "unilateral adoption by a country of the currency of another nation as the only legal tender." He also referred to it as "asymmetric monetary union,"[37] because the governors of the anchor currency give no representation to the izing currency and no share of the seigniorage. Regardless of the high utility of such an exchange rate solution, it's not a feasible solution for most countries in the political sense, except for small countries, because their expectations of having a meaningful representative voice in the management of a large currency are necessarily low. For larger countries, it's almost as unacceptable a method of monetary union as accepting political domination or military conquest. Napoleon's francs were accepted throughout his empire, as was the ruble in the Soviet Union, but monetary policy at the end of a gun is not a welcome monetary solution.

It may be that some interim stages might be developed between pure ization, with its lack of political representation and lack of seigniorage, and monetary union. For example, something like an "associate" membership in the EMU might be established for ized countries or monetary unions, where they might share a single vote, just as do groups of countries represented on the Executive Board of the IMF. Similarly, some formulas might be developed for the European Central Bank to allocate seigniorage to associate member countries, just as the International Monetary Stability Act of 2000 sought to do for izers to the US dollar. Perhaps such seigniorage could be included as part of international foreign aid programs, which might be appropriate for an associate membership in the EMU for the African monetary unions. Foreign aid could be conditioned upon joining a monetary union.

Benn Steil and Robert Litan report that the EMU is hostile to euroization because it evades the Maastricht criteria for officially joining the Eurozone.[38] Perhaps, however, the ECB's concerns will subside as the euro's place in the world financial system is further solidified and the strength of the euro is seen as based upon the credibility of the bank rather than of the incoming or the existing member states.

When countries are coming out of a political or economic crisis, it might be a good time to consider joining a monetary union or izing with a solid anchor country. After the 2003 Iraq war, there was some consideration given to izing Iraq to the euro or US dollar, but the decision was made to resurrect the Iraqi dinar.[39] An additional choice might have been to join the planning for the Gulf Cooperation Council's common currency. Similarly, Zimbabwe, currently the worst example of hyperinflation, might consider ization to the South African rand or another stable currency.

The pace of launching new countries has declined to nearly zero since the end of the European and Soviet colonial eras, but more will surely come. A challenge for the world monetary system will be to replace the lingering habit of planning a new currency with a recommendation to join a monetary union. One of the next countries to be launched will be Palestine, and planning for a new currency has begun. Currently on the West Bank and Gaza, the primary currency is the Israeli new shekel.[40] One commentator suggested that both Palestine and Israel ize to the US dollar.[41] As a monetary union with Israel seems politically infeasible, Palestine could consider joining with the financial powerhouse of Lebanon or with Jordan or with the Gulf Cooperation Council countries. Establishing a new currency for Palestine would be a step in the wrong direction, in relation to the movement toward a Single Global Currency.

Expand Existing Monetary Unions

If a major global reserve currency, such as the US dollar or the yen or euro combines with another or with a currency of a monetary union, such as the GCC monetary union or the West African monetary unions, such a joining would be called a merger, rather than an accession.

As noted earlier, the EMU is entirely within the European Union, at least so far, and it's committed to expand to its twenty-eight member countries. The next of the remaining ten countries is likely to be Lithuania in January 2015. John Edmunds and John Marthinsen wrote in 2003, "Once a currency union is formed, we predict that it will exert a force of attraction on countries that have not joined...."[42]

Beyond the twenty-eight, the potential for further additions to the EMU will grow as the EU grows. Negotiations have begun with five recognized applicants for membership: Iceland, Macedonia, Montenegro, Serbia and Turkey. Potential candidates are Albania, Bosnia/Herzegovina and Kosovo.[43] With those named countries, the EU would grow to 36, and with EU accession would come monetary union for least 33, if the three initial holdouts--Denmark, Sweden and UK--remain outside.

If the United Nations membership stays at 193, a Eurozone membership of 33 would constitute 17 percent of the nations of the world. If the euroized UN members (Andorra, Liechtenstein, Monaco and San Marino) are included, that would bring the number to 37 or 19.2 percent of the UN membership.

At some point, Russia will join, as it is Europe's largest country with about one-third of Europe's landmass within its boundaries from Poland to the Urals. The entire country of Russia, with 17.1 million square kilometers, is almost four times the size of the current 28 countries of the EU. Bordering European Russia are the former Soviet and European states of Armenia, Azerbaijan, Belarus, Georgia, Kazakhstan, and Ukraine. Once Russia joins as a European member, the euro will extend to the Pacific Ocean, and four more Asian countries will then border the Eurozone: Afghanistan, Mongolia, China, and North Korea.

Maybe Israel will be considered, as it has a cultural claim to being a "European State," thereby further breaking the symbolic barrier of continental contiguity, already breached by Cyprus and Malta. Canada, with its longstanding interest in monetary union, but averse to digestion by its giant neighbor to the south, might consider joining, as might Caribbean countries and former European colonies in South America.

Every expansion of the European Monetary Union increases the size of the world's largest monetary union in terms of the number of countries, the total population and total GDP. There seems little doubt that the European Union and the EMU will continue to grow.

The EMU and its European Central Bank have been careful not to publicly seek a larger role in the global financial system, as that could be perceived as detracting from its primary goal of monetary stability and might subject it to being accused of being imperialistic or anti-American. As ECB Executive Board Member Lorenzo Bini Smaghi said in March 2008, "... the policy of the ECB is neither to encourage nor to discourage the use of the euro."[44] However, there is a "middle ground" that the EMU/ECB/Eurosystem could take, which is to urge the world to plan for a system where it will rely not upon a single national or regional currency, but to a system with a Single Global Currency, managed by a Global Central Bank within a Global Monetary Union. With such a goal, the Europeans would not be accused of being competitive or anti-American or imperialistic.

Even without accepting the goal of a Single Global Currency, it's widely recognized that the euro's role in international finance is increasing, even if stalled by the 2008-2013 crises. Jeffrey Frankel and Menzie Chinn wrote, albeit before the crises, that the euro may surpass the dollar as the international reserve currency by 2022.[45] As the euro's and the yuan's international roles increase and that of the dollar declines, the next option will not be merely the ascension of the newest monetary power, but to ask whether it is time to stop the competition and declare a new winner: the Single Global Currency, and the trophy can be retired.

Similarly, other monetary unions will likely expand, now that such a solution to the exchange rate puzzles has emerged and endured. The Eastern Caribbean Monetary Union could expand to include all of the Caribbean,[46] and the West and Central African monetary unions can expand.

If the European Central Bank were to set for itself the goal of becoming the Global Central Bank, it could likely do so. A change in name for the bank and the currency would be helpful and symbolic. There would need to be significant indications that the doors are open to those who wish to join in the movement toward a 3-G world. For such an invitation to be successful, it would have to go beyond the accommodation of izing, and toward real, even if minor, participation in ECB monetary decision making.

Somewhat playfully, "in my little thought experiment," Brad Setser, anticipated such a merger when he wrote about "Chimerica" and "Chieuropa" and noted that such combined currencies would eliminate balance of intra-currency payments problems.[47]

At some point, the regional currencies will see more benefits than costs in merging.

Establish New Monetary Unions

As described in Chapter 4, there are growing movements to establish regional monetary unions in the Arabian Gulf (GCC), East Asia, South Asia, South Africa, West Africa, all of Africa, South America, North America, and across regions, such as for G-2, G-3, etc.

Robert Mundell's proposals on the next step of creating a super-monetary union among the larger economies are referenced extensively here.

He wrote in 2000,

> "A G-2 Monetary Union? I want to emphasize, however, that achieving price stability and fixed exchange rates among the G-3 is much easier to achieve--from at least a technical point of view--than people generally think. It might be hard to think of a currency union of the three currency areas at the same time. But in fact a union of any two would be sufficient to set the trend. The three currency areas have monetary masses more or less corresponding to their respective GDPs, the ratio of about $9.5 trillion, $7.0 trillion, and $5 trillion respectively, together making up perhaps 60 per cent of world GDP. A monetary union of any two of the areas would make it the dominant currency area and thus make it very attractive for the third area to join because the

alternatives would be worse. Any one of the three could
opt out and accept the number two position."[48]

However, perhaps because he was apprehensive about the political
feasibility of EMU-like monetary union of the G-3, he wrote that the union
could be a currency area, where the value of the three currencies would be
irrevocably fixed to each other. "My ideal and equilibrium solution would be
a world currency (but not a single world currency) in which each country
would produce its own unit that exchanges at par with the world unit."[49]
Further, he wrote, "Everything would be priced in terms of intors, and a
committee--in my view, say, a G3 open market committee designated by the
Board of Governors of the International Monetary Fund--would determine
how many intors produced each year would be consistent with price
stability."[50] (As noted in Chapter 5, one of Mundell's proposed names for
the G-3 currency is "intor," combining "International" and "or," from the
French word for gold.[51])

> "How would monetary union between two of the G-3
> countries come about? The clue is provided by what the
> EU-11 did. To do that, they had to have a common
> agreement on 1) the targeted inflation rate; 2) a common
> way of measuring the inflation rate (Eurostat's
> harmonized index of consumer prices, HICP); 3)
> redistribution of the seigniorage (in proportion to equity
> in the ECB); 4) locked exchange rates; and 5) a
> centralized monetary policy. Europe did that. Why would
> it be more difficult to do it between, say, the dollar and
> the euro, or the dollar and the yen, or the yen and the
> euro? The rate of inflation is close enough, the inflation
> target is about the same, why not just lock exchange
> rates and organize a common monetary policy? It would
> be administratively and institutionally easy and the
> politics would not be more difficult than, say, the
> organization of D-Day."[52]

Such a step toward a 3-G world by the G-3 would be very helpful.

In 2005, Professor Mundell further clarified his vision of the transition,
and concern about the feasibility, with an interim stage of coordination of
currencies, with the DEY, for Dollar/Euro/Yen:

> "My approach is rather to start out with arrangements
> for stabilizing exchange rates, and move from there to a
> global currency. It would start off from the situation as it
> is at present and gradually move it toward the desired
> solution. We could start off with the three big currencies
> in the world, the dollar, euro, and yen, and with specified
> weights, make a basket of them into a unit that could be
> called the DEY. Bearing in mind that there is no
> important inflation in the DEY area, I would propose that
> the three DEY central banks undertake to minimize
> currency fluctuations, using a combination of
> unsterilized currency intervention and monetary policies.

The DEY could then become the platform on which to build a global currency, which I shall call the INTOR."[53]

Mundell continued,

"Let us make a leap of the imagination and consider the possibilities of a monetary union of the FRB, ECB, and BOJ, i.e., a G-3 monetary union. Of course the argument will be made that these areas are too different to have a monetary union. But in terms of economic reality, they are much more similar than the twelve countries that now make up the EMU and a different magnitude from the diversity of the 25 countries that now make up the European union and which will probably at some future date all be members of the same currency area.

"The first point it is necessary to make is that the G-3 monetary union I am thinking about is not a single-currency monetary union. I am not proposing that the United States give up the dollar, that Europe give up the euro or that Japan give up the yen. It is rather a multi-currency monetary union, a fixed exchange rate area with a common monetary policy.

"Formation of a monetary union for members of either a closed economy or an open economy with flexible exchange rates requires five conditions:
1. Consensus on an inflation target (e.g. 1–3 percent);
2. Construction of a common index for measuring inflation (e.g., euro area's harmonized index of consumer prices (HICP));
3. Locking of exchange rates, as EMU did in July 1998;
4. Establishment of the DEY central bank to determine monetary policy as the ECB did in 1999–2002; and
5. Mechanism for distributing seigniorage (in EMU it is proportionate to equity in ECB).

"The duty of the DEY central bank would be to pursue monetary stability in the DEY area, which represents nearly two-thirds of the world economy. Successful monetary unions need some arrangement to prevent free-rider fiscal policies.[54] The problems should not be insurmountable in an arrangement with three central banks. There would be a great increase in efficiency and the gains from exchange and payments once the huge gyrations of exchange rates are removed and an enormous gain to the rest of the world. The DEY unit should become the platform on which to base a multilateral world currency in which every country would have a share."[55]

Mundell continued,

"A strong case can be made for making provisions for widening, extending and generalizing the monetary union to other countries. First, the other countries would benefit from stability of exchange rates among the three largest currency areas because it would serve as a more stable anchor for their own currencies. Second, all countries would benefit from the adoption and use of a global unit of account. Third, countries outside the G-3 (especially the larger countries) might resent trilateral dominance in money matters in which they have no voice. Fourth, a world currency is in the nature of a social contract in which every country has a juridical stake in proportion to its economic size.

"The board of governors of the IMF, composed of the finance ministers or central bank governors of each member country, represents a broad-based international monetary authority in which all countries have votes. The adoption of an international currency with a name like INTOR, sanctioned by the board of governors of the IMF, freely convertible into dollars, euros, yen and DEY, would mark a great advance in the creation of an international financial architecture.

"The board of governors of the International Monetary Fund could make whatever changes are necessary in the IMF articles of agreement. Instead of emphasizing the necessity of flexible exchange rates to its clients, the IMF executive board would be asked to stress the advantages of achieving stable exchange rates to an INTOR that is stable in terms of the main world currencies.

"The process could start bilaterally between the United States and Europe, Europe and Japan, or United States and Japan, or simultaneously, with all three. The core basket of the three DEY currencies would not be fixed for all time and it could be altered at the discretion of the board of governors. As the economies in the basket expand or contract in relative terms, weights in the basket would be duly adjusted.

"Consideration could also be given to the changes in the currencies in the basket. At the present time, Britain's pound and China's yen represent, respectively, the fourth and fifth largest currency areas and consideration could be given to those two areas, allowing for the possibility that Britain might join the euro, and that China's currency might become convertible.

"The basic plan for the world currency could be implemented in three stages:
• Stage I: Transition to stable exchange rates;
• Stage II: The G-3 monetary union based on the DEY; and
• Stage III: Creation of the INTOR.

"Stage I would be inaugurated with steps preparatory to the G-3 monetary union. A gradual process could start with ceilings and floors on the G-3 currencies.

"Stage II would involve the steps outlined above: the fixing of an inflation target and definition of the price level in terms of the DEY; the locking of exchange rates; the establishment of the joint monetary policy committee; and the arrangement for the division of seigniorage.

Stage III would begin after Stage II has been completed. It would involve the selection of a definitive name and value of the currency, the mechanism and agency by which it will be introduced, the system and criterion for controlling its quantity, its backing in terms of currency or commodity reserves, and the location of its central authority."[56]

The largest problem with Professor Mundell's interim step of a monetary union using fixed rates among the major G-currencies is that their currencies will still be in the foreign exchange marketplace and will require central bank intervention to achieve stability, where they will be subject to intense pressure from speculators, and large capital flows.

Another problem with the interim steps is that public support would be needed and the concept of fixing exchange rates among currencies is far more difficult to understand than the concept of a single currency. People around the world understand the concept of the euro, but not the complications of fixing exchange rates by unelected boards of governors of central banks. As the amount of public support necessary for a G-3 multicurrency monetary union would be nearly the same as for a Single Global Currency, why not skip the interim steps? A major lesson of the successful emergence of the euro in 2013 from the debt and bank crises was that the people of the Eurozone wanted stable money. They didn't like recession, but they wanted solutions with the euro and not without the euro.

The idea of a monetary union between the dollar and the euro was also proposed by Bryan Taylor, who proposed in 1998, before the adoption of the euro, a "eurodollar" combination with the dollar, to be managed by a "Global Reserve Bank."[57] He argued that the best exchange rate for such a union would at parity, i.e., 1:1, but foresaw that the union could be successful even if the pre-union exchange rate was not at parity. At the time of the October 1988 article, it was known that the euro was to begin its life at the rate of $1.16. Since the 1 January 1999 adoption of the euro in the ledgers of Europe, that magical 1:1 parity point has been crossed on 19 trading days, nine of which were on the journey "down" against the dollar in 1999 and 2000 and 10 of which on the return journey "up" against the dollar.[58] However, the euro hasn't approached parity with the USD since late 2002.

For the sake of simplicity, 1:1 parity has great appeal for a G-2 union, and also for the timing of a union between Canada and the United States. The difficulty is that artificially closing the gap among currencies can be expensive, and even if parity is reached by market forces, it's never known when it will happen--until it does. Decimal simplicity can also come with a 1:100 parity for the euro or US dollar and the yen.

However, fixing exchange rates among the currencies of independent countries can be very difficult as the pre-existing currencies still exist and are subject to the currency markets and speculation. The European Commission report *One Market, One Money* explicitly chose to pursue a single currency, rather than a monetary union of fixed exchange rates, and used six criteria to support that decision: transaction costs, transparency of prices, economies of scale, currency credibility, visibility, and external benefits (of having one).[59]

C. Fred Bergsten proposed in 2004 a "Finance G-2" between the euro and the dollar, noting, that such an association "will inevitably become a necessary feature of the international monetary policy of both and thus a central element of the global monetary system of the 21st century."[60]

While a G-2 or G-3 monetary union would, by itself, create the critical mass to thrust the world rapidly toward a Single Global Currency, other new monetary unions can be established as well. We can expect to hear soon of such developments in Africa, Asia, and South America.

Another monetary union route for the United States is to join with Canada and Mexico as has been proposed. The NAFTA trade agreement is a sound start, just as was the Common Market for the EMU. The timing may come when the currency competition with the euro becomes more intense and the United States, like any modern global corporation whose #1 status is threatened, will look for merger partners to bolster its "market share." At that point, the United States may be more willing to give other countries a voice on the Federal Reserve decision making committees.

Even before joining such a North American Monetary Union, the Federal Reserve would enhance the status of the USD as well as the movement toward a Single Global Currency, by providing voting or non-voting representation for non-nationals on its important committees. For example, having a representative from the EMU, and another from China, help assure the world that its current "global currency" is being managed with the world's interests in mind, as well as the relatively narrow concerns for the US economy.

Establish a Global Central Bank and a Global Monetary Union

One of the biggest stumbling blocks to one country "izing" its currency to that of another currency is that one never knows what is going to happen to that other currency. The anchor currency may decline in value, as has distressed some El Salvadorans and some Ecuadorans, or it may increase in value as some Montenegrins and Kosovars have found to their regret.

Several economists have written that small countries should abandon their currencies, for which the maintenance of an independent monetary policy is not worth the operating cost and certainly not worth the risk of a currency crisis. But where to go? There has been much discussion of izing, but there are political disadvantages to that route, the most serious of which is the choice of anchor. As a common currency, the euro would seem the safest politically, but the European Central Bank is intent on getting its own, growing, house in order without taking on challenges beyond its original charter.

In the meantime, the IMF, the Bank for International Settlements, the United Nations or other suitable international organization could establish an explicitly named "Global Central Bank," to be run initially by the founding organization, but later by its cooperative members, which would, by definition, become members of what could be explicitly called a "Global Monetary Union." Robert Mundell has suggested that such a Global Central Bank could issue credible currency which could be "an international asset backed by reserves of dollars, yen, euros, and gold."[61]

One useful step to assist small countries which are interested in "izing" to a more stable currency would be for the IMF or the Bank for International Settlements, or the proposed prototype Global Central Bank, to establish a new currency with a value set as a combination of currencies, weighted in a "currency basket." The proportions in the basket would be public information. Such a currency would be less subject to the fluctuations of single currencies.

The name of the currency of the GCB could be picked through a large international search, as described above, or through a less cumbersome process. Eventually, when the work of this GCB is merged with that of other monetary unions and currency areas, the name of the currency could be changed through the larger selection process, if desired. This GCB currency could be explicitly defined as a basket of the major currencies, such as the euro, US dollar, yen, and yuan, and it could be backed by the resources of the IMF, and operate as a currency board.

The GCB could begin its work when just one country decides to SGCize to the GCB currency. Then a second country would join and a third, and so on. As part of the IMF's Article IV consultation process, it could recommend to countries that they join the new GCB/GMU.

Allocation of seigniorage would be a simple matter, comparable to current levels of foreign aid.

Just as a level of trade or other economic integration is not required for ization, it would not be required for countries joining the GCB/GMU. For example, the existence of an economic relationship between Grenada and Tonga would not be required.

The total GDP of the smallest one-hundred nations was $884 billion in 2012, which is less than the GDP of the fifteenth ranked country, Indonesia. The total GDP for the 18 European Monetary Union countries was $12.2 trillion in 2012, which was larger than the GDP for the bottom 162 UN members.[62] Thus, to develop a Global Central Bank to provide monetary services for most of the countries of the world all at once would be a project of manageable size.

Borrowing from a well-known saying made popular in the US film, *Field of Dreams*: if the GCB is built, the members will come.[63]

Expand the use of SDR's and/or Issue Global Greenbacks

Several economists, and the Chinese Central Banker, Zhou Xiaochuan, have urged that the IMF's SDR's be more utilized as a global reserve, although no one has recommended that SDR's be expanded into a global currency for the people of the world.

Warren Coats, a former economist at the IMF, has recommended that the expanded SDR used be backed by a commodity or basket of commodities. He summarized his proposal:

> "that interest in the SDR could be transformed by replacing its valuation basket of currencies with a basket of goods and replacing the allocation of SDRs with issuing them under currency board rules. Rather than buying and selling SDRs for the items in its valuation basket (à la the gold or other traditional commodity standards), the IMF would sell and redeem these 'real SDRs' for the basket indirectly (against government or other triple A financial assets of equivalent value). Such an SDR, with a relatively constant real value, is likely to be adopted as the anchor currency for fixing the exchange rates of many, if not most, national currencies and to augment or replace the US dollar and euro in countries' foreign exchange reserves."[64]

Similarly, but with different terminology, 2001 Nobel laureate Joseph Stiglitz wrote in *Making Globalization Work* in 2008, "There is a remarkably simple solution, one which was recognized long ago by Keynes: the international community can provide a new form of fiat money to act as reserves. (Keynes called his new money 'bancor')."[65] Stiglitz called them "global greenbacks," which are similar to the IMF's SDR's. He wrote that the concept of global greenbacks, "simply extends the concept" of SDR's, and that global greenbacks would be issued annually, unlike SDR's which are issued "episodically."[66]

> "I envision global greenbacks being held only by central banks, but a more ambitious version of this proposal would allow global greenbacks to be held by individuals, in which case there would be a market price for them and they could be treated like any other hard currency."[67] This "ambitious" global greenbacks version seems close to the Single Global Currency as proposed here.

> "Each year, each member of the club - the countries that signed up to the new global reserve system - would contribute a specified amount to a global reserve fund and, at the same time, the global reserve fund would issue global greenbacks of equivalent value to the country, which they would hold in their reserves."[68]

> "The problems of the global financial system are systemic and have much to do with the global reserve system. The world is already moving out of the dollar system, but that doesn't mean that it is moving toward a better system and, sadly, little thought has been given to

where it is going or how it should evolve. This single initiative [the 'global greenbacks' system] could do more to make globalization work than any other. It would not eliminate the problems faced by developing countries, but it would make things better. It would enhance global stability and global equity. It is not a new idea, but it is an idea perhaps whose time has come."[69]

Ensure that Currency Area Competition is Healthy

In his "On Why Not a Global Currency," Kenneth Rogoff wrote of the benefits of having competition among a few major currencies, such as encouraging monetary innovation. He envisioned those currencies vying for the No. 1 spot and perhaps to become the major foreign reserve currency.[70] As growth is usually a major measurement of success in organizations, another focus of such competition would be to see which currency will take the lead toward a Single Global Currency. Two can merge to become larger than the third, or one can find other merger partners to move ahead. When a leader of the sponsoring country or central bank of one of the major currencies announces a goal of becoming THE Single Global Currency and looks for partners, a seismic shift will occur.

Given the head start of the Eurozone in the dynamics of currency area growth, it may be hard for the United States or Japan or China to catch up. That is, Europe has shown how nations can work together for the common good on the issue of a common currency. Joseph Nye's "soft power"[71] might be just the right mix of economics and politics that will transform the euro into the Single Global Currency. At least in monetary terms, Mark Leonard's book, *Why Europe will run the 21st Century*, may be entirely on the money.[72] He focused on the European model of negotiation and consensus and voluntary agreements. Titles of books can sometimes be misleading, and Leonard really means that the techniques of cooperation developed by the post-World War II Europeans have become very successful and those techniques will dominate the world in the twenty-first century, but not the "hard" power of the European nations which formerly dominated the world.

Whether the managers of the US dollar or the euro or the yen or yuan work together for the stability of the world's financial system, or whether they view the power, influence, and success of their own currency as the sole goal, will help determine not only the eventual outcome of the journey to the Single Global Currency, which is certain, but how we will all get there--cooperatively and proactively, or competitively and reactively.

It's not known how the central bankers *really* view their roles as custodians of the currency. If they were oriented solely toward the power of their own currency, then why, even if retired, would former US Federal Reserve Governor Paul Volcker strongly support a global currency? Perhaps he was thinking of transforming the dollar into that pre-eminent global currency; but there is no evidence for that view. He was thinking as a genuine global citizen.

For some in Europe, the potential global role for the euro was one reason for Europe's adoption of a single currency. There are many in Europe who appreciative US support during the two World Wars and the Cold War but who resent the US influence in the world, including the omnipresence of the US dollar. Included in that resentment is surely the view that the ability to avoid the requirements to balance its payments is undeserved, and that the US hubris deserves its comeuppance. A problem with that view is that the comeuppance may endanger financial stability for the world. Thus, the international currency competition should focus on the larger goal of worldwide financial stability rather than relative ranking for a currency. Several economists have cautioned that "competition with the dollar for monetary leadership should not be a motivation for euro area policies."[73]

One champion of North American monetary union, Herbert Grubel, argues monetary union consolidation should stop at the point of regional monetary unions so that currency competition could continue to generate monetary innovation. He wrote, "As Hayek noted, there are no substitutes for competition as a process for discovery of successful innovations in markets and, by extension, economic policies."[74]

When that competition reduces the number of currencies to "three to four if not n," as Kenneth Rogoff might say, it will then be apparent whether the competition should continue or whether the monetary system should finally become a unitary system, like the worldwide calendar/time system or the worldwide metric system.

Role of the International Monetary Fund

In the short and medium term, it could take the lead in encouraging nations to either join monetary unions or anchor, peg or "ize" their currencies to another stronger currency. Its support of the GCC and East Africa monetary unions should be expanded to more assertive support of other existing and future monetary unions.

The IMF conducts numerous studies of the member nations and their currencies, including the annual Article IV consultations. In such consultations, the IMF should urge that the countries, especially the small countries, abandon their own monetary policies and, for the sake of their own financial stability and for international monetary stability, join that of other currency areas, or an IMF-created anchor currency.

So far, the IMF's support for such currency consolidation has been tepid. Wrote an IMF spokesperson in reply to my mailing to Managing Director de Rato a copy of the 06 Edition,

> "The IMF has generally supported common currency
> arrangements when they have been established by a
> group of member countries, but it neither promotes nor
> discourages their use by others. As you may know, the
> Second Amendment to the IMF's Articles of Agreement,
> which took effect in 1978, gave members broad latitude
> to establish currency arrangements of their own
> choosing, including cooperative arrangements."[75]

Other steps the IMF could take:

1. Stop Article IV consultations with countries which are already members of monetary unions. The focus of the IMF should be re-centered on currencies and not national economies. The IMF already does provide consultation to monetary unions, so the continued redundant consulting with their member nations does not make cents/sense.

2. Internal voting, SDR allocations and other obligations and benefits of IMF membership should reflect the membership of monetary unions, rather than the member countries of those monetary unions.[76] For example, the European Monetary Union should be the official member of the IMF, and national memberships for the 18 member countries should cease. A precedent for this change was the decision to make the euro one of the SDR basket currencies to replace the deutschmark and French franc.

3. Stop or reduce research on issues that might be characterized as "more of the same," such as fluctuations of exchange rates or exchange rate regimes, and focus research on the 3-G world.

For example, the IMF analyzed the effects of expatriate remittances to Jordan on the real effective exchange rate. The authors concluded in 2006, "We estimate a long-run equilibrium model for the Jordanian REER by applying the Johansen cointegration estimation methodology over the period 1964 to 2004 to a newly calculated and expanded REER data set."[77] Such an analysis does not help move Jordan toward the best future exchange rate system - a monetary union.

It may be, incidentally, that 3-G research will bring insight into the current system, just as spending for "pure" research in other disciplines has led to technological breakthroughs for civilian products.

The IMF needs to refocus on solving the problem which led to its creation: the multiple currency foreign exchange system, and reduce its other well-intentioned, but secondary efforts, such as the Mali "Poverty Reduction and Growth Facility (PRGF) arrangement.[78] By helping the world move to a 3-G world, the IMF can do far more for the developing countries of the world than all of its macroeconomic and fiscal consulting.

The IMF is chartered to maintain global financial stability, and assist countries as they cope with the multicurrency world. Such assistance has typically been in the form of loans and advice to assist countries through a currency crisis and how to avoid one. As the Single Global Currency is the best means to global financial stability, the IMF should be helping the world move toward that goal. One dilemma is that the world will need a Global Central Bank to manage a Single Global Currency within a Global Monetary Union (the 3-G world), and not an IMF. Thus, the dual challenge for the IMF will be to move the world toward a 3-G world and to transform itself into some part of that Global Central Bank. The challenge for the Bank for International Settlements will be the same.

The IMF could do several things to further these changes:

1. Announce publicly that its primary goal is to move the world to a Single Global Currency.

2. Initiate research on the implementation and operation of the Single Global Currency. Without spending additional IMF funds, economists could be redeployed from doing Article IV reviews of very small countries, and of countries which are already in monetary unions. Authored by

economists in several IMF departments, the 2010 IMF paper, "Reserve Accumulation and International Monetary Stability" briefly mentioned the future option of a "Global Currency."[79] Calling it "bancor," in honor of the proposal of John Maynard Keynes at Bretton Woods, the paper discussed the creation of a Global Central Bank and the development of "bancor" as a reserve currency, based on SDR's, or a full common currency or parallel for the people.[80] The paper asked that the IMR Directors respond to the ideas presented, but there was no recommendation to further research the proposed global currency.

3. Immediately begin recommending to its smaller IMF members that they either "ize" to an existing international currency, join a monetary union, or join in the formation of a new international currency which could be established by the IMF for this purpose. The reserves of the new currency could be openly and explicitly set as a combination of specific shares of the current international currencies, such as the US dollar, euro, yen, Swiss franc, etc. The proportions of such currencies in the reserves could be set by a pre-existing and public formula, perhaps based on the proportional amounts of trading of those currencies in the foreign exchange marketplace.

4. Begin planning with the Bank for International Settlements for its own transformation into the Global Central Bank or portions of that bank. If the European Central Bank eventually becomes the core of the Global Central Bank, then the IMF and BIS can be merged into that bank.

To show how far the IMF is from these steps, there is not one economist among the approximately 2,000 economists at the IMF who is known to be dedicated full-time to the Single Global Currency "project."

Twice a year, the IMF publishes its "Global Financial Stability Report,"[81] but that report has yet to comment on the goal of a Single Global Currency which would bring a substantial amount of that sought-after stability. Neither has the group, Financial Stability Forum, addressed the 3-G goal, which would achieve the much of the purpose for its existence, i.e. financial stability.[82]

At some point over the next several years, these groups, and economists in general will take notice, as might be observed by the 1960's rock group, "Buffalo Springfield." Their 1967 hit, "For what it's worth," began, "Something's happening here, What it is ain't exactly clear..."[83] Indeed, something is happening to the international monetary system, and it is "exactly clear" as the number of the world's currencies continues to decline.

At bottom, it's important to get started and keep our "Eyes on the Prize," to use the expression from the US Civil Rights movement of the mid-twentieth century. What Wolfgang Munchau said about the efforts for Asian monetary, trade and financial integration applies for the Campaign for a Single Global Currency, "Apart from the many technical features, there is one important lesson from Europe. Monetary integration is difficult, it takes time and it may appear impossible at times. But once the process is under way, it develops its own momentum."[84]

The IMF should lead the world out of the existing multicurrency world and into a stable 3-G world, and thereby achieve its work, as established in the Articles of Agreement. Just as the 60th anniversary of the IMF in 2004 generated a new look at strategy, albeit only for the medium term, the 80th anniversary in 2024 can be viewed as the time for implementing the inevitable goal of a long term strategy: A 3-G world, with a Single Global Currency to be managed by a Global Central Bank within a Global Monetary Union.

Convene International Conference(s)

Prior to the 1944 Bretton Woods International Monetary Conference, the 1867 Conference in Paris was the best known such conference, but a series of conferences called to plan and implement a Single Global Currency would become the best known of all.

Such a conference cannot be scheduled in a vacuum. As Todd Sandler has noted in *Global Collective Action*, there would need to be sufficient preconditions and incentives for a successful conference.[85]

The first such named conference might be held to initiate the process to determine a name for the currency, and to establish a goal date and a schedule for implementation.

The legal foundation for such a conference could be the Articles of Agreement of the IMF which provide for their amendment upon approval by the Board of Governors. The Articles also provide for the establishment of a special Council to consider such amendments, upon approval of 85 percent of the voting power of the Board of Governors.[86]

In October 2008 at the urging of French, and EU President Nicolas Sarkozy, US President George W. Bush requested a meeting of the leaders of the G-20, the twenty countries with the largest economies for 15 November 2008, in Washington, DC. The G-20 countries comprise 90 percent of the world's GDP, and 85 percent of the world's trade and 67 percent of the world's population.

At the one-day conference and photo-opportunity, the expectations for substantive progress were low. Nonetheless, a few leaders and columnists urged that the meeting become the first step for a major monetary conference on the scale of the 1994 Bretton Woods conference. Sarkozy called for a "refoundation of modern capitalism" and British Prime Minister Gordon Brown appealed to establish "a new Bretton Woods [by] building a new international financial architecture."[87]

The *People's Daily,* which reflects the views of the Chinese Government, stated, "The world urgently needs to create a diversified currency and financial system and fair and just financial order that is not dependent on the United States."[88]

Other leaders cautioned that such changes would have to take time. Said IMF Managing Director, Dominique Strauss-Kahn, "Lots of people are talking about a 'Bretton Woods 2,' but we won't be concluding a new international treaty... Things aren't going to change overnight."[89] However, he also sent a letter to the G-20 participants a week before the conference which stated,

"There have been numerous calls in recent months for a "new Bretton Woods agreement," which I strongly endorse. However, one important lesson of the original

Bretton Woods agreement was that its foundations were carefully laid through serious and vigorous discussion of the underlying issues. I therefore very much welcome the initiative taken by the President of the United States to bring together the G-20 leaders, to follow up with various working groups, and culminate these efforts in a conference, hopefully within the year ahead."[90]

The IMF Research Director, Olivier Blanchard, looked slightly forward, "Longer term reforms of the financial architecture should touch upon: (i) the design of financial regulation; (ii) a better way of assessing systemic risk; and (iii) mechanisms for more effective actions for crisis prevention and resolution."[91]   However, not a word was said about the best long term solution to global monetary instability, the Single Global Currency.

The resulting "Declaration" of the conference considered the need for reforming the voting powers at the IMF and World Bank, but said little to indicate that substantial reform was being considered. "The IMF, in collaboration with the expanded FSF [Financial Stability Forum] and other bodies, should work to better identify vulnerabilities, anticipate potential stresses, and act swiftly to play a key role in crisis response."[92] The Finance Ministers and others who were charged with implementing the goals of the G-20 "Declaration" should consider the systemic vulnerability of the multicurrency system, but such a broad review was unlikely, at least before the scheduled reconvening of the G-20 leaders in London on 20 April 2008.

Similarly, the "Declaration" called for standardizing accounting standards, "The key global accounting standards bodies should work intensively toward the objective of creating a single high-quality global standard."[93] However, it's unlikely that it will consider the international accounting standardization which be achieved with a Single Global Currency, as is recommended by the former Single Global Currency Assn. Director, Ratnam Alagiah in his article, "A theoretical justification for a uniform and universal system of currency in accounting for inflation." He, and co-authors, Ludwig Reinhard and Paul Shum, concluded,

> "Overall, the introduction of a single global currency seems to bring considerable economic benefits especially for developing countries, which will (among others) not only benefit from an increase in trade flows and economic growth, but also from an improved monetary policy and the elimination of currency crises. The introduction of a single global currency will, however, undeniably result in short-term, possibly 'painful' economic adjustments in some countries and regions especially through increases in unemployment and economic migration processes. In the light of the overall positive effects of a single global currency, those adjustments seem however to be justifiable, especially if a single global currency would be introduced in steps through inter-regional currency unions, such as in ASEAN or ASEAN+5 first, in order to alleviate countries

from the negative burden of short-term adjustment costs. It thus appears to us that it is not a question of whether but when a single global currency will become a reality."[94]

Mobilize Stakeholders to Encourage the Tasks Above and the Implementation of the Single Global Currency

Fundamental to any political effort is the need to mobilize stakeholder groups such as those in the partial list presented below: consumers, economists, accountants, investors, international corporations, travel and trade organizations, international bankers, central bankers, nations, international humanitarian organizations, international finance organizations (IMF, World Bank, WTO, Bank for International Settlements). In short, everybody in the world can be mobilized.

The role of the IMF is discussed earlier in this book. Two goals of the World Bank are to "end extreme poverty within a generation and boost shared prosperity."[95] A goal of the World Trade Organization, which is descended from the International Trade Organization which arose from the 1944 Bretton Woods Conference, is "to ensure that trade flows as smoothly, predictably and freely as possible."[96]

The Financial Stability Board (FSB), based in Basel, Switzerland, is chartered to "coordinate at the international level the work of national financial authorities and international standard setting bodies and to develop and promote the implementation of effective regulatory, supervisory and other financial sector policies in the interest of financial stability." In 2013, it was asked by the G-20 countries to review the foreign exchange system and ensure that the "interest rate benchmarks" are properly defined and set.[97] Perhaps the FSB can think "outside the box" and consider the Single Global Currency as a way to solve the problems of the foreign exchange system.

The implementation of a Single Global Currency will help achieve the goals of all four of these organizations

Individuals can work through groups, and can consider other options as presented in Appendix B, "What Citizens of the World Can Do." Even some of the currency traders and speculators can be mobilized as they know that the current system needs to be replaced by a Single Global Currency. As noted earlier, George Soros knows that the world needs a Single Global Currency managed by a Global Central Bank.

Consumers

Of the earth's 7+ billion people, a substantial proportion are consumers of internationally traded goods and services, and they therefore have an interest in monetary and price stability and low prices. Consumers International (CI), headquartered in London, "is the only independent global campaigning voice for consumers."[98] CI represents 240 organizations in 129 countries.

Another organization for consumers, and business too, and as described in the previous chapter, is the International Organization for Standardization (ISO), in Geneva. It "...is the world's largest developer of voluntary International Standards. International Standards give state of the art specifications for products, services and good practice, helping to make industry more efficient and effective. Developed through global consensus, they help to break down barriers to international trade."[99] The ISO has a subcommittee for financial services which could have an interest in standardizing money, but the ISO's practice is to wait for member requests for standardization rather than proceed on its own initiative.

Economists

While most international economists have not publicly stated their views about the Single Global Currency, and while most of those who have made statements have been cautious about the utility and/or the feasibility, the world can change due to the actions and thinking of a few.

Robert Mundell has written extensively about the Single Global Currency and has conducted several annual panel discussions at his Tuscan home, "Santa Columba."

During the run-up to the euro, German economist Peter Bofinger "organized economists to speak out publicly in support of the euro."[100] Andrew Rose has urged similar activism in support of monetary union, though not to the global level, and has written,

> "At this point, academics should be persuading policymakers to lower the perceived political benefits of national money. Any debate on monetary union must leave the ivory tower of the academy; policymakers must raise it publicly if the discussion is to be serious. Succinctly, academics should be trying to get policy-makers to raise monetary union to the level of national debate."[101]

It's time for such economists to present the case for the Single Global Currency, especially its economic utility. Let the people and the politicians worry about the political feasibility. In 2003, several economists endorsed a letter to the finance ministers of the OECD countries urging them to begin planning for the Single Global Currency.[102] As was seen with the euro, it was the people and the politicians who led the effort, and now most international economists support the euro, even if not all its characteristics.

Accountants

Accounting for the international trade and investments of individuals and corporations will continue to be a challenge even with a Single Global Currency. Without it, the task will remain obviously more difficult. Through their multi-billion dollar/euro losses, the corporate scandals of Enron, Lehman Brothers, and Worldcom in the United States and Parmalat in Italy have reminded the world of the importance of careful, accurate accounting. International accountants, through their employers or through national and international accounting organizations, have a natural motivation to work for the implementation of a Single Global Currency.

There are international standards about how to account for fluctuations of currency values, but they still lead to arbitrary calculations, due to currency value fluctuations.

Investors, Investment Companies and Investment Funds

As individuals and as participants in their mutual funds, retirement funds, and other grouped funds, investors seek a return and/or growth for their investments. They also favor stability over instability and knowledge over ignorance.

In the United States, mutual funds and retirement funds have become more active in the management of the companies in which they hold stock. The California Public Employee Retirement System (CALPERS), with $271 billion in assets, has an international reputation for pressing its interests in good governance.[103]

With trillions of dollars in assets increasingly invested internationally, this industry can accelerate the movement toward the Single Global Currency by actively pursuing its interest in international financial stability.

International Corporations and their Associations

European corporations and their associations supported the planning for the euro and its implementation, which is a worthy precedent for what needs to be done for the Single Global Currency.

Guidliemo Carchedi explained the lobbying efforts for the euro in some detail in his book, *For Another Europe,*

> "Perhaps the most influential of all these groups is the European Roundtable of Industrialists (ERT), which was founded in 1983 by Umberto Agnelli of Fiat, Wisse Dekker of Philips and Pehr Gyllenhammer of Volvo. The ERT has dramatically increased contacts among European corporations. Its members are forty-five 'captains of industry,' that is, the Chief Executive Officers of the most important European oligopolies, also called transnational corporations, which in 1997 had a combined turnover of ECU 5,501m and three million employees world-wide. The ERT has some ten working groups covering major areas of interest (e.g., competition, education)....
>
> "This new alliance between the European Commission and the ERT played a crucial role during preparations for the Internal Market. In 1985, ERT chairman Wisse Dekker launched his proposal and timetable for the removal of all obstacles to trade within the European Economic Community. The European Commission was easily convinced. This pressure from industrial leaders for unification of European markets was precisely the momentum towards further European integration that the Commission was seeking.... Alongside the ERT, there is also the Union of Industrial and Employers'

Confederation of Europe (UNICE). While the ERT influences the general criteria informing European legislation, UNICE reacts to specific pieces of legislation and makes sure that they are tailored to business's interests....

"In the autumn of 1993 the ERT prepared its report 'Beating the Crisis'. In December 1993, the Delors 'White Paper on Growth, Competitiveness and Employment' was released. The two reports were prepared in close co-operation between the ERT and the Commission and 'are strikingly uniform in their calls for deregulation, flexible labour markets and transport infrastructure investments'.... As early as 1985, the ERT had argued that the Internal Market must be completed with a single currency. The EMU continued to be a leading ERT demand in its 1991 report *Reshaping Europe.* This report also presented a timetable for EMU implementation which bears remarkable similarity to the one incorporated in the Maastricht Treaty a few months later. However, the main work preparing the ground for the EMU was not done by the ERT, but rather by (one of its off-springs) the Association for the Monetary Union of Europe (AMUE). The AMUE was founded in 1987 by five transnational corporations, each of which was also represented in the ERT. The AMUE enjoys the same privileged access to high decision-making bodies as the ERT and its co-operation with European oligopolies and the EU is close. The Commission not only provides financial support to the AMUE but also frequently consults it on monetary questions. The AMUE also has close contacts with the European Central Bank."[104]

The ERT and AMUE model could be useful for international corporations as they join together in support of the Single Global Currency.

In Switzerland, the chief economist of the Swiss National Bank, Ulrich Kohili, noted in a 2003 speech that there was pressure in his country from industry and the unions to join the euro because the strong Swiss franc was hurting Swiss exports, especially to the Eurozone.[105]

For the campaign for the Single Global Currency, worldwide business and trade organizations, such as the International Chamber of Commerce,[106] will need to be mobilized. Even such support as the publication of articles in business association publications will help generate momentum for the 3-G world. In 1996, the American Chamber of Commerce in Belgium published in its *AmCham* magazine, "The Case for a Single Global Currency" by Brian Warburton.[107]

Even for corporations whose self-interest would appear to be damaged by a common currency, there is often a silver lining. At a 2006 annual meeting of the Directors of HSBC Malta, the Maltese subsidiary of the international HSBC bank, CEO Shaun Wallis was asked about the effect of the upcoming implementation of the euro, and he replied, "Yes, we will have lower foreign exchange profits, that's true. But the introduction of the common currency will create more trading opportunities. It will provide stability because 60 percent of Malta's trade is done within European Union borders."[108]

Finally, corporations do not all have to be "international" in order to support the implementation of a Single Global Currency. In Ecuador in 2000, the Chamber of Commerce supported the dollarization in order to achieve financial stability.[109]

As corporations are the primary organizations which engage in global trade, it's noted in this section that they could encourage the WTO to be a supporter of the Single Global Currency, as the SGC will enhance global trade.

Labor and Labor Unions

Around the world, labor has an interest in fair pay for its work, worldwide. As Noam Chomsky has noted, many labor unions label themselves as "international." Depending upon the country or region, that international interest works in favor of a Single Global Currency. Chinese workers are interested in being paid a wage closer to the world average, and Western workers are interested in a fair representation of the actual wages paid to workers around the world, without the fog of exchange rates, real exchange rates, or Purchasing Power Parity.

In testimony on 23 April 2004 before an Australian legislative committee, Dr Geoff Pain testified on behalf of Scientists for Labor, to the Joint Standing Committee on Treaties at its meeting in Perth, "But something this Committee might like to consider in terms of improving Australia's trade position is my proposal for a Single Global Currency.

"Many of Australia's problems come from the absurd obsession with the 'value' of the dollar against various currencies. A Single Global Currency would end unproductive gambling through hedging and futures markets."[110]

Writing two years earlier in the online Australian labor magazine, *Workers Online*, Dick Bryan, a professor at the University of Sydney, wrote in an article otherwise questioning Australian ization to the US dollar, "There is, for accumulation, a clear logic in having a Single Global Currency. Multiple currencies are as sensible as different rail gauges and different power sockets--they are an anachronistic inconvenience and costly."[111]

In 2002, Philippe Van Parijs, Secretary of BIEN (Basic Income Network), stated at a meeting in Geneva,

> "More worth exploring, in my view, is the idea of combining the move to one Single Global Currency, as advocated, e.g., by Myron Frankman, 'Beyond the Tobin Tax: Global Democracy and a Global Currency,' *The Annals* 581, 62-73, and the use of the seigneurage rights associated with this currency for funding a modest non-inflationary basic income at the level of the annual

growth of the world GDP, along the lines developed by
Joseph Huber at our Berlin congress."[112]

While not addressing the issue of the Single Global Currency directly, Barbara Shailor of the US AFL-CIO wrote in 2003 that currency crises and currency speculation are not in the interests of working people.[113]

Maybe it will be around the issue of the Single Global Currency that workers of the world can truly unite. As Bryan Taylor suggested, their slogan might be, "Currencies of the World Unite."[114]

Travel and Trade Organizations and Corporations
The people who travel and trade have the most obvious interest in making international trade and travel more convenient and less expensive. This group includes the hotel chains, the airlines and passenger liner companies, and the shipping and forwarding companies.

The volume of world trade in 2012 was reported by the WTO to be $18.3 trillion in goods or merchandise and $4.3 trillion in commercial services.[115] Every product and service in those totals went through a currency change transaction, except those which began and ended within the same currency area. If the savings from the implementation of a Single Global Currency are estimated here as a conservative one percent of the above totals, the travel and trade companies and their customers could save annually $183 billion and $43 billion respectively.

International Bankers
Although the banking industry earns billions from the trading of currencies for their customers and for themselves, they also stand to gain from international financial stability. Currency crises are not good for banks or for their customers. Banking used to be a conservative business where risks were avoided where possible.

Central Bankers
Paul DeGrauwe and Jacques Melitz wrote that a major reason for the adoption of the euro was that the central bankers of Europe became convinced in the 1970s and 1980s that the tools of their trade, exchange rate interventions, were not as effective as once thought,[116] and even "that countries that engaged in such monetary activism would experience an inflation bias and macroeconomic instability. From the perch of this new theoretical outlook, relinquishing one's own monetary policy instrument did not seem so costly as before."[117]

Former Turkish central banker Gazi Ercel supports a Single Global Currency, and has participated in Robert Mundell's conferences at Santa Columba.

Another former central banker who supports the Single Global Currency is Paul Volcker, former Chair of the US Federal Reserve Bank, and the source of the aphorism, "A Global Economy Requires A Global Currency."[118]

In New Zealand, a non-executive director of the board of the New Zealand Central Bank, Arthur Grimes, wrote in support of a Single Global Currency before taking his current position.

Benjamin J. Cohen views central bankers as stuck in currency competition and unable to see a cooperative future. He writes, "As the future unfolds, therefore, the worldwide competition among currencies appears destined to grow more intense, not less. Central banks must confront not just one another in an oligopolistic struggle for market share."[119] He seems to view the goal of central bankers as to "exercise independent and autonomous monetary policy"[120] which is really only a means to the overriding goal which is stable money.

On the other hand, Richard Cooper has written that "central bank cooperation has grown extensively, if fitfully and sporadically, since the birth of the BIS [Bank for International Settlements] and the inauguration of monthly meetings of central bankers in 1930," and notes that technology has enabled far more cooperation since then.[121]

The examples of the establishment of the euro and the movement of the New Member States into the Eurozone show that central bankers are more interested in stable money for the citizens of their countries than they are in competing for some kind of competitive advantage for their own central bank or country.

Non-Governmental Organizations

With the regular demonstrations at meetings of the World Trade Organization, it's plain to see that there is a large movement of people in the world concerned about economic fairness and who oppose some or many aspects of globalization.

In arguing for capital controls, Kavaljit Singh urged that "peoples' movements, therefore, have to be galvanized for devising new tools of analysis and action to ensure that global finance capital serves the interests of citizens and democratic states and not the avarice of owners and managers of capital."[122]

While there is no guarantee that the billions/trillions to be saved through the elimination of transactions charges, and foreign exchange reserves, and currency risk will go to the poorer people of the world, there is a guarantee that worldwide financial stability will help the poor.

Establishing a 3-G world where people are able to save their earnings, without loss to ruinous inflation or foreign exchange fluctuations, is like giving every person in the world an implicit micro-loan. In the past, inflation and currency crises had the reverse effects, which could never be outweighed by inadequate foreign aid programs.

As Raymond Baker notes in *Capitalism's Achilles Heel: Dirty Money and How to Renew the Free-Market System,* there is not much that can be said for an international system which provides about $50 billion annually in foreign aid to the poor countries of the world, but which watches the export of $500 billion a year from those same countries to the financially safer countries and investment centers of the world.[123] Even in a Single Global Currency world, people in countries with fewer investment opportunities or with political instability will seek safer havens for their money. However, to the extent that currency risk is a reason for money flight, that money will be more likely to remain in those countries upon the introduction of a

Single Global Currency with zero currency risk, and be available to the citizens of those countries.

Nations

From one perspective, the Single Global Currency is a political project and will be achieved when a sufficient number of governments in the world embark upon the goal of a Single Global Currency.

Again, one can look at the establishment of the euro for guidance. De Grauwe and Melitz noted, "Remarkably, though, politicians pushed through the whole process of monetary integration against the advice of most experts."[124]

Increasingly, nations are seeing that it is in their interest to join a stable monetary union and when the real prospect of a Global Monetary Union emerges, they will seek membership.

International Monetary/Trade Organizations (IMF, World Bank, WTO, Bank for International Settlements)

The roles of these three organizations will change upon the implementation of a Single Global Currency, and most severely the IMF. That's one reason why the IMF should lead the effort for such implementation, and seek to transform itself, perhaps into a part of the Global Central Bank. Ramon Tamames and the author wrote separately in 2005 and 2006 to IMF Managing Director Rodrigo de Rato to urge him to adopt the Single Global Currency as an IMF project.[125] Although the IMF, through Rodrigo de Rato, and his successors, Dominique Strauss-Kahn and Christine Lagarde, have shown increasing interest in the effects of its policies upon the poorer people of the world, it has not yet focused upon the Single Global Currency as a means to that end, nor for any other reasons.[126]

Political Action to Encourage Implementation of the Single Global Currency

It takes time and hard work to change the world. The movement toward a Single Global Currency began long before this book and that movement will continue inexorably. It will be achieved through the efforts of hundreds of thousands of people working individually and through their affiliated groups, nations, and non-governmental organizations. The efforts of the Single Global Currency Association and the publication of this book are only a small part of the movement. If these efforts can accelerate the implementation of the Single Global Currency by only one month, i.e., by December 2023 instead of January 2024, then these efforts will have saved the world $25 billion in avoided transaction costs alone. If the cost of *ALL* the non-governmental efforts over the next 10 years to implement a 3-G world cost approximately $30 million, which is surely an optimistic guess, then the "return" to the world on that investment in the FIRST year will be at least 10,000 fold, or 1,000,000 percent. That sounds like a good investment, and even makes common cents/sense.

The political challenges are to seek acceleration of that implementation and to ensure that the transition goes smoothly. Presented in Appendix B, "What Citizens of the World Can Do," are a few examples of the work to be done by groups and organizations.

Public Opinion Polls

Sometimes just asking questions can provoke consideration of ideas previously thought unthinkable.

Zogby International has polled US citizens about their support of a Single Global Currency. They were asked:

Some financial leaders have proposed using a Single Global Currency, where all of the people in the world would use the same money. They argue that this would eliminate currency trading costs, currency risks, currency misalignments, and currency crises; thereby substantially boosting world prosperity. Would you strongly favor, somewhat favor, somewhat oppose, or strongly oppose a Single Global Currency, where all the people of the world would use the same money?

The question has been asked in three separate polls since 2003, and the answers have been substantially consistent as seen below:

	Dec. 2004	April 2004	Nov. 2003
Strongly Favor	11	9	9
Somewhat Favor	14	16	19
Not Sure	9	10	12
Somewhat Oppose	18	19	17
Strongly Oppose	48	47	42

As with representative politics, expectations are a big part of primary elections and elections. In this case, although a majority in the US opposes a Single Global Currency, the level of support is higher than expected.[127] Such polling should be done internationally, and ask other questions or assertions from this book. Is it true, for example, that citizens of the world desire their money to be stable? If given a choice, would they prefer a stable common currency to their own national, but less stable, currency?

The Single Global Currency Association sponsors an online poll on its website with the same question as above and the results have been pulled from time to time. The sample of voters, from visitors to the SGCA website, is not a random sample, and it is very small, but the results seem to be consistent over time.

	Feb. 2014	Feb 2006	Dec. 2004
Strongly Favor	25%	33%	31%
Somewhat Favor	7%	13%	15%
Not Sure	6%	5%	6%
Somewhat Oppose	3%	5%	5%
Strongly Oppose	59%	44%	44%
Total Votes to date	11,036	1,513	741

When a critical mass of political support is achieved, and when people and countries accept the inevitability of the Single Global Currency, then the movement to join will accelerate. That point will likely come when even less than 51 percent of the world's population supports the idea.

As with all polling, the wording of the questions matters. In 1988, a Gallup poll in the United Kingdom found that 77 percent of the British people opposed the immediate adoption of the euro, but 80 percent believed that Britain would join eventually.[128]

Group Resolutions

Every governmental and non-governmental group can indicate its support of the Single Global Currency by passing a resolution. While it's tempting to think that the only legislative bodies which can vote are those which will establish the Global Central Bank, that's not the case. Every group, such as neighborhood groups, labor unions, fraternal organizations and student groups, can have an opinion and those opinions will count.

Below is sample resolution:

RESOLUTION PROPOSED FOR ADOPTION BY GOVERNMENT AND NON-GOVERNMENT ORGANIZATIONS

WHEREAS the world's monetary system is characterized by multiple currencies which fluctuate in value compared to one another, and

WHEREAS these currencies are subject to manipulation, speculation, international imbalance, and currency crisis thereby causing severe and widespread economic hardship around the world, and

WHEREAS the total annual transaction costs of maintaining such a system are measured in the hundreds of billions of dollars/euros, and

WHEREAS the currency risks among the currencies cause artificially diminished asset values which are measured in the trillions of dollars/euros, and

WHEREAS the implementation of a Single Global Currency will save the world hundreds of billions of dollars in transaction costs, and

WHEREAS the implementation of a Single Global Currency will eliminate the risk of currency crises and the balance of payments problems for every country, and

WHEREAS the implementation of a Single Global Currency will increase the values of assets in those countries in inverse proportion to the level of the existing currency risk.

THEREFORE, BE IT RESOLVED that _____
(name of group)
supports the implementation of a Single Global Currency as soon as possible.

The idea of a Single Global Currency can be proposed in different settings, including *ad hoc* academic forums. In 2004, the Copenhagen Consensus project brought together eight distinguished economists to whom were brought proposals for solutions to problems in ten areas, such as "Climate Change," "Conflicts," and "Financial Instability."[129] The eight were asked, "What would be the best ways of advancing global welfare, and particularly the welfare of developing countries, supposing that an additional $50 billion of resources were at governments' disposal?"

The eight economists considered thirty proposals from ten papers written by others. Barry Eichengreen presented four proposals for "Financial Instability" including "Option 3: Establish a common currency."[130] He focused only on the benefit to developing countries of eliminating currency crises, and found an annual net benefit of $91 billion. Unfortunately, the eight economist panel did not apply their rankings of "Very Good, Good, Fair, and Bad," to any of the four "Financial Instability" recommendations among the seventeen projects due to "the complexities and uncertainties in this area."[131] If endorsed, this one proposal could have contributed a sum almost double the hypothetical $50 billion which then could have been used to solve other world problems. Too complex and uncertain, they said.

Other Issues on the Road to a 3-G World, with a Single Global Currency, Managed by a Global Central Bank, within a Global Monetary Union

Eligibility Criteria for Joining a Global Monetary Union?

The sole criterion for a country joining the GMU should be whether there has been a political decision to use the Global Monetary Union currency as legal tender. Once that decision has been made, then the remaining questions would concern the level of participation in the monetary union. In the European Monetary Union, the eligibility criteria have been used as a way to ensure willingness and ability to comply with the terms of the Growth and Stability Pact.

Hugo Narrillos Roux, a strong supporter of the Single Global Currency, argues that there should be "deep economic integration" among nations joining such a Global Monetary Union.[132] However, the endogeneity found by Andrew Rose and Jeffrey Frankel for smaller monetary unions is likely to be found for a Global Monetary Union as well. Thus, Roux's integration will likely be found after Global Monetary Union, so why insist upon it beforehand? Instead, the level of willingness and ability to adhere to fiscal and monetary standards can be used to determine not whether the Single Global Currency can be used as legal tender within a country, but to determine the level of participation in that monetary union.

A major difference between the commitment to join the Global Monetary Union and current and past decisions to join monetary unions is that the Global Monetary Union will be larger, by definition, and large enough that any new country's addition will not make an appreciable difference to the overall confidence in the Single Global Currency.

If a country's fiscal management is not sufficiently prudent, then a new country can use the Single Global Currency through SGC-ization, just as Ecuador and El Salvador have ized to the US dollar.

If a new country wishes to utilize the full services of the Global Central Bank and wishes to have a vote on decisions on money supply, inflation and interest rates, then further conditions may be required, perhaps in the nature of a Global Growth and Stability Pact.

With such an approach, every willing, responsible, country could use the Single Global Currency as legal tender, but only countries meeting certain criteria could participate on the decision making committees to manage it.

Timetable of Movement to a Single Global Currency.

At its 2003 formation, the Single Global Currency Association set a goal of 2024 for achieving a Single Global Currency. As with many such goals, it's arbitrary and could have been 2023 or 2025 or 2034; but 2024 was used as it's the eightieth anniversary of the 1944 Bretton Woods agreements. Also, it seemed close enough the above referenced predictions of *the Economist* and Richard Cooper.

The 2024 date was established twenty-one years in advance, not because the mechanics of establishing a Single Global Currency would take that long, but because it's estimated that it would take most of those years to develop the political will to formally establish the goal. If a serious international currency crisis occurs in the meantime, the political will might be developed more rapidly.

Once the goal is formally accepted by the governments of the participating countries, whether they be G-2, G-7, G-20, or all 193 UN member countries, the actual implementation could be quite rapid. When an increasing number of commodities are priced in the SGC, or whatever its future name, and as worldwide financial transactions, including World Bank loans, are conducted in that new currency, the incentive to all countries to join the SGC-area, if not the Global Monetary Union, will be overpowering. What incentive would remain to stay out?

In several respects, the EMU is an exceedingly realistic test site as it provides real data about how to establish, maintain, and expand a large monetary union. As noted before, not all monetary unions are alike, and there is no necessity that the Global Monetary Union must look exactly like any of them. Nonetheless, with the accession of the ten New Member States, the EMU will be large and contain a wide variety of economies, and can be considered as simply a smaller version of the coming Global Monetary Union.

From several key vantage points, a few of which are listed below, the organizers of the Global Monetary Union can learn much from the EMU:
The formation process for the EMU;
The creation of the European Central Bank;
Setting the exchange rate for all participating currencies to the euro
Introducing the new currency;
Adding new countries/currency areas to the existing EMU;[133]
Managing inflation; and
Managing international reserves.

Below is a table showing the dates of euro implementation and proposed dates of implementation for the Single Global Currency.

Task	Euro	Single Global Currency
Estab. implement. date	January 1994	January 2016
Adopt name for currency[134]	16 December 1995	16 December 2017
Announce exchange rates	May 1998	open timing
Establish central bank	1 June 1998	1 June 2020
Convert to new currency	1 January 1999	1 January 2021
Coins & bills to public	1 January 2002	1 January 2024
Old currencies stop (opt'nal)	1 March 2002	1 March 2024

If it can be done for 18 countries, and 335 million people, why not 20 or 30 or 100 or 193 countries, and 7+ billion people?

Another aspect of timing is the stage of development of countries joining the Global Monetary Union. Because the EU countries passed through a fifty-year transition from the Coal and Steel Pact to Common Market to monetary union, it's commonly thought that such trade-oriented steps are pre-requisites to participation in the Global Monetary Union, but that need not be the case. As Edmunds and Marthinsen stated, "A monetary union can be formed at any stage of economic development, and it can be formed with other nations that may be at different stages of development. It is not necessary for the nations unifying their currencies to have previously integrated their economies in other ways."[135]

The Mechanics of Implementation

By 3 January 2002, two days after the distribution of euro cash, 96 percent of all automated teller machines were dispensing the new euro currency. By 8 January, 50 percent of all cash transactions were being conducted with euro coins and bills.[136] By the end of February 2002, more than 6 billion legacy currency banknotes and 30 billion coins had been withdrawn from circulation. This process went extraordinarily smoothly, to the surprise of some. As with other aspects of the EMU, the process is a good model for future implementation of the Single Global Currency.

The implementations of the accessions of the subsequent EMU members have gone even more smoothly, as lessons were learned from 2002.

Assure the Public that Prices will not Increase During a Changeover from one Currency to Another.

During the conversion from the initial twelve national currencies to the euro, many citizens and media articles questioned whether prices were actually being raised and whether merchants were using the confusion of the transition to camouflage the process. One technique was "rounding up" a fraction to the next largest coinage of the euro. For example, the price of a euro was set as 1,936.27 lira in Italy, so when a merchant changed the price of a shoe which cost 149,000 lira, the exact price in euros would become 76.952 euros. However, instead of rounding mathematically and posting a price of €76.95, a merchant might have posted the price at €80. A merchant might have posted such a price in the spirit of easy-to-understand pricing, but s/he might also have posted the price at €70 or

€75, too. It's the belief of many Europeans that many merchants raised their prices in that manner.

While studies of consumer prices in Europe have found that actual price increases were substantially less than the public's perception, there were pockets of significant increases, such as for food in Italy where the average increase from November 2001 to November 2002 was 29 percent.[137] It's the perception of inflation which must be anticipated during the coming transition to a Single Global Currency. Paul De Grauwe concluded that some part of the price increases came due to an implicit understanding that such increases were permissible and collectively implemented. He also noted that the increases were not expected by economists, and has recommended price controls to deal with this problem for the ten accession countries.[138] Now, with awareness heightened of this problem, future expansions and creations of monetary unions should include preparations to discourage such opportunistic price increases. For the subsequent accession countries, consumers were better informed about the pricing changeover to the euro, than was the case in 2002, in order to be vigilant against inappropriate price increases.[139]

Fear of price increases is a major reason why people in the accession countries are hesitant about the adoption of the euro. Only 38 percent of Eastern Europeans believe that the euro will be positive for them at home, but 92 percent believe that the use of the euro will help travelers and 80 percent expect that shopping abroad will be easier.[140] The 2006 poll did not ask about any feelings of loss of sovereignty due to the prospective loss of national currencies.

In preparation for the Slovakian accession into the EMU, the OECD prepared in 2008 a "How To" document which shows the depth of understanding now available about monetary union accession. The last several paragraphs of "The Euro Changeover in the Slovak Republic" are presented here, as they contain much general guidance about such changeovers for future accession countries to other monetary unions, including the future Global Monetary Union.

"Policy recommendations for the short term – From now to mid 2009

- Rounding effects should only exert a minor upward pressure on prices. A pure mathematical rounding procedure would lead to rounding up in five out of 10 cases while rounding down in four out of ten cases. Public information campaigns as well as negotiations with retailers should therefore emphasize that euro adoption does not automatically mean rounding up prices. The same logic also applies to the transition to a system of new "attractive prices".
- Publicly administered prices as well as prices and fees for public services still play an important role in the consumption basket for Slovak citizens. The changeover for such price items in the public domain should be presented as show case. For such prices the need to charge "attractive" numbers is less evident. Publicly determined prices and fees should be changed strictly according to the conversion rate. The euro adoption should be used as an opportunity to introduce publicly available price

and fee comparisons for public services, like public and municipal utilities.

- International retail chains are already operating in the Slovak Republic. Most of them offer price information which is available via the internet. Consumer protection organizations could consider to put together representative samples of consumer baskets and maintain a "beauty contest" for retail chains, which is publicly accessible. Such comparisons should also include neighbouring countries, especially Austria and Hungary, which are in reach for a large share of consumers in Western Slovakia.

- Calculations show that those socio-economic groups which are likely to experience a larger increase in the costs of their consumption expenditure also have a higher income. Programs to compensate for the price level effects of euro adoption should be limited to low income groups, especially families with children. General transfer increases would only stimulate price increases and should be avoided.

- If suppliers want to increase their profits by gaining market share (and not by increasing prices) during the changeover period then any obstacles to bring the additional supply to the market will deter firms from choosing such a strategy. Remaining administrative obstacles to increase supply should be removed and arguments in their favour, referring to health and safety concerns should be carefully examined to avoid that such concerns are misused as entry barriers which protect insiders. Unavoidable changeover costs, like menu costs, as well as costs related to the handling of a new currency for some time in parallel with the current Slovak koruna, are equivalent to a one-off cost increase, which – under conditions of perfect competition – will be shared among suppliers and consumers according to the slopes of demand and supply schedules. Such cost increases cannot be rolled forward into wage increases without increasing wage costs throughout the economy and thus putting employment at risk. Social partners should be encouraged to exclude changeover costs from wage and price negotiations in the current and next rounds.

Policy recommendations for the medium term

- Competition is limiting the scope for misusing the euro changeover for an increase of mark-ups and to reap extra profits. A competition friendly regulatory environment, which keeps entry barriers low and avoids administrative overheads and red tape, is a powerful ally for the changeover campaign. While past reforms have achieved a lot already, much remains still to be done and this also includes network industries. Although regulatory changes need time to exercise an impact it is now the time to use this opportunity. The government should use the euro changeover to reduce and remove altogether entry barriers and accelerate its efforts to remove administrative barriers. Where competition is not yet possible due to the existence of natural monopolies, regulators should be endowed with sufficient powers to allow the use of private networks at fair conditions and to set prices which do not include excessive monopoly rents.

- Financial market integration should lead to lower spreads, not the least because of the removal of any exchange rate risk within the euro area. Currently lending rates are above the euro area average, while deposit rates are below. Experience from the euro area demonstrates that financial sector integration takes time and that it more often takes the form of takeovers than cross border expansion. This process has been more or less concluded insofar as domestic (Slovak) banks and financial institutions are involved. However, there may be some scope for consolidation among the foreign banks. The government should investigate in co-operation with the central bank and financial market supervision in how far barriers for the establishment of a more competition friendly market structure in financial services exist. In order to reap these potential benefits from a pro-competitive market structure it will also be necessary to make sure that the associated cost cutting opportunities can be exercised.

- Adopting the euro will eliminate the opportunity to pursue real appreciation via nominal appreciation. This is important for catching up economies, which have lower prices in domestic services sectors than in richer euro area member countries. This Balassa-Samuelson effect will damp real interest rates and can possibly contribute to a boom-and bust cycle. In order to avoid such a scenario the government should prepare a comprehensive policy package in order to compensate for the loss of monetary policy and the elimination of the nominal exchange rate as a channel for real appreciation. Such a package should include:

- Measures to increase the scope for competition in domestic services sectors in order to close the gap of productivity growth with the (international competition exposed) export manufacturing sector. Such a measure would reduce the Balassa-Samuelson effect directly.

- Measures to reduce the attractiveness of loan financed asset bubbles, in particular a capital gains tax. Such a measure would reduce the attraction of investing in a bubble market.

- Maintaining a prudent fiscal stance and avoiding in particular to expand general transfer programs. The government should continue to improve the incentives to work as well as to search for work and to participate in lifelong learning in order to be employable longer.
  Such measures would increase the overall supply of labour and avoid a premature overheating of the labour market.

- Establishing a regulatory environment which allows the development of a rental housing market. This would reduce the need to enter the housing market as a buyer in order to satisfy a housing need."[141]

By the time there is a consensus or agreement that a Single Global Currency has been born, it may be that the leading monetary system candidate, if through an anointing process, will be so stable there will be less concern about such inflation. With the creation of the euro, there were no such reassurances of stability, and, in fact, the euro varied in price relative to the dollar by as much as 60 percent during its first five years.

If the Single Global Currency is to be a new currency, like the 1999 euro, then it will, by definition, include several very large currencies which will, together, ensure its stability, and reduce the fear of inflation.

Assure the public that adverse effects of the implementation of a 3-G world will be addressed

To the extent that there are individuals or groups who might be adversely affected by the implementation of the Single Global Currency, they should be identified and appropriate remedial measures should be planned. Such measures could be financed through the savings achieved through the 3-G implementation.

Why is a Global Monetary Union feasible NOW?

As noted in the beginning of this book, money has different functions and attributes. As we move toward the third decade of the twenty-first century (Gregorian calendar).[142] money is far less important as a medium of exchange, as the most important medium now used is the digit in the form of an electron in a cable or wire or in the form of a radio or other electromagnetic wave. As a store of value, it's far less important, too, as very few people speak openly of the virtue of placing one's savings under the mattress. That leaves the third leg of the standard definition of money as the most important: unit of account. As a unit of account, money is failing the people of the world who are increasingly oriented to buying, selling, and sending money internationally where the units of account are constantly fluctuating. It's time for at least one worldwide unit of account: a Single Global Currency.

A Global Monetary Union is more feasible now because the technology of computers and communications has enabled the faster distribution of information to a vastly larger audience than ever before. Robert Mundell wrote that the lack of such technology was a major reason why a global currency was not created at Bretton Woods in 1944.[143]

One of the earlier perceived obstacles to monetary union had been the incongruence of nations' business cycles, but over the past twenty years, the severity and volatility of business cycles have moderated by about fifty percent,[144] thus reducing that barrier. The effect is so dramatic that it's called by economists "the Great Moderation."[145] A major cause has surely been the computerization of the world which enables companies to avoid unnecessary inventory accumulations, formerly a basic cause of recession.

The total cost of the multicurrency foreign exchange world is now more visible and no longer acceptable. Despite being dwarfed by the $2.5 trillion of daily foreign exchange trading, the annual $300 billion cost of the current system is still a vast amount of money. That is $42.86 for every human being, more than half of whom subsist on $2 or less a day.[146] Even more attractive are the potential gains of $trillions in worldwide asset and GDP growth.

The risks of the global imbalances are growing. What might China and Japan DO with their huge foreign exchange reserves of $3.73 trillion and $1.3 trillion, respectively? In comparison, the United States, with most of its currency outside its borders, has only $.2 trillion in foreign exchange reserves.[147] Governments talk about fixing "global imbalances," but it sometimes takes voter interest and pressure to ensure that governments act properly. More effective than nations pressuring nations to change their behavior will be pressure to abandon an obsolete, often harmful multicurrency foreign exchange system in favor of a Global Monetary Union. Such a union will have zero destabilizing global imbalances, at least in the sense that such imbalances of payments, current account deficits, and trade imbalances are currently understood. With such imbalances set aside, the world can pay more attention to far more human and serious imbalances and inequalities in the world where the richest five percent of the world's population earn as much income as the poorest eighty percent.[148]

The multicurrency foreign exchange system is more like a horse-driven five-wheel cart to carry people from different airports serving the same city, e.g., Gatwick and Heathrow. That is obviously not acceptable, nor even thinkable. We don't need the obsolete, though charming, horse, nor the fifth wheel of the international financial system.

The importance of the US economy to the economy of the rest of the world is diminishing as is its claim to be the legitimate issuer of the world's primary reserve currency. It has gone from being a wealthy creditor nation to being an "empire of debt."[149]

At the time of Bretton Woods, the US economy accounted for approximately 40 percent of the world's GDP.[150] By 1984, the year of Richard Cooper's article, "A Monetary System for the Future," that percentage had shrunk to 25 percent, and he wrote, "...as the United States shrinks in relation to the rest of the world, as it is bound to do, the intrinsic weaknesses of reliance on the US dollar will become more apparent, especially in the United States, where the possible reaction of foreign dollar-holders will become an ever greater constraint on US monetary policy."[151] Cooper forecast that by 2009, the year in which his world currency was to be implemented, the percentage would be 17 percent. By 2013, the percentage had actually decreased only to 22.4 percent ($16.5-73.8 trillion).[152] The dramatic growth of the emerging world over the next several years will surely bring that percentage down, though not as rapidly as Cooper foresaw.[153]

The world now has an alternative to the dollar: the euro. Despite the difficulties with the euro in the years 2008-2013, no countries seceded, and several countries joined. While there are many who argue that the euro is the best candidate to be the next primary international currency,[154] the choice should no longer be which national or multinational currency will be the primary international reserve currency among other major currencies, but whether that competitive model is becoming obsolete and whether a multinational currency ought to be designated as the Single Global Currency.

Summary
The world is ready to begin preparing for a Single Global Currency, just as Europe prepared for the euro and as the Arabian Gulf countries are preparing for their common currency. After the goal of a Single Global Currency is established by countries representing a significant proportion

of the world's GDP, then the project can be pursued like its regional predecessors. If pursued with the investment of time and money on the scale of the US flights to the moon (and economics is not "rocket science") or the Allied invasion on D-Day, as suggested by Richard Cooper; then the path to the Single Global Currency could be greatly shortened.

One of the temptations during the pursuit of a 3-G world is to bundle additional goals into the effort, but those other goals must stand on their own. The chances of their implementation may be improved in that 3-G world, where monetary and fiscal policies will not be burdened by the multicurrency foreign exchange albatross. For example, it may be that the groundbreaking theories of Louis Kelso[155] will improve the chances of increased economic growth and fairer distribution of income and wealth, but those goals will be enhanced in the 3-G world. Bundling Kelso's "binary economics" theories with the drive for a Single Global Currency will not help either effort. Borrowing from a 1970s environmental movement slogan: whatever the international economics cause, it's a lost cause until we implement a Single Global Currency.[156]

It's important that the idea of the Single Global Currency be researched and pursued without regard to the interests of those invested in the current system. Borrowing from President Barak Obama, who stated, "Don't tell me words don't matter," and who asked rhetorically, "Just Words?" "[157] and as argued by Dani Rodrik, ideas do matter.[158]

Once the pieces of the 3-G puzzle begin coming together, as described above, then the momentum will accelerate. As the inevitability of the 3-G world emerges with a common currency servicing countries containing somewhere around 30-40 percent of world GDP, then the "tipping point" rush to join will increase. Many great social and political movements have been successful with less than majority support. During the American Revolution, approximately one-third of the colonists supported independence, one-third wanted to remain a British colony, and one-third was neutral.

It is now time to seriously pursue the goal of a Single Global Currency as managed by a Global Central Bank within a Global Monetary Union. As the title of Lester Thurow's book states, "fortune favors the bold."[159]

What that world will look like is addressed in Chapter 8.

ENDNOTES

1. The title of this chapter is related to a well-known Maine joke, as related by Marshall Dodge in his routine, "Bert and I." When an out-of-stater asks for the way to Millinocket, the local Mainer attempts to respond with three sets of directions, but finally concludes, "Come to think of it, you can't get there from here." Well, despite the reluctance of some, we will, of course, get to a Single Global Currency from here. See Marshall Dodge and Robert Bryan, *Bert and I and other stories from Down East*. Camden, ME: Down East Books, 1981, and listen to the selections, "Which Way to East Vassalboro?" and "Which Way to Millinocket?" on the CD, *Bert & I/ More Bert & I*, Bluewater Books & Charts, Fort Lauderdale, FL. The chapter title

also echoes the last sentence of the article "One World, One Money" in *The Economist*, 26 September 1998, "Fine, you say, but how would the world ever get from here to there?" at http://www.economist.com/node/166471

2. Sisira Kanti Mishra, "Towards a Single Global Currency," Social Science Research Network, 8 December 2010, at http://papers.ssrn.com/sol3/papers.cfm?abstract_id=1722126

3. Ambrose Evans-Pritchard, "The G20 moves the world a step closer to a global currency – The world is a step closer to a global currency, backed by a global central bank, running monetary policy for all humanity," *The Telegraph*, 3 April 2009, at http://www.telegraph.co.uk/finance/comment/ambroseevans_pritchard/5096524/The-G20-moves-the-world-a-step-closer-to-a-global-currency.html

4. Mark Twain, "...the report of my death was an exaggeration," Wikiquote, "Mark Twain," at http://en.wikiquote.org/wiki/Mark_Twain

5. Jeffrey Garten, "Toward a post-dollar world," McKinsey Global, 17 December 2009, at http://whatmatters.mckinseydigital.com/currencies/toward-a-post-dollar-world and "We must get ready for a weak-dollar world," 29 November 2009, *Financial Times*, at http://www.ft.com/intl/cms/s/0/d7c5b756-dd14-11de-ad60-00144feabdc0.html#axzz2uXkbqImj

6. Cover Story, *The Economist*, "Get Ready for the Phoenix," 9 January 1988, pp. 9-10.

7. See the table of "Currencies by Country" at the Single Global Currency Association website at http://www.singleglobalcurrency.org/currencies_by_country.html

8. Bryan Taylor, "The Eurodollar," 1998, p. 5, at http://www.emuenzen.de/forum/574004-post185.html.

9. Paul De Grauwe and Jacques Melitz, editors, *Prospects for Monetary Unions after the Euro*. Cambridge, MA: MIT Press, 2005, p. 2.

10. Robert E. Litan and Benn Steil, *Financial Statecraft*. London and New Haven, CT: Yale University Press, 2006, p. 143.

11. Robert Mundell, "Exchange Rates, Currency Areas and the International Financial Architecture," remarks delivered at an IMF panel, 22 September 2000, Prague, Czech Republic, at http://www.usagold.com/gildedopinion/mundellprague.html.

12. Robert Mundell, "The Case for a World Currency," *Journal of Policy Modeling*, June 2005, pp. 465-75, at p. 474, at http://ideas.repec.org/a/eee/jpolmo/v34y2012i4p568-578.html. These ideas are summarized in a 3 March 2009 97 slide presentation, "Financial Crises and the International Monetary System" at http://www.normangirvan.info/wp-content/uploads/2009/03/mundell.pdf

13. "Catching the Eagle," *The Economist*, 20 November 2013, at http://www.economist.com/blogs/graphicdetail/2013/11/chinese-and-american-gdp-forecasts

14. Robert Guttmann, *How Credit Money Shapes the Economy, The United States in a Global Economy*. Armonk, NY: M. E. Sharpe, 1994, p. 431.

15. "Kyoto Protocol to the United Nations Framework Convention on Climate Change," at http://unfccc.int/resource/docs/convkp/kpeng.html

16. Robert Mundell, "Currency Areas, Volatility and Intervention," Columbia University, Discussion Paper Series, Discussion Paper #0102-09, January 2002, p. 2, at http://academiccommons.columbia.edu/catalog/ac%3A114118.

17. "President proposes Single Currency," *TEMPO Interactive*, 5 November 2008, at http://www.tempointeractive.com/hg/nasional/2008/11/05/brk,20081105-144210,uk.html

18. Babajide Komolafe, "Again, a radical reform prescription from Professor Soludo," *Vanguard*, 3 November 2008, at http://www.vanguardngr.com:80/content/view/20735/116/

19. "What Should Bretton Woods II Look Like?" by Jose Antonio Campo, *Guatamala Times*, 4 November 2008, at http://www.guatemala-times.com/opinion/syndicated/the-frontiers-of-growth/498-what-should-bretton-woods-ii-look-like.html

20. "Scenarios - Possible featured of new world financial order," *Reuters*, 6 November 2008, at http://www.reuters.com/article/marketsNews/idUSL630935420081106?sp=true

21. "Top Ten 2008/2009 Global Economic Challenges facing America's 44th President," edited by Lael Brainard, Brookings Institution, 2008 at http://www.brookings.edu/reports/2008/~/media/Files/rc/reports/2008/10_global_economics_top_ten/top_ten_2008.pdf

22. "Transcript: President Obama's News Conference," *New York Times*, 24 March 2009 at http://www.nytimes.com/2009/03/24/us/politics/24text-obama.html?pagewanted=all&_r=0

23. Rebecca Christie, "Geithner Remarks on IMF Currency Roil Foreign-Exchange Market, 26 March 2009, at http://www.bloomberg.com/apps/news?pid=newsarchive&sid=aSZTgpL48TZQ

24. See, for example, "Explaining Exchange Rate Dynamics--The Uncovered Equity Return Parity Condition" by Elizaveta Krylova, Lorenzo Cappiello, and Roberto A. De Santis. The abstract begins, "By employing Lucas' (1982) model, this study proposes an arbitrage relationship--the Uncovered Equity Return Parity (URP) condition--to explain the dynamics of exchange rates," European Central Bank, Working Paper 529, September 2005, at http://www.ecb.int/pub/pdf/scpwps/ecbwp529.pdf.

25. See Egil Matsen and Ragnar Torvik, "Optimal Dutch Disease," 27 April 2004, at http://www.svt.ntnu.no/iso/Ragnar.Torvik/emrtjderev2.pdf

26. Maurice Obstfeld and Kenneth Rogoff, "The Six Major Puzzles in International Macroeconomics: Is There a Common Cause?" *NBER Macroeconomics Annual 2000*, pp. 339-390, at http://www.nber.org/chapters/c11059.pdf.

27. See the list of 215 Economics Departments, Institutes and Research Centers in the World, for International Economics at the EDIRC database, maintained at the University of Connecticut at http://edirc.repec.org/.

28. Robert Mundell, "Financial Crises and the International Monetary System," 3 March 2009 97 slide presentation at http://www.normangirvan.info/wp-content/uploads/2009/03/mundell.pdf, op. cit.

29. Martin Wolf email, 6 July 2005, in response to question from the author regarding Mr. Wolf's estimate of the implementation date of a Single Global Currency Association, he wrote,"Half a century, perhaps." In his 2008 Book, *Fixing Global Finance,* Wolf wrote, "A return to the gold standard is out of the question in the foreseeable future. So too is the creation of a global currency union on the model of the European Union. … the monetary environment is unlikely to be transformed within the next decade or two." Johns Hopkins University Press, p. 184.

30. "Mahathir Proposes Single Global Currency," *DowJones*, 9 June 2001, at http://www.nikkei-events.jp/future-of-asia/2001/010608_08.html

31. "IMF Executive Board Concludes Article IV Consultation with Germany," Public Information Notice No 13/299, 6 August 2013, at http://www.imf.org/external/np/sec/pr/2013/pr13299.htm. See also IMF Article IV of Agreement, at http://www.imf.org/external/pubs/cat/longres.aspx?sk=40860.0

32. "El Salvador: 2013 Article IV consultation," International Monetary Fund, 22 May 2013, at http://www.imf.org/external/pubs/ft/scr/2013/cr13132.pdf

33. Alex Brummer, "Financial Notebook: Birth Rites," *The Guardian*, online, 11 January 1994, at http://www.guardian.co.uk/euro/story/0,11306,616489,00.html, according to timeline at http://politics.guardian.co.uk/euro/story/0,9061,617173,00.html.

34. See http://www.new7wonders.com/

35. Benjamin J. Cohen, *The Future of Money.* Princeton, NJ: Princeton University Press, p. 221.

36. Mark Leonard, *Why Europe Will Run the 21st Century.* London, UK: Fourth Estate, 2005.

37. Willem H. Buiter, "The EMU and the NAMU: What is the Case for North American Monetary Union?" September 1999, Canadian Public Policy, pp. 285-306, at p. 286, at http://qed.econ.queensu.ca/pub/cpp/sept1999/Buiter.pdf.

38. Robert E. Litan and Benn Steil, *Financial Statecraft*, op. cit., p. 156.

39. Simon Gray and Jacob Nell, *A New Currency for Iraq.* London, UK: Central Banking Publications, Ltd., 2005.

40. Malcolm Lowe, "Palestine Declares Independence and Its Currency Is: the Israeli Shekel?" Gatestone Institute, 25 May 2011, at http://www.gatestoneinstitute.org/2138/palestine-currency-shekel

41. Sever Plocker, "Dollarization in Israel-Palestine," May 2005, Brookings Institution, at

http://www.brookings.edu/research/papers/2005/05/01middleeast-plocker.

42. John Edmunds and John Marthinsen, *Wealth by Association--Global Prosperity Through Market Unification*. Westport, CT: Praeger Publishers, 2003, p. 146.

43. "Enlargement of the Eurozone," *Wikipedia*, at http://en.wikipedia.org/wiki/Enlargement_of_the_eurozone

44. "The international role of the euro and its potential in Latin America," by Lorenzo Bini Smaghi, at conference, "The Euro: Global Implications and Relevance for Latin America," Sao Paolo, 17-18 March 2008, at http://www.ecb.int/press/key/date/2008/html/sp080318.en.html

45. Menzie Chinn and Jeffrey Frankel, "Will the Euro Eventually Surpass the Dollar as Leading International Reserve Currency?" National Bureau of Economic Research, 16 August 2005, at http://www.nber.org/papers/w11510.

46. Andre Baladi, "Realizing a Caribbean Monetary Union," Business, *Finance & Economies in Emerging Economies*, 2007, at http://www.ccmf-uwi.org/files/publications/journal/2007_1_2/1_30.pdf. See also speech by ECCB Governor K Dwight Venner, "The economics of nationhood – the political economy of economic union in the Eastern Caribbean," 5 February 2014, at http://www.bis.org/review/r140205c.htm

47. "Chieuropa?" by Brad Setser, *RGEMonitor*, 20 December 2008, at http://www.rgemonitor.com/asia-monitor/254828/chieuropa

48. Robert Mundell, "Exchange Rates, Currency Areas and the International Financial Architecture," remarks delivered at an IMF panel on 22 September 2000 at Prague, at http://www.usagold.com/gildedopinion/mundellprague.html.

49. Robert A. Mundell, website, "World Currency" page, at http://robertmundell.net/economic-policies/world-currency/.

50. Robert A. Mundell, website, "World Currency," ibid.

51. Robert A. Mundell, website, "World Currency," ibid.

52. Robert Mundell, "Exchange Rates, Currency Areas and the International Financial Architecture," op. cit.

53. Robert Mundell, "The case for a world currency," op. cit, p. 472. Mundell continues to call for the creation of DEY. See Shehab Al Makshleh, "Economist calls for a new world currency," *Gulf News*, 1 June 2013, at http://gulfnews.com/business/economy/economist-calls-for-a-new-global-currency-1.1191382.

54. The term "free-rider fiscal policies" refers to the undeserved benefit for a member of a group who declines to contribute to a course of action, but benefits regardless. In the context of monetary union, Robert Mundell appeared to refer to countries which engage in reckless fiscal policy, but continue to use the currency of the monetary union which is made sound by the prudent fiscal policies of the other members. The EMU Growth and Stability Pact seeks to address this problem by preventing "free-riders."

55. Robert Mundell, op. cit., p. 472-73.

56. Robert Mundell, ibid., p. 473-74.

57. Bryan Taylor, "The Eurodollar," 1998, at http://www.emuenzen.de/forum/574004-post185.html

58. The 19 days were: 2, 3, 29, 30 December 1999, 24, 25, 26 January and 23 February 2000 on the "down" journey and 25 July, 3 September, 1, 4, 5, 6, 21 and 22 November, and 3, 4, 5, December 2002 on the "up journey. Source: Bank of Canada online currency conversion utility at http://www.bankofcanada.ca/rates/exchange/10-year-converter/.

59. Michael Emerson, Daniel Gros, Alexander Italiener, Jean Pisani-Ferry, and Horst Reichenbach, *One Market, One Money--An Evaluation of the Potential Benefits and Costs of Forming an Economic and Monetary Union.* Oxford, UK: Oxford University Press, 1992, p. 37.

60. C. Fred Bergsten, "The Euro and the Dollar: Toward a Finance G-2?" 26 February 2004, p. 9, at http://www.iie.com/publications/papers/bergsten0204.pdf. This paper later became a chapter in Adam S. Posen, editor, *The Euro at Five: Ready for a Global Role?* Washington, DC: Institute for International Economics, 2005.

61. Robert Mundell, "Currency Areas, Volatility and Intervention," Columbia University, Discussion Paper Series, Discussion Paper #: 0102-09, January 2002, p. 11, at http://academiccommons.columbia.edu/catalog/ac%3A114118.

62. "GDP Ranking," The World Bank, 2012, at http://data.worldbank.org/data-catalog/GDP-ranking-table

63. The saying is, "Build it, and they will come." In the film, *Field of Dreams*, about a man's love for the game of baseball, the "it" was a rural baseball stadium. See website of filming location, http://www.fieldofdreamsmoviesite.com/distance.html

64. Warren Coats, "The Case for a Real SDR Currency Board," *Central Banking Journal*, 11 November 20211, at http://www.centralbanking.com/central-banking-journal/feature/2123796/real-sdr-currency-board

65. Joseph Stiglitz, *Making Globalization Work*, op. cit., page 260.

66. ibid, page 261.

67. ibid, page 263.

68. ibid, page 263.

69. ibid, page 269.

70. Kenneth Rogoff, "On Why Not a Global Currency," 8 January 2001, presented to the American Economic Association Meeting on "Exchange Rates and Choice of Monetary Regimes," published in the *American Economic Review*, Vol. 91(2) pp. 1243-247 and on the web at http://scholar.harvard.edu/rogoff/publications/why-not-global-currency.

71. Joseph Nye, "Europe's Soft Power," in *Globalist*, 3 May 2004, at http://www.globalpolicy.org/empire/analysis/2004/0503softpower.htm.

72. See Mark Leonard, *Why Europe Will Run the 21st Century.* London, UK: Fourth Estate, Ltd., 2005.

73. See Jean Pisani-Ferry and Adam S. Posen, *The Euro at Ten: The Next Global Currency?* Peterson Institute for International Economics and Bruegel, 2009, p. 99.

74. Herbert Grubel, "The Merit of a North American Monetary Union," in *The Dollarization Debate*, edited by Dominick Salvatore, James W. Dean, and Thomas D. Willett. Oxford, UK: Oxford University Press, 2003, pp. 318-40, at p. 345.

75. Letter from Kathleen White, External Affairs, IMF, 12 September 2006 to the author, as posted at http://www.singleglobalcurrency.org/latest_news.html

76. Dennis Leech and Robert Leech, "Voting Power Implications of a Unified European Representation at the IMF," Warwick Economics Research Paper Series, No. 720, January, 2005, at http://www2.warwick.ac.uk/fac/soc/economics/research/papers/twerp720.pdf

77. Tahsin Saadi-Sedik and Martin Petri, "To Smooth or Not to Smooth - The Impact of Grants and Remittances on the Equilibrium Real Exchange Rate in Jordan," IMF Working paper 06/257, at http://www.imf.org/external/pubs/ft/wp/2006/wp06257.pdf

78. International Monetary Fund, "Statement by IMF Staff Mission to Mali, Press Release No. 06/260, 21 November 2006, at http://www.imf.org/external/np/sec/pr/2006/pr06260.htm.

79. Several IMF Depts, and approved by Reza Moghadam, "Reserve Accumulation and International Monetary Stability," International Monetary Fund, 13 April 2010, at http://www.imf.org/external/np/pp/eng/2010/041310.pdf.

80. ibid, pp. 26-28.

81. "Global Financial Stability Report (SGSR), IMF, April and September 2007, at http://www.imf.org/External/Pubs/FT/GFSR/2007/02/index.htm

82. The Financial Stability Forum was founded in 1999 and is based at the Bank for International Settlements, at http://www.fsforum.org/home/home.html

83. "Bruce Palmer, Buffalo Springfield Bassist, Dies at 58," Douglas Martin, *New York Times*, 16 October 2004, at http://www.nytimes.com/2004/10/16/arts/16palmer.html?pagewanted=print&position=

84. "Monetary Integration Poses many questions," Wolfgang Munchau, *Financial Times*, 13 May 2007, at http://www.ft.com/cms/s/0/fb22f734-fc36-11db-93a4-000b5df10621.html

85. Todd Sandler, *Global Collective Action*. Cambridge, UK: Cambridge University Press, 2004, p. 269.

86. Articles of Agreement, International Monetary Fund, Article XII--Organization and Management, Article XXVII--Amendments, and Schedule D--Council, all at http://www.imf.org/external/pubs/ft/aa/index.htm

87. "Europe's Hopes for G-20 Summit Risk Being Dashed," by Bruce Crumley, *Time* magazine, 13 November 2008 at http://www.time.com/time/world/article/0,8599,1858863,00.html

88. "China paper urges new currency order after 'financial tsunami'," from *Reuters*, 17 September 2008, at http://www.reuters.com/articlePrint?articleId=USPEK4365020080917

89. ibid.

90. "Letter from IMF Managing Director Dominique Strauss-Kahn to the G-20 Heads of Governments and Institutions," Press Release No. 08/278, International Monetary Fund, 9 November 2008, at http://www.imf.org/external/np/sec/pr/2008/pr08278.htm

91. "The Tasks Ahead," by Olivier Blanchard, IMF Working Paper, 08/268, November 2008, at http://www.imf.org/external/pubs/ft/wp/2008/wp08262.pdf

92. "G-20 Statement Following Crisis Talks," *Wall Street Journal*, online, 15 November 2008, at http://online.wsj.com/article/SB122677642316131071.html

93. ibid.

94. Ratnam Alagiah, "A theoretical justification for a uniform and universal system of currency in accounting for inflation," 2009, http://www.davidpublishing.com/show.html?8758

95. World Bank, at http://www.worldbank.org/en/about

96. World Trade Organization, at http://www.wto.org/index.htm

97. "Press Release: FSB to review foreign exchange benchmarks," 14 February 2014, at http://www.financialstabilityboard.org/press/pr_140213.htm

98. Consumers International, London, at http://www.consumersinternational.org

99. International Standards Organization, Geneva, at http://www.iso.org/iso/home.

100. Carter Dougherty, "Spotlight: 'Painless Doctor for German Economy,'" *International Herald Tribune*, 16 December 2005, at http://www.nytimes.com/2005/12/16/business/worldbusiness/16iht-wbspot17.html.

101. Andrew Rose, "What should Academics tell Policy-Makers about Monetary Union? Discussion of Coleman and Wyplosz," 28 July 2001, at http://faculty.haas.berkeley.edu/arose/RBADisc.pdf. Note that Rose has stated that he is not in favor of a single global currency, in an email to the author, 15 August 2004.

102. Letter from the Single Global Currency Association, 6 September 2003, at http://www.singleglobalcurrency.org/documents/OECDLetterassenttoOECDFinanceMinisters.doc.

103. California Public Employee Retirement System, at http://www.calpers.ca.gov/index.jsp?bc=/about/press/news/invest-corp/home.xml.

104. Guidliemo Carchedi, *For Another Europe*. London: Verso Publishers, 2001.

105. Text of 1 December 2003 speech by Mr. Ulrich Kohli, chief economist, Swiss National Bank, as posted on internet by "Swiss Plus," of the Swiss Bankers Association at http://www.swissplus.ch/newsletter-nov-2003?newsid=5531.

106. International Chamber of Commerce, Paris, at http://www.iccwbo.org/.

107. Brian Warburton, "The Case for a Single Global Currency," *AmCham* magazine, American Chamber of Commerce, Belgium, 1996, No. 514, p. 28.

108. Michael Carabott, "HSBC Announces Lm36.7 Pre-Tax profit," *The Malta Independent Online*, 17 February 2006, at http://www.independent.com.mt/articles/2006-02-17/news/hsbc-announces-lm367m-pre-tax-profit-87444/.

109. Email to author from Jose Luis Cordeiro of Venezuela, 15 February 2006. Jose was an advisor to the Ecuadorian Chamber of Commerce at that time.

110. See the 23 April 2004 testimony of Dr. Geoff Pain, to the Joint Standing Committee on Treaties. This is no longer available on the internet, but is referenced at http://www.aph.gov.au/binaries/house/committee/jsct/usafta/report/full report.pdf.

111. Dick Bryan, "Currency Unification: Dollarize or Die?" in *Workers Online*, 27 April 2001, at http://workers.labor.net.au/93/c_historicalfeature_dollar.html.

112. Philippe Van Parijs, "Does Basic Income Make Sense as a Worldwide Project?" at the IXth Congress of the Basic Income European Network, International Labour Organization, Geneva, 14 September 2002, at http://www.globalincome.org/English/VanParijs-WorldwideBI.html.

113. Barbara Shailor, AFL-CIO, United States, "Internationalism for Working People," in the August 2003 *OECD Observer* at http://www.oecdobserver.org/news/fullstory.php/aid/893/Internationalis m_for_working_people.html.

114. Bryan Taylor, "The Eurodollar," 1998, at http://www.emuenzen.de/forum/574004-post185.html.

115. "World Trade Report 2013," World Trade Organization, 2013, at http://www.wto.org/english/res_e/booksp_e/world_trade_report13_e.pdf

116. See, for the example of Japan, Toshiaki Watanabe and Kimie Harada, "Effects of the Bank of Japan's Intervention on Yen/Dollar Exchange Rate Volatility," *Journal of the Japanese and International Economies*, March 2006, pp. 99-111, at http://www.sciencedirect.com/science/article/B6WMC-4DVBGXH-1/2/41970dd0a1129ac691062228b2d11e62. See also Michael Hutchison, "Is Official Foreign Exchange Intervention Effective?" FRBSF Economic Letter 2003-20, Federal Reserve Bank of San Francisco, at http://www.frbsf.org/economic-research/publications/economic-letter/2003/july/is-official-foreign-exchange-intervention-effective/.

117. Paul De Grauwe and Jacques Melitz, editors, *Prospects for Monetary Unions after the Euro.* Cambridge, MA: MIT Press, 2005, p. 2.

118. While the quote is by Paul Volcker, and he stands by it, as confirmed in a telephone conversation with his assistant, there is no precise source for it. The closest was in his Op-Ed in the *International Herald Tribune*, on 31 August 2000, where he wrote, "In fact, if we are to have a truly globalized economy, a single world currency makes sense." (He also wrote, echoing the feasibility concerns of others, "That is not a world I will live to see, but the underlying tendencies are in that direction...." 31 January

2000, at http://www.nytimes.com/2000/01/31/opinion/31iht-edpaul.2.t_0.html.

The phrase, "a global economy requires a global currency," may also be derived from the pro-euro slogan of the 1990s, "One Market, One Money," which is also the title of the book by Michael Emerson, Daniel Gros, Alexander Italianer, Jean Pisani-Ferry, and Horst Reichenbach, about the 1990 European Council study of the single European currency, Oxford University Press, 1992.

119. Benjamin J. Cohen, *The Future of Money*. Princeton, NJ: Princeton University Press, 2004, p. 202.

120. ibid., p. 207.

121. Richard N. Cooper, "Almost a century of Central Bank Cooperation," BIS Working Papers, No. 198, February, 2006, at http://www.bis.org/publ/work198.pdf. See also Beth A. Simmons, "The Future of Central Bank Cooperation," BIS Working Papers, No. 200, February, 2006, at http://www.bis.org/publ/work200.pdf.

122. Kavaljit Singh, *Taming Global Financial Flows*. Hong Kong: Hong Kong University Press, 2000, p. 221.

123. Raymond Baker, *Capitalism's Achilles Heel: Dirty Money and How to Renew the Free-Market System*. Hoboken, NJ: John Wiley & Sons, 2005.

124. Paul De Grauwe and Jacques Melitz, editors, *Prospects for Monetary Unions after the Euro*. Cambridge, MA: MIT Press, 2005, p. 1.

125. Ramon Tamames, "Monetary Simplification Euro/Dollar: Towards a Global Currency," November 2004, Instituto Europeo De Estudos Economicos, and emails from the author to Rodrigo de Rato, 10 November 2005 and 22 March 2006, both at http://www.singleglobalcurrency.org/latest_news.html

126. See IMF press release, "Strengthening Our Commitment to Low-Income Countries," by Rodrigo de Rato, 30 November 2005, International Monetary Fund, at http://www.imf.org/external/np/vc/2005/113005.htm.

127. Letter from Zogby International to Single Global Currency Association, 16 December 2004, at http://www.singleglobalcurrency.org/news_prev.html.

128. "The Euro Has Landed," *The Guardian* online, 31 December 1998, at http://www.guardian.co.uk/euro/story/0,11306,616452,00.html

129. See the website of the Copenhagen Consensus Project at http://www.copenhagenconsensus.com/

130. Barry Eichengreen, "Financial Stability," a Copenhagen Consensus Challenge Paper, April 2004, at http://emlab.berkeley.edu/~eichengr/policy/copenhagenjun9-04.pdf.

131. "Copenhagen Consensus: The Results," at http://www.eldis.org/go/home&id=15478&type=Document#.UwOJzcKYadI

132. Hugo Narrillos Roux, "Divisa Unica y Establidad Economica Mundial," translated as "Single Currency and Worldwide Economic Stability," April 2004, Ph.D. thesis in Spanish, with abstract in English, at http://www.singleglobalcurrency.org/academics_and_economists.html.

133. ECB Staff team led by Peter Backe and Christian Thimann and including Olga Arratibel, Oscar Calvo-Gonzalez, Arnaud Mehl, and Caroline

Nerlich, "The Acceding Countries' Strategies towards ERM II and the Adoption of the Euro: An Analytical Review," February 2004, at http://www.ecb.int/pub/pdf/scpops/ecbocp10.pdf.

134. The spelling of "euro" in several of the EMU member countries, e.g. the newest member, Latvia, was a sensitive matter. See "Linguistic issues concerning the euro," Wikipedia, at http://en.wikipedia.org/wiki/Linguistic_issues_concerning_the_euro.

135. John Edmunds and John Marthinsen, *Wealth by Association, Global Prosperity through Market Unification.* Wesport, CT: Praeger Publishers, 2003, p. 34.

136. European Central Bank, "Cash Changeover," at http://www.ecb.europa.eu/ecb/legal/1004/1020/html/index.en.html.

137. Paul De Grauwe, *Economics of Monetary Union.* Oxford, UK: Oxford University Press, 2005, 6th edition, p. 70.

138. ibid., p. 71.

139. Joaquin Almunia, "Seven Years of the Euro: Main Lessons and Future Challenges" at the EMU Governance and Euro Changeover Conference," Ljubljana, Slovenia, 17 March 2006, at http://ec.europa.eu/economy_finance/events/2006/conference170306/almunia_speech_en.pdf

140. James Gomez, "East Europeans Cool to Euro as Governments Prepare for Currency," *Bloomberg.com*, 3 January 2006 at http://www.bloomberg.com/apps/news?pid=71000001&refer=europe&sid=aRMXyySy4gE4.

141. Felix Hufner and Isabell Koske, "The Euro Changeover in the Slovak Republic: Implications for Inflation and Interest Rates," by, OECD Economics Department Working Papers, No. 632, 12 August 2008, at http://titania.sourceoecd.org/vl=5380334/cl=22/nw=1/rpsv/cgi-bin/wppdf?file=5kzfxw92r3mr.pdf

142. The "21st Century" is another example of a globalized standard, which came from the European/Christian timekeeping system which ostensibly begins with the birth of Jesus Christ. It's now commonly believed that he actually was born several years before the date considered to be the first day, A.D.

1 January 2006 in the Christian/Gregorian calendar was 8 Kislev 5766 by Hebrew calendar, 8 Dhu I-Qa`da 1426 by Islamic calendar, 18 Azar 1384 by Persian calendar, and 18 Agrahayana 1927 by Indian Civil calendar. (See Index Librorum Liberorum, at Fourmilab, at http://www.fourmilab.to/documents/calendar/.

143. Robert Mundell, "The Case for a World Currency," op. cit., p. 475.

144. Andres Arias, Gary D. Hansen, and Lee E. Ohanian, "Why have Business Cycle Fluctuations Become Less Volatile?" NBER Working Paper No. 12079, March 2006, National Bureau of Economic Research, Cambridge, MA, at http://papers.nber.org/papers/W12079.

145. Peter M. Summers, "What Caused The Great Moderation? Some Cross-Country Evidence," 3rd Quarter 2005, *Economic Review*, pp. 3-32, at http://www.kc.frb.org/publicat/econrev/PDF/3q05summ.pdf

146. Anup Shah, "Causes of Poverty: Poverty Facts and Stats," last updated 7 January 2013, at http://www.globalissues.org/TradeRelated/Facts.asp.

147. "List of Countries by Foreign Exchange Reserves," Wikipedia, at http://en.wikipedia.org/wiki/List_of_countries_by_foreign-exchange_reserves.

148. Promotional Materials, Branko Milanovic, *Worlds Apart: Measuring International and Global Inequality*. Princeton, NJ: Princeton University Press, 2005, at http://www.pupress.princeton.edu/titles/7946.html.

149. See Bill Bonner and Addison Wiggin, *Empire of Debt*. Hoboken, NJ: John Wiley & Sons, 2006.

150. J. Bradford DeLong, "Estimating World GDP, One Million B.C. to the Present," at http://www.j-bradford-delong.net/TCEH/1998_Draft/World_GDP/Estimating_World_GDP.html and Ralph Zuljan, "Allied and Axis GDP," at http://www.onwar.com/articles/0302.htm. Both indices are expressed in 1990 dollars.

The 1944 percentage is calculated from the nominal $219 billion US GDP (from Louis D. Johnston and Samuel H. Williamson, "The Annual Real and Nominal GDP for the United States, 1790--Present." Economic History Services, October 2005, URL : http://www.measuringworth.com/usgdp/).

From a third source comes the calculation of 35 percent, in the article "The Trajectory of the United States in the World-System: A Quantitative Reflection," by Chris Chase-Dunn, Rebecca Giem, Andrew Jorgenson, Thomas Reifer, John Rogers, and Shoon Lio at University of California Riverside, 2002, p. 13, at http://irows.ucr.edu/papers/irows8/irows8.htm.

151. Richard Cooper, "A Monetary System for the Future," *Foreign Affairs*, Fall 1984, pp. 175, at http://scholar.harvard.edu/cooper/publications/reform-international-monetary-system-modest-proposal See also, Richard Cooper, "Toward a Common Currency," June 2000, at http://onlinelibrary.wiley.com/doi/10.1111/1468-2362.00053/abstract.

152. "List of Countries by GDP (Nominal)," Wikipedia, at http://en.wikipedia.org/wiki/List_of_countries_by_GDP_(nominal).

153. Other parts of Cooper's article were remarkable prescient. Richard Cooper, "A Monetary System for the Future," *Foreign Affairs*, Fall 1984. He wrote, "The world will be very electronic," at p. 176, and "English will become even more widespread as the language of commerce," at p. 177. Also, he foresaw online purchasing, albeit through a television rather than a computer screen.

154. Alexander Gorlach, "If the Eurozone pursues greater integration and common financial policies, then the Euro will be the next global reserve currency," 10 July 2012, at http://d.repec.org/n?u=RePEc:ner:lselon:http://eprints.lse.ac.uk/46122/&r=mon

155. See Norman Kurland's summary of the Kelsonian binary economics perspective in "A New Look at Prices and Money: The Kelsonian Binary Model for Achieving Rapid Growth Without Inflation," 1972, revised 2002, at http://www.cesj.org/binaryeconomics/price-money.html.

156. The original slogan was, "Whatever Your Cause, It's a Lost Cause Until We Control Population Growth."

157. Jeff Zelney, "An Obama Refrain Bears Echoes of a Governor's Speeches," *New York Times*, 8 February 2008, at http://www.nytimes.com/2008/02/18/us/politics/18video.html

158. Dani Rodrik, "When Ideas Trump Interests: Preferences, World Views, and Policy Innovations," National Board of Economic Research (NBER) Working Paper 19631, November 2013, at http://www.nber.org/papers/w19631?utm_campaign=ntw&utm_medium=email&utm_source=ntw

159. Lester Thurow, *Fortune Favors the Bold*. New York, NY: HarperCollins, 2003.

Chapter 8. The Single Global Currency World-in 2024?

For the people of the world, a Single Global Currency will be legal tender which can be used to buy anything anywhere within the Global Monetary Union without the need to convert to a foreign currency. In some parts of the world, there may be a second or third currency which may be acceptable as legal tender, but one Single Global Currency will be accepted within the Global Monetary Union. As proposed previously, the Single Global Currency can assume that mantle when it achieves usage in countries whose populations comprise a specified percentage of the world. Fifty-one percent would be a good start, but the benefits of the Single Global Currency will grow as that percentage moves toward 100 percent.

As the usage of the Single Global Currency increases, international trade and investment contracts increasingly will be denominated in the Single Global Currency (SGC). For such major commodities as oil, this change will be significant. People and corporations from every country within the GMU will be able to purchase oil with their own currency, assuming either that the oil-producing countries are members or that oil is priced in the Single Global Currency, or both.

Global Central Bank (GCB)

Richard Cooper, among others, foresaw the need for a Global Central Bank. He wrote in 1984, "... a single currency is possible only if there is in effect a single monetary policy, and a single authority issuing the currency and directing the monetary policy. How can independent states accomplish that? They need to turn over the determination of monetary policy to a supranational body, but one which is responsible collectively to the governments of the independent states."[1] Today, he would likely add that the GCB responsibility would be to the participating monetary unions and to the IMF.

The primary office of the GCB likely would be located in one of the major financial centers of the world or in Basel, Zurich, or Geneva, Switzerland-- assuming that Switzerland decides to join the Global Monetary Union as well. Switzerland has a reputation for sound money, and locating the GCB in Switzerland just might be the necessary incentive for that country to join the Global Monetary Union as a member.

Governing Structure of the Global Central Bank

Richard Cooper suggested, "The governing board would be made up of representatives of national governments, whose votes would be weighted according to the share of the national GNP in the total gross product of the community of participating nations. This weighting could be altered at five-year intervals to allow for differences in growth rates."[2]

One model for the structure of the GCB is the International Monetary Fund which is governed by the Board of Governors, which is made up of one governor from each of the 188 member countries. Voting power is allocated on the basis of the allocation of SDRs, which, in turn, is done on the basis of the size of a nation's economy. As the board meets once a year, the operations of the IMF are managed by the Executive Board which has twenty-four members. Five are appointed by five larger nations, and the other nineteen are elected by groups of nations.[3]

Another model is the European Central Bank where the key rate setting decisions are made by the Governing Council composed of a six- member Executive Board and representatives of the national central banks of the 18 EMU member states. The Executive Board is composed of the President and Vice-President of the ECB and four other individuals.[4]

The governing structure of the GCB should be relatively easy to design, given the available, successful models of the US Federal Reserve, European Central Bank, International Monetary Fund, World Bank, United Nations, and associated organizations such as the World Health Organization. Not everyone is happy with the structure of all those organizations, but it's a negotiable political question and not one to be decided in this volume or by any theory of economics. The IMF has published a good summary of structures of central banks in "Central Bank Governance: A Survey of Boards and Management." by Tonny Lybek and JoAnne Morris.[5]

To be accepted as legitimate, the governing structure must be representative of all of the stakeholder interests.

Duties of the Global Central Bank

A major responsibility of the Global Central Bank will be to ensure price stability around the world. The wording of that goal and of other goals will be the subject of extensive negotiations at future international monetary conferences, but the outcome will be substantially similar to the charters of the European Central Bank and other successful monetary union central banks.

Even without calling for a Single Global Currency, former US Undersecretary of Commerce Jeffrey Garten proposed in 1998 the establishment of a Global Central Bank with the duties of regulating lending practices around the world and, generally, promoting worldwide financial stability.[6]

Wrote Richard Cooper about the work of the GCB,

"...to stabilize the macroeconomic environment and to avoid or mitigate liquidity crises by acting as a lender of last resort, just as national central banks do today. The debate on the relative weights to be attached to output and employment as opposed to price stabilization, and on how monetary policy should actually be managed, could continue just as it does at present, without prejudice.... The Bank of Issue need not engage in detailed regulation of the banks throughout the system covered by the new currency. That could be left in the hands of national regulators."[7]

Operations of the Global Central Bank

Of no small import is the future financing of the Global Central Bank. As it will be independent of national governments, it will be easier for the bank to self-finance through the seigniorage benefit.[8] The Global Central Bank could be funded entirely with seigniorage, as long as the usage of cash currency continues without severe decline. Even as the use of cash declines, there should be surplus revenue from that source which can be used as the governors of the GCB, or other international body, direct.

As Alain Ize has explained, one significant cost of central banking is the cost of maintaining cash reserves of other currencies.[9] With a Single Global Currency, that cost to the future GCB, and other central banks, will disappear.

One of the issues facing every central bank is the degree that its deliberations and decisions about interest rates, inflation projections, and money supply should be open to public inquiry.[10] Petra Geraats of the University of Cambridge wrote in 2001 that while there should be some level of "Monetary Mystique" to insulate central banks from political pressures, the operations of central banks should be open to the public, i.e., transparent. Its data and forecasts on interest rates and inflation should be available.[11]

Similarly, in a December 2005 paper presented at the American Economic Association meeting, Anne Sibert stated, "I find that, no matter what their preferences, central banks and societies are made better off by more transparency."[12] On the other hand, cautions Alex Cukierman, "Although transparency is currently hailed as an important feature of best practice policymaking institutions, there are several aspects of modern monetary policymaking that are not as transparent as current rhetoric would lead us to believe. In addition, there are circumstances in which excessive transparency is actually detrimental."[13] Michael Ehrmann and Marcel Fratzcher of the European Central Bank agree that transparency is important, but have found in their review of the operations of the US Federal Reserve, the Bank of England, and the European Central Bank that it's also important that central banks and their governing committees communicate with one voice."[14] Communications from members of those committees might better remain opaque.

To be researched is the question of how the need for transparency will be affected by the reduction of currency competition with other central banks as the Single Global Currency acquires more and more market share. What will be the effect on central bank communications if there is no substantial need to manage an exchange rate for the Single Global Currency, nor a concern about a balance of payments or international reserves? Presumably, without currency competition, there would be less need for secrecy.

Frederic S. Mishkin wrote in 2006 that six ideas about monetary policy and central banks have now been accepted around the world:
  1) there is no long-run tradeoff between output (employment) and inflation;
  2) expectations are critical to monetary policy outcomes;
  3) inflation has high costs;
  4) monetary policy is subject to the time-inconsistency problem;

5) central bank independence helps improve the efficacy of monetary policy; and

6) a strong nominal anchor is the key to producing good monetary policy outcomes."[15]

Thus, the world of central banking converging, and number "7" should be the acceptance of the inevitability of a Single Global Currency, managed by a Global Central Bank, within a Global Monetary Union.

Global Central Bank Reserves

One question that arises frequently is the question of whether a Single Global Currency should be backed up by monetary reserves of some kind, such as gold or a non-metallic commodity such as cocoa.[16]

One of the ironies about fiat currencies is that they are not "backed" by commodities with value such as gold, but that same fiat currency has become a commodity itself. For example, the value of the euro rises and falls like the fluctuations in values of gold and aluminum, even though the euro is a fiat currency and the bills are only paper with images printed on them. It will be the movement to a Single Global Currency which finally stops currency from being a commodity by itself, except as collectors' items.

Initial Valuation of the Single Global Currency

The Single Global Currency promises to have lower inflation due to the absence of foreign exchange fluctuations and "price-stickiness," but the psychological scars of the lowered purchasing power of the 20th century currencies remain. One cure might be to set the value of the Single Global Currency at a multiple of ten times the current values of the US dollar, the euro or even the pound. Thus, when established, it might take .06 "SGC," or 6 SCG cents, to purchase a US mail letter stamp, instead of what is likely to be the US dollar cost of 60 cents in 2024. Six cents was the price of a US first class stamp in 1968.

The psychological downside of such a revaluation would be than incomes would also drop by a factor of ten, and it may constitute too much change too quickly. A revaluation could wait until the SGC is firmly established.

Stability and Growth Pact

The European Union has a Stability and Growth Pact (SGP) with its most publicized provision that member and applicant countries cannot permit their annual government budgets to be imbalanced by more than three percent of the Gross Domestic Product and that they must keep their public debt no higher than 60 percent of GDP.[17] In an interesting illustration of the relationship between the EU and EMU, the Stability Pact applies to the non-EMU members of the EU, but the pact's enforcement mechanisms can be applied only to members of the EMU.[18] Efforts to enforce the SGP's requirements against EMU countries has led to considerable controversy, which led to relaxation of the requirements in March 2005.[19]

The Eastern Caribbean Monetary Union does not have a Growth and Stability Pact. If the other existing monetary unions have them, they are not as contentious as is the SGP in the EU. The Gulf Cooperation Council is considering whether to have such a provision in its charter documents.

As the size of a Global Monetary Union increases, it will matter less to the currency's value whether any of its member states is fiscally irresponsible. Just as it does not matter now to the value of the dollar whether there is a bankruptcy of a corporation or even a state government, it will not affect the value of the SGC when a member state in the GMU has financial difficulty. There was no serious effect on the US dollar in the 1970s when New York City nearly defaulted on its debt payments, or in the 2000s with the bankruptcies of Enron, Lehman Brothers, Worldcom, and Global Crossing. The foundation for faith in the value of money in a monetary union is confidence in the soundness of the union's central bank, and not the political and financial status of member countries or constituent corporations.

There are powerful forces within countries to ensure member states are fiscally responsible: the citizenry and the financial markets. The citizens know that the final cost of borrowing will be greater than the current cost and that it will be borne by their children. For various cultural reasons, countries view their national burdens quite differently, as can be seen by comparing the 2013 national debt to GDP ratios of EMU members Luxembourg (20 percent) and Greece (158 percent).[20]

The markets efficiently digest the numbers, and they understand the ability of debtors to pay. When that ability is questioned, the interest rates on bonds increase, and citizens and governments will be forced to take notice by either paying more interest or by borrowing less or both. During the first few years of the euro, yields from member states' bonds converged with the unwritten assumption that the EMU would bail out irresponsible countries. Without ever testing that assumption, the yields began diverging in 2005 as investors realized that even with a common currency, countries are responsible for their own fiscal policies and debt.[21] J. Bradford DeLong argued in 2006 that the markets were still not correctly valuing the risks of individual EMU countries, and that "In the long run, this is dangerous. Both market discipline and sound fiscal policy are needed to create a reasonable chance of long-run price stability."[22] To the extent that the 2008-2013 Eurozone crisis was caused by overborrowing and overlending because of misunderstanding and misrepresenting the risks, DeLong was prescient.

One major question is whether the Global Central Bank will be a bank of last resort to a mismanaged national bank. That will be for the framers of the charter of the bank to determine. Even if the future Global Monetary Union has a Stability and Growth Pact, the principle of members' fiscal responsibility might be preserved with a less restrictive deficit to GDP ratio, such as five percent.

Secession from the Global Monetary Union.

There are no provisions for member secession from the European Monetary Union, but there was considerable discussion during the 2008-2013 Eurozone crisis about such a drastic move for several EMU members:

Cyprus, Greece, Italy, Spain and even Ireland. As all pre-twentieth century monetary unions have vanished,[23] except for those which were also political unions, such as the United States, it seems prudent to plan for the option for secession from the Global Monetary Union by a member country. A secession process should be designed that fairly assesses the seceding country for the costs of secession. The principle that monetary unions are voluntary associations is important to their democratic processes.[24]

In a 3-G world, however, what could be the incentives for seceding? What would a seceding country do for foreign exchange? How would it handle its large currency risk, compared to that of countries within the Global Monetary Union? These are just a few of the questions for further research and thinking. These are the questions that 21st Century economists should be asking and not what level of exchange rate fluctuation volatility is optimal.[25]

Name of the Single Global Currency

Names are important, as one can see when looking at the names of buildings on university campuses or of bridges, airports, and public buildings. The EU chose the name "euro" at the December 1995 meeting of the European Council at Madrid. Other possibilities included "Europa"[26] and the name of the previous European basket currency, "ecu," for European Currency Unit.

An ideal name for the Single Global Currency would be one that is easy to pronounce and spell in all major languages. Of the proposed options on the Single Global Currency website, "Geo," as proposed by Charles Goldfinger,[27] was leading with 33% (22) of a total of 73 votes, as of 23 March 1006.[28] The other proposed names listed on the original 2003 ballot are: Alitinonfo, Bancor, Eartha, Global, Globo, Intor, Mondo, Mundo, Only, Terran, UNA, UNIT, and Worldo. Other suggested names, but not on the ballot, are: Cosmos, Dey, Eartho, Esperanza, Galacto, Harmoney, Phoenix, Unitas, and even SiGiC.

The name of the Single Global Currency is one element that can easily be opened to an internet-based nominating process and electronic voting around the world. It's estimated that in 2013 there were 6.8 billion mobile phones in the world, for 7+ billion citizens.[29] Even if distribution is uneven and obviously distorted by global income equality, there are digital ways to permit every person in the world to vote at least once on the preferred name of the Single Global Currency.

Electronic Money

When the Single Global Currency is implemented, money will be even more digitized than it is in 2014, and there will be less cash. However, the format of money should make no difference regarding the successful operation of the Single Global Currency. Digital money requires a unit of account in order to store value and in order to transfer payment.

Alternate Currencies

There are thousands of non-currency area, non-state currencies which are perfectly compatible with the existing multicurrency world and will be similarly compatible with a Single Global Currency. Benjamin J. Cohen calls these currencies, "Local Money" and notes that they are also called, "private currencies" and "complementary currencies." He writes, "Local currency systems can be created in one of two ways. One approach offers a specialized medium of exchange, generically labeled 'scrip' as a means to underwrite purchases of goods and services, often at a discount. The other, typically referred to as barter-based money, is explicitly based on an updated multilateralized form of the primitive bilateral transaction that preceded the invention of money."[30]

An example of a scrip system is the Canadian Tire Store's "Canadian Tire Money™" which can be used to purchase items at any of the company's stores.[31] Another is frequent flier miles on major airlines, of which there are estimated in 2005 to be 14 trillion "in circulation," worth about $700 billion.[32]

A barter-based currency began in Vancouver, Canada in 1983 called the "Local Exchange Trading Systems (LETS)," where members could trade labor for the goods and services of other members.[33] In the United States, "Ithaca Hours," from Ithaca, New York, became the model for many similar systems which value the currency unit as an hour of labor by a member. An "Ithaca Hour" was the unit of account and the name of the currency, and each hour of any member's work was worth ten US dollars.[34] Support for these systems depends upon the energy of their founders and managers, and the willingness of people and businesses to accept the paper notes as money. Some systems have collapsed or died, leaving the holders of the alternate currency with worthless paper.[35]

In 2013-2014, support grew for the mysterious computer-based bitcoin currency, the supply of which is derived from a complex computer program developed by an unknown person. The bitcoin exchange rate has been volatile and subject to intermittent speculative bubbles. In late 2013, governments began to scrutinize the bitcoin system for illegal transactions.[36] In February, 2014, the largest bitcoin exchange, Mt. Gox, closed its doors after reporting the digital theft of over 744,000 bitcoins, which represented about six percent of the total in circulation at the time, and which were worth about $400 million.[37] The future of bitcoin is uncertain, but the hunger of the world for a global, non-national currency and easy inter-currency transfer is not uncertain.

Remaining Foreign Exchange Trading

As most of the world's trade and most of the international financial transactions will be conducted with the Single Global Currency, by definition, the scope of foreign exchange trading will be vastly reduced in quantity and in importance. Sam Cross put it simply in his book, *All About The Foreign Exchange Market in the United States*, "In a universe with a single currency, there would be no foreign exchange market, no foreign exchange rates, no foreign exchange."[38] The world's financial health will no longer be jeopardized by uncertain fluctuations of the major currencies of the world.

Thus, for the first time in 2,500 years, foreign exchange will not be necessary for most of the world's financial long distance transactions.

The decline in foreign exchange trading upon the adoption of the euro is a precedent for the upcoming Single Global Currency-induced decline in the volume of foreign exchange trading. In 1998, the reported daily volume of foreign exchange trading by the Bank for International Settlements was $1.49 trillion, but by the next triennial report in 2001, it had declined to $1.20 trillion.[39] Most, if not all, of the decline must be attributed to the substitution of one European currency for twelve.

The existing foreign exchange market fills a vast need and the market will continue to exist as long as there is a need; and the market will not be legislated away. Instead, it will just fade away as the people of the world increasingly use the Single Global Currency for all their transactions. Eventually, foreign exchange trading will be relegated to the same role as is now occupied by stamp and expired-currency collectors.

Bank Reserves: Foreign Exchange and Cash

Barbados Central Bank Governor Marion Williams summed up the necessary amount for foreign exchange reserves by saying "Enough is enough," in response to the tendency among many central banks to accumulate more than enough reserves.[40]

There will be no more need for international reserves, by definition, so the only remaining need for reserves will be for sufficient cash and deposits to ensure that national banks and their local banks have sufficient amounts of cash to meet customers' needs.

Juan Luis Moreno-Villalaz estimated that Panama's dollarization had reduced the need for bank reserves from a level of 13 percent of GDP to 8 percent--a significant savings.[41]

What will be done with the excess foreign exchange reserves after they are all converted into SGCs? Some would be retained by national banks for liquidity reserves, and the rest could be disbursed as each country determines.

The Role of Gold

Economists remain divided over the utility of gold, even though the phrase "gold standard" continues to evoke nostalgic fondness for a more stable period, despite John Maynard Keynes' label of the gold standard as a "barbarous relic."[42] A recent article by Natalia Chernyshoff, David Jacks, and Alan Taylor, "Stuck on Gold: Real Exchange Rate Volatility and the Rise and Fall of the Gold Standard," suggests that the gold standard was useful before World War I, but not between that war and World War II.[43]

The role of gold in the international monetary system has declined over the years as central banks and governments, with some exceptions, have learned how to make their money more stable--and it is stable money that the people of world want. Presumably, with the advent of the most stable money ever, the Single Global Currency, gold will finally be relegated to its deserved, rather than inflated, role as a wondrous metal that is resistant to corrosion, transmits electricity, and attracts the admiring eyes of people of all races.

Effects on Financial Markets

The adoption of a Single Global Currency would tend to synchronize yields in different countries' bond markets.[44] As all the financial markets would be run with the same currency, further consolidation of markets would be expected. Philip Arestis and Santonu Basu have written about financial globalization and that to reduce financial dislocation, "it is necessary to introduce a single currency that would allow international financial markets to adopt a uniform credit standard for all countries. To introduce a single currency and to implement uniform standard credit requirements, there is a need to establish a world central bank for the global financial markets."[45]

As John Edmunds and John Marthinsen predict, the values of assets worldwide would increase by trillions upon the establishment of a Single Global Curreny. The amount of increase by country would be roughly in reverse proportion to the pre-SGC level of currency risk.

Prices

While there is a "Law of One Price" in economics which states that the price of a good or service will be the same everywhere, other things being equal, it's rare that other things are equal. Thus, prices for the same goods and services vary from place to place. The source of some disappointment in the euro is that prices still vary by geography as much as they do, but it was the expectation of "one price" that is the problem, not the geographic variation. It's been noted that prices in the United States, a large common currency area, also vary substantially among and even within the fifty states.[46] A recent survey by the author of the price of hot chocolate/cioccolata calda, found prices centering around €2.50, but which varied from a low of €1.40 to a high of €5.80.

Also, the fluctuations of prices are not likely to be affected by Global Monetary Union. Kenneth Froot, Michael Kim, and Kenneth Rogoff have found that the price volatility for basic food commodities in England and Holland has not varied substantially over the past 700 years.[47]

Inflation

One of the mysteries of economics (which economists might call a puzzle) is why there must be inflation. Prior to becoming US Federal Reserve chair in 2006, Ben S. Bernanke said in 2002, "Since World War II, inflation--the apparently inexorable rise in the prices of goods and services--has been the bane of central bankers. Economists of various stripes have argued that inflation is the inevitable result of (pick your favorite) the abandonment of metallic monetary standards, a lack of fiscal discipline, shocks to the price of oil and other commodities, struggles over the distribution of income, excessive money creation, self-confirming inflation expectations, an 'inflation bias' in the policies of central banks, and still others. Despite widespread 'inflation pessimism,' however, during the 1980s and 1990s most industrial-country central banks were able to cage, if not entirely tame, the inflation dragon."[48] One possible cause he didn't mention was the fluctuations of exchange rates.

It defies common cents/sense that a product must cost more units of money in the future than in the past. The people of the world may have become used to it, but that doesn't mean that it's right or that the system must continue, as Thomas Paine would argue. He wrote, "...a long habit of not thinking a thing *wrong,* gives it a superficial appearance of being *right* and raises at first a formidable outcry in defence of custom."[49] Why should the people of the world remember that when they were children they paid X units for a loaf of bread and that now the same loaf of bread costs 5X or 10X? Another way to look at it is to ask why people cannot see as many prices going down as up? One of the reasons is that it's hard to see that a product with more functionality and costing the same as last year actually represents a price-per-functionality decrease than the previous year.

For example, a radio might have cost €25 last year, and this year the same model radio might cost €27. However, it may now include new features, such as a travel plug conversion from European to US electric circuits, which would have added €4 to the cost of any other radio. Thus, an increase of the price to €27 actually represents a price decrease per functionality for a radio which could have cost €29.

It is this creeping worldwide inflation that has driven people to continue to wish longingly for the world of gold with its illusion of stability. Perhaps in a Single Global Currency world, the price of gold will become more stable, too.

The effect on inflation rates by the establishment of a common currency, as shown by a study of the Eurozone is not yet clear, and requires more study.[50] One other element of inflation needing further clarification in the Single Global Currency world will be the products and commodities whose prices are included in any inflation index. For example, some measures of inflation use wholesale prices and others used consumer price indices, with or without energy and food.[51]

The question is: How much of the economists' expectation of an annual inflation rate of two percent arises because of the needs of the multicurrency foreign exchange world and system? In a Single Global Currency world, would there be as much concern about deflation?

If it's found that a Single Global Currency world can operate with an inflation rate of zero percent, then the question will arise of whether the people of the world really want such a low rate, and a governing board of the Global Central Bank will respond to their wishes, through its open, transparent operations.

Monetary stability has always been a goal of central banks, and it was almost universally thought that controlling the size of the money supply was the best means to that end. Now, however, many of the world's central banks are now explicitly using "inflation targeting" with a goal of two percent inflation or less, as a method of operation.[52] It's not known how the future Global Central Bank will operate, and how its work within a 3-G world will differ from that of its multicurrency predecessors. Still, it's safe to predict that some type of inflation targeting will be a major part of its work for global monetary stability. The remaining question will be the desired and feasible inflation targets that will be established.

One of the widely acknowledged reasons for central bankers' success at lowering inflation around the world is the increased independence of central banks from national governments. In the 1990s, several countries passed laws which made their central banks less susceptible to temporary political pressures. John Edmunds and John Marthinsen summarized this development, "To control inflation, central banks have to control their money supplies, and one of the most important lessons we have learned from monetary history is that the more independent a central bank is from the government, the greater are its chances of controlling inflation."[53]

In a Global Monetary Union, the Global Central Bank will be even more independent of the politics of national governments by virtue of being one entity among 193 UN member state governments. This is one of the elegant realities of a monetary union, and its truth becomes more evident as a monetary union grows.

Deflation

One of the recent concerns among central bankers has been the risk of deflation, which Lester Thurow calls "capitalism's worst disease."[54] Early twenty-first-century Japan is exhibit #1, where, stated Ben Bernanke, before becoming chair of the US Federal Reserve,

> "what seems to be a relatively moderate *deflation*--a decline in consumer prices of about 1 percent per year-- has been associated with years of painfully slow growth, rising joblessness, and apparently intractable financial problems in the banking and corporate sectors. Japan's 15-year experience with deflation or stagflation is the most recent and severe of recent years and economists' understanding of Japan's struggle is important as other nations, and the future Global Monetary Union seek to avoid the same fate."[55]

The basic problem is that if consumers and corporations believe that prices will be lower in the future, they will be less likely to make current purchases.

In early 2014, European Central Bank President Mario Draghi, made it clear that the ECB will take the necessary steps to avoid Japan's deflationary fate.[56]

Even if deflation is not a serious risk in a Global Monetary Union, it will take a long time for central bankers to believe that to be the case. Therefore, it can be expected that inflation will be targeted at some level greater than zero.

Interest Rates and the Availability of Credit

Interest rates are typically about two percent higher than inflation, so the key to low interest rates is a low inflation rate.

A major concern of economists and others about whether a country should join a monetary union is the loss of an independent monetary policy and thus the ability to lower interest rates in order to promote investment and spur economic growth. However, if a country has the prospect of joining a Global Monetary Union with low inflation and low interest rates, the loss of the option to lower interest rates does not seem to be a substantial loss.

For most people in the developing world, interest rates for longer term loans do not matter because such loans are not available, due to lenders' aversion to currency risk. Benn Steil and Robert Litan report that "15-30-year fixed-rate mortgages...are unavailable elsewhere in the developing world."[57] With a Single Global Currency, and its near-zero currency risk, mortgages and shorter risk loans of all types will be more available.

Global Inequality of Wealth and Incomes

To the extent that the poor live in poor, high-currency-risk countries, they will be helped as their countries benefit from the 3-G world. States Jose Cordeiro,

> "Countries with more fluctuation in their currencies
> show less economic development, about two percent less.
> If we can introduce a global currency, poor countries
> wouldn't pay so much to keep these national currencies,
> and their economies would grow more. Believe me, the
> poor will benefit more from a Single Global Currency."[58]

One by-product of economic growth for emerging countries is that their currencies rise in value as the currency markets assign value to a currency when their source economies improve. The rising currency values then tend to thwart economic growth as exports become increasingly expensive to international customers.[59] In a 3-G world, the value of the currency will not fluctuate according to the currency markets' assessments of national economies.

The Single Global Currency will not, by itself eliminate poverty. However, it will expose to the light of day the true price of labor and goods and services throughout the world. For example, we may know. hypothetically, that a day laborer for construction work in New Delhi can be hired for SGC .50 an hour and one can be hired in Cape Town for SGC 5.00 and in London for SGC 10.00. Those rates can be relied upon to be stable and not subject to the day to day ups and downs of currency fluctuations. Such knowledge will assist investors and others in making their investment decisions. Using Thomas Friedman's terms in *The World is Flat*, and Paul Volker's words from his 2000 Op-Ed, "Toward a Single World Currency to Level the Playing Field," the Single Global Currency will level the world's economic playing field, and perhaps be part of "Globalization 3.0."[60]

While inflation is decreasing around the world and is less likely to impair the lives of the poor, it is still a major problem for most of the people in the less-developed world. The poor have no ability to send their savings to Switzerland or Monaco or Miami, so they suffer the loss of earning and saving power by themselves. With a Single Global Currency, such unavoidable losses will not occur, and the poor and all of us can safely save whatever we can.

War and Peace

Thomas Friedman noted in *The World is Flat* that countries with McDonald's restaurants did not go to war with each other, and similarly, countries in the Dell Computer supply chain have not fought each other; and are not likely to do so.[61]

Would membership in a Global Monetary Union effectively preclude going to war against another member? When the southern states of the US rebelled in 1861 and became the Confederate States of America, they were forced to develop their own money system. It wasn't easy, and the hyperinflation of the CSA was one of the reasons for the failure of the infant country. In all the major nineteenth- and twentieth-century wars, the combatants used different currencies, and they were invariably national currencies. A 2006 news article about a renewal of bus service between Punjab cities in India and Pakistan looked forward to the day when those cities will share a common currency and noted, "When businessmen from both sides of the border gain a common currency in money, then war will just not make any business sense."[62]

Just as the Maastricht treaty does not provide for the withdrawal of a member state from the European Monetary Union, it does not contemplate war among member states either. Assuming a two-country war, there are only three possibilities for management of their currencies: they both continue to use the euro, or one is cut away from the system, or both are cut away. It's hard to imagine how a war between two European Union or Global Monetary Union nations could continue for long without severe sanctions being imposed upon one or both, including restrictions on the money supply.

If a member country exited a Global Monetary Union, and quickly created, or recreated, its own currency, it would likely need to purchase war materials or other supplies from other countries, but the lack of a functioning foreign exchange market would make that more difficult. Barter would likely be used to some degree, albeit inefficiently. Thus, one could argue that one likely effect of Global Monetary Union would be a decrease in the use of war as a political tool or weapon.

Summary

The 3-G world will be more efficient, without the costly burden of a multicurrency foreign exchange system. Money will flow even more easily to all corners of the globe, and there will be no resulting currency crashes. Money may still flow to Switzerland and other money centers for investment and safety, but it will not be due to a fear of a currency crisis at home.

The 3-G world will not be Nirvana nor Utopia, but it will be a better world; and the goal should be pursued as soon as possible.

ENDNOTES

1. Richard Cooper, "A Monetary System for the Future," *Foreign Affairs*, Fall, 1984, p. 177, at http://www.jstor.org/discover/10.2307/20042091?uid=2129&uid=2&uid=70&uid=4&sid=21103479588527

2. Richard Cooper, "A Monetary System for the Future," ibid., p. 178.

3. International Monetary Fund, "IMF Executive Directors and Voting Power" at http://www.imf.org/external/np/sec/memdir/eds.htm.

4. "Governing Council," European Central Bank, at http://www.ecb.europa.eu/ecb/orga/decisions/govc/html/index.en.html and "Executive Council," European Central Bank, at http://www.ecb.europa.eu/ecb/orga/decisions/eb/html/index.en.html

5. Tonny Lybek and JoAnne Morris, "Central Bank Governance: A Survey of Boards and Management," IMF Working Paper WP/04/226, at http://www.imf.org/external/pubs/ft/wp/2004/wp04226.pdf.

6. Jeffrey A. Garten, "Needed: A Fed for the World," Op-Ed, *The New York Times*, 23 September 1998, at http://www.nytimes.com/1998/09/23/opinion/needed-a-fed-for-the-world.html

7. Richard Cooper, "A Monetary System for the Future," *Foreign Affairs*, Fall, 1984, p. 178, op. cit.

8. For an analysis of how national central banks have spent their seigniorage revenue, see Alain Ize, "Spending Seigniorage: Do Central Banks Have a Governance Problem?" IMF Working Paper 06/58, International Monetary Fund, March 2006, at http://www.imf.org/external/pubs/ft/wp/2006/wp0658.pdf.

9. "Spending Seigniorage: Do Central Banks Have a Governance Problem," Alain Ize, IMF Staff Paper Vol 54, No. 3, at http://www.imf.org/External/Pubs/FT/staffp/2007/03/pdf/ize.pdf. This paper was IMF Working Paper 06/58 and that version was referenced in the 06 Edition at page 312.

10. Petra Geraats, "Why Adopt Transparency? The Publication of Central Bank Forecasts," Working Paper 41, January 2001, European Central Bank, at http://www.ecb.int/pub/pdf/scpwps/ecbwp041.pdf. For a sample "Minutes of the Federal Open Market Committee" of the US Federal Reserve, see the 17-18 December 2013 report at http://www.federalreserve.gov/monetarypolicy/files/fomcminutes2013121 8.pdf

11. Petra Geraats, "Political Pressures and Monetary Mystique," November, 2005, at http://www.econ.cam.ac.uk/dae/repec/cam/pdf/cwpe0557.pdf. See also her analysis of the theory and practice of transparency in central bank operations, "Transparency of Monetary Policy: Theory and Practice," Center for Economic Studies, Munich, Working Paper No. 1597, November, 2005, at http://papers.ssrn.com/sol3/papers.cfm?abstract_id=869207

12. Anne C. Sibert, "Is Central Bank Transparency Desirable?" 14 December 2005, presented at the annual meeting of the American Economics Association, Boston, MA, 6-8 January 2006, at http://www.aeaweb.org/annual_mtg_papers/2006/0107_1015_0902.pdf

13. Alex Cukierman, "The Limits of Transparency," 25 December 2005, presented at the annual meeting of the American Economics Association, Boston, MA, 6-8 January 2006, at http://www.aeaweb.org/annual_mtg_papers/2006/0107_1015_0903.pdf

14. Michael Ehrmann and Marcel Fratzscher, "How Should Central Banks Communicate?" European Central Bank Working Paper Series, No. 557, November 2005, at http://www.ecb.int/pub/pdf/scpwps/ecbwp557.pdf.

15. "Monetary Policy Strategy: How Did We Get Here?" Frederic S. Mishkin, National Bureau of Economic Research, 2006 Working Paper No. 12515, at http://papers.nber.org/papers/w12515

16. "Currency Regimes and currency crises: What about cocoa money?" Mark S. LeClair, *Journal of International Financial Markets, Institutions and Money*, Vol 17, Issue 1, February 2007 at http://ideas.repec.org/a/eee/intfin/v17y2007i1p42-57.html

17. The EMU Growth and Stability Pact is composed of a number of documents, beginning with the Maastricht Treaty and then European Council Resolutions and regulations in 1997, 1998 and 2005. See "Council Regulation No. 1177/2011 of 8 November 2011 amending Regulation (EC) No 1467/97 on Speeding Up and Clarifying the Implementation of the Excessive Deficit Procedure," EC No. 1467/97, at http://eur-lex.europa.eu/LexUriServ/LexUriServ.do?uri=OJ:L:2011:306:0033:0040:EN:PDF.

18. "EU ministers Tell Britain to Cut Budget Deficit," *Reuters*, 24 January 2006, at http://www.abcmoney.co.uk/news/2620061797.htm.

19. See Michele Chang, "Reforming the Stability and Growth Pact: Size and Influence in EMU Policymaking," *European Integration*, March 2006, pp. 107-20, at http://www.tandfonline.com/doi/abs/10.1080/07036330500480664#.UwTbkcKYadI

20. "List of countries by public debt," *Wikipedia*, at http://en.wikipedia.org/wiki/List_of_countries_by_public_debt

21. Joanna Chung, "Eurozone Bond Yields Diverge," *Financial Times*, 26 February 2008, at http://www.ft.com/intl/cms/s/0/8a9f7b16-e49f-11dc-a495-0000779fd2ac.html

22. Ed Dolan, "How Germany Free Rides on the Euro," 28 August 2008, *Econ Blog*, at http://www.economonitor.com/dolanecon/2011/08/28/how-germany-free-rides-on-the-euro/.

23. Volker Nitsch, "Have a Break, Have a . . . National Currency: When Do Monetary Unions Fall Apart," Chapter 12, in Paul De Grauwe and Jacques Melitz, editors, *Prospects for Monetary Unions after the Euro*. Cambridge, MA: MIT Press, 2005.

24. William Fuchs and Francesco Lippi, "Monetary union with voluntary participation," Bank of Italy Working Papers No. 512, September 2005, at http://haas.berkeley.edu/faculty/papers/fuchsunion.pdf.

25. Kyuil Chung, "Capital Inflows and Exchange Rate Volatility in Korea," at http://www.economicdynamics.org/meetpapers/2013/paper_890.pdf

26. "Europa" was the name proposed in 1975 by Giorgio Basevi and others for a parallel European currency. The proposal was summarized in *The Economist*, 1 November 1975, as, "The All Saints' Day Manifesto for European Monetary Union." See Giorgio Basevi, Lorenzo Pecchi, and Gustavo Piga, "Parallel Monies, Parallel Debt: Lessons from the EMU and Options for the New EU," Tor Vergata University Research Paper Series, Working Paper No. 68, January, 2005, at ftp://www.ceistorvergata.it/repec/rpaper/No-68-Basevi-Pecchi-Piga.pdf. The name "Europa" was also proposed by Robert Mundell in a presentation to the American Management Assn, "A Plan for a European Currency," on 8 December 1969, at http://ec.europa.eu/economy_finance/emu_history/documentation/chapter3/19691208en35planeuropecurrency.pdf.

27. Charles Goldfinger, "Intangible Economy and Electronic Money," Chapter 4 of *The Future of Money*, OECD, op cit. In chapter 4, see sub-chapter 4 at p. 111, "Core Alternatives for Future Money Landscape" and at p. 113, sub-chapter "Single Global Currency: the Geo," undated, at http://www.oecd.org/futures/35391062.pdf.

28. See Single Global Currency Association website, "Feedback on SGC Names" at http://www.singleglobalcurrency.org/feedback_names.html.

29. "List of Countries by number of mobile phones in use," *Wikipedia*, at http://en.wikipedia.org/wiki/List_of_countries_by_number_of_mobile_phones_in_use

30. Benjamin J. Cohen, *The Future of Money*, Princeton, NJ: Princeton University Press, 2004, p. 180.

31. Canadian Tire Money™, "Canadian Tire 'Money': A History of Loyalty Program Innovation – Canadian Tire 'Money' Highlights," at http://corp.canadiantire.ca/EN/AboutUs/Pages/Loyalty.aspx.

32. Loren Steffy, "Frequent flier programs a bright spot amid gloom," 25 January 2005, *Houston Chronicle*, at http://www.chron.com/business/steffy/article/Steffy-Frequent-flier-programs-a-bright-spot-1676738.php.

33. Local Exchange Trading Systems, LETS, at http://www.transaction.net/money/lets/.

34. See the Ithaca Hours website at http://www.ithacahours.com/. Its currency has now issued smaller denomination notes such as "1/8th Hour."

35. See Emily Lambert, "Funny Money," *Forbes* Magazine, 14 February 2006, at http://www.forbes.com/2006/02/11/local-currencies-ithaca_cz_el_money06_0214local_print.html

36. "Bitcoin," Wikipedia, at http://en.wikipedia.org/wiki/Bitcoin

37. Sophie Knight and Takaya Yamaguchi, "Japan says any bitcoin regulation should be international," *Reuters*, 27 February 2014, at http://www.reuters.com/article/2014/02/27/us-bitcoin-mtgox-idUSBREA1Q1YK20140227

38. Sam Y. Cross, *All About The Foreign Exchange Market in the United States*. New York, NY: Federal Reserve Bank of New York, 1998, p. 3.

39. *75th Annual Report*, Bank for International Settlements, 27 june2005, p. 81, at http://www.bis.org/publ/arpdf/ar2005e.htm.

40. Marion Williams, Governor, Central Bank of Barbados, "Foreign Exchange Reserves: How Much Is Enough?" remarks delivered at the 20th Adlith Brown Memorial Lecture at the Central Bank of the Bahamas, 2 November 2005, at http://www.centralbank.org.bb/Publications/Adlith_Brown_Lec.pdf.

41. Juan Luis Moreno-Villalaz, "Lessons from the Monetary Experience of Panama: A Dollar Economy with Financial Integration," *Cato Journal*, Cato Institute, Winter 1999, at http://www.cato.org/pubs/journal/cj18n3/cj18n3-12.pdf.

42. John Maynard Keynes, wrote "In truth, the gold standard is already a barbarous relic." in Monetary Reform, 1924, at p. 187. Note that this phrase is often mis-quoted as referring to the metal gold rather than to the gold standard, to which the value of money can be fixed.

43. Natalia Chernyshoff, David Jacks, and Alan Taylor, "Stuck on Gold: Real Exchange Rate Volatility and the Rise and Fall of the Gold Standard," National Bureau of Economic Research, Working Paper No. 11795, November 2005 at http://papers.nber.org/papers/W11795.

44. Frank Fabozzi, Editor, *Professional Perspectives on Fixed Income Portfolio Management*. Hoboken, NJ: John Wiley & Sons, 2002.

45. Philip Arestis, Santonou Basu, "Financial Globalization: Some Conceptual Problems," Levy Economics Institute Working Paper 397, December, 2003, at http://ideas.repec.org/p/lev/wrkpap/wp_360.html

46. John H. Rogers, "Monetary Union, Price Level Convergence, and Inflation: How Close is Europe to the United States?" October 2002. Board of Governors of the Federal Reserve System, International Finance Discussion Paper 740, at http://www.federalreserve.gov/pubs/ifdp/2002/740/default.htm. For the case of US and Canadian prices, see Charles Engel and John H. Rogers, "How Wide Is the Border?" *American Economic Review*, vol. 80, 1996, pp. 1112-25.

47. Kenneth Froot, Michael Kim, and Kenneth Rogoff, "The Law of One Price over 700 Years," IMF Working Paper 01/174, International Monetary Fund, Washington, DC, at http://www.imf.org/external/pubs/ft/wp/2001/wp01174.pdf.

48. Ben S. Bernanke, "Deflation: Making Sure 'It' Doesn't Happen Here," speech before National Economists Club, Washington, DC, November, 2002, at http://www.federalreserve.gov/boarddocs/speeches/2002/20021121/default.htm.

49. Thomas Paine, *Common Sense, Rights of Man, and Other Essential Writings of Thomas Paine*, New York, NY: New American Library, 2003, p. 3, Introduction.

50. I. Angeloni, L. Aucremanne, and M. Ciccarelli, "Price setting and inflation persistence: did EMU matter?" May 2005, at http://www.ecb.int/events/pdf/conferences/emu/sessionV_Angeloni_Paper.pdf.

51. See Pietro Catte and Torsten Slok, "Assessing the value of indicators of underlying inflation for monetary policy," OECD Economics Dept. Working Paper No. 461, 25 November 2005, at http://search.oecd.org/officialdocuments/displaydocumentpdf/?doclanguage=en&cote=ECO/WKP(2005)48. See also, Robert Rich and Charles Steindel, "A Review of Core Inflation and an Evaluation of Its Measures," Staff Report No. 236, December 2005, at http://www.ny.frb.org/research/staff_reports/sr236.pdf.

52. "Inflation targeting," *Wikipedia*, at http://en.wikipedia.org/wiki/Inflation_targeting

53. John Edmunds and John Marthinsen, *Wealth by Association--Global Prosperity Through Market Unification.* Westport, CT: Praeger Publishers, 2003, p. 118.

54. Lester Thurow, *Fortune Favors the Bold.* New York, NY: Harper Collins, 2003, p. 48.

55. Stanley White, "Japan out of deflation now, no guarantee it won't return: economy minister," *Reuters*, 20 January 2014, at http://www.reuters.com/article/2014/01/21/us-japan-economy-amari-idUSBREA0K01W20140121

56. Brian Blackstone and Todd Buell, "European Central Bank Ready for New Stimulus," *Wall Street Journal*, 5 February 2014, at http://online.wsj.com/news/articles/SB10001424052702304680904579366481785544034

57. Benn Steil and Robert E. Litan, *Financial Statecraft.* London, UK, and New Haven, CT: Yale University Press, 2006, p. 127.

58. Marco Visscher, "Everyone Should Pay in Mondos," *ODE* Magazine, Netherlands, November, 2005, an interview with Jose Cordeiro, an economist in Venezuela.

59. Marialuz Moreno Badia and Alex Segura-Ubiergo, "Real Exchange Rate Appreciation in Emerging Markets: Can Fiscal Policy Help?" IMF Working Paper 14/1, at http://www.imf.org/external/pubs/ft/wp/2014/wp1401.pdf

60. Thomas Friedman, *The World is Flat.* New York, NY: Farrar, Straus and Giroux, 2006.

61. Thomas L. Friedman, *The World is Flat,* ibid. See Chapter 6, "The Dell Theory of Conflict Prevention," pp. 414-38, and Paul Volcker, "Toward a Single World Currency to Level the Playing Field," New York Herald Tribune, 31 January 2000, at http://www.nytimes.com/2000/01/31/opinion/31iht-edpaul.2.t_0.html.

62. Hemangini Gupta, "Humble Jutti Bonds Two Punjabs," *CNN-IBN*, 20 January 2006, Uttar Pradesh, India.

Chapter 9. CONCLUSION

This book has emphasized common sense and common cents, and that is what the people of the world understand, just as they quickly grasp the concept of the Single Global Currency, "You mean, like the euro?"

A primary goal of the leaders of the international financial system is stability, the essential economic foundation for people who seek to earn, spend, trade, save, and invest. That international financial stability has been the goal of the International Monetary Fund from its beginning in 1945,[1] and it will be substantially achieved upon the implementation of the Single Global Currency. That is, the money will be stable, even if local financial institutions or countries fail or go bankrupt.

The proverbial person from Mars would not design such a multicurrency foreign exchange system as we have today. Robert Mundell wrote in 2005, with commendable acknowledgment of changing gender roles,

> "If some spaceship captain came down from outer space
> and looked at the way international monetary relations
> are conducted, I am sure she would be very surprised....
> But it would strike her as very strange to find the
> complete disorganization of currency markets, the
> recurrent currency and debt crises, and wonder why
> more than one currency was needed to conduct
> international trade and payments in a world that aspired
> to a high degree of free trade."[2]

Willem Buiter wrote in 1999, "From a microeconomic efficiency point of view, if one were to design the world from scratch, a single currency would be adopted."[3]

Money is a human invention of immense utility. Without it, trade would be severely hampered. The problem addressed in this book began approximately 2,500 years ago when traders began exchanging the newly developed coins of the emerging currency areas.

People understand the value and simplicity of barter, but barter for international trade of primary goods in a $73.9 trillion GDP[4] world is impossible, despite the increased automation of even that basic transaction.[5] Similarly, bartering for money, a secondary good, on the foreign exchange markets, is also incompatible with other financial goals. What the people want is a return to a simple system of trade, and that means a Single Global Currency. The 2,500-year multicurrency foreign exchange transition between barter and the Single Global Currency must soon end.

During those 2,500 years, the fifth wheel of the international financial system has been oiled, redesigned, and otherwise improved to handle $5.3 trillion per day in exchanged money. However, the two central problems of foreign exchange have never been solved: how to consistently and accurately determine the value of one currency compared to another, and how to predict changes in those relative values over time. Even with all the computers and economists now available, no one has been able in 2,500 years to solve these two puzzles--and it's time to change gears, and discard the fifth wheel. Throwing Tobin's sand into the wheel is not enough, and it must be remembered that it was his second choice, ranked after the development of a common currency. Even if the "Tobin Tax" might have achieved his goals of slowing down worldwide capital flows, it was never adopted and it would not have solved the other problems of the multicurrency foreign exchange world. Developing worldwide support for a tax is a more difficult task than implementing a Single Global Currency, which will save money.

The foreign exchange system can be soon relegated to a special wing of the money museums of the world where people can examine all the techniques to make predictable the unpredictable, until the quest was abandoned upon the arrival of the Single Global Currency.

A world with a Single Global Currency, managed by a Global Central Bank, within a Global Monetary Union is both useful and feasible for the world. There are easily quantifiable benefits and softer benefits, such as the elimination of fear of currency crises. The quantifiable benefits are staggering:

<u>One-Time</u>
$ 10	trillion increase in world financial assets
$ 3	trillion in increased GDP

<u>Annual</u>
$ 90	billion in annual GDP increases arising from asset increase
$300	billion savings from elimination of transaction costs
$330	billion savings from burden of foreign exchange reserves
$200	billion from an estimated one percent increase in trade
$920	billion, total

Such amounts more than justify the effort required for planning and implementation.

Also, there are many risks to continuing the multicurrency foreign exchange system, such as unhedged currency fluctuations and currency crises. There is no logical need for such financial uncertainty. As noted in Chapter 5, Robert Mundell has termed the multicurrency foreign exchange system "an absurd currency system."[6]

Like Plato's prisoner emerging from the cave of shadow-reality who emerges into sunlight,[7] the people of the world have seen in the European Monetary Union the stable money they want, and they cannot go back to the economists' shadows of "real exchange rates" and Purchasing Power Parities and unsolved puzzles.

The people, their unions, their corporations, their non-governmental organizations, and their governments are increasingly saying to the economists, "We want stable money, now that we see how to get it. We want our money back." There is no reason to delay the first meetings of nations, non-governmental organizations, corporations, and individuals to plan the steps necessary to achieve the goal.

If a cure for cancer became known, but which required years of planning to design and build the facilities to produce that cure, would there be any reason to delay the first meetings to plan that result?

The cure for the ills of the multicurrency foreign exchange system is before us and deserves the attention of the world. We are becoming a global village, and a village needs only one currency.

No comprehensive research is now being done on the benefits and costs of a 3-G world. Among the thousands of economists working in universities, corporations, national governments, monetary unions and the international financial institutions (BIS, FSB, IMF, World Bank, WTO), there is not one who is yet working full time on such research. Not one.

The failure, to date, to conduct such research would fit the phrase used by Robert Mundell in in 2006 in another context, "an international monetary crime."[8] When such research is initiated and the results incrementally revealed to the people of the world, they will demand the implementation of the Single Global Currency managed by a Global Central Bank within a Global Monetary Union. They will ask the economists and the international financial institutions, "Why didn't you tell us about this option sooner?" or "Why haven't you been working on its implementation?"

There are many benefits to moving to such a 3-G world and each of them should be evaluated and quantified, as should the costs. It is believed here that the total annual monetary benefit can be measured in the hundreds of billions and the total wealth value in the trillions. The costs will surely be determined to be vastly less.

Ralph Bryant posed the dilemma for supporters of the Single Global Currency with the "complete motto of pragmatic incrementalism...*Don't ask too much, too soon. But don't be too timid either.*"[9] Given what we know about the net benefits of the 3-G world, it does not seem too soon to ask. Indeed, we have a moral obligation to press for implementation as soon as possible.

ENDNOTES

1. Anne O. Krueger, Deputy Managing Director, IMF, "At the Service of the Nations: The Role of the IMF in the Modern Global Economy," speech before the 18th Australasian Finance and Banking Conference, 16 December 2005, at http://www.imf.org/external/np/speeches/2005/121605.htm.
2. Robert Mundell, "The Case for a World Currency," *Journal of Policy Modeling*, June 2005, pp. 465-75, at p. 465, at http://www.sciencedirect.com/science/article/pii/S0161893805000463.
3. Willem H. Buiter, "The EMU and the NAMU: What is the Case for North American Monetary Union?" *Canadian Public Policy*, 1999, pp. 285-96, at p. 288, at http://qed.econ.queensu.ca/pub/cpp/sept1999/Buiter.pdf.
4. This amount is calculated in February 2014 with the nominal 2013 world GDP and projected 2.9 percent growth rate, both from *Wikipedia*, at http://en.wikipedia.org/wiki/Gross_world_product
5. For a sample of software for automating aspects of barter transactions, see the "Ozone" software by XO Limited, from New Zealand, at http://www.barter-software.com/.

6. International Monetary Fund, *IMF Survey*, "Mundell Calls for a Closer Monetary Union as Step Toward Single World Currency," 5 March 2001, p. 76, at http://www.imf.org/external/pubs/ft/survey/2001/030501.pdf.

7. Plato, "Allegory of the Cave," *The Republic*, translated by Benjamin Jowett at http://classics.mit.edu/Plato/republic.8.vii.html.

8. Howard Vane and Chris Mulhearn, "An Interview with Robert Mundell," *Journal of Economic Perspectives*, Vol. 20, No. 4, Fall 2006, pp 89-110, at page 109, at http://pubs.aeaweb.org/doi/pdfplus/10.1257/jep.20.4.89

9. Ralph C. Bryant, *Turbulent Waters--Cross-Border Finance and International Governance*. Washington, DC: Brookings Institution Press, 2003, p. 415.

Appendix A. The Single Global Currency Association

<u>Origin:</u> The Single Global Currency Association (SGCA) was founded in June 2003 to educate the world about the benefits of a Single Global Currency, and to mobilize efforts toward implementation. The only other organization in the world with a similar goal of a Single Global Currency is the Centre Jouffroy, established in 1974 by Jacques Riboud in France. The center has proposed a global currency to be called the "New Bancor" (NB), after Keynes' proposal for the "bancor" at Bretton Woods in 1944. It is to be defined as a "non-national numeraire defined as equal in value to the sum of the values of one half of a constant Euro and one half of a constant Dollar."[1]

Although termed a "scattered dreamer" by David Wolman,[2] it is hoped that the SGCA will be as effective in the area of currency reform as Greenpeace[3] has been in awakening the environmental consciousness of people around the world, and as Transparency International[4] has been to reduce international corruption, and as the Innocence Projects have been in the US in bringing justice to hundreds of wrongfully convicted innocent people.[5] With luck, the SGCA will be as successful as the International Landmine Coalition was in promoting the creation and signing of the 1997 Land Mine Ban Treaty.[6] If the 161 parties of that treaty would all endorse a Global Monetary Union, it would be implemented very quickly.

<u>Website:</u> Critical in the communication of any twenty-first-century message is the internet. The SGCA website, <u>www.singleglobalcurrency.org</u>, was created upon the establishment of the organization, in order to bring to one electronic location as much information as possible about the Single Global Currency and related monetary issues.

<u>Single Global Currency Conferences</u>: The first Single Global Currency Conference was held at the Mt. Washington Hotel in Bretton Woods, New Hampshire, USA, on 9 July 2004, in the Gifford Room, which was used during the 1944 conference. The second and third Single Global Currency Conferences were held there in 2005 and 2006. Future annual conferences will be resumed when interest in the Single Global Currency increases. Perhaps these conferences can be supplemented with regional conferences in other parts of the world.

<u>Contacts with economists</u>: A major activity of the association is to contact economists around the world who have written papers and books about the multicurrency foreign exchange world, and monetary unions and related issues. Through such contacts, the association acquaints them with the Single Global Currency and the association, and urges them to research and write about the Single Global Currency.

<u>Public Opinion Polls</u>: As noted in the text of this book, the SGCA has sponsored a question about the Single Global Currency in three national USA polls in 2003 and 2004 conducted by Zogby International.[7] In the future, similar polls will be conducted worldwide to measure the increasing public awareness of the Single Global Currency.

<u>Currency Area</u> <u>Chapters</u>: The SGCA seeks to establish a chapter in every currency area in the world. That is, one chapter is anticipated for the Eurozone, and one for the Eastern Caribbean Monetary Union, and one

each for countries and monetary unions which have their own currencies. Local chapters might be established in countries within monetary unions. The only requirements for establishing such a chapter are a strong interest in the goal of a Single Global Currency and an informal agreement to work together with the SGCA, and others within that currency area. At the end of 2013, there were chapters in several countries or currency areas.[8]

Contributions: The SGCA welcomes contributions and support from interested individuals, corporations and foundations. Contributions to the association are not yet tax-deductible according to the US Internal Revenue Service through Chapter 501(c)(3) of the US tax code.

A contribution to the SGCA provides an opportunity for uniquely large "returns on the investment," even if the return does not return to the actual contributor. That is, looking only at the potential $300 billion annual savings to the world arising from elimination of transaction costs, we suggest to potential contributors that if all the work of the SGCA over the next ten years (until 2024) nudges the implementation date forward by only one week, our efforts will have saved the world $5.8 billion. If a single donor were to fund the entire annual SGCA budget at the rate of $100,000 for those next ten years, for a total of $1 million, that would mean a return on investment of a multiple of 5,769.23 or 576,923%. That's a staggering "return." It would also give a donor, or donors, considerable worldwide visibility, if desired.

The future: For the Single Global Currency Association to be successful it must add members and build global support and coalitions among related groups, organizations and governments. The movement to the Single Global Currency must be a massive, cooperative effort.

ENDNOTES

1. Centre Jouffroy, at www.centre-jouffroy.com.
2. David Wolman, "The case for a global currency – Would it make more sense to have one currency for the entire world?" 11 February 2012, at http://www.salon.com/2012/02/11/the_case_for_a_global_currency/ See also Wolman's book, *The End of Money*, 2012, pp. 120-21.
3. Greenpeace International is based in Amsterdam, with website at http://www.greenpeace.org/international/.
4. Transparency International is based in Berlin, with website at http://www.transparency.org/.
5. Founded by attorneys Peter Neufeld and Barry Scheck and based in New York City, the original Innocence Project chose a precise strategy to challenge wrongful convictions in the US of innocent people--focus only on cases where exculpatory DNA is available. This strategy is slowly forcing the US legal system to confront its wrongful convictions of thousands of innocent people. See http://www.innocenceproject.org. There are now many local Innocence Project and related organizations, most of which are associated in the Innocence Network, with website, www.innocencenetwork.org. Many of these organizations are now working on non-DNA-based claims of innocence, which constitute the vast majority of such claims.

6. International Campaign to Ban Landmines is based in Belgium, with website at http://www.icbl.org/. The full name of the 1997 treaty is the "Convention on the Prohibition of the Use, Stockpiling, Production, and Transfer of Anti-Personnel Mines and on Their Destruction." Currently, 161 countries are "parties" to the treaty and 36 (including China, India, Russia, and the United States) are not.

7. Zogby International was acquired in 2010 by IBOPE International of Brazil. The Zogby website is at http://www.zogby.com/.

8. See "About Us" section of website of Single Global Currency Assn., at http://www.singleglobalcurrency.org/about_us.html.

Appendix B. What Citizens of the World Can Do to Help Move the World toward Implementation of the Single Global Currency

"Never doubt that a small group of thoughtful, committed citizens can change the world; indeed, it's the only thing that ever has."(TM)[1] by Margaret Mead (1901-1978)

Despite the persuasive powers of Margaret Mead and the knowledge of how a few large changes have occurred in the world, such as the American, French, and Russian Revolutions, it is still daunting to commit to working for a large scale change for the international monetary system.

Below are suggestions for actions which might be available to most human beings. One inspiration for such a list was the book, *Rules for Radicals* by Saul Alinsky.[2]

In the spirit of innovative activism, this Appendix has a list of twenty recommended activities which individuals and/or groups can initiate in support of the implementation of a Single Global Currency. There is one for each letter in the term s-i-n-g-l-e g-l-o-b-a-l c-u-r-r-e-n-c-y.

Send a copy of this book to a friend and ask that person to read it and pass it on; and then buy another, and another, and pass those on, too. If a thousand people read the book in a week and   then buy two more and pass on the three books to others, and those 3,000 do the same the next week for 9,000, and so on, it will take only 15 weeks for every human being on the earth to read the book. In the 16th week everyone would have a chance to read it again.

Initiate discussions with friends and others, "What do you think of a Single Global Currency?" Then ask them to read this book and visit the SGCA website.

Next time you purchase something from another currency area, try to determine the amount and percentage of the transaction charge for the foreign exchange barter, and then multiply that percentage by $2.5 trillion and then by 260 trading days.

Go to the Single Global Currency Association website, www.singleglobalcurrency.org., and explore, including the links in the online END NOTES to this book.

Learn more about the Single Global Currency, beyond what is in this
   book.

Elect representatives who understand that the people want international financial stability and that the 3-G's are necessary elements of that future stability.

Google "monetary union," "Global Monetary Union," "Robert Mundell," "Single Global Currency," "single world currency", "Global Central Bank" and related topics and learn all you can about this important international financial reform. Also, try www.yahoo.com or any other search engine.

List your provincial, regional, state, and federal government representatives and then ask them what they are doing to promote the implementation of the Single Global Currency, and ask them to sponsor the SGC resolution in Chapter 7.

Organize a chapter of Single Global Currency Association, with one to a country or monetary union. The primary goals of such chapters are to support the goals of a Single Global Currency and to encourage the home country or monetary union to take steps toward that goal.

The SGCA is a non-profit corporation in the United States, but there are no requirements about how other chapters must be organized. All it takes is for one or more persons to join together and then notify the Single Global Currency Association of the establishment of a country/monetary union chapter. The organizational structure might be an informal group or an incorporated, tax-exempt corporation. The SGCA recognizes chapters by listing them in the "About Us" section of the website, www.singleglobalcurrency.org.

Buy more copies of this book and loan them to friends and give them to libraries, and when the 2007 edition is published, buy that, too. And the 2008 edition, etc.

Ask governments and economists and newspaper editors and everyone else why we don't yet have a Single Global Currency, and then ask them to explore the issues.

Listen to those who have questions about the utility and feasibility of the Single Global Currency and respond with either answers or promises to get more information from the Single Global Currency Association.

Contribute to the Single Global Currency Association, a non-profit organization seeking to save the world trillions.

Understand that the multicurrency foreign exchange barter system is obsolete, and that it will be replaced by a Single Global Currency.

Request legislators to pass a law which would require each country's treasury department and central bank to provide a semi-annual report of the progress made toward a Single Global Currency. Such a report would be similar to the report required semi-annually in the United

States from the Treasury Department, which identifies those countries/monetary unions where the currency is manipulated to have a lower value to finance exports. Instead of semi-annual finger-pointing, why not a semi-annual report on progress toward the 3-G future?

Request that groups, organizations, and legislative bodies pass resolutions urging implementation of a Single Global Currency.

Engage others in discussion and inquiry about the solutions to the costs and risks of the existing multicurrency foreign exchange system.

Network with others to spread the word about the 3-G world.

Consider devoting a few minutes a day to this large enterprise which will bring so much benefit to so many people.

Yell from your window or rooftop that you are "mad as hell"[3] and that you are not going to tolerate an expensive, risky, multicurrency foreign exchange system anymore, and that you want a stable 3-G international financial system with a Global Monetary Union with a Global Central Bank and a Single Global Currency.

ENDOTES

1. I had the privilege of being a student in a large, introductory anthropology class taught by Margaret Mead. The force of her personality, and the memory of her swaggering with her walking stick to the podium makes her quoted statement the more powerful for me. This exact quote from Margaret Mead generated 28,300 "results" in a Google search. With the word "people" substituted for "citizens," there were another 848 results. However, the citation is unknown for the original quote, now trademarked by the intellectual caretaker for Mead's work, the New York-based, Institute for Intercultural Studies, Inc. From the Institute came this email about the source of the quote:

"The Institute has received many inquiries about this famous admonition by Margaret Mead, which has become a motto for many organizations and movements. However, we have been unable to locate when and where it was first cited. We believe it probably came into circulation through a newspaper report of something said spontaneously and informally. We know that it was firmly rooted in her professional work, and that it reflected a conviction that she expressed often, in different contexts and phrasings. This quote is now trademarked, and the trademark is held by the Institute for Intercultural Studies.

We appreciate hearing about members of your family having been students of Dr. Mead, and appreciate your question concerning this most famous quote attributed to her.

Sincerely yours,

Betty Howe

Administrative Assistant

Institute for Intercultural Studies, Inc.

67A East 77th Street, New York, NY 10021"

2. Saul D. Alinsky, *Rules for Radicals: A Pragmatic Primer for Realistic Radicals*. New York, NY: Vintage Books, 1971, revised edition, 1989. One memorable demonstration of those rules came when a neighborhood group in Chicago, in opposition to the expansion of an airport, made its voice heard when members engaged in a sit in/sit down in all the toilets in all the restrooms available to the public at that airport. While it caused discomfort to some, the authorities responded affirmatively to the group's grievances.

3. This a reference to Howard Beale's (played by Peter Finch) speech as a newscaster in the movie *Network*, where he urged viewers "get up right now and go to the window, open it, and stick your head out and yell, 'I'm mad as hell, and I'm not going to take this anymore!'" at http://www.americanrhetoric.com/MovieSpeeches/moviespeechnetwork2.html

Appendix C. AUTHOR'S AFTERWORD

After founding the Single Global Currency Association in June 2003, Morrison Bonpasse was often asked, "How did you think of THAT idea?" The first part of the answer is that there are few original ideas, and even if he thought at the time that he might be among the first to articulate it, he knew that it surely was not original with him--and it wasn't, as this book has shown.[1]

The second part is that in October 2002, while running for the Maine State Legislature (United States), the issues of the campaign focused on taxes, education, health care, ... taxes, education, health care and taxes. Thinking that some other issues might invigorate the discussion, he proposed a Single Global Currency in the following letter to the *Wiscasset Newspaper* and *Boothbay Register*:

A Vote For One Currency
Dear Editor:

...we are distracted from the really important long term issues facing humanity. Species become extinct, the earth warms and the environment deteriorates, but these issues are not so dramatic as war and weapons of mass destruction. It's hard to win elections on those issues.

Somewhere in between those two poles is a goal, which, if reached, can dramatically improve the lives of everyone on the earth: a single currency. That's right, a single currency. Actually, for the United States it's not so revolutionary a goal, as we transitioned from a 13 currency system to a single currency after the Revolution.

This time, Europe has led the way with the euro. One currency now exists where before there were many. When traveling from Germany to France to Italy, there are now no money changers and no associated changing costs and no time spent translating from an unfamiliar currency into one's home currency. Also, but less visible, there are no currency exchanges, and their speculators, for francs or marks or lira; and the rate of inflation is the same for all the euro countries. Soon, more European countries will be added.

The logical next step, but not on the Washington radar screen, is a world currency. Let's call the basic unit a "mundo," or "eartha," or whatever name we can choose from a worldwide contest. No more Canadian dollars, nor Mexican pesos, nor US Dollars, just one currency.

All this requires fiscal discipline in each participating country, but the rewards would be great for their citizens. As a single currency would require a truly multi-national effort, ...

Let's move to a single world currency by the year 2010.

Morrison Bonpasse
Newcastle
Democratic Candidate for the House 58th District[2]

Despite the logical appeal of that issue, he lost the election.[3] However, the seed was planted. While the idea had been conceived long ago and discussed by many eminent persons, it became clear to him there was not a single organization in the world entirely dedicated to that one goal: the Single Global Currency, despite its large potential benefits to the people of the world.

The next spring, he sold his small business and returned to the idea of a Single Global Currency. There were other non-profit options, but, paraphrasing the twentieth-century bank robber in the United States, Willie Sutton, the issues involving foreign exchange are "where the money is,"[4] even if not for him personally. After further research, the Single Global Currency Association was founded as a non-profit corporation in Maine, USA, in June 2003, with a website at www.singleglobalcurrency.org.

Now, after eleven years of learning, and several Single Global Currency conferences at Bretton Woods, it's time to share the bad news and the good news. The bad news is that the existing multicurrency world financial system is very expensive and is in danger of suffering some type of a collapse or crisis. The good news is that the long term, elegantly simple, clean solution is available and stands in front of us, in the form of existing monetary unions. What is needed is to make the transition from many monetary unions and currencies to one Global Monetary Union.

The models and inspiration for this book are the books which inspired economic, social, or political movements, among them:

Common Sense, by Thomas Paine (British colonialism)
The Communist Manifesto, by Karl Marx (unregulated capitalism]
Uncle Tom's Cabin, by Harriet Beecher Stowe (slavery abolition)
The Jungle, by Upton Sinclair (slaughterhouse conditions)
The Other America, by Michael Harrington (poverty in the US)
Silent Spring, by Rachel Carson (DDT, pollution of environment)
The Feminine Mystique, by Betty Friedan (feminism)
The Second Sex, by Simone de Beauvoir (feminism)

For some of these books, the solution was presented, as in *Common Sense*, and as is the case in this book. John Maynard Keynes' *The Economic Consequences of the Peace* would have been listed above, but its cogent analysis of the post-World War I peace imposed upon Germany regrettably did not lead to sufficient political action, in order to avoid World War II. Another inspiration for Morrison was the book, *The Territorial Imperative* by Robert Ardrey, which brought to the people the findings of ethology, the study of animal behavior, and its relationship to humans.

Just as John F. Kennedy's *Why England Slept* sought to explain the United Kingdom's slow reaction to Hitler's early aggressions, the book in your hands seeks to explain why the world sleeps with respect to the issues of the multicurrency foreign exchange system; and it seeks to wake up those who can be stirred.

It is hoped that this book has met the standards of Roger Lowenstein's "Off the Shelf" column in *The New York Times*, "Exposing the Economics Behind Everyday Behavior," where he noted that "A funny thing seems be happening to economics writing: it's getting better."[5] In addition, it's hoped that this book will lead to substantial research on the topic of the Single Global Currency and to political progress toward that goal. Perhaps the readers who are international economists will be inspired to do the research necessary to inform the decision makers about the timing of implementation and operations of the Single Global Currency. My third hope is the same as stated by Paul De Grauwe in his Introduction to *Economics of Monetary Union*, "...that I have conveyed to the reader the same sense of excitement that I have when I study the subject."[6] If the readers of this book are not now excited by the subject of the Single Global Currency, then your assistance is requested on how to make the book better--because the subject is monumentally exciting, and important.

This 2014 edition of *The Single Global Currency – Common Cents for the World* is the fourth, as it follows the original edition in 2006 and updates in 2007, 2008, and 2009. Future editions, which are planned for 2019 and 2014, will include improvements as suggested by readers. Please send comments to Morrison at morrison@singleglobalcurrency.org. Criticisms and identifications of errors are especially welcome. All comments, unless requested otherwise, will be posted on the Single Global Currency website at www.singleglobalcurrency.org, and additions and corrections will be included in subsequent editions.

Morrison Bonpasse
Founder
Single Global Currency Assn.
P.O. Box 390
Newcastle, Maine, USA
15 March 2014

ENDNOTES

1. The idea of a single global currency is elegantly simple and many people around the world have surely already thought of it, independently from economists and science fiction writers.
2. "Letters--A Vote for One Currency," *Wiscasset Newspaper*, Wiscasset, Maine, 17 October 2002.
3. For those who seek more information about the author, Googling "Bonpasse" will work, and his resume is on the Single Global Currency Association website at http://www.singleglobalcurrency.org/about_us.html
4. "Famous Cases: Willie Sutton," Federal Bureau of Investigation, at http://www.fbi.gov/about-us/history/famous-cases/willie-sutton. See also "The Bank Robber, the QUOTE, and the Final Irony," on the website of the American Banking Association, at http://www.ababj.com/blogs/reporter-s-

notebook/item/256-the-unexpurgated-search-for-willie-sutton. According to the latter article, Sutton never said, "because that's where the money is," in response to the question, "Why do you rob banks?" After finally being released from his last of several prison terms due to poor health, he wrote two books and in one he stated that it was a newspaper reporter who made up that quote and attributed it to him. In his book, Sutton wrote, "If anybody had asked me, I'd have probably said it. That's what almost anybody would say... it couldn't be more obvious." The story of the origin of this quote parallels that of three other quotes cited in this book, by Senator Everett Dirksen ("Take a billion here, and a billion there and pretty soon, you are talking about real money") and Federal Reserve Bank retired chair Paul Volcker ("A global economy requires a global currency"), and Margaret Mead ("Never doubt that a small group of thoughtful, committed citizens can change the world; indeed, it's the only thing that ever has"). The originators of all four did not clearly write or speak those words, but confirmed subsequently what others recorded for them.

5 . Roger Lowenstein, "Off the Shelf: Exposing the Economics Behind Everyday Behavior," *The New York Times*, p. BU 7, 18 December 2005. He also wrote, "In recent books like *Freakonomics* and *The Travels of a T-Shirt in the Global Economy*, economists have taken it upon themselves to explain something of how the world works. They even tell little stories." at http://www.nytimes.com/2005/12/18/business/yourmoney/18shelf.html

6. Paul De Grauwe, *Economics of Monetary Union*. Oxford, UK: Oxford University Press, 1992, p. 2.

Appendix D. Acknowledgments

I gratefully thank those who assisted my journey toward creating the Single Global Currency Association and the writing of this book, and its earlier versions.

Throughout the journey, my wife, Leah Sprague has claimed to retain the common sense in the family as she patiently endured marriage to a champion of causes.

In 2003, Babson College professor Alan Cohen graciously responded to my request for networking help. "Might you know someone who is interested in the topic of the single global currency?" Indeed, he did, and referred me to Professor John Edmunds a Finance professor at my MBA graduate school, Babson College, and whose initial interest in the Single Global Currency was an important step. We met in his office on 23 June 2003, and subsequently planned to write this book together, but when his schedule did not open up as anticipated, he graciously encouraged me in October 2005 to go ahead and write.

Thanks go also to the members and Boards of Directors and Advisors of the Single Global Association, especially Jose Cordeiro, Ted DeStefano, and Ramon Tamames.

Thanks also to the occasional encouragement that came from people over the past eleven years with no previous familiarity with the idea of a single global currency, but who immediately responded with support. One such person was Jeannette Poe, an employee of a bank in South Carolina whose response was, "Well, Yeah!".

In the summer and fall of 2003, my late sister, Barbara, encouraged me to continue working for Dennis Dechaine and for the Single Global Currency.

Jennifer Bunting provided crucial editing and publishing help for the publication of the first four editions.

Finally, despite the efforts of the above, the book remains imperfect, and such failings are solely the responsibility of the author.

APPENDIX E				

This book priced in 140 Currencies, starting with €16,
with other prices calculated from www.oanda.com using
thu "bid" rates as of 2 Jan. 2014, rounded to nearest hundredth.

Price of Book	Curr Code	Currency Name	Currency Area	no. of nations using
16.00	EUR	Euro	Europe	23
22.08	USD	Dollar	United States	8
10,495.52	XOF	CFA Franc	West African	8
59.36	XCD	E.C. Dollar	Caribbean	7
10,495.52	XAF	CFA Franc	Central African	6
24.64	AUD	Dollar	Australia	4
27.84	SGD	Singapore Dollar	Singapore/Brunei	2
0.00				
1,238.24	AFN	Afghani	Afghanistan	1
2,213.12	ALL	Lek	Albania	1
1,722.08	DZD	Dinar	Algeria	1
2,147.84	AON	New Kwanza	Angola	1
143.68	ARS	Peso	Argentina	1
8,931.68	AMD	Dram	Armenia	1
17.28	AZN	Manat	Azerbaijan	1
21.92	BSD	Bahamian Dollar	Bahamas	1
8.32	BHD	Bahraini Dinar	Bahrain	1
1,680.00	BDT	Taka	Bangladesh	1
42.88	BBD	Barbados Dollar	Barbados	1
209,564.80	BYR	Belarusian Ruble	Belarus	1
43.20	BZD	Belizean Dollar	Belize	1
1,364.64	BTN	Ngultrum	Bhutan	1
149.44	BOB	Boliviano	Bolivia	1
31.36	BAM	Mark	Bosnia & Herzegovina	1
191.20	BWP	Pula	Botswana	1
51.84	BRL	Real	Brazil	1
31.20	BGN	Leva	Bulgaria	1
33,836.32	BIF	Burundi Franc	Burundi	1
86,100.80	KHR	New Riel	Cambodia	1

23.52	CAD	Canadian Dollar	Canada	1
1,764.32	CVE	Escudo	Cape Verde	1
11,588.00	CLP	Chilean Peso	Chile	1
134.72	CNY	Yuan	China	1
42,529.76	COP	Peso	Columbia	1
7,871.52	KMF	Comoran Franc	Comoros	1
19,983.04	CDF	Congolese Franc	Congo, Dem. Republi	1
10,801.60	CRC	Colon	Costa Rica	1
122.24	HRK	Kuna	Croatia	1
490.24	CUC	Cuban Peso	Cuba	1
437.76	CZK	Koruna	Czech Republic	1
119.36	DKK	Krone	Denmark	1
3,881.28	DJF	Dijibouti Franc	Dijibouti	1
929.44	DOP	Dominican Peso	Dominican Republic	1
152.80	EGP	Egypt Pound	Egypt	1
330.88	ERN	Nakfa	Eritrea	1
414.72	ETB	Birr	Ethiopia	1
41.28	FJD	Fiji Dollar	Fiji	1
829.44	GMD	Delasi	Gambia	1
38.24	GEL	Lari	Georgia	1
51.84	GHS	Cedi	Ghana	1
169.44	GTQ	Quetzal	Guatamala	1
4,411.84	GYD	Guyanese Dollar	Guyana	1
948.64	HTG	Gourde	Haiti	1
439.84	HNL	Lempira	Honduras	1
4,748.64	HUF	Forint	Hungary	1
2,530.40	ISK	Krona	Iceland	1
1,358.56	INR	Rupee	India	1
268,032.00	IDR	Rupiah	Indonesia	1
546,491.20	IRR	Rial	Iran	1
25,220.16	IQD	Dinar	Iraq	1
76.32	ILS	New Shekel	Israel	1
2,164.00	JMD	Jamaican Dollar	Jamaica	1
2,321.92	JPY	Yen	Japan	1
15.52	JOD	Dinar	Jordan	1
3,362.72	KZT	Tenge	Kazakhstan	1
1,878.24	KES	Shilling	Kenya	1
2,977.92	KPW	Won	Korea, North	1

23,266.56	KRW	Won	Korea, South	1
6.24	KWD	Kuwaiti Dinar	Kuwait	1
1,084.48	KGS	Som	Kyrgyzstan	1
173,448.00	LAK	New Kip	Lao Peoples' Dem Re	1
32,559.20	LBP	Lebanese Pound	Lebanon	1
231.20	LSL	Loti	Lesotho	1
1,785.76	LRD	Liberian Dollar	Liberia	1
26.88	LYD	Dinar	Libya	1
55.20	LTL	Litas	Lithuania	1
979.20	MKD	Denar	Macedonia	1
48,518.88	MGA	Ariayry	Madagasgar	1
9,435.36	MWK	Kwacha	Malawi	1
72.32	MYR	Ringgit	Malaysia	1
321.60	MVR	Rufiyaa	Maldives	1
6,315.52	MRO	Ouguiya	Mauritania	1
643.52	MUR	Rupee	Mauritius	1
288.80	MXN	Mexican Peso	Mexico	1
282.88	MDL	Moldovan Leu	Moldova, Republic of	1
36,176.80	MNT	Tugrik	Mongolia	1
176.16	MAD	Dirham	Morocco	1
655.20	MZM	Metical	Mozambique	1
21,445.60	MMK	Kyat	Myanmar	1
231.20	NAD	Namimbian Dollar	Namibia	1
2,157.76	NPR	Nepalese Rupee	Nepal	1
26.72	NZD	NZ Dollar	New Zealand	1
552.64	NIO	Cordoba	Nicaragua	1
3,487.36	NGN	Naira	Nigeria	1
133.76	NOK	Krone	Norway	1
8.48	OMR	Rial	Oman	1
2,298.72	PKR	Rupee	Pakistan	1
54.40	PGK	Kina	Papua New Guinea	1
99,520.00	PYG	Guarani	Paraguay	1
60.48	PEN	New Sol	Peru	1
976.80	PHP	Phillipine Peso	Phillipines	1
66.40	PLN	Zioty	Poland	1
80.32	QAR	Riyal	Qatar	1
71.84	RON	New Leu	Romania	1
724.64	RUB	Ruble	Russian Federation	1

14,718.40	RWF	Rwandan Franc	Rwanda	1
50.08	WST	Tala	Samoa	1
393,246.40	STD	Dobra	Sao Tome & Principe	1
82.72	SAR	Saudi Riyal	Saudi Arabia	1
1,835.84	RSD	Dinar	Serbia	1
249.76	SCR	Rupee	Seychelles	1
94,589.12	SLL	Leone	Sierra Leone	1
161.60	SBD	Solomon Is Dollar	Solomon Islands	1
24,367.84	SOS	Somalian Shilling	Somalia	1
231.20	ZAR	Rand	South Africa	1
69.92	SSP	So. Sudanese Pnd	South Sudan	1
2,883.04	LKR	Sri Rupee	Sri Lanka	1
125.12	SDD	Dinar	Sudan	1
71.68	SRD	Suriname Dollar	Surinam	1
231.20	SZL	Lilageni	Swaziland	1
141.76	SEK	Krona	Sweden	1
19.52	CHF	Swiss Franc	Switzerland	1
3,116.96	SYP	Syrian Pound	Syria	1
105.28	TJS	Somoni	Tajikistan	1
34,242.24	TZS	Shilling	Tanzania, Republic of	1
720.32	THB	Baht	Thailand	1
40.96	TOP	Pa'anga	Tonga	1
139.20	TTD	T&T Dollar	Trinidad & Tobago	1
36.16	TND	Tunisian Dinar	Tunisia	1
47.36	TRY	New Lira	Turkey	1
62.88	TMM	Manat	Turkmenistan	1
55,160.80	UGS	Ugandan Shilling	Uganda	1
179.84	UAH	Hryvnia	Ukraine	1
80.96	AED	Dirham	United Arab Emirates	1
13.28	GBP	Pound Sterling	United Kingdom	1
457.76	UYP	Uruguayan Peso	Uruguay	1
48,467.04	UZS	Uzbekistani Sum	Uzbekistan	1
2,103.36	VUV	Vatu	Vanatu	1
138.72	VEF	Bolivar Fuerte	Venezuela	1
459,600.00	VND	Dong	Viet Nam	1
4,738.24	YER	Rial	Yemen	1
120.48	ZMK	Kwachi	Zambia	1
0.00		multiple currencies	Zimbabwe	1